Routledge Revivals

The Economy of Israel

First published in 1960, *The Economy of Israel* presents a critical account of the first ten years of Israeli economy. The book starts with a short description of the physical nature of the country and an examination of the Zionist ideas which played a decisive role in the formation of Israel. Part I of the book surveys the economy of Israel and traces the significant features of its development between 1948 and 1958. Part II is not a photograph of Israel's exchange regulations at one particular date, but an eclectic account of the variable features of a flexible system that had but one constant factor, namely, the absence at any time of an effective unitary exchange rate. Part III of the book contains some general observations that are largely speculative. The book concludes with an examination of the prospects of Israel's economy with special reference to the charitable aid which has provided it with its life blood during the first decade. This is an important historical account for scholars and researchers of economics, Middle East economics, and history of Israel.

The Economy of Israel

A Critical Account of the First Ten Years

Alex Rubner

Routledge
Taylor & Francis Group

First published in 1960
by Frank Cass & Company Ltd.

This edition first published in 2024 by Routledge
4 Park Square, Milton Park, Abingdon, Oxon, OX14 4RN

and by Routledge
605 Third Avenue, New York, NY 10017

Routledge is an imprint of the Taylor & Francis Group, an informa business

Publisher's Note
The publisher has gone to great lengths to ensure the quality of this reprint but points out that some imperfections in the original copies may be apparent.

Disclaimer
The publisher has made every effort to trace copyright holders and welcomes correspondence from those they have been unable to contact.

A Library of Congress record exists under LCCN: 60004327

ISBN: 978-1-032-67674-6 (hbk)
ISBN: 978-1-032-67678-4 (ebk)
ISBN: 978-1-032-67676-0 (pbk)

Book DOI 10.4324/9781032676784

THE ECONOMY OF ISRAEL

A CRITICAL ACCOUNT OF THE FIRST TEN YEARS

ALEX RUBNER

B.Sc.(Econ.), Ph.D.(Lond.)

Formerly Adviser to the Ministry of Finance and the Ministry of Trade and Industry in Israel

FRANK CASS & COMPANY LTD.

LONDON

1960

First published by FRANK CASS & COMPANY LTD.

First published 1960

Printed in Great Britain by
Ebenezer Baylis & Son, Ltd., The Trinity Press,
Worcester, and London
Bound by Garden City Press

TO
MY FATHER

"Tell it not in Gath,
publish it not in the
streets of Askelon;
lest the daughters of
the Philistines rejoice,
lest the daughters of
the uncircumcised triumph"

II Samuel, Chapter I, 20

CONTENTS

CONTENTS

PREFACE

THE material for this book was mainly collected during my stay in Israel from the summer of 1948 to the spring of 1957, and I have had the opportunity of feeling Israel's economic pulse during my work as an editor, adviser to the Ministry of Finance and the Ministry of Trade and Industry, business consultant, member of various investigating government commissions, etc. During this period I advanced the arguments, presented in this book, in several hundred articles, broadcasts and lectures. Like others, who have written critically of official policy, I have found the Israeli authorities prepared to accord liberal freedom of expression to all shades of opinion—a rare occurrence amongst the states of the Middle East. Unfortunately this tolerance is not always extended to critics of Israeli life who express their views in a language other than Hebrew.

Part B of this book, completed in February 1958, was accepted by the University of London as a thesis in partial fulfilment of the requirements for the degree of Ph.D.(Econ.) London.

Mr. D. Core, Professor E. Devons, Mr. W. Koenigsberger, Mr. H. H. Liesner, Mr. R. Ney, Dr. O. Rabinowicz, Mr. B. S. Yamey and two senior Israeli civil servants, who wish to remain anonymous, read part or all of an earlier draft of this book; whilst I have benefited greatly from their comments and advice, they clearly bear no responsibility for the contents of the book. To Mr. B. Temkin fell the unenviable task of saving the reader from having to plough through a book full of linguistic monstrosities. Miss R. Johnson laboured on the preparation of the Index. Only I can be aware what debt I owe to my wife, for without her encouragement this book would never have been started and without her co-operation would never have been completed.

The publishers and editors of *Commentary* (New York), *Daily Telegraph* (London), *Davar* (Tel-Aviv), *Economic Quarterly* (Tel-Aviv), *Haaretz* (Tel-Aviv), *Jerusalem Post* (Jerusalem), *Jewish Chronicle* (London), *Land Economics* (Wisconsin), *Mondes d'Orient* (Paris), *Spectator* (London), are thanked for permitting the reproduction of material which first appeared in articles in which I tried out those ideas that form the theme of this book.

ALEX RUBNER

Jerusalem/London, February 1959.

ix   A*

MAJOR STATISTICAL TABLES

GLOSSARY OF HEBREW AND TECHNICAL TERMS

Average rate . . *Vide rate*; this IL *rate* per $ is the weighted average of all effective import and export *rates*.[1]

Black market . . Used as a collective term to connote semi-legal and illegal (commercial) activities.

Bank of Israel . The central banking institution of the country.

C.B.S. . . Central Bureau of Statistics and Economic Research; part of the Prime Minister's office and responsible for the collation of most official statistical data.

Clearing-dollar (Cledo) A currency denomination of varying value used as the accounting standard in most Israeli trade treaties.

Cost-of-living index . Published by the C.B.S. with a base of September 1951 = 100.

Development Budget . The capital outlays of the Government dealt with in a special budget to separate them from the current outlays in the Ordinary Budget.

Dollar ($) . . U.S. currency. In Israeli economic literature and official regulations the dollar is often used as a synonym for "foreign currency". Also frequently employed as a standard of measurement for the economic performance of Israeli production, exports and imports.

Dunam . . 1 dunam = 0.247 acres.

Economic Advisory . A body of about twenty economists—
Staff (E.A.S.) mostly from America—which was called

[1] My estimates of the *average rates* are as follows:

1948: 0.350	1954: 1.700
1949: 0.450	1955: 2.000
1950: 0.600	1956: 2.250
1951: 0.750	1957: 2.500
1952: 1.100	1958: 2.750
1953: 1.400	

xiii

	into being in order to constitute the nucleus of an economic planning centre. Functioned in 1953 and 1954.
Foreign Currency Controls	Import and export licences were issued by several ministries of which the Ministry of Trade and Industry was the most important. The allocation of foreign currency and the overall conduct of these controls were directed by the Ministry of Finance.
Histadruth	A confederation of trade unions with a centralized executive. It has established numerous cultural, welfare, distributive and manufacturing institutions—these account today for one-third of Israel's National Income.
IL	Israeli Lira (Pound) = 1,000 Prutoth.
Import(s)-for-export (licences) abbreviated *IfE*[1]	A special type of licence (administratively separated from general import licences) in order to provide manufacturers with imported materials for production of exports.
Import(s)-without-pay (licences) abbreviated *IwP*	A special type of licence for the import of goods for which the foreign currency controller is not required to allocate foreign currency. The goods either belong to, or are financed by, non-Israelis who wish to transfer capital to Israel.
Import content	The foreign currency inputs of an Israeli product.
Institution	A collective term for non-profit-making organizations which seek material aid outside of Israel for academic, charitable, cultural, political and religious bodies active in Israel.

[1] In this book a difference will be made between direct *IfE* and indirect *IfE*. Direct *IfE* refers to the materials imported under the provisions of this special licence; the foreign currency value of direct *IfE* as a proportion of the foreign currency proceeds of the exported product can be more or less accurately established. Indirect *IfE* refers to the import content that is bought locally by the Israeli manufacturer for IL, e.g. fuel.

Jewish Agency . . The political executive of the World Zionist Organization (with the participation of some non-Zionist individuals). In this book the term is used indiscriminately for all organized Zionist efforts.

Kibbutz(im) . . A communal, rural settlement which has been likened to a "rural monastery" (153). The members receive no money wages, eat in communal dining halls and elect their managers at general assemblies by open voting. All property is owned jointly and every member is available daily for work assignment.

Knesset . . Israel's parliament.

Mapai . . Israel's socialist labour party headed by Ben-Gurion and the dominant force in Israel's Government, the Histadruth and the Jewish Agency.

Moshav(im) . . A co-operative smallholders' settlement with joint marketing and supply organs. The constitution of a moshav does not permit the members (with rare exceptions) to employ hired labour.

Nominal-dollar . The foreign currency unit in which all Israeli official trade statistics are reckoned. The statistics do not distinguish between the differing values of the clearing-dollars and the dollar.

Pamaz (account) . "Import-Entitlement-Accounts"; i.e. foreign currency accounts of individual exporters at Israeli banks to which they are entitled to transfer some or all of their foreign currency earnings. Some of the exporters are permitted to finance with their *pamaz* holdings, the import of (usually "luxury") goods for resale in the domestic market.

(Exchange) *rate* . The exchange rate of the IL expressed as a function of $1. Thus "IL1 = $0.56" is equivalent to "a *rate* of 1.800".

Reparations (Company) Western Germany is paying, partly in the form of goods, annual reparations to the

	Israeli Government of about $70 million. The administration in Israel and Cologne is handled by this Government concern.
Standard III (*rate*) .	The *rate* on the black market for Israeli currency. This *rate* refers to pure money transactions, measuring the sum of IL involved in the illegal sale of $1.
Standard IV (*rate*) .	The *rate* on the black market for Israeli currency. This *rate* refers to legal, semi-legal and illegal imports of "luxury" goods, measuring the sum of IL exchanged for an imported article with a (c.i.f. Haifa) value of $1. The Standard IV *rate* is not necessarily the same for all imported goods.
Tozereth Haaretz .	The policy of affording a maximum of protection to domestic industry and agriculture by the State restraining, or prohibiting, the import of competing products.

INTRODUCTION

THE lowest point on the earth is located in Israel and its Ministry of Finance has instituted the highest number of exchange rates for any known currency; it numbers world-renowned atomic scientists among its citizens and its divorce laws are reminiscent of the Middle Ages; the official language is Hebrew, a dead tongue which has been revived, and in this living medium the slogans for the building of a socialist society in the Holy Land are shouted; Israel's army has on two occasions repelled the onslaught of invaders from the neighbouring territories; its economy is propped largely by the aid of the German and American Governments and its rising standard of living financed by the donations of Jewish philanthropists. What other country in the world is so full of contradictions, incongruities, abnormalities and charm? What social scientist can fail to be fascinated by the drama of the welding of a new society in the first state ever to be proclaimed by the United Nations? Where else can the economist find so many practical illustrations for an analysis of the implications of a distorted price-and-cost structure?

Part A of this book surveys the economy of Israel and traces the significant features of its development between 1948 and 1958. This is preceded by a short description of the physical nature of the country and an examination of the Zionist ideas which played so decisive a role in the past, and may aptly be depicted as the social prime mover of Jewish colonization in Palestine/Israel. The social and political factors dominating the life of the Jews in their National Home, before and after 1948, are sketched insofar as they have left a discernible stamp on the economic structure and policies of today. I should point out that my treatment of these politico-historical data is neither authoritative nor comprehensive. The specialists on Israel may not wish to read these passages, but those readers desirous of obtaining some non-economic background information on the subject may find them useful before tackling the main themes of the book.

A small poor country like Israel (faced with the problems of a flow of immigrants that trebled its population within a decade, while beset by hostile neighbours) is not the type of economy in which the working of the price mechanism can be expected to bring about the optimum use of resources. Government intervention in economic life (and particularly government participation in major investment projects) has inevitably been on a larger scale than in more fortunately placed countries. But the conclusion is inescapable that, even when the operation of the price mechanism was technically feasible and economically advisable, it was rejected as the proper regulator of economic organization.

The distorted price-and-cost structure and the dominating influence of the "public" sector (consisting in Israel of Government, Jewish Agency, Histadruth and municipalities) can be detected in every branch of the Israeli economy. The descriptive part of this book illustrates this fully; moreover, wherever possible, I present quantitative estimates of the economic damage[1] caused by the deliberate and unnecessary suppression of market forces and the market mechanism.

Foreign aid, received in cash and materials, dominated the Israeli economic scene since 1948. Israel's dependence on unrequited imports (i.e. imports not paid for with exports) is unparalleled in modern history. This heavy dependence on foreign aid partly explains the importance in the Israeli economy of its foreign currency controls; for the foreign currency, derived mainly by way of aid, is made available to the domestic economy *via* these controls. The operation of these controls, moreover, has contributed greatly to the distortions in the price-and-cost structure of the economy. For these reasons an extended treatment of the foreign currency controls constitutes an important part of this book. This treatment is also warranted in a wider context than that of the particular economy of Israel. Multiple exchange rates, as in Israel, are frequently in operation in underdeveloped countries, and the experience of Israel, analysed and documented in some detail, has this wider relevance. In Part B I have indeed attempted to do for Israel what Yang (112) has done for Thailand: to present a case-study of the operations of a multiple exchange rate system. I know, however, that not all readers will wish to work through the detailed discussion in the somewhat inhospitable pages of Part B. For this reason Chapter VII in Part A presents a short summary of the analysis and conclusions elaborated in Part B. Readers who are not particularly interested in the detailed case-study, but are mainly interested in a non-technical survey of Israel's

---

[1] When resources can be allocated to produce either a small or a large product, and, in fact, a small product is generated, one measures the economic damage by the difference between the actual product and the potentially larger one. I do not regard the production of Israeli eggs by the feeding of bread to hens as an economic waste. When, however, (cheap) milicorn is available to do the same job performed by bread baked from (expensive) hard Canadian wheat, the difference in the price of these two inputs provides a measure of economic waste.

economic development, problems and policies, can, therefore, omit Part B, leaving that Part for the professional economist or for the general reader whose interest in the apparatus and implications of foreign currency control has been aroused.

Apart from Chapter XVII, the analysis of Israel's foreign currency controls is not presented in historical sequence. The tools used for this analysis are described in Chapters XV and XVI. As the IL (Israeli Pound) does not perform the function of a clearly defined standard of measurement for the Israeli currency, I have constructed five different yardsticks (on an index basis) for indicating its changing value. The concept of "value-added" is treated separately because it has a distinct connotation in the decrees and regulations of the Israeli Ministry of Finance, the latter employing a special staff to calculate the value-added of products, the economic performance of which, it seeks to measure. Chapter XVIII is devoted to an exposition of the motives which inspired the behaviour of those who drafted the regulations and operated the foreign currency controls. In later chapters it will be shown that the "aims" which the controls were intended to serve were only partly realized. The effects of the control system are examined in Chapters XX–XXIII which deal respectively with domestic production, the composition of imports and the volume of unrequited exports, i.e. exports involving the Israeli economy in a loss of real resources. The final chapter of Part B deals with the beneficial effects of the past devaluations of the IL.

Part B is not a photograph of Israel's exchange regulations at one particular date, but an eclectic account of the variable features of a flexible system that had but one constant factor, namely, the absence at any time of an effective unitary exchange rate. In Chapter XIX a classification of exchange rates is presented but it is neither complete, nor is the space devoted to each exchange rate necessarily indicative of its quantitative importance in Israel's external trade. It should be remembered that Israel does not publish a list of its effective exchange rates, and persistent research was needed to turn up the several hundred rates that I chose to cite. Like a detective searching for clues, for years I have been on the look-out to discover new *rates*. I have not, however, been primarily concerned in preparing a codex of exchange rates but in presenting an account of the reactions that followed upon the introduction of certain *rates*. The varying prices for foreign currency in terms of IL are grouped in accordance with the type of distortion in the price structure to which they gave rise. Many of these regulations and *rates* will seem inconceivable to the reader unacquainted with Israel's economy. Hence, I have combined

xix

a theoretical formulation of each group of *rates* with a practical example to indicate its significance in commercial life. The illustrations which have been chosen from a particular trade do not necessarily tell us about the behaviour of the average member of that trade—they merely show the possible consequences of the application of a particular *rate* in a given set of circumstances. However, the quoted instances indicating illegal procedures portray practices believed to be more than marginal phenomena. My narrative tells of overlapping and contradictory regulations in an untidily arranged "system" of foreign currency controls. I have deliberately omitted the description of certain *rates* and cut the frills off many regulations —all in the hope of simplifying a complex picture. Nevertheless, the analysis of the many cross-rates and confusing government edicts is not one which makes it always easy to follow the thread of the argument or to present a clear-cut exposition. To some extent, however, this is inevitable if the confused state of affairs brought about by incongruous controls is to be portrayed faithfully.[1]

A government that does not control the economy of its country completely cannot efficaciously operate a multiple rate system—that is the chief conclusion which can be drawn from my analysis of the Israeli case study. When the foreign exchange regulations were effectively enforced in Israel, they often led to the uneconomic employment of local resources (in the uncontrolled sector). Many of the regulations, however, were not effectively enforced and large-scale black market activities followed. The ability of the private entrepreneurs to make a stand (especially before 1954) against the powerful competition of the public sectors was largely due to their successful manœuvres against the controls.

Part C of the book contains some general observations that are largely speculative. Some of the features recorded in this study are recognized as being specific to the Israeli scene, yet most of them can be traced to the typical traits of under-developed countries and/or

[1] In January 1959 the Supreme Court of Israel came to the sad conclusion that it was impossible to establish with any certainty what had been the country's *legal* exchange rate on the 4th September 1953. On that day died a Mr. M., leaving a bank account with a credit of 37,000 dollars. His heirs later received a request to pay Israeli estate duty at the *rate* of 1.800. The matter was challenged and evidence was produced in court by the Authorised Foreign Exchange Dealer of a leading bank that the official *rate* on that day had been only 1. The representative of the Ministry of Finance gave evidence that in practice the *rate* was 1.800. Although the Supreme Court felt no doubt that the latter *rate* was the effective one in operation, it ruled against the Ministry of Finance for the Ministry could offer no proof that the effective *rate* was also the *legal* rate.

of economies in which foreign currency controls operate without a unitary exchange rate. In Chapter XXVI an attempt is made to link Israel's specific experience with the general complex of problems facing under-developed countries. The preceding chapter, XXV, indirectly deals with an issue that, despite its Israeli setting, also cannot be limited to the geographical boundaries of my case-study: the relationship between a parliamentary system of government and the workings of multiple exchange rates.

The book concludes with an examination of the prospects of Israel's economy with special reference to the charitable aid which has provided it with its life-blood during the first decade. It seemed to me worthwhile reflecting on how far external forces might play a larger role than internal political changes in altering the present course of the Israeli economy.

It would have proved well-nigh impossible to make a serious analysis of the Israeli economy by referring only to the sources available in English. Several writers have indeed attempted to do this as they were misled by the abundant quantity of economic publications in English. The failings of most of these publications, however, are that they primarily serve to further the publicity aims of official bodies. I quote a Swiss critic:

> "There are relatively many official publications (in Israel); one cannot but notice that they evade a deeper analysis of economic problems. Israel is economically very dependent upon the outside world—especially as regards capital imports—and these publications are clearly aimed at creating by this propaganda a favourable atmosphere for the maintenance and intensification of the necessary aid. . . . Sooner or later the hard facts manage to get through outside Israel and the propaganda character of such publications or of the lectures of such officials becomes apparent." (120).

It, therefore, seems essential to refer to original data published in Hebrew, but even they often do not give a full picture. Statistical data are collected almost solely by the Government and facilities for economic research depend for the most part upon access to archives controlled by the Government.

In the past both the restricted and published material of the Government proved unsatisfactory on many counts, of which the following two are the most important: the distrust of many citizens of the assurance of secrecy given by the Central Bureau of Statistics, and other Government bodies, collecting statistics from private firms and individuals, and the deliberate neglect by the Government statisticians of the existence of the black market. (In fact, the Central Bureau of Statistics later changed its practices and, after 1953, sometimes included data on the black market in its publications; I have found some data on the black market in its files for before 1953, from which it can be deduced that they were collected but that it had been decided not to use them in official computations.) My research has shown that in certain fields the black market accounted for a major part of the transactions; if this was the case, much of the official economic data must be treated with reserve. The following four instances may illustrate this:

A. The Central Bureau of Statistics (185) published figures in English showing that the IL value of the imports in 1951 was IL 123 million. Few will dispute today that the figure of IL 285 million gives a truer picture. (The Bureau at the time also knew their figure to be divorced from reality but they had to use an unrealistic official exchange *rate*.)

B. When the Government appointed Bavli to make a survey of the building and metal industries and official questionnaires were sent out, he had to admit, on the completion of the survey, that the "data supplied by the manufacturers are of a doubtful nature and no reliance can be placed upon them" (15).

C. In one of my writings I queried certain official data and described them as worthless since they excluded transactions on the black market. In a spirited reply the Central Bureau of Statistics admitted that "official statistics do not take account of black market prices insofar as wages, materials and services are concerned; everyone will agree that we could not possibly do so" (152).

D. In a publication sponsored by the Government Printer, the American economist Clawson comments:

> "It is generally believed that there are far more chickens than are officially reported. Some informed observers believe that in the fall of 1954 there were some 3.5 million[1] laying hens, rather than the 2.1 million shown in table 20 [a reference to a publication on agricultural data by the Central Bureau of Statistics]" (16).

In such circumstances (and they are not uncommon in under-developed economies) the research worker must rely—to a larger extent than he would in a developed country with statistical data of

---

[1] There is other evidence according to which the number of laying hens was even larger, i.e. 4 million.

fair accuracy—on field work, intelligent guessing, newspaper reports, proceedings of the law courts and the reporting of private estimates by experts who, understandably, do not wish to be identified by name. Indeed, rich, unvarnished material in the weekly and annual supplements of the leading newspapers deserves a more intensive study than many of the official publications.

A favourable turn in the fortunes of economic research came about in 1953 when the Economic Advisory Staff was founded. The work of this body of professional economists was financially well supported and it initiated independent research which included studies of single firms and of whole branches of economic life. If, until then, guess-work and the mere expression of opinion had been the mainstay of much of the economic writing about Israel, this tradition was broken by the Economic Advisory Staff which measured quantitatively the processes it studied and applied cost-accounting principles in its analyses and projections. The hundreds of reports and job-analyses of this body—I was accorded the courtesy of perusing most of these—laid the foundation for a more rigorous treatment of applied economic problems in this part of the world.

In 1953, the first issue of the *Economic Quarterly* was published, and thus a regular medium was provided for the publication of original research on local matters. In the same year the Central Bureau of Statistics—which had greatly extended the scope of its collection of economic data—began, more realistically, in its publications to take account of transactions on the black market. In 1954 the well-endowed "Falk Project for Economic Research in Israel" was launched in Jerusalem and, under the guidance of S. Kuznets and D. Creamer, initiated a programme of ambitious projects, some of which have already borne fruit. In 1955 the Bank of Israel started to recruit a staff of economists for its research department and some of their work has been cited in this book. By 1957, this research depart-ment had become the chief source of published data on economic indicators.

PART A

CHAPTER I

THE TENETS OF ZIONISM

THE Jews, though dispersed for two thousand years in different regions of the world and speaking many languages, have, nevertheless, retained emotional, religious and national bonds tying them to Jerusalem. Throughout these years the ancient tongue of Hebrew was in some form or another used as a language of prayer and, as the faithful turn to Mecca, so religious Jews throughout the ages turned three times a day in their prayers towards the East, the direction of Jerusalem, and recalled the memory of the sovereign Jewish state before the "dispersion into the diaspora".

Until this century, despite these bonds, no serious attempts, apart from the calls of a few false Messiahs, were made to organize the return of the Jews to what had become known as Palestine. Occasionally a rabbi would make a pilgrimage to the Holy City and pious Jews might transplant themselves at the end of their lives to Jerusalem in order to die there. Collections were made amongst the Jewish communities of the world for the maintenance of those of their brethren who prayed near the Wailing Wall—an alleged remnant of the ancient temple. These were known as the "Halukah Receivers"[1] as they depended for their upkeep on the generosity of Jews abroad. This devotion and the persecutions notwithstanding, the mass of Jews preferred to move from country to country and await outside the Holy Land the coming of the Messiah who would gather them into Jerusalem, and whose advent must not be hastened by voluntary and premature acts of "return".

The last two decades of the nineteenth century saw philanthropic movements organized by Montefiore, Rothschild and the Hilfsverein, which laid the foundation for the later settlement policy of the Zionists to help found Jewish villages in Palestine. Despite Turkish

[1] "Halukah Receivers" later became a word of contempt in the Zionist dictionaries. When Livneh and G. Schocken wanted to protest against Israel's dependence on charitable support, they recalled the Zionist settlers' contempt for those who had come to the country to die and pray, whilst the Zionists had come to work and live. *Vide* particularly (57).

1

obstruction some tens of thousands of Jews from Eastern Europe came into the country in those years; most left again for the American continent, and the majority of those who remained became prosperous farmers who employed the cheap, indigenous Arab labour; it was far from the ideal of a Jewish political state.[1]

The World Zionist movement was founded at an international congress held in Basle in 1897 and developed into a movement with a paid membership of several millions in all continents of the world. It was primarily a political movement and the important leaders at its head were mostly assimilated men who professed no religious faith; even those of its leaders who adhered to the Jewish religion saw in the national aspirations of the Jewish group the fuel for the Zionist motor. The founder of the Zionist organization, Herzl, travelled throughout the world seeking to obtain a concession to build a Jewish state in Palestine; important negotiations led him to meet the Sultan, the anti-Semitic Russian minister Plehve, Joseph Chamberlain, the Kaiser and others. The famous Balfour Declaration[2] of the British Government in November 1917 seemed to point to the success of the diplomatic campaign which Herzl had initiated.

The anti-Semitism to which Jews were subjected in one form or another was the main recruiting agent of the Zionist movement. This was closely linked to another important element that was to become the ideal of all Zionist groups, and not only of those professing socialist views: the restratification of the Jewish occupational structure. In the diaspora Jews were found predominantly in commerce and finance, in certain light industries and the professions; they were not engaged in manual labour in heavy industry, mining and agriculture. This was regarded as a deplorable abnormality by the Zionists who believed that the Jewish occupational structure could only be remedied in a Jewish state where Jews would "be like non-Jews". (B. Borochov, J. Lestschinsky and A. Ruppin are among the better known writers on this subject who have made specific studies of this abnormality.) Public utterances on this aspect of Zionism have often been couched in language reminiscent of anti-

---

[1] The hostility between the Socialist-Zionists and these non-socialist farmers—who regarded themselves as no less true sons of Zion—played an important role in the history of the Jewish community of the Holy Land during the twentieth century. Even today the hatred, which had been generated by these past quarrels, is not entirely forgotten, and only recently the Socialist Minister of the Interior, Bar-Yehudah, referred contemptuously to those who had come to Palestine in order to "change the occupation of a merchant for that of an Effendi landowner" (251)—both being inferior occupations to the speaker.

[2] ". . . His Majesty's Government view with favour the establishment in Palestine of a National Home for the Jewish People . . ."

2

Semitic writings;[1] expressions like "parasites", "non-productive characteristics", "building on the toil of others", will be found in Zionist literature to castigate the Jewish occupational structure [*vide* (156) Lipovetsky].

Before the establishment of the State of Israel, a study by Y. Kaufman aroused considerable controversy (155). In this article he said that "Zionism actually based the national movement on a rationale of charges that it took over from the anti-Semites, and attempted to find a core of justice in the hatred of the Jews". Further, he derided Zionism for speaking slightingly of the economic functions of the Jews so that it would have arguments to induce Jews to leave the countries of their domicile. He illustrated his thesis, *inter alia*, by quoting *Davar*, the official organ of the Histadruth, which used the following headline on a festive occasion: "National renaissance, the regeneration of a parasitic nation". A leader of the Histadruth is quoted as having given the following explanation in 1933 of what "occupational preparation for Palestine" meant: "First of all, preparation for Gentile jobs, the self-preparation of the Jewish worker to become a Gentile . . . to do Gentile work . . . to make a profit the way Gentiles do. . . . The Jewish village girl shall live like a Gentile country lass," etc.

Kaufman, who is today a Professor at the Hebrew University, was a teacher in a Haifa Secondary School at the time this study was published, and no doubt spoke from personal experience when he said that "these falsehoods infect all our Hebrew literature and the mind of our youth. If you were to open the notebook of a Hebrew school student, you might read such phrases as these: 'The Jews in the diaspora are living unhealthy lives . . . they are corrupt . . . the Gentiles around them are living healthy lives'."

This national sentiment and the alleged need for the economic restratification of the Jewish group were gradually accepted as basic tenets of Zionism.

Religious Zionists found in their faith an additional reason to support this Return to Zion.

Socialist-Zionists, a minority in the world movement but probably a majority of the actual immigrants until 1948, had a further set of

[1] The following is a quotation from the head of the American Labour Zionists: "There was a time when it used to be fashionable for Zionist speakers . . . to declare from the platform that 'to be a good Zionist one must first be somewhat of an anti-Semite' . . . To this day, Labour Zionist circles are under the influence of the idea that the Return to Zion involves a process of purification from our economic uncleanliness. Whosoever does not engage in so-called 'productive' manual labour is believed to be a sinner against Israel and against mankind" (157).

3

reasons to support the Zionist aims. They argued that the Jews outside a sovereign state had no useful role to play in the economic, political (and military) struggle of the proletariat because of their abnormal occupational structure. Borochov (154), as the best-known exponent of this theory, postulates it as the duty of a Jewish Socialist to build up a sovereign Jewish state with a Jewish proletariat in heavy industry, mining and agriculture in order that the Jews might become effective fighters in the anticipated world socialist revolution. The men who are today at the head of the Israeli Government came in their youth to Palestine in order to become voluntary proletarians; they were inspired by these socialist ideals as vigorously as by the nationalist and religious content of Zionism. They chose, first and foremost, agricultural labour for their proletarian vocation; they did so because in the Zionist handbooks agriculture was regarded as the most essential economic activity of a sovereign nation and, as pioneers, they took upon themselves the hardest lot in the process of the occupational transformation of the Jewish group. It is no accident that these voluntary proletarians chose the communal village, the kibbutz and the moshav, for their new lives.[1]

Yet, in immigrating to Palestine, few Jews did so in response to the nationalist, religious, socialist or "occupational structure" ideals I have referred to. The overwhelming majority of those who entered Israel (Palestine) came because of severe persecution and the impossibility of immigration to other lands (e.g. German and Austrian Jews) or because the standard of living in Israel was higher than in the countries of their origin (e.g. oriental Jews). Nevertheless, the specifically Zionist ideals did inspire a handful to immigrate, and the rulers of the State of Israel have come from the ranks of these idealists; the conduct of Israel's economic policy during the years surveyed in this book, was powerfully influenced by their socialist belief.

The Dreyfus trials in Paris and pogroms in Tsarist Russia had attended the birth of the Zionist movement before the First World War; yet—largely through the obstruction of the Turkish authorities—the Jewish community in Palestine did not number more than 85,000 in 1914. When the British left in 1948, more than 650,000 Jews constituted the nucleus of the State of Israel. Now, at the beginning

---

[1] The Socialist-Zionists became agricultural proletarians because of their devotion to socialism. Yet their efforts were financed by the whole of the Zionist movement including those who held distinct anti-socialist views. To the latter the creation of a Jewish farming group seemed of such paramount importance that they were prepared to close their eyes to the socialist forms of the rural villages.

4

of 1959, there are almost 2 million Jews in Israel out of an estimated total world Jewish population of 12 million. More than half live on the American continent, about 2 million in the Soviet Union and 2 million in Western Europe, North Africa, Hungary, Roumania, etc. No emigration from Soviet Russia is permitted. The present chief sources of immigration into Israel are oriental communities and Eastern Europe.

Until the establishment of the State of Israel the Jews outside Palestine could be divided into four categories: those who proclaimed themselves to be Zionists (i.e. who were aiming at the establishment of a sovereign Jewish state and intended to live there as soon as was practically possible); the non-Zionists who did not want to leave their countries but viewed the efforts at colonization sympathetically, contributed to Zionist charities and aided the establishment of the State; the anti-Zionists who actively opposed the work of establishing an independent Jewish state—and, of course, there were those who were apathetic to the happenings in the Holy Land.

In 1952 the Knesset passed a law (140) which enabled the Government to sign at a later stage the "Charter of the Zionist Organization in Israel". The law exempts the Jewish Agency and its subsidiary bodies from the payment of certain taxes and Government dues and ascribes to the Zionist Organization the status of an "authorized agency" which will be entitled to function in the State of Israel in furtherance of "the development of the country and its citizens, the absorption of immigrants from the diaspora . . ." Whilst it is explicitly stated that the historical mission of constructing the Jewish state demands "co-operation and full co-ordination" between the endeavours of the Government and the Jewish Agency, no mention is made in the law that the State of Israel recognizes the Jewish Agency as the sole representative of diaspora Jewry or even as the chief delegate of the Jewish groups in the diaspora active in the cause of Israel; this omission disappointed many veteran Zionists.

By 1951 the technical difficulties in the way of a mass immigration from the Western World had been removed. But, to the surprise of most Israelis, only very few English-speaking Jews took the opportunity of emigrating to the National Home. Some Zionist leaders who did not settle in Israel have since expounded the doctrine that a person can remain a registered member of the Zionist organization without wishing to live in Israel, invest his money there, learn to speak Hebrew, etc.; but this is condemned by most Israelis as worthless sophistry. The head of Israel's Government declared on his last visit to America, in 1951, that "a Zionist is a person who settled in Israel". Since then people, claiming to know Ben-Gurion's inner

5

mind, have attempted to explain away this remark as a slip of the tongue. Notwithstanding these apologists, he wrote in 1953 to the Zionist General Council asking its delegates to clarify "whether a Zionist movement, particularly after the establishment of the State, is feasible without the duty of personal immigration and if so, what is the difference between Zionism without the duty to come and live in Israel and devotion to the State of Israel which is common to almost every Jew wherever he be? What is the philosophical content and the special role of Zionism without immigration and what personal duty is imposed upon a Zionist by the movement which enables one to differentiate between him and a Jew who assists the State of Israel?" On the 28th of November 1958, Israel's Prime Minister declared that the absence of any substantial number of immigrants from the West proved that the Zionist organizations in these countries had failed and had "now lost their *raison d'être*".

The ideology of Zionism, therefore, can be said to have played a decisive role in the pre-State period but is now of little significance. However, the sympathy of the majority of Jews in the English-speaking countries of the world—whether they are registered members of their local Zionist organizations or describe themselves as non-Zionists—for the State of Israel, which expresses itself in political and charitable aid, is today, more than ever, a prerequisite for the existence of Israel.

CHAPTER II

ISRAEL—SOME DESCRIPTIVE DATA[1]

THE area of Israel extends over 8,030 square miles and covers 78% of the area of Palestine which was 10,434 square miles.

The distance between the most northern and the most southern point is 262 miles, but the width of the country is as narrow as $9\frac{1}{2}$ miles in the central plain and extends 41 miles in the north and 69 miles in the south.

As against a sea frontier of 159 miles the land frontiers of Israel stretch along 594 miles. Syria and Lebanon are the northern neighbours; the Hashemite Kingdom of Jordan borders the eastern frontier and Egypt (and Saudi Arabia) the south.

The three principal rivers flowing in or through Israel are the Jordan (157 miles), the Yarkon (16 miles) and the Kishon (8 miles).

Mt. Atzmon (3,962 feet) is the highest point in the country, and the lowest point—which is also the lowest point in the world—is the Dead Sea (1,286 feet below sea level).

Most of Israel has a sub-tropical climate with a long, rainless summer which in the coastal plain is humid. The rain is concentrated during a five months' period in the winter—November to March—and this distribution of the rainfall is considered unfavourable to agriculture. The average annual rainfall in the north is similar to that of Western Europe—24 inches—but in Israel little of the rainwater is absorbed in the soil. In the south there is an average rainfall of 8 inches—typical of an arid region.

The country is poor in natural resources and has no coal deposits. Mineral resources have been located in the southern parts of the country. Potash, phosphates, kaolin, glass sand and bromine are already commercially marketed. Some limited deposits of iron, copper, manganese, gypsum, baryte and felspar have been located. Lately, several drillings have led to the discovery of oil, as yet in small quantities, and the country is regarded geologically as an oil-bearing region; several local and foreign companies are prospecting and drilling now.

The capital of Israel is Jerusalem (population 155,000) which is the administrative centre of the country. Tel-Aviv (a population of

[1] A useful summary can be found in the chapters contributed by Dan Horovitz to (124).

600,000, including that of its suburbs) and Haifa—with a deep sea port—(a population of 200,000) are the two largest towns. Nazareth is the chief town of the region in which most of the Arab population lives.

TABLE I

POPULATION ESTIMATES (in thousands)

	Non-Jews	Jews	Total
Turkish Palestine, 1914 .	(680)	85	(765)
British Palestine, December 1947 . . .	(1,150)	650	(1,800)
Israel, January, 1959 .	225	1,820	2,045

Of the non-Jewish population the largest group is that of Moslem Arabs; the other two numerically significant groups are the Christian Arabs and the Druzes.

The new State was proclaimed as a democratic republic with equality before the law for all, irrespective of creed, ethnic origin[1] or sex.[2] The legislature, known as the Knesset, is elected every four years by a direct, secret ballot. "There are no restrictions upon the legislative powers of the Knesset, for no written constitution has yet been adopted.[3] During the term of the first Knesset there were long and recurrent discussions . . . on the question whether there should be a written constitution or not" (245). The President of the State is elected by the Knesset every five years. The President appoints, *inter alia*, the State Comptroller (upon the recommendation of the Knesset), the Governor of the Bank of Israel (upon the recommendation of the Government), the members of the Civil Judiciary and the Judges of the Rabbinical Courts (upon the recommendations of the Nominations Committee[4]). All of these, but the judiciary in particular, have provided efficacious checks to the power of the executive.

[1] Restrictions on the movement of the Arab minority have been in force in some areas since 1948, but these limitations are being gradually whittled down.—Non-Jews are not liable to army service.

[2] Some exceptions can be noted in connection with the jurisdiction of the religious courts.

[3] The original intention had been to have a written constitution and to "disestablish" the Jewish, and other, religious organs. The clerical parties, however, threatened with a modern version of the "Kulturkampf" if such a constitution was adopted. The socialist parties usually needed the clerical parties as coalition partners; hence, the former acceded to the request of the latter and shelved, at least temporarily, the formulation of a written constitution.

[4] Composed of judges, cabinet ministers, members of the Knesset and lawyers.

In Israel there are civil, military and religious courts. The courts of the several recognized Christian communities, the Moslem Religious Courts and the Rabbinical Courts have exclusive jurisdiction in all matters of personal status affecting the members of their communities. The judgements of the religious courts are executed by the process and offices of the civil courts.

At the last election Israel's Labour Party (Mapai) elected 40 members to the Knesset, two right-wing parties 28, two extreme socialist groups 19, three clerical organizations 17, the Communists 6, a liberal party (the Progressives) 5, and there were also five representatives of the non-Jewish minority who usually voted with Mapai —a total of 120 members. During the eleven years of its existence, Israel has been ruled by coalition governments[1] which have been dominated by the Labour Party. Except for a period when he retired demonstratively to a kibbutz in the Negev, Ben-Gurion has headed every government and also acted as Minister of Defence.

[1] During an interregnum between two coalition governments, the Labour Party once governed alone for a period of a few weeks.

9

CHAPTER III

A POLITICAL GUIDE: 1917–1959[1]

"Israel, then, is a freak of history. When writing about
the events, past and present, which led to the resurrec-
tion of the Jewish State, adjectives like 'unique' and
'unprecedented' are difficult to avoid." (263)

The Jewish religion does not allow the erection of
human monuments. If, notwithstanding this prohibition, the future State of Israel should ever erect
monuments to its founders, it might well erect five
statues—*Moses*, the old national and religious symbol;
Herzl, the visionary of the nineteenth century; *Weitzman*, who laid the political foundation stones of the
National Home; *Bevin* for desisively destroying the
illusion that Zionism can be realized except in a
sovereign Jewish state; and *Ben-Gurion*, who pushed
aside the waverers and pacifists of his people, became
the political and military midwife of the State of Israel
and, within one decade, unified the ingathered exiles into
a harmonious, political entity.

THE Turkish rule over Palestine had lasted exactly 400 years when
it was terminated by the march of Allenby and his troops from
Egypt through the Wilderness of Sinai, which resulted in the capture
of Gaza—the southern tip of the country—in November 1917. A few
days later the Balfour Declaration was published, a political achievement of the Zionist Organization that owed much to Weitzman, a
Russian, who taught chemistry at Manchester University and was
later to become the first President of Israel:

"His Majesty's Government view with favour the establishment
in Palestine of a National Home for the Jewish people, and will use
their best endeavours to facilitate the achievement of this object, it
being clearly understood that nothing shall be done which may
prejudice the civil and religious rights of the existing non-Jewish
communities in Palestine or the rights and political status enjoyed
by Jews in any other country."

There were two discordant notes in this document; one was the
reference to "A" Jewish National Home—while the Zionist move-

[1] Among the sources consulted, I found (42), (257), (259), (262) and (263)
particularly helpful.

10

ment wanted Palestine to become "THE" National Home—and the other was the ambiguous phrase concerning the "rights" of the Palestinian Arabs. In retrospect the task facing the British administration during thirty years was a hopeless one. It had to reconcile the Zionist sentiments of the Balfour Declaration with those of its clauses which lent themselves to the interpretation that Britain was to aid the Zionists only with the explicit consent of the indigenous population. The Arabs organized riots against the administration, accusing it of furthering Zionist aspirations, while the Jewish Agency scorned the mandatory Government for appeasing the Arabs and proving unhelpful in the building of a National Home.

In 1920 the Allied Peace Conference allotted the mandate over Palestine to Britain, and Herbert Samuel went from London to become the first High Commissioner, charged with replacing the military government with a civil administration. In the latter part of 1923 the mandate was formally conferred upon Britain by the League of Nations. The first in the series of grave disturbances, that were periodically to shake the Holy Land during the mandatory rule, occurred in 1921, resulting in the loss of many Arab and Jewish lives; this was followed by the Churchill White Paper of 1922 that reassured the Arabs and appeared to the Zionists to whittle down the obligations of the Balfour Declaration. It declared, *inter alia*, that "His Majesty's Government regarded it as impracticable [that Palestine was to become] . . . as Jewish as England is English". After the Wailing Wall Arab–Jewish clashes in 1929 had cost the lives of 253 persons, the Shaw Commission was sent to Jerusalem and returned with a unanimous report: the fundamental cause of the disturbances was the Arab animosity towards the Jews; the Jewish land policy was found to create a discontented class of landless Arabs; Jewish immigration into Palestine was described in the report as having been larger than the economic absorptive capacity of the country warranted; the administration in Jerusalem was advised that " . . . the special position assigned to the Zionist organization in the mandate does not entitle it to share in any degree in the government of Palestine". The work of the Shaw Commission was supplemented by the Hope-Simpson memorandum, the author of which thought that the natural increase of the Arabs and the immigration of the Jews had produced such pressure on the available cultivable land that there could be no question of adding to the rural population except after extensive development schemes. While these reports were not followed by severe restrictions on immigration,[1] they did encourage

[1] Throughout the mandate the Jewish Agency, other bodies and individuals organized legal, semi-legal and illegal immigration of Jews into the National

11

the Jerusalem authorities to confine "in the meanwhile" Jewish farm settlement to the land already in Jewish possession. The riots of 1936 brought a further commission, known as the Peel Commission, to Palestine; it reported in 1937 to the British Government that the mandate had proved unworkable and proposed that the country be divided, founding an independent Jewish state in those areas predominantly occupied by the Jews, and joining the rest[1] of the country to Transjordan. These recommendations were immediately accepted by Whitehall, but the Arabs refused even to consider them; in 1937, the Zionist Congress split the Zionist movement on the issue of "Partition", and only a small majority was obtained by the Executive of the Jewish Agency for negotiations on this with the British Government.

In order to appease the Arabs, however, the British Government abandoned its policy of implementing the partition of the country; nonetheless the Arab Rebellion against the Palestinian administration broke out and lasted throughout 1938 and 1939, dying out with the publication of the (Malcolm) MacDonald White Paper (just before the outbreak of the war) which buried the Balfour Declaration altogether. This White Paper announced that the British Government aimed at a sovereign, independent State of Palestine at the end of a transitory stage of ten years; during the first five years only 75,000 Jews were to be admitted into the country, and thereafter immigration be allowed only "on the acquiescence of the Arab elements in the population". The MacDonald White Paper divided the country into three zones: zone A (63% of the total area of Palestine) in which the purchase of land by Jews was absolutely prohibited; zone B (32% of the total area) in which land transfers to Jews could only take place with the consent of the High Commissioner, which, in fact, was never given; zone C (5% of the total area) in which Jews could purchase land freely. This brought about an open breach between all sections of the Zionist movement and the British Government. Despite the outbreak of war, land ordinances, in accordance with the MacDonald White Paper, were published in 1940, and the mandatory administration fought unauthorized Jewish immigration more fervently than ever. In spite of

Home; the climax was reached in the early thirties when extreme economic pressure on Polish Jewry and the persecution of German Jews with Hitler's accession to power turned a trickle into a flood—in 1935 alone, 62,000 Jewish immigrants passed through the ports of Jaffa and Haifa.

[1] The areas of Jerusalem, Nazareth, Bethlehem and Haifa were to be placed under a separate trusteeship to which the two partitioned states would have equal access.

12

these measures, which were felt by the Zionist movement to be acts of provocation, a truce in the struggle against the British administration was declared by the Jewish Agency for the duration of the war. Palestinian Jews were encouraged to volunteer for the British army and the economic potential of the country was geared to the war effort of the Middle East.

The truce was called off in 1945 when the anti-Zionist policy of the new Labour Government was put into effect; from 1945 to 1948 a bitter and violent struggle was conducted against the administration in order to force Britain to give up the mandate; illegal immigration was organized on a large scale and tens of thousands of such immigrants, when apprehended, were deported to detention camps in Cyprus; one large ship was even returned to Germany by British troops. Several underground armies, often at loggerheads with one another, fought, each in their own way, for a sovereign Jewish state; the largest force was the (Jewish Agency controlled) "Hagannah". In the winter of 1945, President Truman called on Bevin to permit the immediate immigration of 100,000 Jews; the Foreign Minister of the Labour Government refused this appeal but—in contradiction to the 1939 MacDonald White Paper—allowed a legal immigration quota of 1,500 per month, though the continuation of this trickle was to depend on—to quote Bevin—"the generosity of our Arab friends". The last Palestine Commission appointed by Whitehall was the "Anglo-American Committee" sent to the Holy Land by the Labour Government. To the chagrin of Bevin it recommended the immediate admission of 100,000 Jews and the repeal of the anti-Jewish land ordinances. The Labour Government announced its refusal to implement these recommendations and left the problem to the newly-formed United Nations. When the United Nations dealt with the issue, it considered not only the Arab–Jewish conflict, but also took into account that several hundred thousand Jewish displaced persons, who were waiting in European camps, pressed for admittance to Palestine.

During the mandate the Jewish Agency evolved as a state within the state, building up an apparatus many of the departments of which were "shadows" of government departments; it established a civil service, a machinery for (unofficial) taxation, an immigration department and a war office so that, with only a few adjustments, its executive could at short notice transform itself into a Provisional Government of Israel, as indeed it did. This evolution of the Jewish Agency was gradual, for only slowly were the Zionist leaders themselves convinced that their political aspirations could alone be gratified in a sovereign Jewish state. In the first years of the mandate, the

13

Jewish Agency was recognized as a representative both of world Jewry and of Palestine Jewry, and was consulted officially as such. At one time it was given semi-governmental functions to perform and was entrusted with the responsibility of regulating Jewish immigration; the first two High Commissioners tried, in fact, to get the Arabs to organize a parallel Arab Agency, but these refused. During those years Zionist leaders seriously believed in the Zionist intent of the Balfour Declaration and many thought that the National Home would be built under the auspices of the Palestine administration. The vote in 1937 for Partition by many Zionists was a vote of distrust against the Palestinian administration; even at that time men like Ben-Gurion thought that a small, sovereign Jewish state would serve the interests of Zionism better than the continued rule, in the larger area of Palestine, of a government that only paid lip-service to the building of the National Home—though no one at that time thought of an armed revolt. The White Paper of 1939 induced some dissident groups to start violent operations against the Jerusalem Government but the Jewish Agency was not, as yet, ready for such a far-reaching step. In 1942, at the Biltmore Hotel in New York, Ben-Gurion as the leader of the (Mapai) socialists co-operated with the head of the American right-wing Zionists, Rabbi Silver, in order to announce a programme which pledged the Zionist movement to the building of an independent Jewish Commonwealth, and thus publicly broke with the moderate, but, until then, dominant influence of the Anglophile Weitzmann on the leadership of the Jewish Agency. Matters came to a head a few years later when Weitzmann was dismissed from office in the movement he had led for so long. Sacher describes how, after Bevin's rejection of the recommendations of the "Anglo-American Committee" and the arrest in Palestine of several members of the Executive of the Jewish Agency, the Zionist Congress met in Switzerland in December 1946: "There Dr. Weitzmann urged that they could not have a Jewish State of the whole of Palestine, but should work for a viable Jewish State in an adequate area of Palestine. He begged the Congress not to abandon Britain, no change of orientation would help. But the majority of the Congress had lost confidence in Britain. This became an issue with Dr. Weitzmann, which expressed itself in the question—should the Executive participate in the resumed London Conference (as suggested by Whitehall)? By a small majority participation was negated, and Dr. Weitzmann retired from the Presidency. Mr. Bevin had succeeded in removing from the Jewish Agency the most faithful friend of association and co-operation with Great Britain" (42).

The "United Nations Special Commission on Palestine"—

UNSCOP—was appointed in 1947 and its recommendations for the partitioning of Palestine were accepted by a majority of the members of the United Nations on the 29th November of that year—Russia and America voted together for the resolution, and Great Britain alone of the great powers abstained, while all the countries of the British Commonwealth voted in favour. The area of the proposed Jewish state was to be 5,500 square miles (and to include an Arab minority of 400,000) and the Arab state was to have an area of 4,500 square miles. On the 14th May 1948—*vide* Appendix X—the Provisional State Council declared the State of Israel to be in existence, and on the next day the High Commissioner put a *de jure* end to the mandatory administration. The Palestinian Arabs and Israel's new neighbours refused to implement the second part of the United Nations' resolution which had urged the establishment of an Arab state; armed forces from seven Arab countries invaded the new state but were conclusively defeated after open hostilities lasting ten months. As a result of the fighting, and the non-establishment of a second state, the territory of Israel became larger than had been originally envisaged. The remaining parts of Palestine, not under Israeli jurisdiction, were occupied by the armies of Jordan and Egypt respectively and were, *ipso facto*, annexed to those countries. The overwhelming majority of the Arabs who lived in the areas now part of Israel, left their homes at the onset of the fighting. At one stage they did so in the belief of the imminent defeat of the Zionists and their departure was actually opposed by the Jewish authorities; there is some evidence to suggest that at a later stage the Jewish authorities changed their attitude and, in fact, encouraged some of the Arabs to flee. 700,000 Arabs are said to have left and 900,000 of such refugees[1] (the difference is accounted for by the high birth rate) are now living in great squalor in camps near the borders of Israel, and depend on relief payments from the "United Nations Relief and Works Agency for Palestine Refugees in the Near East".

In 1949, after the fighting had subsided, the Government of Israel came to the sad but certain conclusion that they would have to build their external political relations on foundations that did not include peaceful relations with their neighbouring states. Owing to the mediation efforts of the United Nations, in which the American, Bunche, and the Swede, Bernadotte (the latter was killed by a dissi-

---

[1] In his 1957 report to the United Nations, the director of UNRWA declared that 922,279 were receiving relief. Of this number 500,000 lived in Jordan, 200,000 in the Gaza strip, 105,000 in Lebanon and about 90,000 in Syria (257). The article on "Arab Refugees" in (279) cites useful sources on why the Arabs fled in 1948 and some reasonable estimates are given of the numbers involved.

dent Israeli terrorist group in Jerusalem), played a prominent role, truce arrangements were signed in 1949 with the representatives of the Egyptian, Jordan, Lebanese and Syrian Governments, though their supervision (in later years) by United Nations observers proved ineffective. The years 1949–1956 were years of disguised warfare between the Arab states and Israel—constant skirmishes, boycott, infiltrations, destruction of property on both sides, etc. During these years several attempts were made to negotiate a global settlement and, while the Jews were prepared to sit around the table with the Arabs (as a token of good will they had permitted some of the Arab refugees to return to their homes), the Arab leaders were afraid to parley with Israel. This fear was occasioned by the assassination of King Abdullah of Jordan (in 1951) who had negotiated in secret, and, by this *de facto* recognition of Israel, had stamped himself as a traitor in the eyes of the Arab world.

In 1956, the balance of power in the Middle East was changing— the Russians and their satellites were furnishing arms and other help to the new leaders of Egypt who had begun writing a fresh leaf in the history of the Arab world after the corrupt régime of Farouk had finally been deposed. To forestall an intensified infiltration campaign, organized by Egypt, or an open attack on its territory, the Israeli Government launched the Sinai campaign in the autumn of that year, clearing the Egyptian army from the Gaza strip within a hundred hours, occupying large tracts of the Sinai desert and striking within ten miles of the Suez Canal. The intervention of Britain and France in the campaign—whether by collusion with the Israeli Government or not—is still too much of a live controversy to be evalued dispassionately. Nevertheless, the campaign had this important consequence, that between 1956 and 1959—when these lines are being written—Israel has been free from raids and attacks by infiltrators and has enjoyed three quiet years of military security. However, since the situation in Israel is like sitting on a powder-keg, the newly-acquired freedom of travelling and walking through the countryside is tasted only with mixed feelings.

Is Israel's fate bound up with the West or with Asia? The main proponent of the Asian orientation is the former Oxford don, Eytan, who has directed Israel's Foreign Office since its inception, but so far there have been no signs that Israel's striving along this course has borne any fruit; most Asian countries have not even recognized Israel—this includes India—and certainly did not welcome its birth. The Western bearing is advocated by Peres—one of "Ben-Gurion's young men"—who had been the chief liaison officer with the Quai d'Orsay and was for seven years Director-General of the Ministry of Defence; he left the civil service in 1959 to enter politics.

Since the 1947 vote by Russia in the United Nations Assembly for a Jewish State, and the arms shipments from Czechoslovakia in 1948, much water has flowed into the Volga; a Communist anti-Semitic wave has come into the open, an open pro-Arab policy has been declared, and relations with Israel have become strained—at one time even diplomatic contact was severed. America's friendship for Israel, which was shouted so loudly from the rooftops in the days of 1948, also cooled; desiring to appease the Arabs, Washington has not, on the whole, acceded to Israeli requests for arms, though its liberal attitude to economic aid—which was cut once only for a few months after the Sinai campaign—is profusely illustrated in the coming pages. But Israel gained a new friend in France which sold arms freely and aided it as decisively in the 1956–59 period as Prague did in the years of 1947 and 1948. Britain also began to bury the hatchet and, in 1958, officially sold two submarines to the Jewish State and promised further deliveries of arms. On Israel's side the decade of sovereignty has turned the anti-British animosity of the mandatory days into subject matter now considered only fit to be dealt with by historians.

CHAPTER IV

AN ECONOMIC CHRONOLOGY:[1] 1948–1958

1948

UNLIKE most British colonies where the transfer of power to the sovereign governments of the new states of the Commonwealth proceeded in an orderly fashion, step by step, the administration of Palestine was instructed not to hand over any local executive organs to the Provisional State Council; "on the contrary, its intention was to disrupt all services before departing from the country, leaving chaos behind them" (272). Weeks before the end of the mandate, the Government refused to grant import licences for many goods and no provision was made for a continued supply of food from the Combined Food Board and the International Emergency Food Council. Postal communications were cut—Palestine being excluded from the International Postal Federation—and, with the large American and British companies refusing to maintain services to Lydda, air traffic was throttled; internal travel and travel onward to the neighbouring countries was discontinued by the British directors of the Palestine Railways, the administration of which was wound up. In March, all British shipping lines were ordered not to call at Haifa. The oil refinery in Haifa was closed down early in April and the flow along the pipeline from Kirkuk was diverted—thus cutting off Israel from its petrol supply until the sovereign Israeli Government issued a decree in June reopening the refinery without the consent of the British owners. In many ways the hardest blow came on the 22nd February when Palestine was unilaterally excluded from the Sterling Bloc, thus freezing the sterling balances of Palestinians in England in blocked accounts. A few days earlier the chairman of the Bank Leumi (as it is called today) was sent to America by the Executive of the Jewish Agency, who controlled the bank, to arrange the printing of new banknotes. This operation was carried out in conditions of extreme secrecy, and during the heaviest fighting the banknotes were unloaded in Israel. During the first few months of the new state the old Palestinian pound notes were still legal

---

[1] This is not a comprehensive account of happenings in the economy during each year. It should rather be regarded as a light introduction to the more technical description found in the later chapters.

18

currency; but, after the Government had concluded a charter agreement with the Bank Leumi (on 17th August) for the issue of a new currency through an Issue Department to be controlled by an officer of this bank (Lehmann), the secretly prepared notes gradually replaced the old ones at parity. The old banknotes had had a 100% cover in the form of Sterling securities held by the Palestine Currency Board in London; as the old notes, which were exchanged by the Bank Leumi for the new notes, were sent to London for redemption, the blocked account of the Government of Israel in London increased weekly.

During 1948 total mobilization was proclaimed and men were waiting for arms to be unloaded—more than 100,000 are said to have been called up. None of the economic difficulties which the State was to face in the later years existed during these months: the sympathy for Israel brought in much hard currency, and Israel's Minister of Finance, the late Eliezer Kaplan, could afford to go without the blocked Sterling balances that temporarily could not be drawn upon. The chief difficulty was the procuring of supplies of arms, food and petrol in the face of the blockade erected not by the Arabs but by the refusal of most shipping and air lines to transport goods to a country that was not expected to last many days.[1] Oil from Roumania, arms brought in by air from Red Czechoslovakia, food imported in unseaworthy vessels at exorbitant prices saved the young economy.

1949

As military victory appeared on the horizon, the newly-organized economic ministries began to take stock of their position, and their chief attention was devoted to the subject that was to become a nightmare during the next five years—the balance of payments. The partial destruction of the Dead Sea potash works (some parts of which were also in enemy territory), the closure of the refineries[2] and the preoccupation of domestic industry with the needs of the army and the growing local market, left the new State without many sources of export earnings, the two exceptions being the citrus and diamond industries which accounted for 91% of the gross export

[1] This left a profound psychological impress on Israel; and if anyone in the years to come challenged the feasibility of the State investing in local shipping and air companies, the old files of 1948 were brought out.
[2] In 1950, the British oil companies agreed to bring crude oil from afar to operate the Haifa refinery for Israeli consumption only. They did not agree to bring crude oil to Haifa against the will of the Arabs in order to re-export the oil products; it was probably also not an economic proposition to do so.

19

proceeds in 1949. Palestine had received considerable foreign currency receipts from tourists in the past; but with the Holy Places in two warring countries and reports of violence in the headlines, few foreign tourists provided foreign currency for the newly-founded Ministry of Finance. In addition, the military victories weakened the willingness of Jewish sympathizers to repeat the record donations of 1948 and the incomes of the *institutions* were reduced. A loan of $100 million from the United States Export-Import Bank lifted the spirits of the people, but as the proceeds had to be used to buy machinery the loan could not pay for food and fuel imports. One remarkable opportunity presented itself to the young State—but was decisively missed; this was the visit of hundreds of Jewish entrepreneurs from all corners of the world who, in their enthusiasm for the new State of Israel, offered to found factories and private undertakings. They met with a warm welcome, but discovered such a host of restrictions and limitations on private enterprise that few were even prepared to make further investigations into the possibility of investment in the new State.

In September, Israel followed Britain's lead and devalued its currency to the *rate* of 0.357. This devalued *rate* soon proved to be unrealistically high. To encourage the import of capital which would otherwise be deterred by this unfavourable *rate*, the Government initiated the policy of *imports-without-pay*. Thus began the long history of permission being officially granted to the importers of capital to transfer their capital in the form of luxury goods, and thereby, in fact, to circumvent the official exchange *rate*.

Immigrants came in an unending stream, the economy adjusted itself to peace conditions, the railway from the coast to Jerusalem functioned again and the Israeli airline, "El-Al", made its appearance in Europe. The threat of inflation became the topic of the day, and Ben-Gurion chose a Jerusalem lawyer, Dov Josef, who had proved himself as a Military Governor of the besieged city of Jerusalem, to inaugurate the "Zena-Austerity" programme. This was to raise the internal value of the IL by reversing the price-wage spiral, and, for that purpose, price controls (on the basis of cost-plus) and rationing were introduced. As the Israeli wages were tied to the movements of the cost-of-living index, the reduced price level induced a reduction in money wages.

1950

At first Dov Josef was received like an economic saviour because he accomplished the apparently impossible; between April 1949 and July 1950 the cost-of-living index was reduced by his physical controls from 371 to 317 and, despite left-wing opposition and joint manipulations of wages in some industries by employers and employees, the Histadruth agreed that the wage rates be lowered on three occasions in consequence of the downward movement of the index. As Dov Josef's appetite grew with his "successes", he added more categories of goods to the tender mercies of his controllers.[1] In the meanwhile, an extensive black market evolved which frustrated the controls of Dov Josef's ministry. Things came to a head in the winter when the total rationing of clothing and footwear was introduced; the private merchants closed their shops in protest and declared a general strike against the Government. This failed, however, to move Dov Josef. Nevertheless, the man who only a year before had been hailed as a saviour, had now become a liability to his party, Mapai. The position was aggravated when the food rations were cut, and even the reduced rations were not honoured. Eventually in the winter of 1950 he was dismissed from his post and transferred to the relative tranquillity of the Ministry of Transport; by December the price-wages spiral once more went in an upward direction.

Despite export subsidies, the balance of payments became desperate and the *institutions* (and private importers) were asked to tap foreign sources of credit and import goods from such suppliers as were prepared to do so against long-term letters-of-credit endorsed by the Ministry of Finance; Jewish Agency loans from Scandinavia, Belgium, Switzerland and other countries were obtained conditional upon the import of goods from the countries providing the credit. All eyes were on the Israeli delegation which went to London under the chairmanship of the Director-General of the Ministry of Finance, Horovitz, and which signed an agreement with Whitehall which settled the outstanding issues of financial obligations on the part of the Israeli and British Governments as part-inheritors and trustees of the mandatory administration respectively. All frozen Israeli Sterling accounts were freed. This brought some relief, but the situation was still desperate enough to force Jerusalem to requisition all foreign securities (in November) for sale against hard currency.

Attacks by Arab infiltrators and the need to compensate owners of property for damage during the War of Liberation led to the

---

[1] *Reductio ad absurdum*, Dov Josef's ministry wished to impose a regulated maximum IL price on the dozen copies of *The (London) Times* which were daily flown in. This led to a bitter conflict between the local agent for this journal and the Jerusalem price controllers, but, to the delight of many of the Israeli public, Dov Josef did not succeed in lowering the profit margin on the sale of *The Times*— but this sort of defeat was exceptional.

21

adoption of a compulsory War Damage Insurance. The recruitment of most Israeli earners for reserve duty of, on the average, one-month-service a year necessitated the passing of a law according to which these reservists were not paid by the army, but from the proceeds of a payroll tax.

During this year the Histadruth "Hamashbir" and certain other trading organizations left the Chamber of Commerce and the building of an "autarchic" Histadruth empire was speeded. However, this did not prove a successful venture in future years.

In March, the "Law for the Encouragement of Capital Investments" was passed by the Knesset and aroused great hopes. Later these were to be shattered as few honest foreign entrepreneurs took advantage of its benefits to establish sound enterprises. The law promised new investors reductions in taxes, permits to import freely certain categories of goods and the right to repatriate annually foreign currency profits of up to 10% on the invested capital. It did not apply to investment in real estate.

1951

In 1948 the total circulation of Israeli banknotes was IL14 million; by 1951 this volume had increased to above IL100 million. (According to Patinkin (32) 1948–51 were the years of "suppressed" inflation which were followed by the years of "controlled" inflation.) When the original charter with the Bank Leumi was signed in 1948, it provided that the foreign exchange cover of the notes was not to fall below the ratio of 50%; the rest of the cover to be provided by 91-day Treasury Bills.

As from 1949 the charter agreement was amended and the Issue Department of the Bank Leumi was allowed in addition to hold long-term Government Land Bonds as cover instead of foreign currency.[1] The Issue Department published a weekly Statement, and the gradual decrease in the foreign currency cover—*vide* table on p. 23—accelerated the flight of the Israeli public from the IL. The price of the illegally traded gold sovereign jumped between 1949 and 1950 from IL7 to IL25.

In October Dov Josef took charge of the Ministry of Trade and Industry and was, thus, once more in command of physical controls. This time, however, the black market prices and not the official

---

[1] Between 1948 and 1951 Israel had two published budgets ("Ordinary" and "Development") and a secret defence budget; the internal financial appropriations for the latter were mostly provided from the proceeds of the Treasury Bills and Land Bonds.

TABLE II

MONEY IN CIRCULATION AND ASSETS HELD AS COVER [in thousands of IL (264)]

Date	Total Money in Circulation	Gold with International Monetary Fund	Foreign Currency	Government Land Bonds	Treasury Bills	Palestine Currency Notes
August 1948	14,200	—	1,736	—	—	12,464
November 1949	50,716	—	28,362	16,860	4,740	317
December 1951	101,833	—	2,762	77,136	20,410	—
December 1952	119,887	—	12	77,136	42,740	—
December 1953	138,012	—	4,256	77,276	56,480	—
December 1954	161,306	2,025	51,905	77,266	30,110	—
December 1955	186,482	2,025	60,089	77,258	47,100	—
December 1956	240,981	8,441	81,358	77,279	73,703	—
December 1957	249,806	6,271	71,568	77,249	94,718	—
February 1959	283,282	6,203	118,304	77,279	81,496	—

prices dominated the market; his ministry could not honour the clothing coupons; and the non-distribution for several months of the sugar ration lowered the morale of the people. The wealthier members of the community depended on imported food parcels and the first "Scrip-Dollar-Shops" (*vide* p. 192) were opened during this year. Electricity restrictions, stoppage of factories because imported materials were lacking, half-format newspapers because foreign currency was not available to import sufficient newsprint, the employment of the army to grow vegetables for the urban population, the need to accommodate the Iraquian mass immigration in temporary huts—all this created social tension in the country at a time when Israel's material fortunes were at their lowest ebb.

On the foreign currency front, the Ministry of Finance dropped all pretence of maintaining the sanctity of its official exchange rate, and participated, through intermediaries, in the black market and encouraged the *import-without-payment* of goods which it considered essential. Yet, while the fuel and flour supplies were only sufficient for a few days because of foreign currency difficulties, the first swallows of a brighter future appeared in this, the most dismal of all years in Israel's history: the American Export-Import Bank granted a second loan of $35 million; the first American grant-in-aid was allotted to Israel in the amount of $65 million; Ben-Gurion went to the United States to launch the sale of the Israeli Government bonds and by December purchases of $74 million had been pledged.

1952

This year was the watershed for Israel's economy. In the first few months Dov Josef continued his controls, and also managed to impose new building controls aimed at strangling building for the private sector of the economy. On the black market, foreign currency was traded at the *rate* (Standard III) of IL2.800 to the dollar, a level not surpassed at any time since. The cost-of-living index recorded the greatest annual fluctuation of the period 1948–58; in twelve months it rose from 107 to 178.

In February the "New Economic Policy" was ushered in to the sound of deservedly loud trumpets. The Government promised to stop inflationary credit expansion. It undertook to discontinue further sales of Treasury Bills and Land Bonds to the Issue Department (and by August this promise had been kept); to "request" the commercial banks to increase their liquidity-ratio to 50%; to devalue the currency through the introduction of three new official *rates*, the highest of which placed the IL at par with the dollar; and to incorporate the secret defence budget in the published official budgets. To enforce the disinflationary trend a forced loan (that could be commuted into a smaller-sized levy) of 10% on all bank deposits, most types of property and pound notes (by exchanging ten of the latter for nine new notes) was imposed.

In May Eliezer Kaplan, who had been Treasurer of the Jewish Agency since 1933 and in charge of the Ministry of Finance since its inception, together with his Director-General, Horovitz, were forced to resign because, *inter alia*, they did not wish to comply with the Prime Minister's order to allocate a large percentage of the available foreign currency for the needs of the army. Their places were taken respectively by Eshkol, who has been Minister of Finance ever since, and (some months later) by Saphir—the latter has since been promoted to a political post as Minister of Trade and Industry.

In the autumn, the General Zionists, who at the time had been the main right-wing opposition party, entered the newly-constituted coalition government. Dov Josef, in his last few weeks of office, reversed the policy of physical controls and abolished the clothing and other rationing regulations. This did not help him to regain much favour in his party and he was transferred to a puppet ministry in November.

One of the few serious labour conflicts of Israel in its first decade was the unsuccessful 42-day strike of the men of the merchant marine; this was a rank-and-file movement against the leaders of the trade union section of the Histadruth who were suspected by most of the merchant seamen of acting in collusion with the employer, which happened to be a Histadruth-controlled shipping concern. Several other unofficial strikes against the management of Histadruth-owned companies have since taken place but none have been so bitter and prolonged as this summer dispute of the merchant seamen.

1953

During 1953 the third devaluation was being carried out, though only on the 31st December were the multiple *rates* (ranging from 1.000 to 1.800) officially proclaimed. As in previous years, the American grant was again $70 million, and the first funds from Germany reached Israel—the previous year the (West) German Government had signed a Reparations agreement according to which Israel was to receive German currency and goods to the value of $814 million during the ensuing twelve years. The sale of Israeli Government bonds in America was now a constant annual foreign currency income item to be reckoned in terms of tens of millions of dollars. At the request of the General Zionists the Prime Minister appointed a Commission, headed by Horovitz, to examine whether Israel should abolish its foreign currency controls. The Commission unanimously rejected the complete abolition of the controls. The majority recommended the retention of the controls with a unitary *rate* of 1.800, while the minority wanted some of the controls to be lifted and a free currency market to be established for part of Israel's foreign currency expenditure and income.

Internally, the Ministry of Trade and Industry, which was now controlled by Bernstein (the General Zionist heir of Dov Josef's resort) abolished many physical controls and permitted a "grey" market to co-exist with a market in which official prices ruled for purposes of manipulating the cost-of-living index. The Government opened a new avenue of inflationary borrowing by instructing the Accountant-General to sign Letters-of-Obligation to suppliers promising to pay them within six to nine months, and these were, of course, discounted by the banks. The technique was stopped after about IL15 million of such notes had been issued. It was regarded as an achievement that the cost-of-living index rose by only 19% during this year.

1954

The orderly and (relatively) stable period of the Israeli economy began in this year, and the State became respectable enough to join the International Monetary Fund and its associated Bank, with a quota of $4½ million. Though private foreign investments and substantially increased export earnings had not materialized (despite the anti-socialist partners which Mapai had taken into the Government) the days of foreign currency crises were over. The 1952 "New Economic Policy" had brought about a fundamental change and, from this year onwards, the Israeli inflation was more a cost-inflation than a demand-inflation; henceforth the cost-of-living index only rose annually by about 7%.

In the preceding years smugglers and clever manipulators had harvested rich crops of differential profits by importing luxury products and selling them locally at exorbitant prices. Now the Government entered the sphere hitherto reserved for black market operators. It offered licences and allocations of foreign currency (at widely varying prices) for the legal import of non-essential products.

The gross foreign currency income from merchandise exports in 1954 constituted a considerable advance over that of the preceding

26

period. At this time bilateral trade agreements were in full bloom; the consignment of goods made in "dollar-packaging" plants to Yugoslavia, Finland and Turkey contributed substantially to this "export success".

Ever since the inception of the State, the linking of the value of money contracts to a "stable object" has been an important feature of Israeli life. This now spread to all departments of the economy and, in fact, was encouraged by the Government. The Ministry of Finance accepted the recommendations of the Lehmann Committee according to which part of the value of funds lent by the Government was to fluctuate with the movements of either the official exchange *rate* or the cost-of-living index. Value-linking had arrived.

1955

The foreign currency controls reached their most elaborate point in 1955. Hundreds of divergent exchange *rates* split the buyers and sellers of IL into different compartments and a high degree of price discrimination ruled in the foreign exchange market. Most illegal transactions in foreign exchange were now repressed, and, for the first time, court proceedings were taken against a bank for contraventions of the foreign currency controls; its licence to act as an Authorized Agent was withdrawn. Imports under the *imports-without-pay* scheme no longer played a dominant part in the market for luxuries, as such imports at high *rates* were increasingly permitted. A further step in the same direction was the decision to abrogate gradually the *pamaz* system which had been introduced 2½ years earlier; instead of allowing favoured exporters to utilize part of their foreign currency earnings for the import (and subsequent resale at relatively high prices) of luxury products, direct money subsidies began to be paid on the value-added content of privileged merchandise exports. In July an announcement was made to the International Monetary Fund that the only official exchange *rate* was 1.800; the *rate* of 1.500 was still maintained for the larger *institutions*—in effect, a punitive *rate*.

Immigration was now at its lowest; and in the previous year the growth of the population by the net influx of Jewish immigrants had been smaller than that gained by a high birth rate. The spirit of Israel's population was fired when oil was discovered in marketable quantities in the Heletz fields.

In this year the Bank of Israel, which had begun activities as the central bank of the country in the previous year, was on its mettle to prove that, besides the Ministries of Finance and Trade and Industry,

27

it was the third economic executive organ of the state. The Issue Department had already been transferred to it from the Bank Leumi in 1954, and, with its growing apparatus, it was fulfilling the task of being the Government's banker. A severe regimentation of the banking system with qualitative and quantitative directions by the Bank of Israel made itself felt.

As the General Zionists had left the Government, the Bank of Israel and the Ministries of Finance and Trade and Industry were in the hands of three socialists (namely, Horovitz, Eshkol and P. Saphir); despite departmental friction, they were united on three basic issues: wages must not rise faster than productivity, the high marginal income tax rates must be reduced, demands for cheap money and deficit budgeting must be resisted. While this united front won the intellectual approval of the country, no substantial advances were made on any of these three (theoretical) points.

1956

At the beginning of 1956, the Ministry of Finance was agreeably surprised to find a new source of foreign currency income; the individual restitution payments to former German Jews brought the economy about $60 million annually. However, special rates and income tax privileges had to be promulgated to discourage the emigration of a large section of these rentiers.

The economic ministers were disturbed about the adverse prestige reactions to the sale of many of the large industrial undertakings by their owners to the Histadruth sector. Lest this expansion of the Histadruth empire have an inimical result on fund-raising campaigns in America, a secret meeting of Mapai leaders forbade the Histadruth to purchase further undertakings without special permission from Mapai.

This year saw the largest deficit to date on the balance of trade, 357 million nominal-dollars (255).[1] Stockpiling in anticipation of the Sinai campaign in the autumn partly accounted for this. Much of Israel's industry was employed during these months in preparation for the impending military clash, and tens of thousands of reservists were called to the colours in October. Although the heavy expenditure in preparing for the campaign gave an added impetus to a renewed inflationary upswing, the short duration of the fighting meant that the economy came out unimpaired by this military test.

[1] This includes both services and merchandise trade and is the equivalent of the official estimate of the Balance of Payments on Current Account. The deficit is actually larger; for the reasons *vide* p. 33.

28

1957

As a direct consequence of the victory of the Israeli army, the port of Eilat was opened to international traffic and the improvised port facilities handled 43,000 tons of cargo in its first year. The Government also speeded its plans for the industrialization of the Negev, and announced that enterprises transferring to new towns, like Dimona (or, motivated differently, to the hitherto exclusively Arab town of Nazareth) would receive loans from the Development Budget equal to 80% of the investment.

The most important strike in Israel's history took place at the "Ata" textile works (near Haifa), the largest private undertaking in the country; this industrial conflict was fought by the managing director of the enterprise (H. Moller) on the principle that a factory owner has the right to dismiss inefficient and redundant employees. The strike lasted for more than three months and ended with an inconclusive compromise.

Agriculture flourished, and the large crops of groundnuts, sugar beet and cotton pointed to the future course which the planners were charting, to devote an ever-growing part of Israel's agricultural resources to industrial crops.

In March, the Interest Law was passed in the Knesset, and the Ottoman Law with its 9% maximum interest regulations no longer applied. The Minister of Finance used his new powers to declare 11% as the maximum interest for ordinary loans, 10% for agricultural and industrial loans, and $6\frac{1}{2}$% for value-linked loans.

1958

In December of 1958, Eshkol joined the rebels among agricultural planners and declared himself in favour of "the war against the cow", i.e. to limit further mixed farming, and to replace some of the areas now cultivated with fodder grains by industrial crops.

The Jewish Agency and the Government came to an agreement whereby they would merge their landholding interests; they established a National Land Company that will in 1960 be the landlord of 95% of Israel's land. In a desperate drive to attract private investors it was promised that the existing "Law for the Encouragement of Capital Investments" would be amended in 1959, with retroactive application to April of 1958; *inter alia*, the new law would permit the repatriation of all profits (and not 10% on the investment as hitherto) and would apply also to investments in real estate.

The British-owned Haifa refinery was sold to a Jewish company.

In the autumn an eight-inch pipeline from Eilat—linking the Red Sea and the Mediterranean for purposes of oil transport—was inaugurated.

The foreign currency position of the State of Israel remained unchanged, and it is thought that the financial year of 1958/59 will witness receipts of 600 million nominal-dollars. The Government refused to consummate the fourth process of devaluation and instead multiplied the exchange rates for the IL—thus creating a world record for financial history. Many predict a nominal[1] devaluation to a *rate* of about 2.800 at some stage in 1960.

[1] Until the beginning of 1957, two-thirds of the buyers of value-linked bonds opted for linking their bonds to the fluctuations of the cost-of-living index but, since then, two-thirds of the buyers of value-linked bonds have preferred—in expectation of a change in the official exchange *rate*—the linkage to the dollar.

CHAPTER V

NATIONAL INCOME, BALANCE OF PAYMENTS[1] AND CAPITAL FORMATION

"Ben-Gurion challenged a gathering of Israeli and foreign economists and sociologists to re-examine economic laws in the light of Israeli experience. His words vented the belief, widespread here, that the cold rules of a balance sheet do not apply when people are working in a state of high-development fever" (199).

ACCORDING to my estimates, Israel, in the period between May 1948 and April 1958, imported goods for domestic use and availed itself of foreign services for the amount of $3,300 million. (This sum would be larger by several hundred million dollars had the import content of Israeli exports not been excluded from it; as I am, however, enumerating only the net export earnings below—i.e. total foreign currency proceeds less import content—the import content clearly must be deducted from the gross import bill.) This expenditure of $3,300 million was matched by eleven categories of receipts, for only the first three of which will I venture to make individual quantitative guesses:

(1) Net proceeds from visible and invisible exports: $300–400 million.
(2) The release of blocked Sterling balances and the sale of requisitioned foreign securities: $150 million.
(3) Private investments [this does not include the purchase of bonds issued by the Israeli Government and public institutions for charitable motives—for these *vide* category (6) below] and property brought into the country by immigrants and others less disinvestments and the (legal and illegal) repatriation of property owned by emigrants from Israel or non-Israelis: $300–400 million.

. . . .

[1] I have mostly made use of official data but hazarded some guesses for 1948/49. These estimates correspond roughly with the evidence which was unearthed during the humourless public debate between Eshkol and Livneh in the winter of 1957, concerning the total of Israel's unrequited income; the debate was fully covered in the *Davar, Haaretz* and *Haboker*. (In addition to the published data, I have estimated the size of certain unspecified receipts not officially registered.)

31

(4) Loans by the American Government's Export-Import Bank.
(5) Grants-in-aid of the American Government, surplus food allocations, American books, etc.
(6) German Government payments via the Reparations Company.
(7) German Government restitution payments to individuals.
(8) Organized charitable support by Jews in the diaspora, mainly through the *institutions*.
(9) Individual charitable support by Jews in the diaspora to relatives and friends.
(10) The "investment" for philanthropic reasons of Jews in the diaspora in Israeli bonds issued by the Government, the Histadruth and others.[1]
. . . .
(11) Other receipts; these include contributions by international agencies, overdraft facilities from countries with which Israel has trade agreements, commercial credit from foreign banks and suppliers, loans from Governments other than the United States Government (e.g. France).

It will be noted that categories 4–10 (and partially category 11) are "charitable and political aid" income items; they are estimated to have yielded $2,350–2,550 million. Thus, during its first decade, one-twelfth of Israel's foreign currency expenditure came from receipts of "earned" income, though the proportion has increased to one-eighth in 1957 and 1958. Whilst there is, thus, a slow, but steady, growth in the share of the foreign currency expenditure, which Israel covers with visible and invisible exports, the gap between merchandise exports and imports has widened during this decade; *vide* Table IV. If the "supported society", as now constituted, is to continue with its present outlays on security and immigration, and if its standard of living is to continue to rise at the same annual rate, an annual subsidy of about $300–350 million will have to be provided by Jewish well-wishers and interested political powers.

This is also illustrated in the (ex ante) budget published by the Ministry of Finance for 1957/58; *vide* Table III. In theory these

---

[1] In 1958, the American agents for Israeli Government bonds urged Jerusalem to raise the interest rate of a new series of bonds planned for 1959 from 4% to 4¼%. The Ministry of Finance refused to do this and a special correspondent of the Histadruth journal *Davar* explained the reasons: "The Ministry of Finance and its American advisers are of the opinion that 95% of those who purchase these bonds do not even know what interest the bonds bear; hence, any changes in the interest rates offered on the new bonds will not affect the volume of sales" (284).

budgets include all the legal foreign currency receipts of the State. There is reason to believe that the actual legal receipts are larger. In addition, illegal foreign currency receipts ought to be taken into account. These—in the views of those I have consulted on the matter —exceed the illegal movements of currency out of the country so that a net "income" from the illegal balance of payments accrues to Israel.

TABLE III

FOREIGN CURRENCY BUDGET FOR 1957/58
[in millions of nominal-dollars (37)]

RECEIPTS		EXPENDITURE	
Gross Visible Exports .	130	Consumption Goods .	122
Gross Invisible Exports and Services . .	56	Gross Invisible Imports, Services and Army Supplies . .	149
Institutions . .	89	Investment Goods .	118
Reparations Company	75	*Import-for-Export* .	87
Israeli Government Bonds . .	55	Fuel . . .	60
Individual German Restitution . .	50	Debts (and diverse) Payments. . .	41
American Grant-in-aid .	50		
"Special" Credits .	38		
Other Income . .	34		
TOTAL .	577	TOTAL .	577

So far, in drawing up a balance sheet for the first decade of Israel's economy, reference has only been made to external unrequited receipts. In addition, in 1948 the newly-formed Israeli Government took over abandoned Arab property; this has been valued by Riemer (283) at £120 million (i.e. $500 million) and by D. Cohen (227) at IL1,000 million. The Custodian for this property has adapted for use 58,000 dwelling units and 11,000 shops and offices, and administers farms with 60,000 dunams of plantation, 30,000 dunams of citrus groves, etc.

An estimate by sectors of Israel's National Income for 1957 will be found in Table V. Yet, in view of the large import surplus, it is desirable not to measure Israel's economic growth primarily in terms of the National Income but rather in terms of Total Available

TABLE IV

THE NATIONAL ACCOUNTS OF ISRAEL[1] [1949–1958] (in millions)

Year	National Income		Gross National Product		Import Surplus	Total Available Resources
	IL	$	IL	$	Nominal-Dollar	Nominal-Dollar
1949	240	533	301	670	225	895
1950	338	563	433	722	264	986
1951	528	704	673	897	335	1,232
1952	856	778	1,103	1,009	279	1,288
1953	1,130	807	1,345	961	226	1,187
1954	1,461	859	1,737	1,022	208	1,230
1955	1,752	876	2,122	1,061	245	1,306
1956	2,092	930	2,509	1,115	256	1,371
1957	2,513	1,005	3,030	1,212	293	1,505
1958[2]	2,850	1,040	3,500	1,280	320	1,600
TOTAL	13,760	8,095	16,753	9,949	2,651	12,600

[1] The table has been built from data culled eclectically from the following sources: (20), (85), (108), (124), (129), (140), (142), (148), (150), (158), (159), (238), (239), (255) and (275). The definitions of National Income, investment volume, etc., differ as between the various sources cited but no attempt has been made to reconcile them. These data represent at best rough estimates.

As explained in the text of Chapter V, the dollar values in these tables are imputed dollar values calculated by multiplying the IL values with the *average rates* of p. XIII. The official data for the import surplus are in nominal-dollars. As the addition of nominal-dollars to dollars must be a sum in a currency of lesser value than the dollar, I have described the currency, in which "Total Available Resources" are presented, as the nominal-dollar.

[2] The 1958 figures are based on a forecast.

34

Resources,[1] i.e. the Gross National Product + the import surplus. In order to have a common denominator for these data, the IL figures in this book are usually presented side by side with their imputed dollar equivalents. For the conversion I employed the *average rates*, p. XIII. According to Table IV, the import surplus constitutes about 21% of Total Available Resources. I share the view of those who believe that the real economic weight of the import surplus is substantially higher.[2]

TABLE V

THE NATIONAL INCOME OF 1957 (255)

Source	Millions of IL	Percentage
Agriculture	299	11.6
Industry, mining	560	21.8
Building	165	6.4
Water, electricity	43	1.7
Transport	182	7.1
Commerce, insurance and other services .	814	31.7
Public Administration . . .	505	19.7
Domestic National Income . .	2,568	
Less net payments to factors abroad .	55	
National Income	2,513	100.0

[1] "Total Available Resources" is a concept used indiscriminately in official Israeli statistics in two different senses. According to the definition of Gaaton (today of the Bank of Israel) it is a summation of the Gross National Product and the total imports; according to the definition of Dinur (now of the Central Bureau of Statistics) it is a summation of the Gross National Product and the import surplus. In this book I am using the concept in the latter sense, i.e. as defined by Dinur.

[2] Some critics have argued that the *average rates* understate the value of Israeli production in terms of dollars. As against this, others have expressed the reasoned view—and I share it—that the *average rates* exaggerate the value of Israeli production when measured in dollars. The *rate* of domestic production (*vide* p. 169) is almost certainly higher than the *average rate*. Furthermore, the import surplus is much larger than can be deduced from the official figures cited in

35

Tables IV and VI show that the net investment in the economy during the years of 1949 to 1957 was 26.3%, and gross investment 33.6% of the National Income. If the investment volumes are compared with "Total Available Resources", the proportions are 16.9% and 21.6% respectively. The import surplus for these years was larger than net investment and equal to gross investment. It follows[1] that during this period there was dissaving in the domestic economy. Moreover, but for the charitable and external political aid, not only would no (net) capital formation have taken place, but the existing productive capacity would not have been maintained. I judge that the investment decisions concerning 80–90% of the $2,000 million net investment were made by officials of the Government, the Jewish Agency and the Histadruth. This tallies with other estimates; Darin (210), for example, arrived at a proportion of 75% for 1955 and the Ministry of Finance[2] forecast for 1956–1960 even considers $87\frac{1}{2}$% a likely figure. The decisions on how to invest public investment funds were made by officials, but not all of these funds were channelled into the public sector. A new private entrepreneur,[3] or one wishing to extend an existing enterprise, stood a good chance of obtaining the necessary capital if, instead of offering shares or bonds on the capital market, he linked himself to persons—or strong

Table IV. Official data do not include important imports of a military nature and certain other items; they do not correct the intentional (fraudulent) under-valuation of many imports, and, of course, do not take account of illicit imports.

[1] These conclusions check with those arrived at by Dulberg in her two studies (63) and (144) and by Gaaton (148), though both differ between themselves and from my work in the estimate of the degree of domestic dissaving.

[2] The Ministry of Finance forecast in 1956 (205) that during the subsequent four years an investment volume of IL1,800 million would be needed to consolidate the enterprises already founded and to found places of employment which would absorb 60,000 new earners; only 12.4% of this amount was expected to be recruited from private sources.

[3] An illustration will be found in Appendix I. The following is a quotation from a remarkable article published in the official Histadruth journal by a leading Mapai economist (250): "The State of Israel has inherited a grotesque tradition from the Jewish Agency. Was there some organized body to which (in the pre-State days) the Jewish Agency did not allocate loanable funds? Every group that received tens of thousands and hundreds of thousands of Pounds—when the Palestinian currency was still equal to the Pound Sterling—regarded these funds as capital which was now owned by the political or economic group that initiated the enterprise. Only very rarely did the enterprise regard it as its duty to pay interest, or a dividend on that capital to the Jewish Agency. Since the State came into existence, it has become the fountain of finance for all sorts of economic undertakings. Everyone regards the State as his partner whose only duty it is to make loans and provide investment capital. The Government has not taken an active part in the management of those enterprises to which it has entrusted millions. . . ."

pressure groups—who knew how to enlist the financial resources of the State. Today there is unanimity among Israeli economists that a substantial portion of the investment funds available during this decade were not efficaciously invested. I am prepared to go further than that and contend that the chief cause for this failure to invest wisely is linked directly to the abundance of investment capital, relative to the available entrepreneurial skills and tested investment projects. This, however, is part of a general problem affecting under-developed economies, and is discussed in a wider context, in Chapter XXVI. The enthusiasm, at times ludicrous, for investments *per se* which characterized many official actions in the economic field during this decade, very often led to severe distortions in the price-and-cost structure. Public capital was provided, in the first years, for undertakings which, on completion, could not employ their modern imported machinery economically, because the Ministry of Finance lacked the foreign currency to make allocations for spare parts or raw materials. Reports made on the employment of equipment, supplied through loans of the U.S. Export-Import Bank, in the building branch, the metal trade and in the Government-owned Tel-Aviv port, all tell the same story of failure to utilize the new capital goods economically. Until 1955, the Government did not, as a rule, offer to lend prospective investors capital with the alter-native of disposing of it to purchase either local or foreign goods;[1] in practice the State offered to furnish investment capital at *low rates of interest and at low (exchange) rates* on the stipulation that the machinery be obtained from a foreign source. No such favoured treatment was given to entrepreneurs who wished to employ local resources for similar purposes.

Public authorities have been known to grant mortgage facilities of up to 100% on the value of new houses, whilst 95% was not an uncommon proportion in the case of the standardized houses which

[1] A concrete example may demonstrate this farce. The Government, wishing to lower the price of bread, was gratified when, in 1954, five Haifa bakeries decided to merge and establish a joint mechanized workshop; on application, they were immediately granted a credit of IL80,000 to buy a stove in Germany. At a later stage when a sub-committee of the Knesset investigated this Government credit, it found that a similar-quality stove could have been built locally at an IL price that was even lower than that which the bakers had contracted to pay for the Marks involved in the purchase. The bakers, however, did not even interest themselves in the local alternative for they knew that the credit *only* applied to a purchase abroad, and the costs of raising capital from a non-Government source were prohibitive. (Because of the protests of the Knesset, the Ministry of Trade and Industry agreed, as an exceptional measure, to make an additional cheap loan from the Development Budget if the bakers wished to purchase a second stove locally.)

were sold to impecunious immigrants. (According to one estimate, the average participation of the public sectors in the financing of houses in 1955 was 89%.) In agriculture some new settlers obtained 100% of their capital from the resources of the Jewish Agency and the State; an authorized estimate for the 1949–54 period indicates that only 9% of the investment in colonization, irrigation and agriculture came from "own finance of farmers" (16), while another source cites a percentage of 2% for 1955. Agricultural economists pointed to the wasteful handling of expensive machinery by inexperienced persons who, they suggested, should work for a period of transition as trainees or hired labourers, instead of receiving as soon as in the first stages of settlement, capital goods from the public bodies. This seemingly sensible suggestion could not, however, be put into practice until very recently, because the political ideology of the Israeli socialist parties saw in the institution of wage labour in general, and in agriculture in particular, an evil of abysmal perversity; hence, the Jewish Agency prided itself on bringing (often illiterate) immigrants straight from the bowels of their boat in Haifa to the paradise of "owning" a farmstead in the Negev. The delegate of the Food and Agriculture Organization in Israel was a very sympathetic onlooker; but he was so struck by the policy of forcing new immigrants to become independent farmers that he found it necessary to comment on this in his report to the Israeli Government:

> "It is generally assumed that best results will derive from individually-owned and operated farms. Certainly, this is a desirable objective, but it should be realized that among those engaged in agriculture will be a considerable proportion who are not qualified either by capability or desire to be managing owners of farms. To force such persons to become owners and managers would be a waste of resources" (145).

No data on the average participation of the State and the Jewish Agency in the financing of privileged industrial projects have been published, but cases of a special nature with a participation of 90% are known. In 1956, the Government wished to scale down its percentage participation in industry and announced that, henceforth, it would not finance any enterprise that could not raise at least one-third of its required capital from private or Histadruth sources. Yet, in July 1957, the Minister of Trade and Industry boasted that he had put up the percentage of loans, that would be granted from the Development Budget to new industrial enterprises in certain areas, to above 70%. In April 1958, the same Minister declared that new entrepreneurs would be granted a whole list of remunerative privileges and Government loans for 80% of the new investment if they allowed his ministry to direct them to certain industrial areas.

TABLE VI

THE INVESTMENT VOLUME[1] 1949–1957 (in millions)

Year	Net Investment[2]		Gross Investment[2]	
	IL	$	IL	$
1949	60	133	80	178
1950	112	187	150	250
1951	158	211	214	285
1952	272	247	316	287
1953	276	197	331	236
1954	349	205	449	264
1955	431	216	551	276
1956	465	207	615	273
1957	630	252	806	322
TOTAL	2,753	1,855	3,512	2,371

[1] *Vide* explanatory notes to Table IV.
[2] These data include semi-durable goods (of immigrants and agricultural settlers) which are not always included in comparative statistics of other countries.

CHAPTER VI

THE HISTADRUTH

THE Histadruth was founded in 1920 as a socialist-led trade union movement. It found little scope, however, for waging a class struggle in Palestine against an exploiting bourgeoisie of the sort that its leaders had learnt about in European socialist literature. Inspired by Zionist ideas, thousands of young men and women from predominantly middle-class families, streamed to the country to become manual workers and build the National Home; but they found few employers ready to give them the chance to become "wage-slaves". Those who did employ Jewish labour—at a time when cheaper Arab labour was readily available—did so mostly through Zionist convictions; few entrepreneurs could afford this generosity and, in any case, in the early years Palestine lacked the financial resources to employ many new citizens on capitalistic forms of production. Hence, from the very first days of its existence, the Histadruth had to concern itself less with defending the interests of its employed members than with creating workplaces for Jewish workers. It accomplished this objective in four ways: (1) It encouraged members to organize themselves under Histadruth guidance as co-operatives (particularly in agriculture and transport) with outside charitable aid—and later self-financing—providing the means. (2) Pressure (and sometimes force) was exerted to induce Jewish entrepreneurs to employ Jewish instead of Arab workers. (3) As the Jewish immigrants could not subsist on the wages paid to Arabs, the Histadruth (with the aid of the Jewish Agency) offered the services of its Jewish members to employers (e.g. the mandatory Government) at the current wages paid to Arab labourers, and paid these members a subsidy from its own funds. (4) Zionist charitable funds were used to found industrial, and other, enterprises for the purpose of employing immigrants. This last point is worth elaboration; the present entrepreneurial empire of the Histadruth owes its origins to this technique that was originally associated with the alleviation of unemployment. The Histadruth opposed the payment of money relief or unemployment pay.[1] It founded (sometimes in conjunction

[1] "It was always difficult to estimate unemployment in Palestine. Apart from the absence of practically all machinery for the purpose, there was always, even in the periods of the greatest depression, a tendency to minimize and even conceal the Jewish share in it, mainly for political reasons. With a large shifting popula-

40

with the Jewish Agency) special construction and contracting firms—the forerunners of Solel Boneh, the largest Histadruth firm in the country today—and saw to it that relief funds were utilized through the medium of these firms for the allocation of "x workdays per unemployed".

In its early days the leaders of the Histadruth did not deliberately set out to acquire factories for their organization. This course seemed to be forced upon them when some existing enterprises were planning to move to Egypt and others were about to become bankrupt; the fear of losing workplaces for several hundred members drove them to seek funds to buy these enterprises. Only at a much later stage, when it was part of socialist strategy to seek to acquire industrial undertakings did the Histadruth use all its influence and power to compel private owners to sell out to them at bargain prices. If the Jewish Agency built "a state within a state", the Histadruth was by 1947 "a state within the Jewish community".

One further crucial point should be mentioned, a point by which through an historic accident the Histadruth was subsidized and built up by non-socialist forces. The animosity between Jews and Arabs during the mandatory period meant that the Government of Palestine could rarely found joint social services for the two communities. This was coupled with the unwillingness of the *institutions* to have part of their relief funds used for the non-Jewish sector. Consequently, the Histadruth was encouraged by the Zionist movement, as a whole, to build up social services that in the Western world would be administered by the state. General Zionist funds helped to subsidize the Histadruth sick funds, elementary, secondary and vocational schools, labour exchanges, public housing, cultural organs, etc.

tion with no homes anywhere, sometimes in Tel-Aviv, at others in a communal settlement, partly seeking employment, partly in hiding from the few Immigration or Labour Department inspectors, this was not difficult. Among the Arabs there was also a political incentive, but to increase not diminish the number of the unemployed. One of their arguments against Zionist immigration was that it took employment from the Arabs and threw them out of work. The powerful Zionist Labour Organization was always claiming the right to dictate to employers whom they might employ, and to send to them not the same man every day, but him whose turn they considered it was for employment. When employment was scarce the Histadruth Haovdim rationed it among their members giving them four, three, two and even one day's work a week and claiming that in calculating the next half-yearly Immigration Schedule they were all equally employed" (262).

These historical reasons for the Histadruth's opposition to unemployment insurance are hardly good grounds on which the old Histadruth leaders could rationally continue to oppose—even in the sovereign State of Israel—the payment of (cash) unemployment relief as a breach of socialist and Zionist faith. Yet these views prevail and the antiquated and expensive method of providing unemployment relief through the "allocation of workdays on special projects" continues.

THE ECONOMY OF ISRAEL

When the State was ushered in during 1948, the Histadruth had become an umbrella under which a trade union section, co-operatives, enterprises owned by its executive and miscellaneous social and cultural services existed side by side. After 1948, as the number of factories signing "closed shop" contracts increased, it became practically compulsory for a worker looking for work to be a member of the Histadruth; and it was even more important to the poorer sections of the population that only members of the Histadruth could make use of the services of its sick fund—the Kupath Holim. As employees in the "Ata" strike in 1957 learned (when some refused to participate in the Histadruth-led strike), the most powerful weapon of the Histadruth was to exclude them from the union and inform the dispensaries and doctors of Kupath Holim that the miscreants were not to receive further medical treatment. In the mandatory days it was possible to pay dues to Kupath Holim without being a member of the Histadruth; but the trade union leaders have since learned that the sharpest whip over recalcitrant workers is to prevent them and their families from enjoying, in the absence of state medical services, the amenities of Kupath Holim, and now only trade union members have access to the latter.[1] All three socialist parties are agreed that any future national health scheme must not involve the abolition of Kupath Holim, the strongest reason for an employee in Israel to be a member of the Histadruth. Whilst in 1948 45% of the Jewish population was served by Kupath Holim, in 1959 70% depend on it.

The power of the Histadruth is so effective that no sane employer is likely to resist its demands for long, for there is little sense in risking a strike from an omnipotent opponent; this explains the paucity of strikes in Israel:

Year	Man Days Lost
1949	57,436
1950	55,087
1951	114,290
1952	58,066
1953	35,404
1954	71,946
1955	53,978
1956	112,756
1957	165,469
1958	87,751

[1] The only trade union of any size which still exists outside the Histadruth is one controlled by the "Herut" party, and its leaders have had to resort to similar tactics by providing a sick fund, dispensaries and hospitals of their own.

There were those who thought that the immigration of hundreds of thousands of unskilled persons, most of whom were unacquainted with the political and social ideas of the Histadruth, would menace the hegemony of the Histadruth trade unions. This threat did not materialize, because the immigrants were pressed to join the Histadruth, while still in the transit-camps, in order to benefit from the Kupath Holim services.

Year	Daily Average of Registered Unemployed
1949	6,351
1953	17,680
1957	12,513
1958	9,328

Israel's workers increased their real wages in the 1949–58 period; but an even greater advance was achieved by the Histadruth in the size of the fringe payments, many of which were not made directly to the employees but to union institutions, e.g. provident fund, holiday hotel accommodation, Kupath Holim. The fringe benefits amounted to 30% of the money wage on the average with extreme cases of up to 50%. The payment of severance pay, at the rate of one month for every year's service, became a general practice in Israel but the Histadruth severely limited the right of employers to lay off workers on grounds of redundancy or inefficiency even when the employers offered to pay more than this traditional severance pay. The trend towards egalitarianism is striking when a study is made of the differential wage rates negotiated by the unions. This is not unconnected with the only defeat[1] ever suffered by the Histadruth in a major conflict since 1948: the strike of the Kupath Holim and Government-employed doctors for appreciable salary increases; the combined power of the State and the Histadruth neither prevented this strike breaking out nor its being waged by the Medical Association to a successful end.

There are two explanations for the relative moderation which the union leaders have shown in the exercise of their powers. One is the influence exerted on them by their party colleagues who head the economic ministries, and the other is the representation on the executive of the Histadruth of the managers of its enterprises, who,

[1] Whilst the employers seem unable or unwilling to stand up to the union leaders, the absolute power of the latter is challenged by professional groups which demand organizational freedom, e.g. secondary school teachers, engineers and others have gone on strike against the will of the Histadruth, whereupon the leaders were threatened with exclusion from the Histadruth and Kupath Holim.

as large-scale employers, are direct beneficiaries from union restraints on wage claims.

The producers' section of the Histadruth can be roughly divided into four parts: (1) the co-operatives in which the equity capital is held by the members but the general control over which is vested in the central organs of the Histadruth, e.g. industrial co-operatives, retail trading co-operatives, kibbutzim and moshavim; (2) enterprises which are owned by the executive, and the employees of which have the status of wage and salary earners as in any private enterprise, e.g. Solel Boneh (Koor), Workers Bank, *Davar*; (3) companies owned, wholly or in part, by small co-operative groups, e.g. Hamashbir (Wholesale Co-operative Society), Tenuvah (for farming produce); (4) corporations in which the executive of the Histadruth is a partner of the Jewish Agency and/or the Government, e.g. Mekoroth Water Company, Zim shipping concern. There is no economic or social field in which the Histadruth is not represented, and its interests range from the production of a daily paper to the making of pipes, from being a landlord to importing drugs, from owning aeroplanes, hotels, cement factories, convalescent homes, kindergartens, insurance societies, a fishing fleet to oil wells; it has its own auditing bodies and private law courts. While about 20% of the National Income of the Jewish economy was derived from its activities in 1947, in 1957 one-third of Israel's National Income had its origin in this organization (273). Before the State came into being, the Histadruth embraced 60,000 workers and in 1959 about 180,000 persons work within its orbit; more than 450,000 men and women are members of the trade union section.

Theoretically the economic institutions of the Histadruth are subject to extensive control and supervision by the members of the co-operatives and/or the executive. In practice things look quite differently. The managers of the large corporations enjoy a salary which, after income tax deductions, may not even be double that of the doorkeeper; but their power to rule is more absolute, ruthless, unchallenged and continuous than that of the heads of private enterprises in Israel or, for that matter, elsewhere. Men like Dan, Efter, Kav-venaki, Verlinski and others, who have stood for a quarter of a century at the helm of monopolistic firms, laughed contemptuously at attempts of the executive to impose its will on them. The Histadruth has always been united on external symbols like the general strike on the 1st of May and the hoisting of the Red Flag, but the powerful bosses of the large corporations never sufficiently co-operated with one another to give the dreamers of a centrally-planned and controlled Histadruth empire a working

44

chance. One Histadruth company allied itself with private groups in a search for oil and competed with a similar venture of another Histadruth group; the Hamashbir and Tenuvah fought bitter battles over the marketing of farm products by kibbutzim; when Dan, the manager of Solel Boneh, did not get sufficient credit from the Histadruth's Workers Bank he bought up a competing bank so that Solel Boneh could have its own credit institution; when the Hakal company did not like Tenuvah's terms it had its vegetables marketed by private firms; when Solel Boneh was too dear for the Shikun housing company, the latter gave a housing contract to private builders; and so innumerable examples could be quoted which point to the absence of central co-ordination and control, and the failure of the executive to build an autarchic empire.

Since 1935 the Jewish Agency has been effectively controlled by Mapai, as has been the Israeli Government since its inception. The important decision-makers in the Histadruth—all the important union leaders, the heads of the commercial, financial and industrial trusts, the managers of its social services and the editors of its journals—are members of Mapai too. This Holy Alliance has had an obvious advantage in helping to harmonize the three competing executive organs of the State, and the boundaries between the three have not always been discernible to an outsider. Conflicts between Mapai leaders in their capacity as economic directors of government, Jewish Agency, or Histadruth corporations, were often settled by the secretariat of Mapai.

It is undoubtedly correct to say that the Histadruth undertakings were more enterprising than those of the private sector, more daring in their ventures and prepared to risk more; but it must also be remembered that the captains of the Histadruth industry were more independent in their ability to make quick and personal investment decisions than any other person in Israel and, unlike the Government, did not have to defend themselves in the Knesset for the numerous misinvestments (owing to an over-supply of public funds on which little or no interest had to be paid) that can today be found in their wake. It is said that in the early years of the State many prospective private investors were frightened by alleged Histadruth threats, according to which only those who would take the Histadruth in as a 51% partner would be allowed to open up in Israel. No convincing evidence has been offered that a minister of the Israeli Government ever told a foreign entrepreneur that he could not invest in the country unless he did so jointly with the Histadruth. What was, however, proved beyond a shadow of doubt was that those who did work on a partnership basis with the

Histadruth led an easier life and received in larger quantities and with less delay the many bounties which the Ministries of Finance and Trade and Industry distributed. Many of the Histadruth concerns behaved as if the foreign currency controls existed only for the private sector and not for them; Dan, the head of Solel Boneh, dared the Minister of Finance to punish him for currency offences.[1] When Dan was appointed head of the Reparations Company in Germany, he staffed it with officials on loan from his company, while he continued at the same time to be the managing director of Solel Boneh. He was dismissed from this (German) post in 1955 because the Mapai secretariat was satisfied that he misused his position in discriminating, *inter alia*, against a competing Histadruth company!

Between 1954 and 1958 the private sector experienced a serious crisis; and many firms, in the face of bankruptcy, went, cap in hand, to the Histadruth begging to be bought out. The supplicants included prominent industrialists who, as executive members of the Manufacturers Association, had only a few years before spoken out against the domination of Israel by the Histadruth. Now they turned to the only address which had sufficient command of liquid financial resources to offer payment if it happened to be interested in an enterprise. Critics in America misunderstood this sale of private enterprise to the Histadruth, thinking that the firms were being browbeaten into selling; in fact, the Histadruth had become fastidious and rejected some enterprises even when they were offered on a plate at bargain prices. Nonetheless, to avoid the bad impression which was made on Zionist philanthropists abroad by the sale of these private firms, a meeting of Mapai leaders accepted the demand of the ministers, Eshkol and Saphir, that in future the Histadruth trusts were not to be permitted to buy private enterprises. The Israeli public was amused by the ludicrous situation in 1957, when a bankrupt Israeli industrialist of some prominence, who thought that he could only save himself from insolvency by selling out to the Histadruth, was informed by a director of the latter's purchasing trust that the Mapai decision bound him and he could not finalize the sale. This time Shenkar, the aged president of the Manufacturers Association, pleaded with Mapai minister, Saphir, asking him to intervene with the Mapai secretariat to permit the Histadruth to purchase this enterprise as an exceptional case.

In the summer of 1956 Pinhas Lavon was appointed Secretary-

---

[1] There are isolated instances in which Solel Boneh, Hamashbir, Tenuvah and other Histadruth companies have been convicted for breaches of the foreign currency controls, black market activities and other economic offences, but these can be regarded as exceptions that prove the rule.

General of the Histadruth. Few thought at the time that he would within a year become one of the handful of powerful men, who could aspire to succeed the present Prime Minister. Lavon was not tied to the traditional[1] patterns of thought of Israeli socialists, most of whom argued that the path to socialism lay in the strengthening of the Labour sector of the economy and who fought against the growing power of the State itself. Lavon has entered into an alliance with Saphir and Eshkol against the old guard of the Histadruth trusts and plans to cut down the Histadruth so that it will become a predominantly trade union body, and insofar as it retains entrepreneurial functions intends a strong executive to direct and control them. In the winter of 1958 Lavon succeeded, not exactly by the use of kid-glove methods, to depose Dan and his henchmen, split up Solel Boneh into autonomous divisions and appoint his own nominees to the management. A similar fate is predicted for the other trusts where analagous purges are seen to be in the offing. Lavon and some younger members of his party feel that Mapai has compromised itself as a socialist party by appearing to many Israelis in the guise of an employer, and not always a benevolent one. Already the Histadruth has been divested of certain powers by the new Ministry of National Insurance and the socialist-directed school system has also been taken over by the State. A majority of Mapai support the nationalization of the labour exchanges and transport co-operatives, though only a minority, so far, is in favour of letting the Kupath Holim be handled by a national body for all citizens. Upon Lavon's decision that, in these new times, the Histadruth does not need to maintain a theatre of its own, the Histadruth has paid the members of its theatre "Ohel" generous severance pay. Already there have been cases of the State taking over small Histadruth industrial enterprises. A slightly different attitude is also noticeable in Government offices towards Histadruth undertakings. It would be an exaggeration to claim that they are no longer privileged and have to wait their turn in the queue with private applicants. Nonetheless, Histadruth demands on the allocation of public resources are now more carefully scrutinized and not automatically confirmed. How far the Lavon policy (of turning the Histadruth into a trade union federation and checking its dominating influence over production and commerce) will be allowed to proceed, will largely depend on the internal political deliberations within Mapai.

[1] Paradoxically enough, non-socialist circles in Israel prefer nationalized industries to Histadruth trusts; and, while orthodox Israeli socialists are disgusted, the non-socialist parties are delighted at the present trend whereby services are increasingly being transferred from the Histadruth to the administration of the State.

47

CHAPTER VII

FOREIGN EXCHANGE CONTROLS

ISRAEL inherited its foreign exchange regulations from the Palestine Government which had moulded them in the pattern of those in the United Kingdom. However, while these controls were almost exclusively employed in Britain to overcome balance of payments difficulties, in Israel they were used for a variety of other purposes. The government restrictions on free external trade between Israel and the rest of the world, through the operation of these controls, helped it more than any other means (excluding the distribution of foreign aid) to intervene effectively in economic life.

The foreign exchange regulations enabled the Government to further its political aims by subsidizing some activities without the specific consent of parliament or, in many cases, the public being aware of its actions. The published IL budgets voted upon in the Knesset do not give a full picture of the Israeli resources devoted to the army, investment, export promotion and agricultural colonization because the administration of the foreign currency controls was able to manipulate the price at which imported resources were translated into the language of the local currency. The importance for the political fortunes of the Government of the movements of the cost-of-living index will be examined in the next chapter; through the power to import at artificially cheapened prices, the Government was able surreptitiously to influence the fluctuations of the cost-of-living index. Much of the growth of the Histadruth since 1948 can be attributed to the liberal treatment it received, at the expense of the private sector of the economy, from the foreign currency controllers. The controls indeed served a long list of "subsidiary aims".

In theory these controls worked smoothly through two parallel administrative processes: import or export licences were applied for from the Competent Authorities, these being specially designated officials dealing with international trade in a number of ministries (e.g. Ministry of Trade and Industry, Ministry of Agriculture, Ministry of Religious Affairs); once the licence had been granted it had to be endorsed by the foreign currency control division of the Ministry of Finance which undertook to sell foreign currency to the importer to finance this import on a stated day, at an IL price agreed upon for a specified type of currency. This endorsement was often accompanied by a number of conditions that had to be fulfilled by the importer before the Ministry of Finance would honour its obligation.

The most significant feature of these controls was the absence of a unitary price for the currency bought and sold by the Government. The rationale of this policy was the belief of the Government that, being the only legal body in the country allowed to trade in foreign currency, it could act arbitrarily in its determination of the multiple prices which it fixed for the foreign currency. Part B of the book provides much evidence that in practice the Government was not the absolute monopolist and monopsonist in this field as it imagined itself to be. There was a large flourishing black market and illicit arbitage, between the prices laid down by the Ministry of Finance and the black market prices, became a source of considerable profit to many in the trading community.

How did the Government determine different exchange rates? There were no hard-and-fast rules and few of the means were published. Three chief criteria guided the officials in this task: (a) to charge "what the traffic" could bear for the sale of their foreign currency and, alternatively, to pay that IL price for foreign currency that was just low enough not to discourage the foreign supplier from transferring the capital or to drive him to arrange for the transfer through illicit channels; (b) to earn the maximum IL revenue for the State; and (c) to reward by low exchange *rates* those Israeli applicants "worthy" of official support, and to punish by high *rates* the economically "unworthy" members (or economic activities) of the community. The absence of one published unitary price for the buying and selling of foreign currency by the Ministry of Finance gave a tremendous discretionary power to the officials dealing with applications and gave scope to personal and political favouritism and corruptive practices. By 1959 the Israeli controls could boast of hundreds of exchange rates and thousands of discretionary administrative decisions annually; the latter constituted, in their effective application, a further set of individual prices for foreign currency.

In many cases the unrealistic official exchange rates, laid down for the transfer of capital to Israel, led to a demand by such potential transferrers for legal permission to circumvent the formal *rates* for the exchange of foreign currency, and the Ministry of Finance, until 1954, held open (though not enthusiastically) the back door for the entry of capital in a manner which undermined the determined *rates*: many suppliers of capital bought goods with their non-Israeli currency and shipped them to Israel where they sold them for IL on the black and grey markets. This system became known as the *imports-*

49   c*

without-payment technique and, understandably, was limited to luxury products for which a relatively higher IL price per $ could be obtained. The supply of capital from abroad in the form of goods proved inimical to the orderly working of the foreign currency budget drawn up annually by the Ministry of Finance, which presumed that all foreign currency would be concentrated in a common pool from which allocations were to be made to individual applicants on the basis of priorities determined by the Competent Authorities.

A further consequence (of more than just statistical and accounting significance) was the abdication of the Israeli currency as a standard of measurement. The Israeli authorities used the United States dollar in order to calculate whether the economic performance of a domestic process of production or a planned export consignment was to be commended. In Part B I have used five standards by which the purchasing power of the IL can be studied: (1) the movement of the cost-of-living index; (2) the official exchange rates of the IL in terms of the U.S. dollar; (3) the black market quotations for the IL; (4) the price at which a transferrer of capital to Israel (through the import and resale of luxury goods—Standard IV goods as I denote them) could sell his foreign currency; and (5) the *average rate*, this being the average price of the IL, in terms of the U.S. dollar, for all import and export transactions of Israel with the outside world.

An important aim of these regulations was to protect home industry and agriculture. This was usually achieved by the refusal of the Competent Authorities to issue licences for goods that were similar to those produced locally. In rare cases they charged the importers a prohibitive *rate* such that, with legal allocation of foreign currency, few took advantage of the permission to import. (The most recent example concerns "Instant Coffee". In 1958 the Government encouraged a local chocolate factory to manufacture such coffee products locally. The promised Tozereth Haaretz protection was given in January 1959 when the custom tariff for imported "Instant Coffee" was raised to IL50 per kg. A merchant could, therefore, only obtain such an import licence by paying the Ministry of Finance for the foreign currency to finance it at the *rate* of 7.800.)

In a few cases Israel missed the opportunity of executing worthwhile exports because it offered the particular exporters a low *rate* for their earnings; as a rule, however, export proceeds were exchanged by the Ministry of Finance at an extremely favourable high *rate* and unrequited exports were a frequent occurrence in merchandise exporting. This last applied particularly to those of

Israel's factories "which packaged dollar goods" for sale in soft-currency markets.

The high rewards for many exports, the exclusion until 1955 of "luxuries" from the official import programme and the exaggerated Tozereth Haaretz policy all led to the uneconomic employment of local resources on high-cost production (mostly for the production of "luxury" articles) and the consequent neglect of their being utilized in relatively low-cost production.

The number of multiple *rates* has increased progressively over the years. However, since 1955 the circumvention of the Ministry of Finance *rates* by the import of goods through the *imports-without-pay* technique has ceased almost entirely. Since then the Government has also "cornered" (what were formerly) the black and grey markets for Standard IV goods; it now permits these goods to be imported officially provided the currency to finance their import is bought from the Ministry of Finance at such high *rates* as to provide the State with considerable extraordinary revenue.

Officially the IL has been devalued on three occasions and it is expected that at some time in 1960 a further *de jure* devaluation will follow on the *de facto* devaluation which, measured by the (Standard V) *average rates*, depreciated the value of the IL (in terms of $1) from 0.350 in 1948 to 2.750 in 1958. In "normal" economies, devaluations of such proportions would have severely curtailed the import volume and/or (at least in the short run) have lowered the standard of living of the economy which devalued its currency so radically. In Israel the devaluations have neither reduced the import volume nor have they caused the standard of living to fall, but have had a beneficial effect by raising the price of foreign goods relative to local products.

CHAPTER VIII

THE COST-OF-LIVING INDEX

DURING the Second World War the Histadruth signed an agreement
with the Manufacturers Association for automatic increases in the
cost-of-living bonus following rises in the cost-of-living index.
This set a precedent which has been followed throughout the Jewish
economy both before and after the formation of the State; important
modifications have been introduced in the original agreement and,
at different times, varying proportions of the total wage (for different
wage levels) have been tied to the fluctuations of the index. The
frequency of the adjustment (one month, three months, six months)
has also been altered in the yearly agreements between the employers
and the Histadruth. The latest agreement, signed in the spring of
1957, ties the major part of the wages and salaries to the cost-of-
living index and promises an adjustment of the wages, twice a year,
if the index rises by more than 3%, and a three-monthly adjustment
if it has gone up by more than 5%. The pegging of the wages to the
cost-of-living index was to give employees an immediate compensation for the reduced purchasing power of the IL. But this did not
deprive the unions of the right to bid up wages for other reasons, and
the increase in wages has, since 1948, been greater than the upward
movement of the index.

The cost-of-living index, published monthly by the Central Bureau
of Statistics (C.B.S.) is not a reliable measure of the short-term
fluctuations of the internal purchasing power of the IL; it is, however,
the only available index in Israel by which the relatively long-term
changes in the domestic price-level can be measured consistently with
some degree of accuracy.

Between 1949 and 1952 Dov Josef led the "war against the
index" (for purposes explained in the next chapter). Those officials
in the C.B.S., who monthly computed the index of retail prices, were
professionally permitted to consider only those prices that "were
the true and representative market prices". The chief worry of
Dov Josef's officials was whether their maximum prices and the
size of the rations they were distributing would pass the scrutiny
of the C.B.S. officials, i.e. whether the official prices would be
regarded as the sole "true and representative market prices".
(The majority of the population also bought goods, distributed by

52

rationing, on the black market—at prices exceeding three to ten times the price of the official ration.) Until professional pressure changed these practices, the C.B.S. was then prepared, for example, to regard as the effective market price for chocolate the price of the two-ounce low-quality chocolate bar distributed once a month only to children. When the Food Division of the Ministry of Trade and Industry learned that it was sufficient for 250 grammes of rice to be distributed as a ration, for children only, it subsidized this ration heavily so that it would qualify for index purposes as the average price of rice ruling in the country. Similarly, imported baby food with a heavy weight in the index was sold at a *rate* of 0.250 when the *average rate* was several times as large. This policy was not limited to food; in July 1951, for example, a certain type of shoe was sold, retail price-controlled, at IL4 while the manufacturers were paid a subsidy of IL2.

In 1952, with the break-up of many of the physical controls, the manipulation of the cost-of-living index was entrusted to a specially created department in the Ministry of Finance. This department sought to "influence" the movements of the index and its actions were largely determined by the criterion of whether an expenditure of ILx in subsidies (to prevent the index from rising) was likely to be greater or smaller than the averted increase in the payroll of the Government and its corporations.

By 1954 the C.B.S. was no longer prepared to give docile recognition to the "official" prices, associated with the distribution of small quantities of rationed commodities, as the only market prices; it took account of prices in the grey and black markets. Nevertheless, the above-mentioned department continued to arrange for the distribution of dummy rations[1] (i.e. rations at a low price which constituted but a part of the expenditure of the consumer on this article) and authorized the expenditure of tens of millions of IL on "index subsidies". The cultivation of the art of "influencing" the index was developed to a fine degree and pursued on several fronts. Thus in 1955 and 1956 the rationing of certain vegetables, for a few weeks only, was reintroduced in the "decisive month", i.e. the month laid down in the national wage agreement as being that in which the size of the cost-of-living bonus during the coming period would be determined. (It was, of course, a fictitious form of rationing as the machinery that could have supervised such rationing had been dissolved in 1953.) When threats of the Ministry of Trade and Industry in 1957 failed to persuade farmers to aid in the "index battle" by

[1] While the *average rate* in 1956 was 2.250, the *rates* for the import of "index rations" were fixed as follows (107): meat, 0.500; fish, 0.800; rice, 0.450.

53

reducing the price of eggs, temporary rationing was introduced and twenty million eggs were imported; the effect on the index was highly beneficial. In the winter of 1957 the Government promised the Kitan company a lucrative loan from the Development Budget provided it reduced the price of certain of its articles that happened to appear with a heavy weight in the cost-of-living index.

Rationing, for manipulating the index, was still in existence for the following products in January 1959 (255): sugar, jam, rice and chocolate and cocoa for children only, cooking fats, margarine, coffee, imported cheese, meat and fillet fish. A partial abolition of these rations has been promised for the near future.

How far have these improper methods of influencing the cost-of-living index (*vide* Table VII) distorted the index as a reliable guide to the movements of the domestic price-level? Between 1949 and early 1952, the index undervalued the rise of local prices; between the second part of 1952 and 1955 the upward movement of the cost-of-living index overestimated the actual rise in the cost of living; this was because the C.B.S. was at last taking into account black and grey market prices. Since 1955 the manipulations and large disbursements on subsidies have again twisted the cost-of-living index, and the actual decline in the internal purchasing power of the IL is larger than that indicated by the rise of the index.

In more than one sense the cost-of-living index has become the golden calf of the Israeli economy. As is explained in the discussion on value-linking (p. 93), not only the wages but also most medium and long-term contracts are tied to the cost-of-living index (or the exchange rate of the IL). Thus upward movements in the cost-of-living index are of general significance as an outward symbol of cost inflation, and are of specific budgetary significance in that they cause the Government to finance a larger payroll and higher interest payments on its value-linked loans.[1] The movements of the cost-of-living index are not mere statistical exercises but headline news in the Holy Land. Deliberations on possible alterations in the statistical weights of certain items in the "index-basket", proceed on the highest political level, just as the disbursements of large subsidies

[1] Actually the sensitiveness of the Ministry of Finance to fluctuations in the cost-of-living index should have been reduced after the adoption of the recommendations of the Lehmann Committee (*vide* p. 95), for the additional expenditure following upon a rise in the index was likely to be offset, partly or wholly, by increased interest payments on loans made by the Government. Berger (268), who was for many years economic adviser to the Manufacturers' Association, suggests that many industrialists sign the value-linking clauses of the Government loans because they believe that these contractual obligations for increased interest payments will not necessarily be enforced.

TABLE VII

THREE INDICES

	Old C-o-L Index (1939=100)	New C-o-L Index (Sept. 1951 =100)	Building Costs Index[1] (July 1950 =100)
May 1948 .	337	(94)	—
December 1948 .	365	(102)	—
April 1949 .	371	(104)	—
December 1949 .	321	(90)	—
July 1950 .	317	(89)	—
December 1950 .	324	(90)	—
September 1951 .	358	(100)	—
December 1951 .	(383)	107	125
December 1952 .	(637)	178	211
December 1953 .	(759)	212	276
December 1954 .	(816)	228	354
December 1955 .	(856)	239	393
December 1956 .	(895)	250	452
December 1957 .	(942)	263	482
December 1958 .	(989)	276	478

INDEX WEIGHTS

Old C-o-L Index[2]	New C-o-L Index	Building Costs Index
Food . . 528	Food . . 410	Wages . . 600
Clothing . . 50	Clothing . . 130	Transport . 110
Rent and Muni-	Rent and Elec-	Gravel . . 50
cipal Taxes . 234	tricity . . 76	Sea Sand . . 30
Electricity . 10	Furniture, house-	Cement . . 65
Education, Cul-	hold utensils . 73	Timber . . 80
ture . . 39	Education, Cul-	Iron . . 65
Union dues, etc. 54	ture . . 40	
Miscellaneous . 85	Union dues,	
	municipal	
	taxes . . 65	
	Miscellaneous . 206	
TOTAL . 1,000	TOTAL . 1,000	TOTAL . 1,000

[1] Data of Building Costs Index of 1951–1956 are yearly averages (267).
[2] Adapted from (65).

for index-manipulations are personally supervised by the two economic ministers. In the autumn of 1958 one of the left-wing parties threatened to resign from the coalition government if the C.B.S. proceeded with its plan to re-define the item "vegetables" so as to exclude from it the high-priced "early vegetables". This was not such a blatant interference with the intellectual independence of Israel's government statisticians as it might, at first sight, appear to be; the C.B.S. proposal was only put forward when, following on long and drawn-out deliberations within the leadership of Mapai, the leaders of Histadruth had previously agreed to support this change.

CHAPTER IX

PRICE AND PHYSICAL CONTROLS

BETWEEN 1949 and 1952 Dov Josef constructed, and in the larger part of this period had the ministerial responsibility for, a body of domestic controls that bore upon almost all raw materials, consumption goods and services.[1] The officials who issued and administered the orders concerning maximum prices, rationing and the allocation of materials by internal licences made (with the aid of the police forces at their disposal) valiant efforts to thwart the resulting black markets through mass arrests, road blocks, the checking of personal luggage of travellers on inter-urban traffic, the publicizing of the names of accused (but not necessarily convicted) offenders, threats to search private refrigerators, etc. The reasons adduced in other countries for the imposition of such severe regulations could not honestly be put forward in Israel; no one seriously dared to suggest that it was physically difficult to import goods (a consideration used to justify rationing in a besieged city) nor was the deficit on current account in the balance of payments proclaimed as the decisive reason. There is overwhelming evidence to show that the cabinet authorized Dov Josef to draw liberally from the then small hard-currency reserves for importing goods that could have been economically produced with local resources, provided that this advanced the chief purpose for which these controls were instituted.

What was the openly proclaimed chief aim of these physical controls? It was part of Dov Josef's economic philosophy that the internal value of the currency could be raised if the price-wage spiral were rolled back, i.e. if prices were cut down this would bring down wages, and reduced wage rates would again lower prices. Dov Josef and some of his chief collaborators in the 1949–52 period wanted these physical controls *also* to serve in the redistribution of the National Income in favour of the poorer classes. (However, this genuine social consideration played no role in the post-Josef period, after 1952, when the physical controls were only exercised for cost-of-living index manipulations). When Dov Josef joined the Government he announced that he aimed at pushing down the cost-of-living index

[1] Some important articles (e.g. fuel, bread, flour—*vide* Appendix VI) with a high import content were not rationed but price-controlled at a subsidized level such that it invited buyers to consume them wastefully.

THE ECONOMY OF ISRAEL

by 25%. He started from a base of 371 in the (old) index in April 1949, and by July 1950 the index had fallen to 317—a reduction of 15% in fifteen months. Though after this month it again rose gradually, it only reached the base from which Dov Josef had launched his campaign in November 1951, after thirty-two months. As a result of this downward movement of prices,[1] the national agreements between the Manufacturers Association and the Histadruth provided for reduced money wages on three occasions. In the beginning, a genuine attempt was made to reduce the cost of the controlled goods, but later the announced reductions in prices were ordered from above just by arbitrarily cutting those profit margins of manufacturers and distributors, which appeared to be too high to the officials in Jerusalem. In 1952 the controls apparatus was being trimmed and shortly before being forced out of office Dov Josef signed an order which abolished clothes rationing.

It has been suggested by some commentators that Dov Josef began to abolish the physical controls which he had inspired because of advice proffered to him by his economic advisers and particularly by Mosak.[2] From first-hand knowledge this can be dismissed as a piece of unfounded speculation. Two fundamental reasons alone explain the somersault in the summer of 1952. The first was the growth in the vote for the main opposition party, the General Zionists, at the general election of the previous year, which was attributed to the popular appeal of their anti-controls platform.[3] The second cause was the emergence by 1952 of a black market of such dimensions

[1] Milk, eggs, fish, cotton yarn had their prices reduced three times. Most other articles had lower prices fixed on two occasions. Fodderstuffs, for example, had their price reduced by 30% but the prices of most food and textile goods were lowered, on the average, by 10%. At first the merchants and manufacturers reacted noisily to these price reductions. In time many became apathetic as they discovered that the Control Division established by Dov Josef's ministry was largely inefficient (and, to some extent, corrupt). They reacted, therefore, to reductions in the controlled prices of their goods by lowering the quality of the goods sold at the official prices, and by selling their better quality products in the black market at much higher prices.

[2] Goldberger (120) even claims to know that a report by Mosak (167) was suppressed in Israel ". . . because its masterly analysis of the inflationary character of the Israeli economy . . . was followed in the report . . . by recommendations for the handling of price control and rationing. Substantially these recommendations were followed to the benefit of the Israeli economy . . ."

[3] "The General Zionists . . . built their propaganda efforts on the anger felt by the public because the rationing and the austerity régime caused difficulties, the serious defects in the supply of goods and their (orderly) marketing, the economic policy of Mapai which is seen to strive for the construction of a socialist society . . . in which the monopolistic companies of the Histadruth would rule" (271).

Table VIII

A COMPARISON OF OFFICIAL AND BLACK MARKET PRICES[1]

Commodity[2]	Sept. 1951–August 1952			May–August 1953		
	Official Prices	Black Market Prices	Ratio of $\frac{II}{I}$	Official Prices	Black Market Prices	Ratio of $\frac{V}{IV}$
Column	I	II	III	IV	V	VI
Cement (ton)	10.08	60.0	6.0	44.48	65.0	1.5
Building timber (cm.)	60.00	280.0	4.7	135.00	300.0	2.2
Iron bars (16 mm.)	78.00	310.0	4.0	222.90	330.0	1.5
Refrigerator	260.00	1350.0	5.2	500.00	1000.0	2.0
Woollen utility trousers	..	..	..	17.00	35.0	2.1
Men's utility shoes	..	..	..	10.05	15.0	1.5
Men's pyjamas	..	..	..	10.36	23.8	2.3
Sheet	..	..	..	3.27	8.0	2.4
Diaper	..	..	..	0.66	1.5	2.3
Fresh meat	0.90	6.0	6.8	2.00	6.0	3.0
Frozen meat	0.70	6.0	8.6	1.00	6.0	6.0
Poultry	2.00	6.0	3.0	2.40	5.0	2.1
Sausage	1.60	6.0	3.8	2.00	5.0	2.5
Eggs (ten)	0.50	2.0	4.0	0.70	1.5	2.1
Margarine	0.30	3.5	11.7	0.70	2.0	2.9
Edible oil	0.30	3.5	11.7	0.70	2.8	3.9
Sugar	0.09	2.0	22.2	0.18	1.4	7.8
Rice	0.12	2.1	17.5	0.14	2.0	14.3
Washing soap	0.15	0.6	4.0	0.25	0.4	1.6
Coffee	2.16	6.0	2.8	4.00	6.0	1.5

[1] All prices are in IL.
Sources include (32), (93), (162) and (163).
[2] All food items, except eggs, are in units of kg. 1.

that it could no longer be dismissed as a marginal phenomenon;
it had become so powerful and widespread as to break down the
dams erected to protect the price and physical controls.

Clearly no conclusive evidence can be presented on the amplitude
of the black market, but the various testimonies, cited below have a
convincing ring. It is especially notable that the judiciary was hostile
to the wishes of the administration that heavy prison sentences be
imposed on convicted offenders. It could in good faith only mete out
minimum fines to offenders against rationing orders when it was
well known that some cabinet ministers openly flouted the regulations
of Dov Josef's ministry by eating black market meals in public
restaurants. In 1950 the research department of the Ministry of
Finance published the first authoritative estimate of the black market
for food[1]: the population was said to consume 26% more than the
official rations, paying for the excess at black market prices which
exceeded the official ones by 129%. The nutritionist, Bavli, showed
discrepancies (193) between actual consumption data and official
marketing-and-rationing figures which had come to light when the
C.B.S. made a consumer survey in the spring of 1951:

Article	Actual Consumption[2] (as per C.B.S. survey)	Rationing Allocations (as per Food Division)
Eggs . . .	94	100
Bread and cereals .	89	100
Fats . . .	94	100
Milk and milk products . .	118	100
Potatoes and vegetables . .	109	100
Sugar . .	112	100
Meat. . .	130	100
Fish . . .	125	100
Fruit. . .	160	100

In 1953 whole sectors of the economy were dominated by black

[1] I believe that the black market in those days was already more powerful and
these estimates are only quoted because of the official status of the investigators.
[2] The Bavli figures for actual consumption have been computed into index
figures, taking the official allocations at a base of 100.

market practices and prices. The Ministry of Trade and Industry admitted (in its unpublished communications to the Finance Committee of the Knesset) that the majority of building materials for the private sector were traded at prices appreciably above the official ones. 90% of the chocolate consumed in Israel was said to have originated on the black market. A group of American consultants presented a report to the Jerusalem Government in which they noted that "90% of the meat consumed . . . moved through the black market" (171). Rokach, a leader of the General Zionists, declared in the Knesset in June 1952 that "today . . . at least 80% of the population buy on the black market". The position in 1954 can be inferred from Lowe's calculations of the per capita consumption of the following products; his report was published (16) by the Government Printer:

Produce	Annual Official Ration	Annual Actual Consumption
	kg.	kg.
Fats . . .	14	16
Sugar . .	12	18
Eggs (in units) .	150	240
Meat and poultry .	1	10
Fish . . .	2	15
Coffee . .	0.6	1
Tea . . .	0.5	1

Finally, two sets of quotations shed light on the public attitude towards Dov Josef's controls:

"The municipality buys essential materials on the black market for the maintenance of its waterworks, hospitals and schools; necessary instructions to that effect have been given to the heads of the departments—declared yesterday the Mayor of Tel-Aviv, I. Rokach, at a meeting of the City Council" (6).

A report of the parliamentary proceedings for 1951 (92) tells the following revealing story:

"Dayan . . . said that when a price of IL45 per ton was the maximum controlled price for hay, trading in hay had been going on for a year at IL70. The Deputy Minister of Agriculture knows of this. The kibbutz Geva (of which he is a member) has bought hay for IL70 from the village of Mishmar Hasharon.

The Deputy Minister of Agriculture, Ephrati . . . said that Member of Parliament Dayan had mentioned as an example his kibbutz which had bought hay at IL60 (probably a misprint for IL70) per ton. This is correct. When I was asked about it, I said it was not so terrible . . ."

Today there is hardly an economist or politician in Israel who does not regard this period of controls as an unfortunate episode. The wage-and-price spiral (except for a limited period) was not rolled back; the lower income groups did not improve their position at the expense of the wealthier classes; Israel's balance of payments certainly did not benefit. The economic damage caused by the controls may be divided into two categories; that which was bred when the controls were efficiently executed, and that which was generated when the controls were not enforced and engendered black market production.[1] Six features of this damage will be examined below:

(1) The Dov Josef period strengthened a latent trend among the *institutions* and the new civil service to strip as many commercial transactions as possible of their monetary garbs and to make allocations in kind. During the years 1949 to 1952 this practice also proved useful in avoiding the letter of the price controls, and helpful in evading the proper payment of direct and indirect taxes. The following are three categories illustrating such arrangements:

A. The Government offices, the Jewish Agency and some other *institutions* were given licences for the purchase of building materials at official prices in more or less unlimited quantities. Hence, these organizations could afford to invite tenders from contractors with the proviso that the former would supply the materials. It became an unwritten rule for the quantity of building materials issued to exceed the quantity actually used on the project, and it was understood that building contractors would submit low bids for such work as they had the right to expect an additional (unspecified) payment for their work through the opportunity to sell the "superfluous" materials at

[1] There is no general agreement among economists that a large black market necessarily leads to a dissipation of resources. Michaely (105), for one, argues that when an inflation is to be repressed by rationing and price controls, the success of the policy may depend on the existence of the "unhappy" black market. A United Nations report (68) regards the black market as a beneficial factor when it acts as a brake on consumption.

black market prices, or use them for construction of houses for the private sector.

B. Similarly, employees were sometimes rewarded with, in addition to their meagre salaries, the right to buy, at official prices, scarce goods over which their public employers had effective control.[1]

C. Attention has already been drawn to the practice of the Jewish Agency of supplying agricultural settlements with goods rather than with financial resources. The goods delivered were not always those needed by the farmers; but the settlements learned to accept any type of goods given by the Jewish Agency as part of the "settlement budget", rather than wait indefinitely for the articles most needed. From police reports and other sources it is learned that the kibbutzim specialized in bartering on the black market those Jewish Agency materials, not needed by them, for goods in urgent demand.

(2) Some regard the strong and persistent temptation for the businessman and citizen to break the law as the worst feature of this period. It was demoralizing for those few firms who obeyed the letter of the law to make losses (as did, for example, the efficient "Ata" company in the textile trade) while the majority reaped illicit profits. Forgeries and frauds were rampant in the food industries. Thus, once when the price controller gave publicity to a further reduction in the price of coffee, Dov Josef had, at the same time, to announce at a press conference (in December 1950) that out of 21 coffee-roasters checked by his investigators, 18 had been found guilty of "serious frauds and the mixing of imported coffee beans with harmful materials".

(3) On the whole the maximum prices were fixed by highly arbitrary methods. These were supplemented by the establishment, in most trades, of price equalization funds into which the efficient importers or producers had to pay the difference between their low costs and the official maximum prices (fixed by the controllers) to compensate those importers and producers whose costs were above the maximum prices. The "points scheme" and the "value system" (as used with

[1] An inquiry (123) into the circumstances by which a senior official of the Jewish Agency had acquired a luxurious dwelling-place in 1951 revealed that his employers had allotted him large quantities of building materials at official prices; he, in turn, handed these over to a contractor who was only too willing to charge him a nominal price for the erection of the house, because his real compensation consisted in the "disposition of the superfluous" building materials. The measure of the hidden remuneration of this official can be gauged by a study of the comparative black market prices in that year in Table VIII. However, this was neither an isolated case nor was it a practice confined to the Jewish Agency.

meat in the United Kingdom) were rejected by Dov Josef; only those products were imported which were technically suitable for the convenient distribution by quantitative rations. (The main argument for importing the dearer fillet fish, rather than the cheaper type of fish which would have saved foreign currency, was that the latter did not fit easily into an egalitarian rationing system.) For the distribution of imported raw materials the Government depended on trade and producers' associations and it forced many importers and manufacturers to join cartels which proved convenient to the administration. The distribution of raw materials sometimes became a function of the personal idiosyncrasies of the responsible officials and was often subject to political pressure. To relate one such example: Dov Josef, who had a sentimental attachment to Jerusalem and aimed at its industrialization at any price, announced that allocations of sugar to food processing factories in Jerusalem would be made on a priority basis and in specially large quantities.[1] The productive capacity of this industry in Tel-Aviv was then only partly exploited, but in any event it was a clear case of a misinvestment to locate new plants in Jerusalem with its high manufacturing and transport costs. Nevertheless, the sweet dew of cheap sugar allocations attracted a dozen astute businessmen to bring machinery into Jerusalem and collect sugar allocations for their "food workshops". However, when, in 1954, the distribution policy in regard to sugar underwent a change, these mushroom factories had to close down.

(4) The inefficiently supervised controls gave unscrupulous, but enterprising, people an opportunity to break the law with impunity by producing for the black market. The black market prices were appreciably so much above the official prices that it became a commercial proposition for entrepreneurs (manufacturing for the black market) to draw factors successfully away from more economical forms of production to employment on their high-cost production processes. Considerable resources were invested for the erection of such plants. The waste of resources that this entailed for Israel only became apparent after several years when the black market ceased to operate in some fields because of the abolition of controls or turned into an officially tolerated grey market. In both cases the relative decline in the black market prices made these uneconomical forms of production no longer profitable. Hundreds of workshops and small factories consequently had to close down; likewise a trading community of thousands, that had been exclusively con-

[1] At one stage during Dov Josef's ministerial responsibility for the Food Division, the price of black market sugar exceeded the official price by two thousand four hundred per cent!

cerned with the marketing of these black market goods, lost its live-lihood.

(5) It would be wrong to regard all entrepreneurs as straining every nerve in order to evade these controls by production for the black market. In some fields producers, for reasons of their own, co-operated with the authorities in making these controls effective. These manufacturers, instead of employing their factors on black market production of controlled articles, simply altered their production schedule and made other articles, which often, because of their being considered inessential, were neither rationed nor price-controlled.[1]

(6) The most fatal of all illusions associated with the physical controls was that they would hold up the inherent inflationary forces. In reality the purchasing power, which was released from paying an economic price for essential articles, was concentrated on accentuating the inflationary atmosphere; it raised the bids for foreign currency and for luxury products (produced locally in an uneconomic fashion or) imported illicitly. This is illustrated in the following table, which has been computed by taking an hourly wage for Israel in 1951—when the distortions in its price-and-cost structure were at their height—of IL0.450 and comparing it with similar data (drawn from United Nations and International Labour Office statis-tics) for the wages of other countries. To take the case of sugar: while an Israeli worker had to labour only seven minutes to purchase kg.1, the Hungarian wage-earner had to toil twenty times as long and the resident of the British Welfare State almost three times as long as his Israeli colleague. These data could lead a superficial observer to presume that either sugar was heavily taxed outside Israel (which it was not) or that the Israeli worker enjoyed a higher standard of living than any European worker (which also was clearly nonsense, for Israel's standard of living was then, as it is now, below that of Western Europe). The real explanation, of course, is that the controls of the Dov Josef period adopted such ridiculous IL prices for some of the imports (financed with foreign charitable and political aid) that the internal balance of the Israeli economy was seriously thrown out

---

[1] The profits of the manufacturers of drinking glasses—the latter appeared as an item in the cost-of-living index—were severely cut when a (low) maximum price was imposed on the article. Not surprisingly the manufacturers switched to the production of liqueur glasses and ornamental goods which were uncon-trolled and sold easily in this period of a pronounced demand inflation.

In 1950 and 1951 only limited irrigation facilities were available. Potatoes and vegetables were distributed in rations and maximum prices fixed with no reason-able profit margin to the farmers. Some, who disdained the production of black market goods, turned their valuable irrigation facilities to the production of such uncontrolled luxuries as flowers.

of equilibrium. These unrealistic prices for the distributed rations not only caused foreign imports to be wastefully employed and domestic factors to be diverted to uneconomical forms of production, but they aggravated the evils of the Ministry of Finance's inflationary policy.

MINUTES-OF-WORK NEEDED TO BUY
PRICE-CONTROLLED AND/OR RATIONED GOODS

Country	1 kg.				Ten Eggs	1 litre Milk
	Bread	Meat	Sugar	Mar-garine		
Hungary .	34	251	137	293	..	37
Poland. .	32	140	114	244	260	39
France. .	23	154	61	212	100	22
West Germany.	25	150	47	92	80	15
Italy . .	35	315	97	197	100	25
U.K. . .	13	74	18	52	60	15
Israel . .	7	60	7	30	42	13

CHAPTER X

SIX CENTRAL THEMES

Immigration—the Army—the Arab Boycott—Housing
—Israel's Occupational Structure—Taxation.

I—IMMIGRATION

ACCORDING to Horovitz (124) the immigration rate during the first years of Israel's existence constitutes a world record. (The highest known annual rate of population growth by immigration is said to have taken place in New Zealand with 4%.) The population of Israel increased both through natural causes and immigration by 17% in 1948, 34% in 1949, 19% in 1950 and 17% again in 1951. About 90% of the immigrants did not pay their own fares and arrived in the country without any means; the State of Israel and the Jewish Agency provided them with the necessities (starting with a bed and mattress), found them temporary and, later, permanent living places, and made relief payments till more permanent employment was arranged. Most of the immigrants were unskilled and included many social misfits and physically and mentally ill persons.[1] All these were permitted to come to Israel thanks to the Law of Return, passed unanimously by the Knesset, which proclaimed the right of every Jew to find refuge in the National Home.[2] The able-bodied and wealthier members of Jewish communities, that were being liquidated, found it easier than their less fortunate brethren to migrate to other countries, and many of them chose Israel only as a transit camp.

In order to place the immigration data for these eleven years into their proper perspective, it should be remembered that 700,000 Palestinian Arabs fled during this period from the territory which is now Israel, about 100,000 Jews emigrated and there was a natural increase (Jews and Arabs) of almost 400,000. (The average rate of natural increase of Israel's population was about $2\frac{1}{2}\%$.)

[1] Until 1952 no aspiring immigrant was refused financial aid by the authorities and his fare was paid automatically. Since that year some chronically ill and aged persons have been rejected in accordance with the "selective immigration policy" which was jointly adopted by the Government and the Jewish Agency.

[2] "... unless the Minister of the Interior is satisfied that the applicant is acting against the Jewish people or is likely to endanger public health or the security of the State, or has a criminal past which is likely to endanger the public peace."

JEWISH IMMIGRATION INTO ISRAEL
(in thousands)

1948	.	119	1954	.	17
1949	.	239	1955	.	36
1950	.	170	1956	.	55
1951	.	174	1957	.	71
1952	.	23	1958	.	26
1953	.	10			

TOTAL . 940

II—THE ARMY

A "neither-peace-nor-war" atmosphere engendered an integrated military machine which, measured in real terms, probably consumes a larger proportion of the national product than the army of any other country in the world in 1959. Jewish transport, water supply, pipes, industrial and farm equipment have been constantly subjected to damaging attacks by infiltrators who have also killed hundreds of settlers and soldiers. Jewish armed groups have made retaliatory raids in the surrounding territory.

The army consists of a small professional core, supplemented by conscripts (boys and girls[1] serving $2\frac{1}{2}$ years) and of an army reserve which, according to published accounts in America, can call on 250,000 men within a few days. All able-bodied men and women up to the age of 50 years must annually serve 30–46 days full-time service in the reserve. There is a one-month-a-year "service" for certain heavy equipment such as lorries (*vide* p. 227). A para-military organization trains schoolchildren. Members of rural settlements, in addition to their ordinary service as reservists, have to perform guard duties in conjunction with the army. During times of emergency hundreds of thousands of work-days are "donated" by the civilian population to the building of fortifications. The impress of the military machine is felt in all walks of life: the lay-out of agricultural settlements, the system of irrigation, the location of industrial plants —all are planned with a view to possible military attacks. The Ministry of Defence is also in charge of numerous ordnance factories that are manned by civilian labour and which are reported to be managed with high efficiency.

[1] Orthodox religious girls may be excused from military service and are then assigned by the Government to civilian tasks.

68

III—THE ARAB BOYCOTT

The Arabs have established an organization for an elaborate economic boycott of Israel (257); its general office is situated in Damascus with branches in other Arab states and it seeks to intimidate companies and individuals from investing in, or trading with, Israel. The Arabs, by threats of economic reprisals, have succeeded in prevailing upon several foreign companies to liquidate their existing branches or assembly plants in the Jewish State: some makers of internationally branded goods refuse to sell to Israel lest they be cut off from the more lucrative Arab markets; Israel has difficulties in obtaining oil from Middle Eastern sources; ships calling on Israeli ports are blacklisted and there are restrictions on the passage of goods to Haifa via the Suez Canal. There are, apart from extensive smuggling, no direct trade relations between Israel and its neighbours. Arab merchants who wish to purchase Israeli goods must do so via a third country (e.g. Cyprus) and Israel acts likewise when buying Arab goods (e.g. it buys Egyptian cotton via European ports).

At one time the Foreign Office of Jerusalem thought it propitious to its political fortunes to adopt the propaganda line that the Arab losses from the cessation of normal commercial relations with Israel were greater than those of Israel [*vide* Meron (18) and Hershlag's appraisal (258) that the boycott had "paradoxically strengthened some elements of the Israeli economy"]. An alternative line of the Israeli Foreign Office is to emphasize the tremendous damage allegedly done to Israel's commercial life by the nefarious boycott of its neighbours. Strangely enough, a United Nations' report echoes this equally exaggerated estimate of the boycott repercussions on Israel. It states that ". . . the breakdown of economic relations with the neighbouring countries deprived Israel of important sources of raw materials and a considerable export market" (160). Some of the propagandists, who believe that they further the cause of Israel by making the damage appear as large as possible, say that the Arab boycott divests Israel of an annual income of $100 million.

The most serious evaluation of this issue has, in my view, been made by the American economist, Patterson, who submitted a report to the State Department in Washington in the latter part of 1953, expressing the opinion that the annual cost of the boycott was between $25–30 million. Israel is hit directly through higher shipping rates and insurance tariffs and the inability to fully utilize the Haifa refinery. If the Arab boycott ended tomorrow few Israeli industrial products could be sold commercially in the neighbouring countries, and the present Tozereth Haaretz protection of domestic agriculture makes it unlikely that extensive imports of agricultural products from Arab states would be encouraged. The real benefits likely to ensue from an end to the boycott are the possibilities of the regional development of soil conservation, irrigation, anti-malaria and anti-locust schemes; tourist excursions to the *whole* of the Middle East would also again become feasible.

So far as can be judged, Jordan is the only Arab country which is seriously harmed by the absence of peaceful relations with Israel, for it is deprived of the Haifa port facilities.

IV—HOUSING

The first wave of immigrants to the new State, i.e. until the beginning of 1950, were mostly accommodated in the 58,000 housing units (abandoned by the Arabs who fled during the fighting) after they had been repaired and, in some cases, improved. The lack of skilled

TABLE IX

BUILDINGS COMPLETED 1949–1957 (255)

Year	Total Area	Residential Area only	
	1,000 sq. metres	*1,000 sq. metres*	*Rooms*[1]
1949 .	843	749	32,431
1950 .	1,249	1,133	48,005
1951 .	2,137	1,946	82,279
1952 .	2,101	1,811	66,667
1953 .	1,158	842	31,667
1954 .	1,412	1,204	42,441
1955 .	1,787	1,575	64,824
1956 .	1,963	1,738	69,730
1957 .	1,911	1,598	68,000
TOTAL .	14,561	12,596	506,044

[1] The following types of rooms are not included: kitchens, bathrooms and toilets, open porches, corridors without windows, work-rooms used for work purposes only and halls of less than eight square metres.

building workers and the limited allocations of building materials[1] delayed the construction of sufficient permanent homes to absorb all newcomers. Hence reception camps for the second wave of immigrants were established near the large towns and most of the indigent immigrants passed through them, staying there for periods ranging from a few days to five years. In 1950 most of the transit-dwellers lived in tents and canvas huts, but these were later exchanged for imported prefabricated houses and corrugated tin huts. At one time 250,000 immigrants were housed in these camps and in February 1959, almost 100,000 still resided there.

Despite the abandoned Arab property, the large volume of building and the slowing down of immigration, the density rate[2] per room in Israel always remained very high; it only fell from 2.5 persons in 1949 to 2.2 in 1955 and 2.0 in 1958. In November 1957 a housing survey was conducted by the Central Bureau of Statistics (239) and this revealed further details about the extreme housing shortage in Israel:

NUMBER OF OCCUPANTS PER ROOM

Per Room	In Percentages of Total Population
Less than 1 person	5.2
1.00–1.49 persons	24.7
1.50–1.99 ,,	12.0
2.00–2.49 ,,	25.4
2.50–2.99 ,,	6.2
3.00–3.99 ,,	11.4
4.00–4.99 ,,	6.4
5 or more persons	8.7
(National Average: 2.1 persons)	100.0

About 70% of the building in Israel is executed with direct labour employed by the Public Works department of the Ministry of Labour, the Jewish Agency and the Histadruth building companies. Less than

[1] Whilst in 1957 Israel exported more than 200,000 tons of cement, in the early days of the State building depended largely on the import of cement.

[2] Judged by Western standards, the Israeli density rate is even higher. Israeli statistical returns do not differentiate between permanent and temporary dwelling-places, and the size of the rooms is much smaller than in Western countries.

one-third of the construction is carried out by private contractors. It is estimated that only about 20–25% of the dwelling places erected since the establishment of the State were built for disposal in the open market. The greater part of residential building is "public housing"; i.e. houses or flats which are not sold to the highest bidder but allocated to specific groups in the population, e.g. immigrants, civil servants, journalists and members of certain political parties. It was considered politically undesirable to encourage the erection of houses for letting by landlords, a social class tainted with the stigma of exploitation. Similarly, it was regarded as improper for the public authorities to own houses that were let for rent. The new immigrants were, therefore, in most cases forced by the Jewish Agency and the State to become the owners of the houses and the flats that were prepared for them; mortgages of 40–95% were given by the *institutions* and the State, and there are instances of immigrants refusing to leave the transit camps for the ownership of permanent dwelling places until they were granted 100% mortgages.

For a different reason the flats built by private contractors for disposal in the open market were not offered to prospective tenants on a "rent only" basis, but were usually sold outright to groups of persons who—for purposes of legal ownership and administration of the property—had organized themselves into "Co-operative Apartment Companies". This was a result of the effects of the Rent Restriction Ordinance (enacted by the Palestine Government during the world war) which froze rents at the 1940 level. Since then the cost-of-living index has risen by about 700%. But this anachronistic regulation was not abolished by the sovereign Jewish State, because the manipulations of the cost-of-living index demanded that the important item "rents" should not move upwards.[1] With the exception of a few housing units constructed by the Rassco company and the "premium system" mentioned below, *not a single house or flat was built in Israel during its first decade for letting.*

In a few cases the building contractor decided not to sell the flats to a "Co-operative Apartment Company", but himself became a member of the parasitical caste of landlords. He would then tell his prospective tenants to make an application to a special tribunal which—with certain adjustments—fixed the (nominal) rent in conformity with the 1940 level of rents and prices. On the basis of the rents fixed by the tribunal, the tenants would receive a lease from their

---

[1] In April 1954 the ordinance was amended to allow landlords to raise the 1940 rents by (an average of) 100%. It is needless to add that this new rent level did not fire a single local or foreign owner of capital with the ambition to become a landlord in Israel.

landlords, but before they could take possession of their new abodes, they had to hand over to the landlord a premium equivalent to 50–60% of the actual building costs. Tenants were entitled to sell their leases at market prices.

V—ISRAEL'S OCCUPATIONAL STRUCTURE

In the opinion of some observers Israel has large untapped labour reserves. The Central Bureau of Statistics give data which show that 39.4% of the Jewish population were in full-time employment when the survey (239), summarized in the table below, was made in November 1957. However, this percentage does not give a true indication of the proportion of the population engaged full-time in pursuits that enhance the size of the national product. It includes

THE JEWISH POPULATION BY LABOUR FORCE CHARACTERISTICS

	Percentage	Thousands
Total Jewish Population	100.0	1,170
Civilian Labour Force[1]	55.3	647
Employed	51.4	601
Full-time	(39.4)	(461)
Part-time	(8.5)	(100)
Temporarily absent	(3.5)	(40)
Unemployed	3.9	46
Non-Civilian Labour Force	44.7	523

those who are doing their reserve duty in the army, hides a great deal of under-employment[2] and embodies 13,000 unemployed (238) who are receiving masked unemployment pay through employment, mostly with low productivity, on "public works specially initiated for unemployed". The composition of the civilian labour force is most unsatisfactory, for a large proportion is employed in services and distribution—these data are seen in their proper light when compared with similar statistics of other under-developed countries.

[1] All over 14 who are either "employed" or "unemployed"; this group excludes those who are doing their national service in the army or those in the regular army.
[2] The Histadruth, in some cases, does not permit employers to lay off workers for whom there is no work. Many employers are also financially unable to give notice to persons to whom severance pay, for several thousand IL, is due.

JEWISH CIVILIAN LABOUR FORCE BY ECONOMIC PURSUIT
[in percentages] (255)

Economic Pursuit	*1947*	*1957*
Agriculture, forestry and fisheries . .	12.6	15.0
Manufacturing (and crafts), mining and electricity	26.5	23.7
Building and public works . . .	8.7	9.5
Transport and communications . .	6.3	7.0
Commerce and banking . . .	19.4	13.5
Government, and other, services . .	26.5	31.3
TOTAL .	100.0	100.0

VI—TAXATION

As a large part of Israel's budget is financed by outside aid, it is largely irrelevant to compare the budget with Israel's National Income. A comparison between the size of the budget and the volume of Total Available Resources is more significant; in 1958 the budget proposal provides for expenditure equal to 28% of Total Available Resources. If "ordinary revenue", i.e. that raised by internal taxes, is compared with the National Income, the proportion is 26%. These dimensions of national tax burdens are extremely high for an under-developed country like Israel,[1] though they are not unusual for most Western economies. It must be remembered, however, that the Central Government imposes several additional monetary and non-monetary burdens on most citizens (e.g. forced loans, reserve duty with consequent loss of income). Municipal rates, too, are high and there are school taxes, for education even in elementary schools is not free except for the very poor. As many social services are not provided by the State, it is in practice obligatory on most to pay (up to 9% of their gross income) to the National Insurance Institute and the Histadruth. The total tax burden is, thus, even by Western standards, extremely onerous and has grown progressively so in each of Israel's eleven years of existence.

[1] The high percentage of Total Available Resources, that served as income sources for the budgets of the Central Government, is a result of the many foreign receipts that flow directly to the coffers of the Ministry of Finance; only half of the Government's budget income is obtained through its tax machinery.

74

TWO ISRAELI BUDGETS[1] (in millions of IL)

Year	1949	1958
Total Available Resources .	403	(4,400)
National Income . .	240	(2,850)
Combined Budget . .	94	1,238
Development Budget .	36	461
Revenue of Post Office and		
Ministry of Transport .	8	25
"Ordinary Revenue". .	50	752
Income Tax . .	9	257
Customs . . .	10	134
Purchase Tax . .	1	80
Other Receipts . .	30	281
Budget as percentage of Total		
Available Resources . .	23	28
"Ordinary Revenue" as percen-		
tage of National Income .	21	26
Income tax as percentage of		
National Income . .	4	9

Despite strenuous efforts to improve collections, the inheritance tax—with marginal rates of up to 70% (260)—is scheduled to net only IL1 million in 1958. A capital gains tax has been enacted but applies only to realized profits from the sale of land, machinery and equipment and not to shares. Some cases of corruption in the customs force, and many cases among the officials of the purchase tax department, have been reported in the press during the last few years, but few serious complaints have been made against the officers of the Income Tax Division. While the administration of the latter was generally lax up to 1953 and considerable profits (including those made on black market transactions) escaped direct taxation, its officers since that year—by paying rewards to informers, maintaining a secret detective force and generally using draconic measures which

[1] (239), (255), (274) and (275) are the chief sources. The period refers to the financial year (beginning on 1st April) but the data for National Income and Total Available Resources are for the calendar year (beginning on 1st January). The 1949 budget figures should be supplemented by the Secret Defence Budget and, following the precedent set in previous years, the 1958 budget proposals may be retroactively adjusted.

75

do not always accord with Western concepts of personal liberty—
have accomplished the remarkable feat of collecting more than 9%
of the National Income in income tax whilst the comparative proportion in 1949 was less than 4%. Both the late and present Minister of
Finance and the successive heads of the Income Tax Division have
pleaded with the Knesset to reduce the high marginal tax rates that
are a disincentive to production and demoralize the higher income
groups without providing the State with much additional revenue.
Only little has been achieved in this direction because socialist
tradition in Israel is interpreted to mean that "the rich must be
soaked", and no Mapai leader has so far dared to go far against this
precept. The marginal rates on income at IL20,000 were 86% in
1952, 77% in 1956 and $76\frac{1}{2}$% ($71\frac{1}{2}$% for married persons) in 1957.
However, these high rates are not indicative of the payments actually
made by the overwhelming majority of those to whom they are
supposed to apply. Income tax settlement has always been a matter of
"bargaining" on the highest level, and although the present heads of
the administration have stated that the days of "bargaining" are
over (and indeed this evil practice has much declined) it has not been
entirely eradicated. The income tax administration has always been
ready to negotiate "special rates" for groups of citizens: lecturers in
approved educational institutions, electricians, stevedores, etc., were
granted flat rates for overtime earnings; judges, cabinet ministers and
journalists were given a "representation allowance"; doctors, lawyers,
architects, engineers were granted a tax-free allowance for "professional literature"; special arrangements were made for residents
in the Negev, the port of Eilat, kibbutz members, foreign investors
and technicians, new agricultural settlements, etc. Considering that
fringe benefits provided tax-free income of up to 50% of the nominal
wage, the scope of introducing certain variations in income tax paid
by different groups was wide.

The joint "company profits" and "company income" tax was 63%
in 1957 and 1958, and divided into 30% for the former and 33%
for the latter. Dividend recipients "gross up" their earnings from
dividends for their tax returns but may deduct from the tax due on
their income (including the augmented amount of dividends) the
30% of income tax paid by the company.

The high marginal rates, deduced at source, are such that unless the
employers can pay in kind, or illegally in cash, or the employees
(through their professional or union organization) succeed in making
special arrangements with the revenue authorities, skilled workers
may have to pay income tax up to 40% on their overtime earnings
and professional people up to 70% on earnings additional to their

76

salaries. The following is an illustration of how much a self-employed person had to earn in Israel during 1957 in order to qualify for a (legally obtained) disposable income equivalent to that enjoyed by middle-class earners in the West:

	IL	£[1]	$[1]
Gross income . . 24,500		3,500	9,800
Income tax payable (after deducting allowances due to a married man with two children; "social tax credits", etc.) . . 14,000		2,000	5,600
Net income but *before* deductions for sick funds, compulsory national insurance, etc. . . . 10,500		1,500	4,200

[1] Computed on basis of *average rate* for 1957 of 2,500.

CHAPTER XI

THE NON-FARMING SECTORS

The Government as an Employer—Electricity Supplies
—Industry—Commerce and Finance—Miscellaneous.

I—THE GOVERNMENT AS AN EMPLOYER

THE data on the direct employment of persons by the Civil Service Commission do not indicate the full impact of the Government's role as an employer, because in many cases Government enterprises are separate legal entities. The following figures on the number of civil servants also do not include several tens of thousands of earners on National Service, in the Regular Army, teachers, 7,000 policemen and several other small groups. Some thousands of employees of the Jewish Agency and the municipalities though, in part, performing tasks as agents of the State are also not incorporated in the table below. The proportion[1] of direct State-employees within the total civilian labour force has increased from 2.5% in 1949 to 5.2% in 1958. Particularly noteworthy is the increase in the staff of the Ministry of Finance from 1,018 to 5,450 and of the Prime Minister's office from 177 to 706.

THE DEVELOPMENT OF THE ISRAELI CIVIL SERVICE

	March 1949	March 1958
Total Civilian Labour Force	368,000	(680,000)
(Majority of) Civil Service .	9,171	34,991
Of this: Post Office . .	2,203	6,326
Health Services .	831	5,593
Transport and Ports	1,358	4,141
Ministry of Finance.	1,018	5,450
Prime Minister's Office . .	177	706

[1] The figures of the civilian labour force of 1949 have been taken from (153) and those of 1958 have been projected from the corresponding 1957 figures in (238); most of the data on the size of the civil service are derived from (255).

Government employees are paid low wages relatively to those in the non-Government sectors and to those of civil servants in the Western world. Though the structure of the emoluments has been modified so that the span between the highest and lowest-paid officials has been widened, the egalitarian tendency is still very pronounced. While Israeli civil servants enjoy considerable fringe benefits, they are unable to increase their effective remuneration by certain practices which augment the wages and salaries of many other Israeli employees without paying income tax on these increments. Many civil servants (from the lowest to the highest divisions) supplement their incomes with additional part-time work.

EXAMPLES OF GROSS AND NET SALARIES FOR SOME CIVIL SERVANTS
(per month[1])

		Gross	Net		
		IL	IL	£	$
Policeman or Postman	.	219.3	200	30.8	86
Clerk or Bookkeeper	.	263.2	234	36.0	101
Medical Officer .	.	368.9	306	47.1	132
Head of Department	.	445.2	354	54.5	152
Chief Medical Officer	.	747.4	504	77.6	217
Director-General .	.	748.4	505	77.6	217

Bernstein (231) makes some apposite comments which confirm my own experience:

"There is too little sense of one public service. Party allegiance here and there may still supersede national loyalty, and newer immigrants in lower ranking jobs have not yet been taught the meaning of national loyalty. Although progress is being made, neutrality and objectivity based on a meaningful concept of the public interest have not yet supplanted official discrimination in

[1] The salaries refer to March 1958 (255) and are calculated for employees with three years' seniority who are married with one child. The *average rates* under-value the purchasing power of the lower-income groups whose expenditure is to a large extent on subsidized food items. I have, therefore, imputed £ (Sterling) values to the IL salaries at the *rate* of IL6½ = £1 and dollar values at the *rate* of IL2,321 = $1. The difference between gross and net reflects the deduction at source of income tax, national insurance, etc.

favour of the official's old friends and associates. Fragmentation of loyalty in the civil service frequently takes the form of 'protekzia' or organized favouritism based on previous associations and values."

II—ELECTRICITY SUPPLIES

The most significant of all indicators of Israel's economic development is the growth of the consumption of electricity. The Palestine Electric Corporation was promoted by the late Pinhas Ruthenberg who obtained the concession for power generation in most of Palestine from the Mandatory Government, and raised capital from Jewish and non-Jewish sources; its shares were among the few Palestinian securities quoted on the London stock exchange. The company has since been nationalized. The old power stations were driven by diesel generators and only in 1935 was the first thermal power station opened in Haifa. Since 1948 two further (steam turbine) stations have been opened in Tel-Aviv and the south, respectively. Since nationalization, the efficiency of the company has been affected by the agreement of the Government—because of political pressure from the extreme left-wing parties—to permit workers' delegates to participate in the management of the company, and by the determination of the tariff policy in accordance with political directives (e.g. disguised subsidies to agriculture and the Acre steel-town through low charges). Apart from the years 1952 and 1953, when the prohibition of electricity for certain uses and its rationing for others had to be introduced, the country's power requirements have been fully satisfied.

THE PALESTINE ELECTRIC CORPORATION (269)

	1938	1948	1958
Total Generating Capacity (thousands of kw.) .	69	78	360
Transmission Lines (km.) .	2,586	3,389	8,000
Total Consumption (millions of kwh.) .	79	261	1,305
Of this: Irrigation . .	32	75	400
Industry . .	20	71	445
Domestic . .	27	115	460

Irrigation in Israel, unlike in most other countries, accounts for a large proportion (30%) of electricity consumption; industry consumes about 35% of total supplies.

III—INDUSTRY

According to official estimates[1] 77,000 workers were employed in industrial enterprises in 1949. These enterprises produced a gross product of IL150 million, of which IL56 million represented the value added.[2] In 1958 there were 142,000 employees in industry which produced a gross product of IL1,720 million of which IL650 million was value added. The nominal value added per worker has risen from IL727 to IL4,590. Using the *average rates* to impute dollar values to the industrial output, the adjusted figures show an increase from $992 to $1,669; when the 1949 data are transformed into 1958 prices by the movements of the cost-of-living index, the industrial productivity per worker is shown to have grown from IL2,204 to IL4,591. There is some independent evidence to suggest that there has actually been an increase in labour productivity, and the above comparisons merely indicate the two extremes between which will be found the true measurement for the real fluctuations of output per industrial worker.

Most firms of the private sector belong to the Manufacturers Association and to this body have been delegated many supply, rationing, importing, investment and credit functions by the economic ministries. Under these circumstances membership for any industrialist in Israel is almost obligatory, except for the very large ones (e.g. "Ata" textiles), which have direct access to the Jerusalem offices. The Government, Jewish Agency and Histadruth enterprises are not members of this association and a special body looks after the interests of the Histadruth industrial undertakings. Most branches of industry are either completely dominated by one "leader" or—with the encouragement of the Government—cartelized. The whole of industry is well protected under the Tozereth Haaretz umbrella, and has cost-plus price-fixing arrangements that enable them to pass on to the consumers most cost increases. Employers and employees have often agreed on voluntary national wage increases—there was very little industrial strife—but in the last few years the Government has expressed its disapproval of this impelling element of cost inflation.

---

[1] These figures are at best a rough guess because official statistics adopt varying definitions of "industrial enterprise" for comparable data.

[2] The value added—measured in IL and not identical with the term value-added, defined on p. 124—is actually exaggerated for official statistics under-value the foreign currency inputs of machinery, fuel and imported materials.

(PARTIAL) SURVEY OF MANUFACTURING 1955
(239), (267)

Branch	Number of Establish-ments	Number of Persons Engaged	Value-Added[1] (millions of IL)	Index of Production December 1957 (Average1955 =100)
All Branches .	6,996	92,000	351	117
Food . .	1,075	16,432	63	93
Wood and Furniture	999	11,569	47	118
Metal . .	814	10,871	40	114
Clothing . .	800	8,117	34	79
Textiles .	690	7,433	23	135
Stone and Cement .	450	5,338	23	115
Miscellaneous .	428	5,068	21	247
Paper, etc. . .	409	4,920	14	104
Leather . .	365	3,849	13	100
Chemicals . .	217	3,056	13	106
Diamonds . .	188	3,044	12	115
Machines . .	151	2,815	11	105
Electrical Equipment	140	2,723	11	142
Rubber and Plastic	110	2,679	10	143
Minerals . .	97	2,577	9	272
Transport Equipment	63	2,368	7	109

As this partial Survey of Manufacturing shows, most Israeli plants are engaged in the assembly or processing of imported materials and concentrate on the production of consumption goods. This applies particularly to the private sector. In so far as Israel has a heavy industry and produces raw materials, this takes place within the compass of the Histadruth and Government sectors—e.g. potash, glass, cement, phosphates, steel, metal and concrete pipes. Whilst the industrial undertakings of the private sector employ about 7 persons per enterprise, the average number employed in Government or Histadruth undertakings is two to three times as large; the

[1] Calculated as the difference between gross revenue and total expenditure on outside factors.

average of the partial Survey of 1955 (which did not embrace the smaller firms) shows a national average of 13.1 persons employed per industrial undertaking.

IV—COMMERCE[1] AND FINANCE

It is officially estimated that more than 20% of the National Income is generated in this sector though some distributive functions in Israel are—for ideological reasons—also performed by industrial, government and agricultural enterprises, so that the true proportion is probably nearer 25%. With a handful of exceptions, foreign banks, insurance companies, accountancy firms, trading companies, etc., do not now maintain branches in Israel. Those that existed before the State were either liquidated or bought by Jews (often former employees). It is difficult to judge to what extent the Government's policy or the fear of reprisals from the Arab Boycott Office have brought about these decisions. Similar considerations also influenced the policies of the three major foreign oil companies which owned extensive distributive channels; these have sold their interests (this includes the disposal of the Haifa refinery owned by Shell and Anglo-Iranian) to a Histadruth oil company, a company the registered owners of which are an American-Jewish group and a new company controlled jointly by the Israeli Government and an Anglo-Jewish charity trust.

Most private importers and wholesalers are members of the Chamber of Commerce which performs delegated functions for the Government similar to those of the Manufacturers Association; its distribution of Government favours, foreign currency allocations and import licences is conducted mostly on the basis of past performance dating back before 1948. As the Chamber is headed by

[1] In other parts of the book the *Weltanschauung* of Israel's rulers is discussed, which regards trading as a parasitical function and has caused the allocation of imports to be tied in many cases to a particular production unit, and licences only to be issued to producers and not to merchants; hence, enterprises in Israel tend to develop vertically and attach to themselves, perforce, importing and exporting functions. This was to revenge itself on industry and particularly on those firms which had been encouraged by this attitude of the Ministry of Trade and Industry, in a period of easy credit conditions, to perform their own merchandizing. A joint American-Israeli report says this of 1956 conditions: "Industry has a relatively large amount of working capital tied up in documentary credits for the import of raw materials and also in export documents in the process of collection. This is mainly the result of a lack of import-export organizations. Most firms do their own importing and exporting and must continually finance these undertakings on their own account. Considering the general credit situation, it is obvious that the financing of imports causes the greatest inconvenience" (270).

persons who are right-wing critics of the Government, it was not surprising that the Histadruth trading corporations seceded from membership of this body in 1950 and established their own association demanding parallel allocations from Jerusalem. (At one time the Government used to keep records of allocations to the private and Histadruth sectors respectively, in order to show the public how impartial it was in its distribution of import licences.) Today the Government and Jewish Agency (owned or controlled) import-cum-export companies account for a larger portion of Israel's external trade than either of the other two sectors.—In the wholesale agricultural field the Histadruth company "Tenuvah" and the Jewish Agency company "Teneh" market 80–90% of the produce.

No reliable data exist on the retail trade, though the co-operative consumers' societies—controlled by the Histadruth's Wholesale Co-operative Society "Hamashbir"—handle, in my estimate, about one-third of this trade and probably a greater proportion in the food section. There are, in the Western sense, no department stores in Israel, though the Tel-Aviv urban area serves three-quarters of a million consumers. Few shops employ more than one or two paid assistants. The ability of the private retail trade to compete with the Histadruth co-operatives consists in their greater flexibility, longer hours worked by the principals and the granting of extensive credit; these advantages would be offset if the shops had to pay their staffs the high wages and fringe benefits laid down by the Histadruth union and paid by the "Hamashbir" controlled stores. The institution of chain stores is almost unknown (Bata-Avnaal is a notable exception). Only in the autumn of 1958 did the supermarket with self-service methods come to the Holy Land; it had been preceded by an acrimonious political debate within the Histadruth as to whether they were to participate in this private venture by a Canadian firm. They decided against a joint company, promising instead to open pure Histadruth (socialist) supermarkets of their own. The aggrieved Tel-Aviv shopkeepers declared a one-day strike when the Canadian supermarket was opened, and provided it with welcome publicity by breaking its shop windows.

V—Miscellaneous

Israel's tourist industry is rightly regarded as one of the natural export "commodities" of the country and, during the first six years of the State, the Ministry of Finance gave extensive credit facilities and subsidies to the hotel industry. Today the Holy Land can boast of 630 hotels, with 17,500 rooms, of which some are modern buildings with air-conditioning and other amenities. In 1958, 70,000 tourists visited the country.

During the mandatory rule the Jews avoided using the railway. This was a patriotic gesture meant to hurt the revenue of the Government and, positively, to patronize the Jewish bus co-operatives. Most of the railroad network was "inherited" in a greatly neglected state. During this decade it was repaired and new lines laid, so that in 1959 Israel has 430 km. of main lines and 200 km. of branch lines which operate services from Nahariyah in the north to Jerusalem and (along the coast) via Tel-Aviv–Lydda to Dimona in the heart of the Negev. Thanks to the equipment brought through the Reparations Company, Israel's railways today operate almost exclusively with diesel loco-motives which have progressively replaced the steam engines. Though rail traffic has grown, only about a quarter of the tons/kilometrage of Israel's goods are carried by rail, and the relatively short hauling distances make transport by lorries in most cases a more economical proposition.

Israel has three major port authorities: Haifa; Tel-Aviv and Jaffa; Eilat in the Gulf of Akaba. Of these Haifa handles about 85% of all cargoes imported and exported.

In 1947 100 Jewish sailors manned four old merchant ships of about 6,000 tons. At the beginning of 1959 about 2,200 men of the Israeli Merchant Marine sail in 35 vessels with a gross tonnage of 210,000; these include mixed passenger-cargo ships, fruit carriers (refrigerated) and oil tankers which were mostly built in German shipyards through credits provided by the Reparations Company. Two-thirds of the tonnage is owned by shipping companies controlled by the Histadruth or the Jewish Agency or jointly. The Israeli Government is considering the expansion of the fleet and contemplating the transfer of new acquisitions to a fully Government-owned shipping concern.

Israel's national airline "El-Al" was founded during the 1948/49 fighting. From its base in Lydda, the international airport of the country, it carried in 1957 46,000 passengers and 1,200 tons of freight on about 1,000 flights.

CHAPTER XII

THE MONEY MARKET

THE money market in Israel during its first decade had three important features: (1) As compared with the prices of other factors of production and particularly of labour, the average price paid for capital was low. (2) The Government[1] operated a differential pricing system for capital; different prices were charged to borrowers with identical credit ratings, and the same price was charged to borrowers with widely varying credit ratings. (3) Some of the distortions which would have resulted from the aforementioned practices were corrected by the refusal of the public and the banks to obey rigidly all the official regulations and a parallel unofficial and unregulated money market flourished.

GOVERNMENT CONTROL OVER THE MONEY MARKET

Until the Bank of Israel was established in 1954, a small department headed by the Controller of the Banks in the Ministry of Finance made the Government's wishes known to the banks. But, in the absence of legislation, it could only "request" the banks to change their policy in conformity with public policy. From 1954 onwards the energetic Governor of the Bank of Israel, who now had statutory backing, began to impose the Government's policy on the banking system; he severely limited the freedom of the banks to lend from their own funds except for those purposes approved in Jerusalem, forced the banks to deposit ever larger funds with the Bank of Israel or hold increased stocks of Government securities, and (*vide* p. 94) tapped a further flow of loanable resources when the Ministry of Finance accorded tax privileges to the buyers of State loans or bonds of public corporations.

Until 1958 the following Bank of Israel "liquidity instructions" applied to all banks (liquid in this context means the holding of cash reserves, deposits with the Bank of Israel or the possession of certain Government securities): 15% of all deposits to be deposited with the Bank of Israel; 100% liquid means to be held against balances by other banks, etc.; 50% liquidity to be maintained

---

[1] "Government" in this chapter refers either to the Ministry of Finance or to the Bank of Israel or to both.

for all time deposits of up to 18 months and all demand deposits made before 31st March 1951; 75% liquidity is required for all

TABLE X

MONEY SUPPLY[1]

Period[4]	Bank-notes and Coins in hands of Public	Demand De-posits	Total Money Supply a + b	Index of Total Money Supply	Total Available Re-sources[2]	Income Velocity[3] $\frac{e}{c}$	Index of Income Velocity
	a	b	c	d	e	f	g
1949	43	97	140	100	403	2.9	100
1950	65	125	190	136	592	3.1	106
1951	91	151	242	173	924	3.8	131
1952	106	151	257	184	1,417	5.5	190
1953	128	162	290	207	1,662	5.7	197
1954	147	202	349	249	2,091	6.0	206
1955	173	247	420	300	2,612	6.2	214
1956	228	289	517	369	3,085	6.0	206
1957	231	345	576	411	3,763	6.5	224

demand deposits accepted between 1st April 1951 and 31st March 1953; 90% liquidity is demanded for all new deposits accepted since 1st April 1953. These draconic regulations meant that *71% of demand deposits had to have a liquid cover.* Additional instructions for the remaining 29% of "free" credits directed that 22% of all outstanding bank credit had to be given to agriculture, forbade marginal

[1] The data in columns a, b, c and e are in millions of IL; 1949 is the base year for the indices of columns d and g; sources *vide* Table XI.
[2] The data in this column were obtai ned by dividing the column Total Available Resources in Table IV by the *average rates.*
[3] The income velocity has been computed by dividing the Total Available Resources (rather than the Gross Natio a! Product) by the "total money supply" of the last day of the calendar year.
[4] The data in columns a, b, c, and d refer to the last month of the year.

87

loans for the purchase of gold and securities (except those expressly approved by the Ministry of Finance) and limited credits for building activities. The discretionary powers of the Government were exercised when individual firms and pressure groups called on the Minister of Finance and the Governor of the Bank of Israel asking that their banks be allowed to extend them loans "below the lines of liquidity" or to discount their bills after they had been assured of re-discount facilities by the central authorities. The latest Bank of Israel reports indicate that, in the future, the control over the banks will shift even

TABLE XI

BANK[1] CREDIT[2] TO NON-GOVERNMENT SECTORS[3]

December	Bank[1] Credit[2]		Total Available Resources[4]	
	Millions of IL	Index (1949=100)	Millions of IL	Index (1949=100)
1949	64	100	403	100
1950	105	165	592	149
1951	127	199	924	229
1952	155	242	1,417	351
1953	197	308	1,662	412
1954	227	356	2,091	519
1955	240	367	2,612	648
1956	264	413	3,085	766
1957	306	478	3,763	934

[1] The term "banks" is used in this book to denote 27 commercial banks, 98 co-operative loan societies and the Government-owned Bank of Agriculture; not included are the Post Office bank, the four mortgage banks and any of the specialized financial institutions.

[2] This volume of credit is extended from "own funds of banks" and is composed of both foreign currency and IL loans; the total is slightly inflated because the returns of the banks (from which these figures are derived) cite the figures for the credit actually extended plus the accumulating interest that is due at the end of the loan period. These credit data do not include the discount of customers' bills which are rediscounted by the banks with the Bank of Israel—at the end of 1955 for IL16 million, at the end of 1956 for IL35 million and at the end of 1957 for IL52 million.

[3] Sources: (20), (100), (138), (158) and (238).

[4] These figures have been arrived at by dividing the column Total Available Resources in Table IV with the *average rates*.

further from general quantitative "liquidity instructions" to qualitative instructions as to whom funds should be lent. Apart from these controls over the loanable resources of the banks, the Government imposed "forced loans" on individuals, insurance societies, provident funds, etc. Moreover, together with the Jewish Agency, the Government disposed of some of the charitable resources on easy credit terms, and some of the property administered by the Custodian of Abandoned Property, as well as other Government properties, were sold on favourable long-term loans. The capital and consumption goods of the Reparations Company were allocated by the Ministry of Finance on long- and short-term credit respectively. Export-Import Bank and other foreign government loans, the IL counterpart funds of the American grants-in-aid and similar loanable resources were all conferred by the Government upon privileged borrowers within the framework of the Development Budget.

THE LEGAL INTEREST RATE

Until March 1957 the maximum legal rate of interest was 9% and the Government exhorted the banks to conform to it. This rate was drawn from the Ottoman law (*vide* Appendix II) which laid down that fiscal contracts involving interest payments exceeding 9% could only be enforced up to the maximum legal rate; aggrieved persons could turn to the courts to force lenders to return the excess interest which had been collected but no penalties were provided for. The Governor of the Bank of Israel opposed the passing of any modern Interest Law, the enforcement of which would fall to his administration, because he was convinced that no useful purpose would be served by the determination of a legal interest rate. Such a law was nonetheless passed in January 1957 because of political pressure by the three socialist parties on the Minister of Finance. In doing this the parties believed that such a law would increase their prestige among the more backward sections of the population. The new law (181) gave the courts power to impose penalties, either on the lender or the borrower, of five times the amount of the (annual) illegal interest. It is notable that in implementing this law the courts are entitled to accept the testimony of one person as sufficient evidence, and are allowed to prosecute in the case of oral money contracts. The Minister of Finance is entitled under this law to publish differential interest rates, and he has used this right by proclaiming the new legal rates for ordinary loans to be 11%, for agricultural and industrial loans 10% and for value-pegged loans only 6½%.

Until Government loans became partly value-linked (*vide* p. 95)
89

most of the public funds had been lent at interest rates of 3–7%[1] and borrowers (with proper credentials) had queued up to be rewarded—e.g. for following a "desirable" occupation, being privileged for some patriotic reason or belonging to a political pressure group—with loans that were, in fact, given at negative rates of interest. Within a decade the domestic purchasing power of the IL was reduced by 90%—if measured by the movements of the *average rates*—and by 67%—if measured by the upward trends of the cost-of-living index. Compared with these depreciation rates of the IL, any rate of interest of 9% or less can only be described as an effectively negative interest rate, and, on that score, all the public loans were a source of potential windfall profits. If these economic depreciation rates of the Israeli currency are linked with the income tax rates that were in force for the upper income groups, it can be deduced that between 1948 and 1958 it was necessary for a legal money loan in Israel to bear an annual interest rate of 35–40% in order to leave the lender with a net return—i.e. in real terms after paying income tax—of 5% on his capital. (Should the lender invest his funds in a manner which involved him in some risk, a gross return of above 40% would have been called for.)

Four inferences can be drawn from this distribution of most of Israel's money resources at cheap interest rates. First, the low interest rate gave an incentive to borrowers to finance with these funds the hoarding of materials in anticipation of a decline in the value of the IL, and many have considered this a subsidiary element in the 1949–52 inflation. Secondly, when a high interest rate prevails, the inclination of the borrowers is to use the loans for Make-Do-and-Mend expenditure which can bring in a quick return. Clearly the reverse process was at work in Israel where cheap money (not generally available for repairs, etc.) helped to finance the purchase

[1] The difference between a 3% Government loan and a 30% money loan on the black market is, in actual business life, even larger than the ratio of 1:10 might suggest. The borrower from banks or on the black market knows that if he does not honour his contract, he faces bankruptcy or, at best, has seriously impaired his commercial standing. The borrower of public funds feels psychologically secure that, should he fail to pay back his loan in time, he will not be dealt with harshly, his farm will not be foreclosed and a petition for insolvency will not be launched. Until recently a loan from the Development Budget was regarded like the receipt of an import licence with an allocation of dollars at a low exchange *rate*, which netted the recipient a differential profit. The Government granted loans from the Development Budget, to quote three examples at random, because it wanted a cantor from South America to settle in Israel; a hotel in Jerusalem to install a kitchen which satisfied the ritual standards; an investor to convert some foreign currency at a low *rate* and to compensate him by subsidizing his investment project.

of expensive new equipment, and the borrower of money to repair old machinery often had to resort to the black market with its high rates. Thirdly, the impact of the Government's exhortations to the banks to lend their own money at interest rates no higher than 9% had the effect—when heeded—of funnelling the limited amounts to old-established customers to whom such loans were the equivalent of a money gift at the discretion of the benevolent bank manager. Fourthly, sub-marginal investment projects were indulged in when subsidized cheap loans were available.

THE ILLEGAL MONEY MARKET

The black market in money can conveniently be considered in its following main aspects: (A) The illegal activities of the banks; (B) the operations of the "second" money market; and (C) loans of real resources (goods) at disguised interest rates.

(A) Most of the Israeli banks somehow evaded the stringent liquidity regulations and the maximum interest charges imposed by the Government. It was not uncommon for the banks to switch funds, derived from Government sources, or their own funds authorized to be lent "below the lines of liquidity", from the specially approved purpose (e.g. to help agriculture or export) to more prosaic and unauthorized uses in the field of industry and commerce. A visitor from the International Monetary Fund commented euphemistically: ". . . It is no secret that the (Israeli) banks have used various devices to defend themselves against some of the more drastic regulations . . ." (125).

In 1954 the Chamber of Commerce appointed a committee to find out what interest charges were actually paid by its members: 50% of the credit was obtained at 9%; 15-35% was given by the banks (!) at 22%; the rest were loans from the "second" money market at between 24-36% (132). In 1957, during proceedings before the Supreme Court, the judges stated that it had been proved to their satisfaction that the accused bank (which, I add, was small and unimportant) in 1953 and 1954 regularly charged interest at "40% or thereabouts" (211). Actually the handling charges of the small banks in Israel were so high that they could not have covered their costs had they charged but 9%. Until 1956 only two banks,[1] the Bank Leumi (predominantly owned by the Jewish Agency) and the Workers Bank (owned by the Histadruth), did not openly defy the Government's exhortations to charge no more than 9%. However, in the spring of 1956, the Workers Bank officially increased its in-

[1] These two banks handled the majority of the country's legal banking business.

terest charges to 10% and in the autumn of that year the Bank Leumi followed suit.[1]

(*B*) The "second" money market had the highest rates of the money black market, but money was more freely available on it than from the two other sources of black market money. This market is also known as the "Iraquian cash market" because of the origin of many of its operators, and the volume of its loanable funds is said in 1955-56 to have been between IL 25-40 million. In this market post-dated cheques and bills—from firms of good standing—were discounted for periods of up to 180 days. The rates were as low as 18% (for bills given to suppliers by the Histadruth or the Jewish Agency) and as high as 45% when no satisfactory collateral could be produced. Kibbutzim, building contractors and manufacturers who had to deliver their products on credit, were the main customers. The General Manager of the Workers Bank said that he knew of kibbutzim which had paid 30% interest (131). Lowe, in his specialized study on interest paid by kibbutzim, says that they refused to state how much they had actually paid, but admitted that it exceeded 20% (134). The Director of the Bank of Agriculture estimated that loans for settlements "from a private source" cost in 1955 between "18-24% and even more" (141).

(*C*) One of the less publicized ways in which the Israeli economy reacted to a maximum legal interest rate was to have recourse to non-banking credit tied to the supply of goods and services.[2] The sources of finance for these "loanable goods" were black market profits made between 1949 and 1952, undistributed profits, amortisation funds and the deliberate investment of money in stocks of goods for the purpose of obtaining a higher interest rate via goods than via the lending of cash money.

The Government, the Jewish Agency and the municipalities forced suppliers to employ a large part of their working capital to extend them credit. Importers, wholesalers and manufacturers competed with one another over their terms of credit to institutional cus-

---

[1] The Bank Leumi was generally known as a law-abiding firm and this open defiance came as a shock to the public. The General Manager of the bank, however, said that he had warned the Government on several occasions that this step was impending: "The many financial institutions which do not adhere to the legal limit on interest charges will in the end force also those, which do adhere today to the 9% limit, to follow in their footsteps" (135).

[2] A Government commission which investigated the bakery trade found that indirectly, via the supply of flour by credit, bakers paid an effective interest rate of 35% (119). Lowe, in his already quoted study (134), says that there are many forms of interest which cannot be discerned from a study of balance sheets, as for example "credit of goods where the interest on the loan is deducted first".

tomers[1] and small merchants and manufacturers.[2] In some cases the effective interest rate in this field of the money black market was very high; in other cases (e.g. oil companies, credit by professional people) it was lower than the legal rate. In most cases, however, it was extremely hard for the credit beneficiaries to ascertain what part of the price was to be imputed to the payment of a credit facility and what part to the payment for the commercial or professional service.

VALUE-LINKING[3]

The search for "purchasing power guarantees for deferred payments" runs like a thick thread through the history of economic theory from Jevons through Keynes to the present practices of the Finnish and French Governments; and even the United States Government has, in at least one case, made contracts with such guarantees. While this concept is not new, I do not know of any other economy which is so completely permeated with the technique of value-linking its contracts as Israel is. In 1959 the IL may truly have completed its abdication as a standard of measurement for all but short-term, "forced" and "lottery" loans.

The most primitive form of monetary value-linking in Israel was the pegging of (oral) contracts to the price of gold and dollars, which were traded illegally on the Tel-Aviv bourses, or to the quotations of the IL in the free money market of Zürich—all of which, despite the expressed displeasure of the Ministry of Finance, were regularly published in daily papers in Israel. This was plainly an unsatisfactory type of value-pegging, because the contracts, being "contrary to public policy" were unenforceable in court.

Until 1950 Israeli residents were permitted to trade in the existing pool of foreign securities. The appreciable premium of the Tel-Aviv-quoted dollar securities over the New York prices were a measure of the Israeli investors' belief that the anticipated depreciation of the IL would exceed that of the dollar, and purchases of such securities provided a legal, though expensive, hedge against inflation.

---

[1] The public bodies bought on credit in order to free themselves from the straitjackets of their budgetary appropriations.

[2] Some small firms, though prepared to pay heavy interest charges, found it impossible to borrow money on the black market. They, therefore, had to finance their transactions by buying supplies from those firms which borrowed money and, in turn, sold goods on easy credit terms.

[3] Historical material will be found in (100) and (265). I have more fully dealt with Israeli value-linking in an article, that is announced to appear in *The Review of Economic Studies*, Oxford in 1960.

The first private value-linking scheme was the issue of bonds by the Land Development Company which were linked to the prices of the urban property owned by the company. The Nesher Cement Company followed suit, pegging its bonds to the price of cement and later the Mehadrin Citrus Corporation tied its bond issue to the market price of orange groves. The Rassco Housing Company offered bonds pegged to the prices of the flats which it sold.

In April 1951 the Ministry of Finance offered for sale to the public IL10 million of value-linked savings bonds—the value of which was adjustable from the basic exchange *rate* of 0.357—which were non-transferable for eight years. The Israeli public did not grasp that this was a given chance to make a large and tax-free capital gain and less than half the issue was taken up before it was withdrawn in 1952.

The aggrieved owners of the foreign securities compulsorily acquired by the Government in 1950, refused to receive compensation from the Ministry of Finance in the form of Israeli Government bonds; and the Government did not wish to pay them in ready money the IL value at which these securities had last been quoted at the Tel-Aviv bourse. The Knesset then authorized the Government to pay for these securities with a new type of bond (given the Hebrew name of Tave-dollar) that had both its interest and capital value linked to the official IL—dollar exchange rate. At that time no one seemed to pay any attention to this deliberate circumvention of the spirit of the maximum interest law. At first these bonds were not well received, but the 1952 devaluation and anticipation of further devaluations drove up their price on the stock exchange and resulted in considerable capital gains for the original recipients of the Tave-dollars. To the Ministry of Finance such value-pegged bonds gave an opportunity to raise capital for its corporations by voluntary means. To ensure an even greater success for the issue of such bonds, the Government gave the specially privileged sponsors of value-pegged bonds (which did not include a single private company but only Histadruth, Jewish Agency, municipalities and state corporations) the right to sell bonds to the interest of which (usually 6–7%) a mere flat 25% income tax rate applied; the increments of capital gains were, of course, not taxed. These bonds were either linked to the official exchange rate or to the cost-of-living index or to both. The effect on the free money markets was tremendous. The Ministry of Finance now successfully competed with the attractiveness of the borrowers on the money black market and, by absorbing available funds, made it well-nigh impossible to raise money by the sale of equity capital or mortgages. In the past the money black market had interfered with the raising of equity capital for private[1] firms; the combination of the 25% flat income tax rate and the value-linked provisions of Government bonds was the death blow to the recruitment of equity capital for the private sector through public issues. By making the working assumption that the IL depreciates by 10% annually, it became a paying proposition for the wealthier members of the community to buy a 6½% linked Government bond rather than a first-class industrial debenture at par with a 45% interest coupon on the gross value of which full income tax was charged. Since 1952 no rational person voluntarily makes an investment in securities except when the income-tax privilege of a maximum 25% applies.[2] In 1959 90% of the securities registered with the Tel-Aviv bourse were either issued (or guaranteed) by the Government or value-linked with income-tax privileges. The securities index (267) shows an increase between 1951 and September 1958 of 8% in ordinary shares (predominantly of companies from the private sector) and a decline of 20% in un-linked debentures while value-linked bonds rose by 188%.[3]

Having adopted the principle that it can borrow voluntarily from the public only on value-linked terms, the Ministry of Finance adapted this technique to its lending. In 1954 a commission, the Lehmann Committee (109), was appointed the recommendations[4] of which were adopted by the Government retroactively to 1st April 1954. These recommendations provided for the linking of most Government loans at the discretion of the borrower either to the cost-of-living index or the official exchange rate in this proportion:

[1] The situation in the first years of the State is described by a banker as follows: ". . . the most obvious explanation (for the failure to place the issue of equity shares on a commercial basis) is the undesirable fact that the black (or grey) money market offers very remunerative possibilities for the granting of short-term advances at high interest rates" (266).

[2] A notable exception of an un-linked bond was the issue in 1957 of three series of bearer bonds, having a variable interest rate of 3–6% which were entirely exempt from income-tax and were intended to absorb black market money; holders of such bonds were exempt from declaring them in statements of property ownership demanded by the income-tax authorities. There are also Government loans (un-linked) which appeal to the gambling instinct of the poor because the interest is paid in the form of a few large prizes drawn by lottery.

[3] Bankers explain the relatively low quotations of value-linked bonds by the fear on the part of the public that the Ministry of Finance will not honour its obligations to adjust the value of the bonds to changes in the exchange rates.

[4] The recommendations were a compromise between those members in favour of linking and those opposed to it. Lerner, who signed the unanimous report but added important reservations, vehemently attacked this compromise; he argued that if the value-linking principle is sound it should apply to the whole amount of all Government lending.

Length of Loan in Years	Percentage of Loan to be Value-tied
Up to 2	0
2–5	50
5–8	60
8 and more	70

With wages and all medium and long-term loans being value-linked the epidemic spread throughout the country after the Zilberg judgement discussed in Appendix II. Rabbinical courts gave judgements for separation allowances "tied to the cost-of-living index"; friends borrowed from one another according to Tave-dollar quotations; the Hebrew University signed an agreement with the Students Union according to which the fees were automatically adjusted with changes in the cost-of-living index; the same applied to annuities and pensions of the Jewish National Fund and the National Insurance Institute; similar provisions were made for severance pay, benefits due from provident societies, etc. Today when a person is asked in Israel to sign a contract with a private builder or with the Government-owned National Building Corporation, this is couched in IL terms that are tied to the "Building Materials Index". In 1955 the Ministry of Finance offered to lend money to certain farmers who undertook to plant orange groves; for this type of loan the value was linked to the "external exchange rate for the export proceeds of citrus in force at the time when repayments are made". Since 1957 almost all Israeli insurance societies issue life policies, the redemption values and premium payments of which are value-linked.

The chief negative aspect of the linking system is the increased rigidity which this monetary jugglery has injected into economic life. The manipulations of the cost-of-living index have become more important in 1959 than at any other time in Israel's history. More far-reaching still is the impact on the overdue modifications of the official exchange rates. The attitude of the Ministry of Finance towards devaluation is entirely divorced from the possible effect on the balance of payments and is now almost entirely influenced by the predictable appreciation in the interest payments and eventual redemption of value-linked loans that would cause immediate structural changes in the internal budget. Value-linking has, therefore, introduced an additional hurdle which must be cleared by an Israeli Government before it can officially consummate a devaluation. As to the positive consequences of this technique many welcomed the institution in Israel of a money market on which persons can offer their loanable resources at interest rates which are effectively higher than the legal ones. The Bank of Israel expressed the fear that these higher interest charges would accelerate the spiralling of the cost inflation (100). Actually the relatively higher costs for loanable funds (including Government loans) may well be regarded as the most beneficial consequence of this new technique, for it is bound to restrain many entrepreneurs from queueing for an allocation of public funds, and thus hinder them from proceeding with undertakings that in the past were worthwhile only because the available finance was likely to be supplied at (effectively) negative interest rates. Finally the anti-inflationary mechanism of this new technique may be noted; this reverses the position of Israel in 1949–52 when the low (or negative) interest rates provided a powerful impetus to the inherent inflationary trend. Lerner, in his reservations to the Lehman Report (109), writes:

". . . one of the effects of linkage and the issuing of linked securities would be that when inflation causes people to flee from money, they are able to buy linked securities instead of hoarding stocks of money . . . so that linkage not only makes a given degree of inflation less harmful, but tends to reduce the degree of inflation itself."

On balance, therefore, the effects of linking may have been salutary. This is written on the explicit assumption that the State of Israel is unable, or unwilling, to check the inflation which the Government is engineering. Indeed, the Ministry of Finance accepts a permanent state of inflation as an inevitable evil. It may be praised for this implied honesty, but most economists will be rightly scandalized by the admission. However, only on the basis of this premise can the value-linking of the IL be seen in its proper perspective and be viewed with some possible degree of sympathetic understanding.

THE FLIGHT FROM THE BANKING SYSTEM

The progressively stricter supervision over the operations of the banks and the attempted enforcement of the legal interest rate on the official money market, led to a flight of the public from the banking system, and some financial resources were transferred to a second, unofficial money market. (Between 1949 and 1957 "banknotes and coins in hands of public" went up by 437%, while demand deposits lagged behind with a growth of 356%.) Taking Total Available Resources as the most significant indicator of general economic activity in Israel, their expansion (*vide* Table XI) of 834% can be fairly compared with the corresponding growth of the credit which the banks could extend from their own resources, 378%.[1] For every IL100 of Total Available Resources a bank credit of IL16 was available in 1949 and of only IL8 in 1957.

Table X shows that Total Available Resources increased during the defined period by 844% (column e) whilst Total Money Supply only rose by 311% (column d); if we regard the 1949 ratio of Total Money Supply : Total Available Resources as a constant, *the Total Money Supply of the country decreased during these nine years by 55%* (derived from column g). This relative decline in the money volume is explained in orthodox language by a change in the income velocity and the latter is shown (in column f) to have risen from 2.9 to 6.5.[2] There are three contributory causes in this development which pulled their weight and defeated the "regular" elements that exert their influence in an inflationary situation by increasing the money volume:

(*A*) The accelerated velocity of the "ordinary" money supply. (The velocity of bank deposits increased by almost 200% between 1949 and 1957).

(*B*) A large volume of clumsy "extraordinary" means of payment was created—or, more accurately, an existing small volume was expanded—in the form of near-money, post-dated cheques, promissory notes, etc.[3] There was also an increase in barter transactions.

(*C*) The strengthened trends to "autarchy" in the Histadruth sector and the consistent growth of the Government-cum-*institutions* sector account for an expanding non-monetized section of the economy.

---

[1] This volume of bank credit includes those loans that have been given at the direction of the Bank of Israel; if an index was constructed of the "free" banking credits extended in 1957, as compared with 1949, the decline would be even more remarkable.

[2] Hansen (151) views the progressive decrease in the rate of income velocity as a function of economic progress. Israel's experience, which was not in accordance with Hansen's long-term prognosis, was similar to that of the United Kingdom after the Second World War.

[3] One of many such examples is the sale of "credit coupons of oil companies". Most large firms in Israel enjoy two to three months' credit from their fuel suppliers and these issue coupons that are cashable at their pumping stations and depots. These coupons form a pool of (several millions of IL) unofficial money and are regarded as being almost as liquid as banknotes.

CHAPTER XIII

AGRICULTURAL POLICY[1]

HOFFIEN, the late chairman of the Bank Leumi, effectively characterized the non-economic nature of the Zionist rural settlements in the pre-State days:

> "The basic aim of our agricultural policy during the Mandate was not the production of foodstuffs but colonization. Except for some periods during the Second World War the Arab fellaheen supplied food in plenty and cheaply. In order that the Jewish farmers might be able to sell their products it was necessary to initiate a campaign of persuasion—and sometimes even use force—to make the urban population buy the dearer Jewish agricultural products. This fact alone shows that other factors apart from the supply of food to the urban population were the decisive element in the development of Jewish agriculture. . . ." (34).

Horovitz in the standard work on the Palestine economy describes at length how the Jewish farmers competed with imported food and the "indigenous cheap Arab labour" (172). The Jewish Agency bought land from the native landowners and settled on it young Zionists who had prepared themselves in training farms outside Palestine for this new life. As land was then a relatively dear factor, the emphasis was on intensive farming.

The establishment of the State changed the economic status of the Jewish farming group. The policy of Tozereth Haaretz afforded most farm products full protection against competitive imports and the "indigenous cheap Arab labour" was no longer to be found within the boundaries of that part of Palestine which had become the territory of Israel. Agriculture, as the privileged occupation of Zionism, was subsidized in diverse ways.[2] (According to Black, the major portion

---

[1] No one writing today on Israeli agriculture can fail to acknowledge his debt to Marion M. Clawson. I have drawn heavily on his analytical studies and the Handbook which he edited: (16), (147), (173), (176) and (192). The writings of the F.A.O. representative Black (145) and (174) have proved helpful. I have also benefited from the work of Israeli agricultural economists, especially Kadar (146), Lowe (177), R. Weitz (189) and Samuel (13).

[2] A sociological evaluation will be found in Ezioni's analysis from which the following is taken: ". . . in the political life of Israel, agrarianism is of great significance but no . . . agrarian party exists. Each party has its agrarian wing. . . .

of the subsidies given to agriculture flow to the older settlements; he deplores this fact and attributes it to the system whereby subventions are linked to the quantity of each farmer's output.) The open subsidies (paid in money) are registered in the budget estimates and amounted to IL21 million in 1956 (158) and to IL31 million in 1957 (238). The disguised subsidies are of much greater significance and include the allocation of public resources at artificially reduced prices (e.g. land, water, electricity, public services, building materials, credit), preferential allocations of investment goods and/or foreign currency, low favourable *rates* for the purchase of foreign currency and, in some cases, high *rates* for the sale of foreign currency obtained from the sale of agricultural exports (other than citrus).

The data assembled in Table XII show that the contribution of agriculture to the National Income has increased from 10% to 11.6% during nine years. The combined Jewish and Arab farming groups constituted $17\frac{1}{2}$% of the total employed civilian labour force at the end of 1957.[1] If the summary of official statistics is followed, 24% of Israel's gross investment will be seen to have been devoted to agricultural and irrigation purposes; however, if—*vide* the comments to Table XII—rural housing is included and realistic exchange *rates* attached to the import content of agricultural investment, the proportion is nearer 35%.[2] The number of Jews who have been added to the labour force as being gainfully employed in agriculture since the establishment of the State can be gauged at 45,000–50,000. Taking the larger number, an investment of $15,000 per new agricultural earner is derived.[3] According to an authoritative announcement, the housing, technical equipment, professional instructions, part-time employment in the first stage of settlement—

Recently a great number of special privileges accorded to agriculture have been subjected to public criticism. These privileges are presented as anachronistic relics from a time when agriculture was the privileged occupation of the nation" (91).

[1] Jews engaged in agriculture are said to be 15% of the total Jewish civilian labour force but, in the view of many observers, this exaggerates the statistical weight of this occupation among the Jews.

[2] Schweitzer has made an interesting, though limited, comparison between the value added which is generated annually per investment of $1 in agriculture and industry respectively; the investments in industry are shown to be $2\frac{1}{4}$ times as productive as those in agriculture (261).

[3] 35% of the imputed import content of Israel's total investments (*vide* Table VI for the years 1949–1957) are $830 million; from this total I have deducted 10% for allocations to Arab farmers and divided the residual sum by 50,000. It is true that part of this investment was destined for farmers who had been settled before 1948 but this consideration is offset by the fact that the 50,000 new settlers will still have to receive additional investment goods (i.e. supplementary to the $830 million) in order to be fully equipped.

all these over a period of five years cost IL30,000 per average settler (182).

THE "PRICE-LESS" LAND

The pattern of land ownership in Israel's 20.7 million dunams is as follows:

	In percentages
Government and Government agencies	76.5
Jewish National Fund (Jewish Agency) .	18.0
Private Jewish landlords . .	3.0
Private Arab landlords. . .	2.5
	100.0

Approximately 4½ million dunams of arable land are being farmed in the agricultural year 1959—of this half a million dunams by Arabs. Only 400,000 dunams of the 4 million dunams cultivated by Jewish farmers are owned privately. Apart from the more intensive exploitation of the already-irrigated areas, Israel's farming output can be further expanded only if (1) some of the sub-marginal land is improved; (2) some of the non-arable land is used for pasture; (3) irrigation projects are executed with a potential of adding a further million dunams to the present area of 1.2 million dunams of irrigated lands. The land reserves for these last-mentioned expansion schemes are almost entirely in the hands of the State and the Jewish Agency. These two public landlords founded in the autumn of 1958 a National Land Company to which they are expected to transfer all their holdings in 1959 and 1960. The new company will thus administer, under joint control, 95% of the total land area and will become landlord over 80% of all farming lands and over 91% of the areas now cultivated by the Jewish farmers.

What is the position of a potential farmer in Israel today who is willing to buy land and able to farm on his own? In practice, unless he joins a kibbutz or a moshav, he can only set himself up by leasing or buying land from the limited resources of the private sector. The weight of the private farming sector is steadily becoming smaller and land held by these two public landlords is—with a handful of exceptions—not allotted to aspiring farmers unless they join a co-operative settlement group, members of which undertake to employ no hired hands, to buy its supplies only from co-operatives, to market its goods exclusively through co-operative marketing bodies, etc. Eight of Israel's political parties each maintain a colonization department which organizes farming co-operatives for new settlers. The co-operatives are constituted to yield the maximum political and/or religious homogeneity, though actual membership of the organizing political party is sometimes not insisted upon. The political parties are rewarded for their labours when "their" villages show a 100% poll in their favour in elections. Farmers who exhibit signs of disloyalty after they have been settled on their homestead have been known to have been expelled from the co-operative for expressing strong dissenting views in public or—particularly in the Mapam party—on suspicion of not voting for the organizing political party.

The basis of Israeli rent policy can be formulated as follows; the average rent charged is far less than the average economic rent, and the rents charged for different prices of land do not reflect differences in economic rent. Gross agricultural rent, according to Noam (8), constitutes 0.6% of the gross value of agricultural output; I estimate that those who lease their lands from the public landowners pay less than 0.4% on the average.[1] Rent is a trivial item of expenditure but the situation of the land in relation to the sources of irrigation water (*vide* Chapter XIV), and its distance to the nearest urban market is of such significance that the arbitrary decision of Jewish Agency officials, where a new settlement should be located, is of paramount importance and may be the source of windfall profits for the lucky group.[2] The theorists of the Jewish National Fund have stated that they regard "2% of the crop value, ex farm" as a "just rental payment", but neither the State nor the Jewish Agency adhere to this rule when granting leases. Usually no long leases are given to capitalist farmers, and the price for short leases of irrigated land to private farmers fluctuates between IL5–8 per dunam, though sometimes for reasons of special privilege as little as IL1 is charged.[3]

[1] In the summer of 1956 I collected comparative data on the rents paid by different farmers in a certain area in the central part of Israel; all the rents referred to below are for more or less similar arable land with access to irrigation facilities: (a) in the Arab village (within the area investigated) the general practice was for the landlord to charge rent in kind—the proportion for rent being one-third of the crop; (b) a Jewish private farmer paid a Jewish landowner IL.24.500 per dunam for a one-year lease; (c) a small strip leased for a short period from a Government agency by a Jewish private farmer had an annual rent of IL5 per dunam; (d) two kibbutzim were charged an annual rent of IL0.400 per dunam for a long lease from the Jewish National Fund.

[2] Milk is the only major produce the transport costs of which are (partially) pooled on a national basis by the marketing bodies.

[3] Between 1950 and 1951 large tracts of Government land suitable for planting citrus groves were leased to three farming corporations each backed by a different political group. The leases provided for a rent of IL1 per dunam during the first five years and for a rent of IL1.6 per dunam subsequently (10).

Special conditions prevail in regard to long leases to kibbutzim and moshavim; these are not charged a rent per dunam but a *unitary rent per land unit*, and each settlement group is allocated a number of land units equivalent to the number of families.[1] The size of a land unit is determined by the concept that each family should be given only that number of dunams which it is capable of cultivating without outside help; therefore, the size of the allocated land unit depends upon the average size of the family,[2] the availability of irrigation facilities and the anticipated main farming activity of the new village—there are "dairy units", "citrus units", "intensive cultivation units", "unirrigated land units", "hill fruit-farming units", etc., and their areas vary from 17 to 50 dunams. The contracts usually consist of a 49-years lease but the right of the public landlord to revise the rents after seven years is stated; the rent per land unit was until recently IL12, i.e. between IL0.250 to 1.500 per dunam.[3] I have found these contracts in reality to provide maximum rents because most settlements succeed, by personal bargaining, to pay even lower rents. As both public landlords abhor the idea of bringing action in court against farming groups for non-payment of rents, it is not unusual for young settlement groups to run up rent arrears for several years.

A WESTERN DIET

The limited land-and-water resources of Israel are the background against which its agricultural economists were called upon to resolve three fundamental questions relating to the national diet and the type of farming output:

[1] By the courtesy of the Head Office of the Jewish National Fund, I was able to examine the 1951 contract (7) signed by its directors with the Histadruth, the latter being the negotiating body representing several hundred co-operative villages.

[2] A family is presumed to consist of enough working hands to provide 450 working days per annum. This may indeed be a correct statistical average of the possible performance of a family, but farming is not carried out by averages. During the first years of married life, the settler—when the wife is not available for help on the farm because she is child-bearing or looking after the small children—can expend a maximum of 300 working days on his holding. When the children are aged 12 to 16 years, and the wife is able to be of substantial help, it is estimated that 900 working days can be supplied by such a family unit. Thus, at different times, the family unit tied to working on its own inflexible holding is either under-employed or the land is not worked to its full capacity.

[3] The contract provides for villages, in which industrial plants are located, to pay increased rents.

A. Should a poor country like Israel encourage the lavish consumption[1] of animal products or rather a diet composed chiefly of vegetarian foodstuffs?

B. Having determined the proportion of animal proteins in the national diet, what type of animal product is to supply most of these proteins? Are they to be produced locally or to be imported?

C. Having decided on those products that are to be produced domestically, are the feedingstuffs for the animal protein producers to be grown locally or to be imported?

A. The proportion of the food budget devoted to expenditure on animal products is in most parts of the world a function of the wealth of the community. If the Government's claim is correct that Israel is so poor in domestic resources (which could be used for food production) and in foreign currency (that could be allocated for food imports) that its intervention in this field is an absolute necessity, surely the consumption of a largely vegetarian diet should have been encouraged. The Government's economic planners urged this course. In practice, however, Israel's distorted price-and-cost structure was such that an extraordinarily large amount of certain animal products was consumed.[2] In 1956 the poor economy of Israel had a greater per capita consumption of poultry than any other country in the world. In the same year the United States and Canada had the highest per capita consumption of eggs in the world (viz. 35 and 23 eggs per month respectively) and Israel was third with 22 eggs per month (12). The value of animal products and of locally grown fodder constitute about 70% of the gross value of Israel's agricultural output.[3]

---

[1] When beasts are fed off land on which crops can be raised for human consumption, a yield of up to ten times as many calories per acre can be realized by eating the crop rather than the livestock products; i.e. the conversion efficiency is as low as 10%.

[2] There are two additional reasons: the need to find an outlet for the high-value products of the moshavim and the European origin of a large part of the population.

[3] The value of poultry products as a percentage of the gross value of agricultural output is shown in an official study to be higher in Israel than in any European country—20% (8). In 1956 almost 25,000 tons of poultry meat were consumed as against imports of 11,000 tons of frozen meat (14), (181); in addition, a few thousand tons of local cattle meat and some imported meat (tinned) were available.

Sea fish is the cheapest source of fish proteins, but whilst its import was limited, the locally-bred carp provided an expensive—though to the Jewish palate,

B. What food products should have supplied Israel with animal proteins? (Milk may be left out of this discussion because, if on the grounds of health, it is considered advisable to encourage the consumption of *pure liquid* milk—and not of tinned milk or milk powder—then this is a product the domestic manufacture of which is impractical to replace by imports. Views on the health argument advocating the drinking of pure liquid milk are divided, but whatever the quantitative verdict on the desirable consumption of this food in Israel, the agreed amount cannot be imported.[1]) For the other animal products the economic alternatives of local production or import do indeed exist.

The consumption pattern of Israel's animal proteins should be: milk, a large quantity of imported cattle meat and small quantities of locally produced eggs and poultry. However, in fact, the Tozereth Haaretz policy determined that if goods could be produced locally (according to physical criteria) then their domestic production should take precedence over cheap imports. Consequently Israel imports small quantities of cattle meat and consumes relatively large quantities of locally produced poultry and eggs.

C. If a decision has been made that a certain quantity of cow-milk is to be produced locally, then the growing of roughage for cows (which, of course, cannot be imported or effectively replaced by an import-substitute) must have precedence over other uses for Israel's irrigated land. Apart from the growing of roughage, it is by no means clear to what extent, in an uncontrolled Israeli economy, the raising of fodder crops would have been superseded by the cultivation of

---

pleasing—alternative. In 1956 7,500 tons of carp were marketed locally; deep-sea fishing and lake fishing yielded 3,500 tons. Only 6,400 tons of herrings and 4,000 tons of frozen fish were imported. The import content of 1 kg. of carp (domestically produced) has been estimated to be equal to 65% of the dollar c.i.f. price of 1 kg. of the (imported) cheaper type of fish. In 1949 R. Ben-Sussan calculated the import content of 1 kg. of Israeli pond-bred carp to be the equivalent of the dollar c.i.f. Haifa price of 1 kg. of frozen Turkish carp.

[1] Despite considerable subsidies the farmers did not find cow-milk production a profitable pursuit, and to the consumers fresh cow-milk was a semi-luxury— the urban per capita consumption is only 75 litres annually. During the first years of the State skimmed milk powder (mostly from American surplus stocks) was used to dilute the cow-milk distributed in the towns. An increase in cow-milk production from 72 to 180 million litres between 1949 and 1957 has stopped the import of milk powder and led to a sharp rise in the price of 1 litre of fresh cow-milk as compared with 1 litre of diluted milk. The further import of milk powder and the sale of cheap diluted milk for the poorer classes have been successfully blocked by the dairy lobby.

TABLE XII

AGRICULTURE IN ISRAEL'S NATIONAL ACCOUNTS[1]

| Year[2] | Gross Investments[3] | | | National Income Originating in Agriculture | Column IV as % of National Income |
	Agriculture, Colonization and Irrigation	Total of Economy	Column I as % of Column II		
	I	II	III	IV	V
1949	16	80	20	24	10.0
1950	36	150	24	32	9.5
1951	47	214	22	39	7.4
1952	75	316	24	104	12.1
1953	120	331	36	140	12.4
1954	136	449	30	203	13.9
1955	121	551	22	220	12.6
1956	135	615	22	250	11.7
1957	158	806	20	298	11.6
TOTAL	(844)	(3,512)	(24)	(1,310)	(12)

Columns I, II and IV are in millions of IL.

[1] Sources drawn on: (16), (20), (100), (158), (159), (165), (185), (238) and (239).

[2] Refers either to agricultural year (e.g. 1956 commences in October 1955 and terminates in September 1956) or to calendar year.

[3] The figures of agricultural investments do not include rural housing whilst the data of column II include investments in housing. The import content of agricultural investments is higher than the import content of the total investment volume of the economy; furthermore the foreign currency is undervalued in the IL (official) statistics from which most of these data have been taken. Considering these three features, it is clear that the true *part of agricultural investments within the total investment volume is much higher* than is indicated by the percentages of column III.

Dulberg (164), in her study of the years 1949–1955 (i.e. covering seven years of our nine-year period) arrives at a percentage of 26% without rural housing and 32% with rural housing.

Eshkol, in his calculations of agricultural investments in the years 1950–1956 (without taking rural housing into account or attaching realistic values to their import content), arrives at 28% as their proportion of total gross investment (254).

alternative crops and the import of animal feedingstuffs.[1] The current position is that the multiple rate system together with the restrictions on the import of animal products are providing the grain farmer with buyers for his output at high prices; these high prices for feedingstuffs are paid by the producers of animal products which are given, by the Ministry of Finance, a Tozereth Haaretz protection *rate* of 8 and above, i.e. it pays to create Israeli value-added at a cost of IL8 per $1 of a similar imported article.[2] Halperin estimates (141) that 80% of the total area under field crops is today taken up with fodder for livestock; 5% is under green manure and no more than 15% of the land is free to grow foodstuffs for direct human consumption.

AT WAR WITH THE COW

Two principles have guided the socialist planners of agriculture in the Jewish National Home since its inception: the settlement of Jews in either kibbutzim or moshavim in such a manner as to obviate the use of hired labourers, and to make each farming unit as "autarchic" as possible. It was intended to prevent a division of labour within the farming sector and to discourage the concentration in different areas on one farming activity. The American grain farmer who—like a town-dweller—buys his milk, bottled, from a shop—is viewed with abhorrence! The farming directors of the Jewish Agency counselled that diaspora Jews could only be turned into a class of farmers when they had become emotionally attached to their new homesteads, and this purpose, it was said, was best served by practising mixed farming—this includes the keeping of livestock and the production of milk for the urban markets. The sacred Jewish cow became an obsession with the planners who insisted that all new

[1] The planting of carob trees along roads and on hills and the growing of non-irrigated sorghum (a summer crop of millet called "dura" by the Arabs) are two ways of providing feedingstuffs without using the scarce factors of irrigated farming (146). The Ministry of Agriculture has shown commendable initiative along these lines.

[2] "The profitable development of these branches has come about largely because of the price distortions which have been caused by the import-and-prices policy. As most of the old agricultural settlements engage in 'mixed farming' (which consists mainly of poultry and dairy production) constant pressure is exerted to protect these products against the competitive imports of milk products, meat and eggs whilst such protection is not extended sufficiently to the industrial crops, on the cultivation of which, as the source of their chief income, depend a part of the newer settlements"—these outspoken comments are taken from the latest Bank of Israel report (238).

farmers on the hills or in the distant south should keep cows and sell dairy produce in the urban market of Tel-Aviv.

The political opposition of the socialist leaders (who were in charge of the Jewish Agency and the Ministry of Agriculture) to wage labour in agriculture, introduced a momentous non-economic element in the determination of the type of product Jewish farmers were encouraged to produce. The kibbutz had the ideal pattern of agricultural production in the eyes of the socialist planners.[1] After 1948 large unbroken tracts of land and a more or less flexible labour force which could be switched from task to task at the instance of labour supervisors, enabled the kibbutzim to produce any *type* of product needed. Unfortunately for the planners the new immigrants were unwilling to choose this form of settlement; they were prepared to work as wage-earners in kibbutzim but not to join as members. While, as a result of more intensive mechanization, output in kibbutzim rose, a further expansion in Israel's total agricultural output (and which would conform to the socialist ideals of the planners) depended on the organizing of new immigrants in moshavim. In these smallholders' settlements with strips of land no larger than could be worked by a family, the *type* of crop which could be raised was a function of the size of the land unit and the employment of hired hands.

The Jewish Agency had behind it 35 years' experience in the establishment of moshavim[2]: most of the new settlers at the start

[1] During the first years of the State many kibbutzim temporarily relinquished their principles and employed some of the new immigrants (who lived in transit camps without employment) to operate their idle factors of production. (Kibbutzim in 1949 and 1950 had received large tracts of land and machinery which they could not operate fully with their own members.) A discussion went on for years within the kibbutz movement to ascertain whether wage labour should be permitted. The judgement of the higher party authorities was as follows: the employment of professional people (doctors, teachers, etc.) is to be permitted; employment of hired labour in industrial undertakings on the soil of the kibbutzim and the employment of wage labour on building tasks, even when this concerns agricultural buildings, is to be "legalized"; the employment of wage labour on agricultural work is proclaimed to be contrary to socialist beliefs.

A compromise solution has been the foundation of corporations owned by a Histadruth subsidiary (the Yachin-Hakal company), the colonization department of the Jewish Agency, two kibbutz federations, etc. Such corporations were granted long leases of land by the Government and the Jewish Agency. They were designated "administrative farms" and had the right to exploit large tracts of land with hired labour—but were considered superior to "capitalist farmers" because their shares were not owned by private individuals.

[2] In 1944 30,000 Jews resided in kibbutzim and 15,000 in all types of moshavim (212), whilst at the beginning of 1958 80,000 Jews resided in kibbutzim and 128,000 in moshavim (239).

were given 1 cow, 50 laying hens and (as the farmer had to be in constant attendance on the livestock) attached to the house, land which included 10–15 dunams with irrigation facilities. In time the settler would increase the number of his cows and chickens and add perhaps another 5 irrigated dunams to his holding. Such farm units were ideally suited to the pre-State policy of settling the largest number of Jews on the smallest number of dunams. They yielded high-value products (milk, eggs, poultry, meat, vegetables); despite the dear production costs a ready market, at high prices, was found for this produce among the Jewish community of Palestine who regarded such purchases as a patriotic act.

During the first four years of the State these high-value products continued, legally or on the black market, to provide a remunerative livelihood for the old and new members of the moshavim. By 1952 the urban market for these high-value products was almost saturated and it was obvious that, if Jewish farming was to continue to expand, it had to employ additional factors for the cultivation of industrial products of a low-value type (wheat, oil-bearing plants, sugar, sisal, cotton, etc.). Such crops could be sold only by replacing imports and the Ministry of Finance, while conceding a large degree of Tozereth Haaretz protection, was likely to object if the prices of the new import-replacements compared unfavourably with those of the hitherto imported goods. In order, however, to grow this new type of crop economically, mechanization was needed and this could be best applied on large tracts of land. Whilst the high-value products of the moshavim require intensive labour, the new products need cultivating by a small permanent staff per large farming unit and a flexible seasonal labour force.

The head of the colonization department of the Jewish Agency rebelled against the old approach to the moshavim and suggested that the new moshavim should have larger land units, and that their traditional practice of mixed farming should cease. It was, therefore, proposed that no livestock be given the new settlers and that, since they would be freed from the responsibility of looking after the beasts in the stables near the house, the allocated land unit could be in large strips away from the immediate vicinity of the dwelling place. The new approach was publicized by R. Weitz (189)[1]

[1] Weitz understood Israel's political reality and did not couple his proposals with the demand for lifting the ban on wage labour in agriculture. Black and Clawson, as experts called in from outside who did not have to adapt their suggestions to political expediency, agreed with Weitz's approach to cultivate staple products on much enlarged farm units, but regarded the introduction of wage labour as a corollary to the new approach.

and evoked strong criticism from those who regarded it as a betrayal of socialist and Zionist principles. The Director of the Bank of Agriculture wrote indignantly:

". . . thus they want to bring about in agriculture a division between the producers of raw materials and those who are to process them; logic and commercial experience will show that the raw materials must necessarily be cheap and the processed goods dear. In this manner there will come into being a further stratum—between the town and the village—and we shall have suburban rings of dairy and poultry farms which will receive their raw materials from distant areas . . . just as the urban industry receives raw materials from the colonies and agrarian countries" (5).

Subsequently some of the new settlements were planned along R. Weitz's suggestions but for political reasons mixed farming on small land units is still regarded as the desirable design for the moshavim. In December 1958 (256) Eshkol joined R. Weitz in an open "war against the cow" and he, who had been R. Weitz's predecessor as the head of the colonization department of the Jewish Agency and had been responsible for executing the policy of "mixed farming" at all costs, now (in his capacity as Minister of Finance) recanted. He is reported to have said at a farmers' conference that the development of the dairy branch had been "altogether wrong. It would be cheaper to import the bulk of our milk, butter and cheese from abroad, and use the land and water needed for cattle fodder for the growing of industrial crops in which Israel has numerous advantages over Europe". Eshkol was listened to with attention, but the lobby of the old farmers again prevailed and no immediate drastic changes are expected.

AGRICULTURAL PLANNING

Planning in agriculture in Israel, as in other spheres, is conceived primarily in terms of physical goals. The Seven-Year Plan[1] which was jointly adopted in 1953 as the official programme of the Ministry of Agriculture and the Jewish Agency, aimed at a level of output in 1960 that would make Israel self-sufficient in *all* foodstuffs and leave a production surplus for exports[2]. In 1956 this autarchic plan was buried.

[1] Three English versions are extant: Clawson's (173), that of the Ministry of Finance (19) and Mayer's (21).

[2] The import of coffee, tea, spices, part of the pulp for the feeding of livestock and some of the wheat were to have been the only exceptions to the planned autarchic idyll.

110

Has there been *one* criterion used by the authorities in the planning of agricultural output and the direction of farmers? I have found a number of objectives which have been declared by responsible leaders to be *the* decisive criterion in planning; they contradict one another and cannot, in my view, be brought on to a common denominator:

A. Maximum income of farmers.

B. Maximum production of calories.

C. Maximum earnings of foreign currency.

D. Maximum value-output per dunam.

E. Maximum value-output per input of 1 unit of water.[1]

F. Maximum number of persons who can be found employment on a given unit of land.

---

[1] This approach has been worked out in a detailed manner by Gevati. He found that the input of 1,000 units of water can generate a value of IL400 in citrus groves and—going down the scale—lucerne for the feeding of cows to the value of only IL144. R. Weitz suggests that this is the most appropriate planning criterion and has asked the Jewish Agency to give up its practice of allocating "land units" and instead allocate "water units" to settlers.

CHAPTER XIV

IRRIGATION

THE WATER POTENTIAL

THE sources of water in Israel are concentrated in the north; the rivers which can be utilized for irrigation, the accumulating ground-water and the rainfall—all decrease progressively southwards. It is possible to dry-farm one crop per year in the north, but the crop value per dunam can be increased many times over by additional irrigation. The Negev, in the south, has an arid climate which allows for practically no farming without irrigation. Organized irrigation schemes are, therefore, an integral part of any plans for agricultural development. The first phase can be said to have ended in 1948 when, with one exception, only local irrigation schemes (which transported water over short distances) were executed. Most of the intensive Jewish farming made use of the groundwater by boring artesian wells while most Arabs engaged in dry-farming. The second phase was initiated in 1949 and was scheduled to be completed by 1960. By the end of this term the large-scale irrigation project of the Mekoroth Water Company[1] will have provided for the transfer from the north and the centre to the south of the firm flow of rivers, the unutilized groundwater and the spring flow surpluses, mainly in steel or concrete pre-stressed pipes, the largest of which have so far been the 66-inch pipes of the Yarkon–Negev line.[2] The third phase, political conditions permitting, aims at transferring the head waters of the Jordan from the extreme north to the south in pipes of 108 inches; this work is projected to be executed in 1966.

The water is transferred, under pressure, by expensive pumping, the power being largely derived from stations with extensive stand-by facilities. A certain amount of power is taken from the existing

---

[1] Until 1957 this company was owned entirely by the Histadruth and the Jewish Agency although the Government had provided most of its financial resources. In 1957 the Government exchanged some of its debentures for shares in the company.

[2] Many of the expensive irrigation schemes in the world provide, as a by-product, important social benefits including the generation of hydro-electric power; in Israel the irrigation schemes are power-consuming. The marginal costs of irrigation projects in America and Asia are relatively low, for they transport surface water by gravity and little of the water is stored in reservoirs.

electricity grid, but for security reasons[1] most of it is generated by independent diesel prime movers. Some of these installations are romantically situated in specially constructed tunnels and are a favourite tourist attraction. Also, allegedly on security grounds, the water is carried in pipes and not in open channels even when the latter is technically feasible. Clawson comments: "I have seen pumping stations constructed in a more lavish manner than I have ever seen in the United States or than anyone there ever dreams of . . . no private water company would engage in such a wasteful practice" (176).—"The fact is that the present plans are wasteful to a degree no private engineering firm would tolerate" (192). What justifies plans being made to convey water under pressure, mainly in pipes, for distances up to 160 miles? Until 1955 it was believed by the Government's advisers on water supplies (particularly by the hydrologist Blass and Amir, the Ministry of Agriculture's expert) that the potential water supply of the country was much larger than could be used on the arable land known to be available. It was then argued that the available surplus of water should be used in schemes to extend the area of arable land. Thus, improvement schemes for sub-marginal land were planned, hill farming encouraged and— because some of the arable land was located in the Negev—the transfer of water from the north to the south was advocated. Blass pleaded in favour of the irrigation of the southern areas "because in other parts of the country there is not enough land on which the available water can be utilized efficiently" (26). Amir then believed "that there was far more water than irrigable land" (27).

In 1944 the Mekoroth Water Company arrived at an estimate of the annual water potential which, adjusted to the present territory of Israel, worked out at *3.450 million c.m.* In 1948 Hays published an alternative calculation which gave the present area of Israel an imputed water supply of *2.340–2.800 million c.m.* (The joint Cotton-Hays memorandum of July 1952 mentioned a potential of *2.435 million c.m.*) At the time other hydrologists challenged these optimistic declarations but the Minister of Finance stated in August 1953 that the investments already made in irrigation projects were undertaken on the assumption of a water supply of *2.700 million c.m.* (25).

---

[1] The Economic Advisory Staff succeeded on several occasions in demonstrating the dishonesty of many "military" arguments adduced by civilian planners who sought to vindicate the more expensive irrigation schemes. This, to cite two important instances, was the case with the advocacy (by military arguments on the part of the Mekoroth Water Company and the Ministry of Agriculture) of conveying water by pipes rather than by open channels, and the installation of diesel motors instead of electric motors.

E*

Clawson and others protested that these were exaggerated figures but an official Ministry of Finance publication, as late as October 1953, cited a corresponding figure of *2.466 million c.m.* (19). Despite attempts to prevent publication,[1] the results of the 1955 water survey made by the Ministry of Agriculture became public knowledge and administered a sharp blow to the complacent farming leaders who still thought water was an abundant factor in Israel. The survey showed that the potential water supply was only *1.800 million c.m.* In the summer of 1958, again in conditions of deep secrecy, the new senior Government hydrologist, Viner, assisted by Dutch experts, arrived at the conclusion that, on completion of the third phase of the irrigation scheme, only a maximum of *1.700 million c.m.* would become available; at least 400 million c.m. are likely to be needed in ten years' time by industry and for private consumption, so that farmers can then expect a maximum of 1,300 million c.m. for irrigation.

Now that water was said to be an existing factor sufficient only for the irrigation of two-thirds of the known arable land, three economic conclusions became self-evident. The diversion of the northern waters to the south had become an absurd economic proposition, and it was clearly desirable to concentrate all arable farming activities as near as possible to the northern sources of water. The improvement of sub-marginal land no longer served any useful purpose once it was established that even some of the better arable land, already awaiting cultivation, would have to remain uncultivated because of insufficient water. Hill farming which depended on the pumping of water to a great height at a heavy cost[2] was also no longer warranted. Yet none of these considerations seemed to affect Government policy, though their economic validity was unchallenged. All that was changed was the justification advanced for the admittedly uneconomic propositions; military and political requirements were the new means of justification. Thus, the carrying of water to the south was defended on the grounds that the Negev had to be populated to resist marauders. Clawson summed up his views on the irrigation plans of the Ministry of Agriculture as follows:

". . . present irrigation programmes are based on large-scale diversions of water southward, out of the areas where the water

[1] Baer (3) disclosed the facts in a newspaper article and thus defeated the object to keep them a guarded secret.
[2] In Manarah, for example, water was pumped to a height of half a mile at a cost which was twenty times as onerous as that of the application of one corresponding unit of water in the plains.

originates to more distant and higher areas, while at the same time leaving unirrigated equally large areas of just as good land nearer the source of water."

The Economics of Irrigation

During the first years of the State the price of water was not of such practical momentousness as it is today. In the days of an intensive black market, a growing population and a rapid inflation it seemed that ready buyers would always be found for all farm products however high the price of water. Furthermore, the costs of water are not a prominent price-component of the high-value products such as were described in the previous chapter. Between 1950 and 1953 the Ministry of Agriculture had to ration the limited water supply to farmers and it demanded the right to intervene in the production schedules of farms and settlements.[1] The Ministry also expressed its views on the utilization of the scarce water factor for "luxury" products and expressed its special dislike for bananas and carp. The Ministry (27) wished to reserve the irrigation water for the cultivation of products that "replaced imports and were likely to increase exports". Steps were taken to measure "the gross value of output of basic foodstuffs per 1 c.m. of water". But before this could be done and an even more comprehensive rationing apparatus was ready, economic considerations recoiled on the planners who had thought only in physical terms. In 1953 the market for high-value products had become saturated and the black market in foodstuffs had either disappeared or offered only diminishing profit margins.

Increasingly farmers had to turn to low-value industrial products in the cultivation of which water is a high price-component. Many of the perishable high-value products were sheltered from outside competition, while Israel's low-value staple products had to compete with imports from areas in which they were grown without irrigation. In 1955 the first signs of strange behaviour of farmers became noticeable, and in 1956 and 1957 this trend was strengthened: although farmers were liable to fines for breach of contract, some did not take up *all the water ordered in advance from the Mekoroth Water Company.* Even at the subsidized price of water—and this applied particularly to the settlements in the south—not all the farmers were prepared to risk cultivating the low-value industrial products at the ruling prices for the products and the cost of the irrigation input.

[1] The effective demand for irrigation supplies was artificially enhanced by the Ministry of Agriculture and Jewish Agency policy to lower the water charges by extensive subsidies.

Amir admitted that the "nearer we come towards solving the techno-logical and engineering problems of water and irrigation, the greater becomes the importance of economics—i.e. the price of water and the water cost as a percentage of the value of the product" (30). At the beginning of 1957 the situation became so serious that the Jewish Agency had to appoint a special commission to provide for the disposal of the surplus water which the farmers in the Negev were not taking up (35).

Those concerned with Israel's irrigation supply have to concern themselves with two sets of tasks: to exploit physically the maximum areas of the available arable land with the limited irrigation supplies and simultaneously to encourage the utilization of the irrigation supplies by the farmer in such a way as to minimize the cost per c.m. of water.[1] In 1958 the expenditure of farmers on subsidized[2] irrigation amounted to 15% of the value of farm products (252). Blass (175), Amir (30) and Kariv (31) have expressed the view that a farmer cannot afford to pay more for water than about 10% of the value of output. Clawson is less dogmatic but even he draws the line at 20%, saying that water costs above this figure are "certainly to be regarded as problematic or worse".

The average price charged by Mekoroth Water company in 1958 per c.m. of water was 43 prutoth. Clawson has made the reasonable assumption in forecasting the average water price in 1960 (the year when the more expensive stretches of the irrigation schemes of the second phase will be functioning) that it will probably be no less than 53 prutoth. On that basis he worked out water costs as percentages of farm prices of different products. His computations (176) show that apart from vegetables and citrus fruit, most farm produce would

[1] The social policy, explained in the previous chapter, of allocating small strips of land to the new settlers in the moshavim, has also had detrimental effects on the economic utilization of irrigation supplies. The initial capital investments in local sprinkler systems is considerably less when effected for large land units. Similarly the energy input for distributing water is higher—per unit of water—for a field split into strips than for one unbroken tract of land. Irrigation costs in the moshavim became even higher because (unlike the orange growers who water economically by surface irrigation) they make an excessive use of sprinklers.

[2] In 1955 a commission was appointed, the recommendations of which were approved by the Ministry of Finance, and which prescribed (retroactively) that one-half of the loans granted from public funds to the Mekoroth Company be regarded as interest-free loans and the other half as long-term loans on which interest of $3\frac{1}{2}\%$ was to be paid—an effective interest rate of $1\frac{3}{4}\%$. Since 1956 various attempts have been made to push this interest rate even nearer to the zero level. (These interest charges should be compared with the current rates enumerated in Chapter XIV.)

A further disguised element which heavily subsidized the price of water was the allocation of foreign currency for equipment and fuel at discriminatory low *rates*.

then have a water-cost content of 24–40%. In the extreme case of lucerne and certain fodder crops, 67% of the anticipated price would be expended by the farmer on irrigation costs.[1]

These figures tell eloquently of the importance of the irrigation payments in the profit-and-loss accounts of Israeli farmers. The comprehensive cost of water to the economy, however, is considerably higher than it is to the farmers, as can be learned from the following description by an official spokesman:

> "It is a fact that the production costs of water exceed greatly the price which the farmer pays for it. Every customer of the Mekoroth Company, without an exception, pays less than the true price. In the agricultural districts near the sources of the water the farmers receive a hidden subsidy because the calculations on which the price of their water is based do not include the real economic value of the employed capital, do not provide for realistic depreciation rates, correct fuel charges, etc. Those who farm in difficult areas— e.g. on the hills or in the Negev—enjoy in addition to the above-mentioned hidden subsidies, the open subsidies which are paid to them, and thus are charged for only a relatively small part of the true costs" (252).

A "FAIR" WATER PRICE

In Chapter XIII it was explained that a family wishing to farm in Israel has, on the whole, no choice but to join a co-operative settlement which is allocated public land. Usually the group cannot decide in which area to settle, but the settlers are directed to their new homes by the planning authorities. As rents are nominal, where they go does not matter from the point of view of rent payments. If farmers had to pay for their water supplies on something approximating their particular costs, the farmers in the south would be heavily hit while those in the north would reap the benefit of paying nominal rents for land favourably located near cheap water supplies. In many influential circles this is felt to be "unfair", and there are several schemes and proposals to rectify the price structure by charging the favourably-located farmers more for their water (i.e. above the cost of the water) and subsidizing that used by the relatively poorly-located farmers.[2] In short, through the manipulation of the cost of

---

[1] Gevati arrived at similar conclusions and estimated that the water costs in Israel were "four times as high as in America", i.e. in irrigated areas like California (33).

[2] The average costs of supplying irrigation water to farms in the north and south respectively are in the ratio of 1:7 (253). To quote the most extreme charges:

water supplies to the farmer, it is hoped to offset one of the anomalous results of artificially low and uniform rents. The three schemes, summarized below, aim at introducing *rent differentials by means of the water price:*

I. The Zionist colonization department and the Ministry of Agriculture pay farmers *in different areas* diverse subsidies *per c.m. of water bought* (and not per dunam farmed). Many of the leaders of the farming community wish to see this scheme extended.

II. On a modest scale, Mekoroth is "averaging" the water prices which it charges though, for institutional reasons, it is unable to do this as comprehensively as most of its directors desire. There is an undoubted trend towards equalizing the water prices though it is unlikely that the public water companies will arrive at *one* mean water charge as some extremists demand. Mekoroth has volunteered its services to the Ministry of Agriculture saying that it is prepared to act on the latter's behalf as an "economic rent collector", i.e. to tax the surplus profits of those who are fortuitously situated in the north by charging them a price considerably above the costs of supplying them with irrigation water. This theory of the "water taxation of land" is very popular but, despite its influential backing, has not been unreservedly accepted by all the Israeli socialist planners. In support of the Mekoroth aspiration to tax the surplus profits of the more fortunate farmers, the Deputy Director-General of the Ministry of Agriculture entered the following plea:

> "It is neither fair nor just that the settler who has by chance been brought to the Hule Basin (in the north) in order to engage in farming there, should reap completely and exclusively the benefit from the cheap water costs of the area, simply because he is accidentally near the source of water supply for irrigation; if the Government pursued such a policy it would force the farmer in the south—who happens to live in an arid area—to bear alone the heavy investment expenditure upon the irrigation projects and the costs of pumping—both of which account for the higher price of the water (in the south). . . . The Government must fix mean water prices" (27).

III. The most recent proposal, now canvassed by farm leaders who wish to inject a disguised rent differential into Israel's agri-

the lowest price charged to a village in the north for 1 c.m. was 7 prutoth; the highest prices were paid in Israel by a village in the remote south, 178 prutoth, and by a hill settlement in the north, 181 prutoth (28).

culture via the water charges, is associated with the name of Kariv (252). He suggests that the Ministry of Agriculture should enunciate the percentage of water charges within the gross agricultural expenditure (i.e. formulate some statistical abstraction of a national "water burden") that could be—or should be—borne equally by all farmers. If the proposal was implemented, the payments for irrigation supplies would become a constant (percentage) item in the production costs of all farm products. Having established such a general, per centum, measuring rod, the Mekoroth Company could then—depending on climatic and soil conditions, and the type of product cultivated—make selective charges to farmers for their irrigation needs that would ensure that the water costs in their production schedule did not rise above or fall below this "water burden".

THE FUTURE

If we make the traditional assumption of Israel's planners that the future population of the country will not exceed three millions, the third phase of irrigation can only be proceeded with on the supposition that the price of water sold to farmers in the south, engaged largely on the cultivation of low-value staple products, will have to be considerably below its *marginal* cost. If, on the other hand, we work with the hypothesis of a population exceeding three millions in about 1970, the utilization of the irrigation supplies (that will then be provided on completion of the third phase) will not necessitate the payment, to the same extent, of public subsidies for conveying water from the extreme north to the south; in that eventuality the effective demand for the traditional high-value products of Jewish agriculture (which can bear relatively high water charges) will be bolstered, and farmers will abandon their present plans to employ most of their resources on the cultivation of low-value produce.

There is yet another course of events which could lead to the abandonment of the present plans to transfer the headwaters of the Jordan to the Negev but would still allow the south to receive cheap irrigation supplies: the possible discovery of a commercial process of desalination of sea water. As the south of Israel borders on the Mediterranean and the Red Sea, the "sweetened sea water" would then only have to be conveyed over short distances to the heart of the arid Negev.

PART B

CHAPTER XV

THE FIVE STANDARDS OF THE IL

A resident of New York in, say, January 1952 who wished to obtain IL1,000 in Tel-Aviv in order to support his aged mother could do so in three ways. First, Standard II, he could transfer dollars at the official *rate* of 0.357; this necessitated an expenditure of $2,800. Secondly, he could transfer dollars through one of the smaller banking institutions which specialized in such transactions or make a private arrangement with an Israeli resident who wished to acquire dollars in New York, i.e. the Standard III procedure (illegal in Israel) which at that date had a *rate* of about 2.500 and necessitated an expenditure of $400. Thirdly, he could have used the Standard IV method; for instance, this could have been done by sending an article (for which there was a great demand in Israel, but for which import licences were not ordinarily granted) that cost, say, $300 in New York, but could be sold in Israel for IL1,000.

Standards II, III and IV play an important role in the Israeli economy, but clearly cannot serve as standards of measurement for the purchasing power of the IL. Standard I measures the value of the IL in terms of the retail prices which are used in the computations of the cost-of-living index to which Israel's wage structure is geared. Standard V measures the purchasing power of the IL in relation to those goods that enter into Israel's external trade transactions.

In a free economy (i.e. one with no foreign currency controls, import and export licensing, government use of public funds to manipulate the cost-of-living index, etc.) it is sufficient to have one standard of measurement for the country's currency. Allowing for market imperfections it is, on the whole, a truism to assert that the internal and external values of the currency of such a country undergo identical fluctuations. The external values of the American dollar

120

and of the Swiss franc in 1959 are inextricably linked to the movements of the retail prices and wages of their countries. In Israel it is necessary (as in other economies with multiple exchange rate practices) to study, in separate compartments, the movements of the currency by five different standards of measurement. The fluctuations of these five standards are independent of each other and do not even always move in the same direction as is evident from Table XIII.

STANDARD I measures the domestic purchasing power of the IL by the fluctuations of the official cost-of-living index.

STANDARD II measures the value of the IL by the official *rates*; i.e. those *rates* declared by the International Monetary Fund to be the legal *rates* of Israel.

STANDARD III measures the value of the IL by the *rates* on the money black market.[1] There are two prices in this market, one for "notes" and the other for "transfers", and both are quoted in the daily press. The former is the *rate* of foreign banknotes and cheques (and gold) in Israel. The latter denotes the *rate* of dollars credited in New York, Milan and Zürich to the account of the buyer, an Israeli resident. The Standard III *rates* in this book refer to the average of these two prices.

STANDARD IV measures the value of the IL by the effective *rates* which are derived from the sale of certain imported goods in Israel. Unlike the Standard III *rate*, this *rate* does not have a unitary value, and it is not a pure money *rate*. The IL receipts from the sale of certain imported goods also contain a payment for the risk taken by the importer and for his enterprise in organizing lucrative imports in a complex and illicit manner.

---

[1] The price of the "notes" *rate* is determined by the demand of (a) Israeli travellers who, risking a search on departure, smuggled out notes mostly to finance their subsistence on short journeys abroad; (b) Israeli residents who hoarded them as a hedge against inflation; and (c)—the greatest demand came from this group—Israeli importers of smuggled goods from the Arab countries who paid the Arab exporters with dollar notes, cheques or gold.

The price of the "transfers" *rate* was determined by the larger (illegal) trading operations—mainly by the abuse of *import-without-payment* or *import-for-export* facilities—and by the net capital movements of non-Israeli residents, who liquidated their holdings in Israel, and Israeli residents who aimed at investing part of their wealth outside Israel.

As Israel had an adverse balance of trade in the smuggling of goods to and from the Arab countries, there was a large demand for "notes" to cover the deficit. Consequently, whilst in most countries (where "notes" and "transfers" exchange rates in the illegal trade of foreign currency prevail) the "notes" *rate* is cheaper than the "transfers" *rate*, in Israel the opposite is the case, and a larger amount of IL is needed to purchase dollar notes handed over in Tel-Aviv than for a credit in dollars in the safety of New York.

It is not a unitary *rate* because the opportunity to introduce Standard IV goods into the country depends on individual circumstances. Thus, a tourist can only obtain this black market *rate* for his foreign exchange from goods which he can bring into the country physically without a licence (e.g. nylon stockings); a relative supported by regular parcels from abroad has an even more limited choice (e.g. sausage); the immigrant is limited to "personal effects" (e.g. refrigerator); an investor with a licence from the Investment Centre may choose from a wide range of building materials for illegal resale in the home market (e.g. cement); etc. Details will be found in Chapter XXI.

STANDARD V measures the value of the IL by the *average rates*, these being the weighted average of all effective import and export *rates*. In order to compute the import *rate* I have taken into account all the legal and illegal payments made by the importer in IL per $1 of import, c.i.f. Haifa. Similarly, in estimating the export *rates*, I have computed the average IL price paid by the economy to earn $1 of value-added export earnings; this IL price includes all direct and indirect pecuniary payments to the exporter.

TABLE XIII

THE FIVE STANDARDS OF THE IL[1]

	STANDARD I[2] C-o-L. Index	STANDARD II Official rates				STANDARD III Money black market rate	STANDARD IV Goods black market rate	STANDARD V Average rate	
		Goods and services			Institutions				
May 1948 .	100	0.248	....	0.333	0.333	....	....	0.333	100[4]
September 1949	98	....	0.357		0.357	0.435		0.450	129
February 1952 .	128	0.357	0.714	1.000	0.714	2.800	1.000	0.800	229
January 1954 .	228	1.000	1.300	1.800	1.300	2.450	—	1.600	457
October 1955 .	253	....	1.800	....	1.500[3]	2.300	15.000	2.100	600
December 1958 .	294	....	1.800	....	1.800	2.450		2.750	826

[1] Sources: current issues of *Haaretz* and Central Bureau of Statistics publications, (44), (48), (50) and (207). Apart from Standard I, all the *rates* express the IL equivalent of one dollar.

[2] May 1948 = 94 of the new cost-of-living index, *vide* p. 55.

[3] Smaller *institutions*, and the transfers of larger *institutions* intended for building purposes, were granted a *rate* of 1.800.

[4] Index of *average rates* with May 1948 as base.

123

CHAPTER XVI

THE ISRAELI CONCEPT OF VALUE-ADDED

THERE are various concepts of the term value-added in Israel. In this chapter I have enumerated them so that it will facilitate both the later study of the various *rates* in their relationship to value-added and also present some sort of idea of the difficulties of formulating economic arguments in the face of these various concepts.

In the terminology of National Income studies "value added" usually refers to the contribution of a particular sector to the Net National Product.[1] Value added is calculated by deducting the value of all the inputs from outside a particular sector from the gross value of the output of this sector. It is, on the whole, measured in terms of the national currency. The National Income statisticians of Israel have no choice but to use the IL as a unit of measurement in the compilation of the National Income and the National Product. The economic sense of such computations has obvious limitations imposed by the distorted price-and-cost structure.

For its own purposes the foreign currency controls administration applies a concept which it calls "value-added". (I shall write this with an hyphen.) This notion is expressed only in terms of dollars, for, in the multiple rate system, computations in IL are of little significance to the operators of the foreign currency controls. There is today in the Ministry of Trade and Industry a "Commission for the Measurement of Value-Added" which issues official certificates to manufacturers confirming the proportion of value-added (and in some cases the IL costs per $1 of value-added) of their products. A product can have a positive value added in terms of IL, whilst it has a negative value-added in terms of the dollar.

In a multiple rate system an exporter may be paid more IL for the export of an article priced at $8 than he spent on the purchase of $10 of imported raw materials to manufacture it. A study which covered ten factories provides some empirical evidence (82): ". . . there is no connection whatsoever between the value-added calculated according to local prices and that at international prices. The highest value-added at local prices occurs at an electric

---

[1] E.g. "value added in manufacture"; "contributed value"; "domestic content"; etc.

124

goods plant B which has a negative value-added at international prices and a low value-added at local prices. This complete lack of correlation between the value-added at local and international prices, shows the degree of distortion of local prices and the negative effect this may have on the development of the economy. From the aspect of the profit motive, which is clearly the main incentive for private investors, it is worthwhile to develop various branches of industry having a high value-added at local prices. In the cases studied here, however, investment in such branches would have sometimes resulted in a net loss for the national economy, from whose viewpoint value-added at international prices is the determining factor of economic worthwhileness for any branch of production."

The question arises as to how the value-added of, say, product X (a product produced domestically and not exported) is computed. This is done as follows: product X is given an imputed dollar price equivalent to the c.i.f. Haifa dollar price at which a similar article can be imported into Israel.[1] The dollar value of the imported inputs of product X is subtracted from this imputed dollar price, and the residual value is the value-added of product X.

The value-added of an article, which is exported, is arrived at by the subtraction of the imported inputs used to manufacture it, from its f.o.b. Haifa dollar price.

In order to test the economic feasibility of producing an article domestically, it would be superfluous in an economy with a unitary exchange rate to calculate the proportion of value-added in the total value of the article. Yet, in Israel the first task of the cost accountant who searches for the *rate* at which a local manufacturer produces import-replacements, is to ascertain the proportion of the value-added. This may be illustrated by the following numerical example: an entrepreneur who owns an assembly plant in Israel wishes to recruit Government funds for an extension of his enterprise. To do so he knows that he must formulate his demand in the language of the Ministry of Finance; his memorandum, therefore, states that the machine which he assembles sells in Israel for IL28 whilst to import it would cost $10. "All I am asking," he proclaims, "is a Tozereth Haaretz protection *rate* of 2.800." At first sight the economic planners in Jerusalem might think this *rate* most reasonable. But a further examination reveals that the proportion of the value-added of this machine is only $1. In order to market his locally assembled product for IL28 the manufacturer has used imported inputs of $9 which he

---

[1] There are some products (e.g. milk) and many services for which no reasonable estimate of value-added can be presented.

purchased at the official *rate* of 1.800. Viewed in this light, and the value-added of this enterprise found to be only 10%, it is possible to make the significant calculation that in this plant $1 of replaced imports costs the economy IL11.800 (i.e. 28 less nine payments of 1.800).—These considerations should have led all Government investigators of the Tozereth Haaretz *rate* (i.e. the relative cost of producing a product locally rather than importing it) to apply themselves exclusively to measuring it on the basis of the value-added. Indeed, this is the practice today of the professional economists in Israel, but is scorned as a method by those manufacturers whose *rate* is shown on a net basis to be appreciably higher than on a gross basis, and whose production is thus considered less worthy of public support.

How was the concept of value-added employed by the Government in its policy of export promotion?[1] Until 1950 the gross receipts of most export proceeds were exchanged into IL at a high (favourable) *rate*, i.e. the Government subsidized not only the domestically produced value-added but also those imported components of the exported products, which were imported on *IfE* licences at a low *rate*. When the radical change was made to subsidize only the value-added of exports, the Ministry of Finance had, at first, (by intelligent guessing) to attribute a "percentage of value-added" to each article; no proper statistics on the allocation of *IfE* were kept.[2] By 1954 the allocation of (direct) *IfE* was registered in the name of each recipient-exporter and a subsidy was only paid on the difference between the allocated *IfE* and the export foreign currency proceeds. In March 1956, the foreign currency controls administration adopted a new definition of value-added in exports which served as the basis for the payment of a money subsidy; value-added became the residual value computed by deducting from the total foreign currency receipts

[1] In 1957 the Zim Shipping Co. demanded that the Government apply the value-added technique also to invisible exports. This company was paid in IL for its services and was allocated currency at the official *rate* for its needs. It asked the Ministry of Finance, in a reasoned memorandum, to consider that an imputed dollar price be given to its services as—in the absence of the Zim and other Israeli shipping companies—the Ministry would otherwise have had to allocate foreign currency for the services of foreign shipping lines. From this imputed dollar price it wanted the Ministry to subtract its actual foreign currency expenditure and have the residue regarded as value-added foreign currency to be paid for at a favourable *rate*.

[2] The principle of the Government paying subsidies only on the domestic component of the value of the exported article was generally accepted as just. Only the Manufacturers Association spoke up against it and demanded the retention of the old system whereby subsidies were paid on the gross foreign currency receipts of the exporters (71).

the registered *IfE* and an indirect attributed *IfE* presumed to have been used additionally in the manufacturing process (*vide* row E, Table XIV).

The "depth" of value-added was to occupy the Ministry of Finance considerably. It has already been remarked that in an economy with a unitary exchange rate the "depth", i.e. the proportion of value-added in the total value of the article, has no administrative importance. From an economic standpoint the benefits of division of labour are such that an enterprise specializing in one process of production (i.e. having a shallow value-added) is often more profitable than one which performs several processes under one roof (i.e. having a deep value-added). Paradoxically the Israeli technique of paying "export subsidies per $1 of value-added" was introduced by a declaration of policy which stated that enterprises with "too deep value-added" (73) were to be discriminated against and paid a low *rate*.[1] By 1955 the wheel had turned and Tsour, who was then the head of the Foreign Trade Division of the Ministry of Trade and Industry, stated that only those exports would be permitted which passed his ministry's criterion of a "minimum depth of value-added".[2] Tsour argued that $40 of value-added earned in a $100 export article are to be preferred to the same net proceeds of $40 in a $400 article—an inefficient factory with a 40% value-added was a greater asset to the country than one with 10% value-added.[3] It was but a logical corollary when Tsour instituted a technique in 1957, whereby (in some cases) exports with a deep value-added were to receive a higher *rate* than exports with a shallow value-added, *vide* p. 160.[4]

The concept of value-added in exports is used independently of the IL costs of producing $1 of value-added. To the head of the agri-

[1] This strange declaration was meant to justify the imposition of a disguised export tax on citrus.

[2] In countries without a unitary exchange rate, it is not uncommon to find regulations which prohibit exports except when possessed of a minimum percentage of value-added. The Allied Administration, for example, imposed such regulations in Western Germany, but abolished them after a short period (59).

[3] Tsour was later to retrace his steps and he became frightened of his own dogma: ". . . we are indeed interested in the deepening of exports . . . but we must be careful lest we place obstacles in the way of the meritorious export branches by forcing them to engage in high-cost production processes. This is not only a theoretical consideration; the efforts made to protect home industry from competing imports hinder the exporter who wishes to bring from abroad materials which are produced in Israel at prices that (should the exporter be forced to use such domestically produced import replacements) would make such exports questionable" (74).

[4] The Economic Adviser to Tsour's ministry pokes fun at these regulations (228) but they are nevertheless being extended.

cultural lobby, Verlinsky (60), the export of high-cost melons, strawberries and flower-bulbs is to be preferred to that of low-cost diamonds because of the deep value-added of the former as against the shallow value-added of the latter. Even so serious an Israeli economist as Dulberg considers it "important to develop especially the production of those goods which have the highest value-added" (63).

Whatever may be thought of the economic soundness of the Tsour theory about the desirability of the foreign currency control of Israel encouraging production with a deep value-added, for years this has in fact guided the administration in its distribution of favours to "commendable exporters". At a later stage the Ministry of Finance discouraged the "packaging of dollar goods industries" and it was aided in this endeavour by scoffing at the profit to the economy of enterprises with a shallow value-added. On p. 199 some details are given of the illegal manipulations by unscrupulous exporters, and the legal manipulations of astute manufacturers with permission to "switch" *IfE* materials from hard-currency supply areas to the soft-currency markets of some of Israel's trade agreement partners. The Ministry of Finance sought means to discourage these manipulations and found a correlation between such (undesirable) exports and the shallowness of the value-added in the goods involved.

CHAPTER XVII

THE STRUCTURE OF THE FOREIGN CURRENCY CONTROLS

FOUR DEVALUATIONS

PALESTINE was a member of the Sterling Area and exchange control regulations, almost identical to those of the United Kingdom, were introduced by the Palestine Government in 1939. The authorities in London excluded Palestine from the Sterling Area in February 1948. When the State was proclaimed, the nominal exchange *rate* was 0.248 (i.e. IL0.248 = $1) although a unitary "unofficial" *rate* of 0.333 was in force for most commercial transactions. The first devaluation occurred in September 1949 and the new *rate* was set at 0.357. Up to the beginning of 1949 there were relatively few illicit currency transactions and the Standard III *rate* diverged by only 10% from 0.333 (44).

In February 1952 the second devaluation took place when three official *rates* were proclaimed. These were 0.357, 0.714 and 1.000.

The country experienced its third devaluation in January 1954, and the new *rates* were 1.000, 1.300 and 1.800.

Unofficially, the fourth devaluation began in 1955. (The two lower exchange *rates* of the previous devaluation were then dropped and 1.800 remained as the only official *rate*.) A gradual process of depreciation brought the *average rate* to 2.750 in 1958. Since 1956 many have urged the Government to consummate this fourth process of devaluation by officially declaring a new *rate* at about 2.800.

THE FOREIGN DEBT

In the first years of the State, the Ministry of Finance, in order to cover the deficit on current account in the balance of payments, called up the two foreign currency reserves of the country: the blocked Sterling balances and the foreign securities owned by its residents. (The foreign currency controller prohibited trading in gold, but gold acquired before this prohibition was not confiscated. There were no takers for the offer by the Government to buy the gold.) Despite charitable and political aid Israel had to borrow extensively to finance its import programmes. In February 1958, the foreign debt of the State (including the non-Government debt guaranteed by the Government) amounted to $538 million (239). There are, in addition, some foreign loans outstanding to Israeli companies which are not guaranteed by the Government.

FOREIGN CURRENCY BUDGETS

The Ministry of Finance draws up an annual (theoretically comprehensive) foreign currency budget, which lists the anticipated receipts of foreign currency and, correspondingly, divides this total into detailed proposed allocations. The allocations are administered jointly by the Ministry of Finance and the Competent Authorities, the latter being designated officials in the ministries which issue import licences. The system of a foreign currency budget worked unsatisfactorily until 1955 for three main reasons:[1]

(1) Many of the anticipated foreign currency receipts were "tied", i.e. the donors or lenders of these funds specified that they be utilized in a particular manner, and thus these "tied" funds were not freely available for allocation among the Competent Authorities for purposes which had been arrived at freely. The Belgian, French, Swedish, Swiss and United States loans were conditional on the funds being used, wholly or partly, for the purchase of machinery in the lending country. Similar conditions accompanied the German reparations.

(2) Since the official *rates* (Standard II) were divorced from the value of the IL, as reflected in the movements of the cost-of-living index (Standard I) or the Standard III and Standard IV *rates*, the Ministry had to agree to the demands of foreign currency suppliers that they (instead of exchanging cash currency for IL) be allowed to transfer goods to the country and receive their IL by selling the goods domestically. Thus there was a further reduction in the sum of foreign exchange at the disposal of the Ministry of Finance for making cash allocations at the direction of the Competent Authorities. It follows that by putting up with these practices, the Ministry of Finance helped to undermine the orderly working of its own budget. But, the Ministry argued, had it not permitted some suppliers of foreign currency to Israel (e.g. investors, tourists, immigrants) to bring in their capital, with more or less official blessing, in the form of goods approved by the Government, they would have chosen the illicit way through the Standard III and Standard IV black markets.

---

[1] In one respect the foreign currency controls left no room for complaint: the Ministry of Finance never defaulted on any of its undertakings to allocate foreign currency.

(It is estimated that in 1951 15% of the total foreign currency receipts of Israel were transferred in the form of Standard IV goods.)

(3) Until, following upon the receipt of German reparations, the foreign exchange position had changed for the better the Ministry of Finance tried to raise as many foreign currency loans as possible. Actually, even at high rates of interest, the cash loans it sought to obtain for the implementation of its budget could not always be secured. In such moments of despair the Ministry agreed to accept foreign currency loans "tied" to goods suppliers were prepared to deliver, at seemingly low interest rates.[1] This was another serious breach in the underlying principle of the foreign currency budget that all the country's foreign currency receipts be paid into a pool to be drawn upon according to criteria to be decided by the Government. The acceptance of short-term loans in the form of goods forced the hands of the Ministry of Finance, so that part of the system of allocation was turned into the distribution of import licences to importers who received credit from their suppliers for goods which happened to be available.

THE PATTERN OF THE DEVALUATIONS

The official devaluations (fixing *rates* of Standard II) were—with the exception of the 1949 devaluation—in the nature of *ex post facto* recognition of what had already happened. They lagged behind the depreciation of the IL as measured by the internal price level or the *average rate*. During the second, third and fourth Israeli devaluation processes—each was a long drawn-out performance and not a statutory act linked to a particular day—the pattern was the same. As the internal price level and the Standard III and Standard IV prices rose, the pressure by foreigners on the foreign currency controls administration to grant special terms for exchanging foreign currency into IL grew more intense. Parallel to this pressure were the no less vigorous demands of Israelis for allocations of foreign currency at the official *rates*, as it was expected that the favourable *rates* would not last long.

The foreign currency controls administration warded off awkward questions from transferrers of foreign exchange by giving them such

---

[1] The Ministry of Finance refused to pay usurious interest and an offer, for example, to supply Israel with commodities at world market prices plus a twelve-months credit at 15% was condemned out of hand. However, the foreign supplier who charged 10% above the world market prices for his goods and granted a year's credit at 5% was certain of a better welcome, for his interest charges were said not to be usurious.

concessions as would improve their *rate* but not with the appearance of officially granting an exchange rate at variance with the official one. Earners of invisible exports, recipients of inheritances and foreign insurance awards and restitution payments were given the right to transfer part of their receipts in the form of Standard IV goods; investors were favoured with *IwP* licences (enabling them to import luxury goods for resale in the black and grey markets); exporters were given *pamaz* benefits (and some of Israel's export earnings were squandered on the import of tinned peaches and expensive fabrics); immigrants were given cash "bonuses" and/or privileged to import Standard IV goods; tourists were given rebates at hotels, in certain shops and by some authorized tailors; etc.

After each devaluation process was consummated and the formal act of devaluation had been proclaimed, the Government, with monotonous regularity, cancelled these bonuses, privileges, rebates, etc., and declared that in future it would not reintroduce them and so evade the official *rate*.

This pattern also recurred in the dealings of the foreign currency controls administration with the Israeli applicants who, by paying for foreign currency at the prevailing *rates*, had aimed at a windfall profit.[1] The Ministry of Finance, using its administrative discretion, progressively imposed surcharges on luxury goods and travel tickets, and gradually spread the net until most non-Government imports were, in fact (before the formal devaluation) already paid for at substantially higher *rates* than the official Standard II *rates*.

It may well be asked what induced the Israeli Government in each cycle to give a *de jure* recognition to a *de facto* devaluation after the lapse of a number of years. One of the reasons was the belief that, by gradually working up to a devaluation through the use of surcharges on existing exchange rates, the blow of the devaluation would be cushioned and would not lead to a sudden jump in the internal price level. There are, however, more weighty reasons for this time discrepancy. In the 1949–52 period the foreign exchange income from the *institutions* was the most important single item of receipts which the Ministry of Finance recorded. The Ministry argued that it would have been bad public policy to impose a tax openly on the contributions to the funds of the Jewish Agency, "Friends of the Hebrew University" and other philanthropic bodies. The officials

---

[1] After the formal devaluation was proclaimed, the Ministry of Finance imposed surcharges on goods—imported with foreign currency allocated at the old *rates*—which had not yet passed into the hands of the final consumer, but could be traced to the warehouses of importers, wholesalers or manufacturers. Nonetheless, every devaluation was a source of windfall profits to many.

of the Ministry admitted privately that a *de facto* devaluation secured the benefit of an overdue devaluation for the economy but, by requiring the *institutions* to sell their foreign exchange at a *de jure rate*, the system (indirectly) provided revenue of tens of millions of IL for the Government. (At a later stage the Israeli Government dropped its inhibition and officially proclaimed a discriminatory *rate* for the *institutions*.)

The *rate* of 1.800 was proclaimed as the sole official *rate* only as late as 1955 for the Government feared, unjustifiably in the light of actual events, that the foreign holders of Israeli Government bonds would exchange these in large numbers for IL cash holdings.[1]

A further reason for the hesitation to proclaim *de jure* devaluations was provided by the obligation of the Israeli Government to pay the counterpart funds of the American grants-in-aid, in IL, into a special account which could be disposed of only at the discretion of the American authorities. At one time the Ministry of Finance thought that the American authorities would be satisfied with an artificially low *rate* if this was equipped with the title *"de jure"*.

In my view, the Government has so far refused to consummate— by the proclamation of a new official *rate*—the devaluation process of 1955–59, for fear of repercussion on the budget of the revaluation of its value-linked loans and the periodic interest payments. In addition the immutability of the official *rate* is said to have a political prestige value internally.[2]

IMPORTS-WITHOUT-PAY (*IwP*)

When import licences with allocations of under-valued dollars (i.e. at low *rates*) were being issued, queues of applicants formed in front of the foreign currency controller's offices. Many of the importers, whose applications were rejected, conquered their disappointment and joined another queue at the same offices to solicit import licences without allocation of foreign currency, i.e. *IwP*.

---

[1] The dollar bonds of the Israeli Government were medium-term ones. Holders, however, had the right to cash them on sight provided they accepted IL according to the official *rate*. As these bonds were traded in America below parity, they provided a legal loophole for non-Israelis to buy, say, one dollar bond for $0.80, sell it in Israel for IL1.800 and thus secure a *rate* of 2.250. Actually, several devices were successfully employed by the Ministry of Finance to frustrate such transactions.

[2] There are, of course, economic arguments against devaluing the IL and I have dealt with these in Chapter XXIII. In any case, those who argue against devaluation are as much opposed to a *de facto* devaluation as to a *de jure* proclamation.

Indeed, the apparatus of the foreign currency controller was employed, from 1949 to 1953, to a considerable extent in examining problematic requests for *IwP* licences. With the collusion of non-Israelis, these licences were financed by the purchase of foreign currency on the (Standard III) money black market.[1] The underlying assumption was that the *rate* of the Standard IV (via the sale of imported goods) would be appreciably above that of Standard III. This was often the case, and hence the possession of an import licence was more important than the question whether imports were to be financed by foreign currency from official sources or from the money black market.

How did the officers of the Ministry of Finance who allowed this system to flourish rationalize the *IwP* licences? For years, the official apologists propounded the view that these licences were necessary to satisfy the needs of the many genuine capital transferrers of goods. (The basic assumption was that goods were not specifically bought for transfer but were already owned.) It was presumed, for instance, that many small manufacturers wished to transfer their plant and stock of raw material to Israel. The Ministry of Finance thought that Jewish shopkeepers in the diaspora, who aimed at liquidating their stores in order to emigrate to Israel, would be prevented from doing so if they could not bring their existing stocks of goods with them. By implication it was suggested that the Ladies Guilds of the Hadassah Organization in Carolina ransacked their homes to find linen for a Jerusalem hospital (but, in fact, the ladies contributed money and the organizers of the *institution* bought American linen for the transfer); naïvely it was thought not at all unusual that rich relatives in the diaspora were not prepared to support their poor relatives in Israel by cash aid, but only through the sending of food parcels which enabled the recipients to sell these on the black market. Apart from the handful of genuine cases, it is now officially admitted

---

[1] An Israeli importer goes to the offices of the foreign currency controller and informs him that Mr. X of New York has decided to invest money in Israel. The latter wishes to effect this by transferring a stock of cement worth $100,000 from New York to Haifa and has appointed the applicant as the importer of these goods. Our Israeli importer is, consequently, given an *IwP* licence for $100,000. This licence is now hawked, i.e. as Mr. X is a dummy figure, a genuine owner of foreign exchange who wishes to receive IL at a black market *rate* is sought. Y wishes to transfer $100,000 to Israel and a *rate* is fixed between the organizer-importer of this project and Y. Y now transfers $100,000 to the account of X in New York. (Alternatively our Israeli importer returns to the offices of the foreign currency controller and informs him that X has changed his mind about investing in Israel, but Y is prepared to invest, and the latter's name must be substituted for that of X on the *IwP* licence).

that the Ministry of Finance policy of granting *IwP* licences has been a policy which was exploited for the enrichment of unscrupulous Israeli merchants. More details of this story will be found in Chapter XXI; it is sufficient to say here that, at best, these imports of Standard IV goods were a method by which non-Israelis, through their purchase of goods with the deliberate aim of selling them in Israel, converted foreign currency into IL. However, in most cases the *IwP* was organized by Israelis who bought the foreign exchange to finance it on the Standard III market and profited from the difference between this price and that of Standard IV. In consequence, it is not surprising that the foreign currency controls administration was sceptical about "presents" which Israelis claimed to be receiving (foodstuffs, cars, sewing-machines, etc.) and, to the chagrin of the few genuine donors, many of these presents were confiscated, or innocent recipients fined because they had no import licences.

In 1949 the Ministry of Finance established a special *IwP* department. Its task was at first confined to checking the genuineness of the ownership of the *IwP* goods, and setting the IL price for the counterpart value of the imported goods which was to be paid into the non-resident blocked accounts.[1] (According to the foreign currency regulations, local currency owned by a non-resident had to be deposited in a blocked account.) It was released upon special application only when the Ministry was satisfied of the use to which the non-resident wished to put these unblocked IL. The Ministry realized that it would be farcical to allow a non-resident, who had been given an *IwP* licence, to sell Standard IV goods on the local market, and block merely that part of his IL receipts which corresponded to the official *rate* of 0.357. This *IwP* department set a *rate* (a compromise between the Standard IV and the official 0.357 *rates*), that certified the IL counterpart which the non-resident transferrer of Standard IV —*IwP*—goods had to pay into a blocked account. In 1950, for example, this *rate* was 1.350.

In 1950 the crisis in the balance of payments brought the Ministry of Finance to a policy that seemed the result of despair. The *IwP* department unofficially promised large importers *IwP* licences for certain goods—with the name of the supplier of the foreign exchange left blank—and encouraged them to seek abroad what were euphemistically called "investment-dollars". This was clearly a travesty of the foreign currency controls and an indirect admission that the official rationale of *IwP* was fallacious. The Ministry privately defended *IwP* as a way of utilizing black market currency for

[1] Not to be confused with a special type of blocked account (instituted in 1953 and mentioned on p. 165) which could be freely sold by the owner.

the import of goods that were more or less essential.[1] In time this *IwP* department was faced with another task. It negotiated with genuine applicants for *IwP*, promising to issue import licences to the suppliers of foreign exchange provided a portion of the currency was sold to the Ministry of Finance at the official 0.357 *rate*.

A further innovation in the winter of 1950 was the readiness of this department to issue blank *IwP* licences for a limited number of articles, of which tyres and cement were the most important. There is reason to believe that the supply of (black market) foreign exchange offered for such *IwP* manœuvres was inelastic, and that the competition among Israeli importers—all armed with blank *IwP* licences— drove up the price of these "investment-dollars".

On 1st April 1951 the Government founded the CONS company which they appointed as the monopsonistic buyer of "investment- dollars" (51). The Ministry dropped all pretence at the sanctity of the official *rate* of 0.357 and set aside its theory of "genuine" *IwP*. Henceforth no more blank *IwP* licences were to be issued to indivi- dual Israeli importers, but traders in cement and tyres could receive import licences from the CONS company with allocations of foreign currency at prices four to five times the official *rate*. The CONS company in turn was empowered to buy "investment-dollars" at a unitary price which was announced semi-officially, the first *rate* being fixed at 1.100. This was during the climax of the immigration of Iraquian Jews, and considerable amounts of foreign currency were offered on the black market by the wealthier members of this com- munity who had transmitted some of their cash holdings to a neutral

---

[1] Large-scale operators worked out their own private versions of *IwP* as will be seen from this summary of the agreement arrived at between the Ministry of Finance and an Israeli company F. (110). The Ministry undertook to issue to the F. company (blank) *IwP* licences for $8 million. In turn the company promised to recruit $9 million abroad and pay the suppliers of these "investment-dollars" no more than IL8½ million which would be entered into the blocked accounts of non-residents. The Ministry agreed to this extraordinary project of issuing blank *IwP* licences because it was deceived by the company's claim that "investment- dollars" could be recruited at the effective *rate* of 0.950. (At the time the Standard III *rate* was 1.500 and the Standard IV *rate*—in textiles which the company proposed to import—2.500). The agreement provided that $1 million or *pro rata* were to be exchanged into IL at the official *rate* of 0.357. In fact, the deal was not completed as the police intervened when it was learned that the F. company was paying the current Standard III price for foreign currency. The F. company sold the *IwP* goods to the local distributors at the nominal price of IL*x* plus an under-the-counter payment of IL*y* to "adjust" the price to the prevailing Standard IV prices. The F. company made an illicit agreement with the owners of "investment-dollars" in that it only paid into their blocked account at the *rate* of 0.950 but supplemented this IL payment with part of the IL*y* and, thus, brought the effective *rate* up to the Standard III market price.

country. The CONS company co-operated with the police and a group of intermediaries dealing with these "Iraquian dollars" was rounded up and informed that the police would grant them immunity from prosecution (for transgression of the foreign currency controls) if they arranged for the sale of dollars to the company at IL1.100 rather than at the Standard III market price of IL1.400. In this way, within a few weeks, the company acquired several million dollars.

The Ministry of Finance postulated that, provided *IwP* and the illicit import of Standard IV goods were stopped, all the foreign currency offered on the black market would be sold to the CONS company. (The company, which bought up dollars at an unofficial *rate*, whilst the Government adhered to the official *rate* of 0.357, was regarded as the agent of the Ministry of Finance in the black market.[1]) The hypothesis about the efficacy of Government intervention in the money black market was never really tested. Encouraged by its initial successes, the CONS company (as the monopsonist it imagined itself to be) thought it could dictate the price of the black market dollar. In the winter of 1951, it arbitrarily reduced its buying *rate* to 1. But,meanwhile, the Standard III *rate* had gone up to 2 and the Ministry of Finance had not succeeded in stopping the gaps through which *IwP* and Standard IV goods continued to flow. Consequently, no more foreign exchange was offered to the company, and with the *de jure* devaluation in February 1952, it was dissolved.

EXPORTS

In an economy which overvalues its currency (as the Standard II official *rate* did to the IL), the government tries to prevent a consequent paralysis in exports by subsidizing them in diverse forms, i.e. effectively devaluing the currency for foreign currency export earnings. Until December 1949 practically the only avenue open to exporters through which to obtain an export subsidy was that of barter transactions.[2] The Ministry of Finance established a

---

[1] Parallel to the hypothesis underlying the work of the CONS company, the Ministry of Finance thought that the effigy of the black market *rates* could be burned by buying against the market. Between 1950 and 1952 the Ministry's representatives in Switzerland were ordered to buy up IL banknotes. The effect upon the black market quotations on the Swiss money market was so slight and the costs in foreign currency so considerable, that this experiment was stopped after three years.

[2] I have been able to substantiate only one case, diamond exports, where the Government paid a money subsidy (the *rate* of 0.478); this subsidy did not appear as an expenditure item in the budget, as the Ministry of Finance "sold" these foreign currency receipts to certain importers.

F

barter commission to confirm each transaction and taxed the bartered imports with a special ten per cent duty. Articles with a high proportion of import content (e.g. tissues made of imported woollen yarn) were bartered for imported Standard IV goods (e.g. fruit). Though these barters were most profitable for the exporters, they often included cases of unrequited exports.

At the end of 1949, the Horovitz Commission, in its report, suggested that a cash premium of 15% be paid on gross export proceeds, but that applications for premiums should be considered "case by case". The Government acted on these recommendations and in December 1949 premiums of 10 to 12% on the 0.357 *rate* were paid. These were financed by a surcharge of 10% on all imports which were considered non-essential. The system was changed in May 1950, from which date only the value-added of export proceeds was subsidized.

A year later the export retention technique made its first appearance in Israel. The Ministry of Finance undertook to grant automatically *IfE* licences for the import content of past or projected exports.[1] One-third of the (attributed) value-added of the export proceeds could then be used by the exporters to import Standard IV goods to be sold in the domestic market, the rest to be sold at the Standard II *rate* to the Government.

With the *de jure* devaluation of February 1952, this method was extended and the value-added of the export proceeds was divided as follows: one-third to be sold to the Government at the Standard II *rate*; one-third to be used for the import of raw materials for the production of "utility" (price controlled) goods; and with the remaining third Standard IV goods for the home market could be imported.

On the 15th of May 1953 the fully-fledged Israeli version of the "one hundred per cent export retention" scheme was launched. The foreign currency controls were adjusted to allow exporters to open *pamaz* accounts at their banks (the denomination of which was not the IL but the dollar) and to pay all their foreign currency receipts into this account. Subject to formal checks the exporter could dispose of all his *pamaz*[2] to finance imports, provided these were in his "line

---

[1] These subsidies did not apply to all exports and among the important exceptions was the citrus industry.

[2] The *IfE* department of the Ministry of Finance was prepared to make foreign currency loans to new exporters. When the export proceeds were paid into the *pamaz* account, the first charge upon them was the *IfE* foreign currency loan of the Ministry. The abuses of the *IfE* system refer to the utilization of these foreign currency loans for imports of goods sold illicitly on the domestic market. When

of production".[1] Thus, the exporter could make his own choice of the proportion of his export proceeds to be used in replenishing his stock of raw materials (in order to execute a new export order) and the proportion to be devoted to the import of Standard IV goods. This *pamaz* system was an administrative improvement for both the exporters and the foreign currency controls officials. It had now become superfluous to calculate what part of the export proceeds was to be attributed to replacement value (direct *IfE*) and what to value-added. In order that an exporter could obtain the highest effective rate for his export proceeds he (a) aimed at the largest foreign currency receipt which the banks allowed him to enter into the *pamaz* account; (b) sought to utilize the smallest portion of the *pamaz* for *IfE* materials; and (c) with the value-added portion of his *pamaz*, chose to import those goods fetching the highest *rate* on the domestic market.[2]—The *rate* for the exporters who did not participate in the *pamaz* scheme was raised to 1,800.

In March 1956 the clock was turned back and a more refined system was introduced. It was decided to abrogate the *pamaz* system in stages and to introduce the payment of substantial cash subsidies for value-added. (This time, however, value-added was not to be defined as the difference between the export proceeds paid into the *pamaz* account and the utilized *IfE* licences.) A group of economists and statisticians was installed in the Foreign Trade Division of the Ministry of Trade and Industry and given the task to analyse the composition of each major export consignment according to (a) its direct replacement value (direct *IfE*); (b) the indirect replacement value (indirect *IfE*, i.e. the import-content bought domestically by exporters for IL); and (c) value-added as a residual factor. Henceforth exporters were paid according to the *rate* of 2.300 for value-added as defined above. In the summer of 1956 this was raised to 2.500, in the autumn of 1957 to 2.650.

In the spring of 1959 the Government discussed whether to raise

the alleged exporter does not carry out his declared exports, he cannot repay the foreign currency loan except by paying in IL.

[1] The "line of production" instruction was to prevent a trade in *pamaz*-dollars. To the extent that the authorities forced the exporters to adhere to this instruction, the *pamaz*-dollars had different *rates*, as the domestic market put different values upon the commodities which could be produced (with the raw materials financed by the value-added). In extreme cases the *pamaz* system did not secure an additional premium for the exporter and he chose to be paid according to the official *rate* or ceased to export.

[2] Some exporters (e.g. in 1958 those of religious articles) were permitted, and found it worthwhile, to pay for local goods with *pamaz*-dollars. The sellers were then regarded as "exporters" and *pamaz*-dollars from the buyers' accounts were credited to the *pamaz*-accounts of the sellers.

the money premium (of IL 2.650) which it paid per $1 of value-added —according to the post-1956 administrative practices—or whether to drop the refined post-1956 definition and return to the original definition of value-added (being the difference between the foreign currency value of the direct *IfE* licences and the gross export proceeds) and pay the 2.650 *rate* on this more liberally-defined volume of value-added.

The foreign currency controls administration adapted most of these export premiums to the reduced value of the numerous clearing-dollars by applying disagios which varied constantly and were subject to individual adjustments. In 1958, only six disagios were still applied to clearing-dollars (30% with Turkey, 15% with Brazil, 13% with Yugoslavia and 10% with Argentine, Hungary and Poland). It is expected that most or all of these will be abolished some time in 1959.

THE MINISTRY OF FINANCE SELLS STANDARD IV GOODS

Until 1954 most of the Standard IV goods came into the country illicitly. From 1955 onwards the Ministry of Finance worked the foreign currency controls in a manner that enabled it to "corner" the Standard IV market. Having successfully ended the *IwP* system, the Government dropped its principle of limiting officially sponsored imports only to "essential" articles. Henceforth, provided the importer paid the Standard IV market prices, he would be allocated foreign currency for "non-essential" articles. Now that the Standard IV market had been legalized, Israeli importers and distributors were prepared to work with a much lower margin than they had been when goods on this market were being imported illicitly. In 1955 the Ministry of Finance sponsored a company, called Amizan, which was entrusted with the imports of so-called luxury foodstuffs. In the summer of the following year, the Ministry allocated foreign currency at the following *rates*:

Green coffee	5.800
Nescafé	5.770
Fish	9.600
Cocoa butter	7.000
Cocoa beans	6.800
Rice	6.000
Dried fruit	6.580
Black pepper	8.100

In 1957 the average *rate* for luxury foodstuffs was IL9 (53).

By the summer of 1957 the officials of the foreign currency controls had, for most purposes, dropped the Amizan company as their agent in selling foreign currency at a high *rate* and allocated foreign currency directly to private importers.[1] In that year the following *rates* were typical: live cattle from Yugoslavia about 8 (64); certain textile fibres 8–9; spare parts for refrigerators 8.400 (106); formica 9; whisky 10.

In 1958 there was prepared an extensive list of "luxury" articles for the import of which the Government was ready to issue licences, provided the foreign currency was bought from its authorized dealers at a *rate* of between 8 and 12. The list included air-conditioners, foreign cigarettes, pepper, pianofortes, panama hats, German (!) cameras, fireworks, perfumes and cinnamon. At a press conference in May 1958, the representatives of the Ministry stated that while foreign currency at the bargain *rate* of 8 was available for the import of gramophone records, Scotch whisky would henceforth only be admitted if foreign currency was acquired at the *rate* of 12.

PRIVATELY NEGOTIATED *Rates*

In 1956, the legal officers of the Ministry of Finance published a

---

[1] Responsible officials of the Ministry of Finance admitted that coercive measures had failed to eradicate the black market; hence, the Government went over to the new system of allocating foreign currency for luxury purposes at *rates* diverging from the official ones and appropriating the profits to itself.

For many years the purchase of a shipping or air ticket was regarded as a foreign currency expenditure which had to be justified before the necessary licence was granted. Experience had shown that after such a licence was refused, most applicants (through accommodating agencies) received these tickets as "presents" paid for in foreign currency abroad, but financed at the Standard III *rate*. The Ministry of Finance obviated these black market transactions by allocating foreign currency automatically after 1954 for the purchase of such tickets. It charged a "tickets tax" which was changed from time to time, but was wisely always kept at such a *rate* that it was more worthwhile to buy the ticket for IL and pay the tax than to buy foreign currency on the blacket market and obtain the ticket as a "present".

A similar deal was made by the Ministry in 1956 with film importers who had hitherto used the Standard III market to obtain some of their foreign currency. They agreed to the Ministry demand to buy dollars "officially" at IL3.500 for they preferred to pay a dearer price (without risk of prosecution) than resort to the cheaper Standard III market.

In the case of watches the new technique did not work. The effective illicit price for foreign watches was determined by the Standard III *rate* of 2.400 plus a small charge for smuggling. In these circumstances Israel's watch importers were not prepared to buy foreign currency, with accompanying legal import licences, from the Government at *rates* of 4–9.

141

codex of the foreign currency controls, but no one in a business office in Tel-Aviv would have dared to make a commercial transaction by merely having reference to this. The essence of the foreign currency controls in Israel was not to be found in published regulations. The effective *rates* were those concluded by private negotiation between the importers and exporters and the officials of the Ministry of Finance and/or Trade and Industry. Consequently, as most of the decisions were of an individual nature, senior officials could delegate few of their powers to their juniors. This helped to overburden the senior officials and accounted for the long delays in dealing with applications. Large firms, including public corporations, retained special employees in the capital who served as liaison officers with the Ministry of Finance, and dealt personally with details that would have been settled by post in the United Kingdom.[1] Usually smaller firms did not plead their own cases but, through the officials of trade associations or political parties, obtained licences collectively. Still other firms made use of what the Americans so aptly describe as "five percenters".

As the published rules of the foreign currency controls were known by the public to be subject to individual modification, the economic ministers and their senior officials became exposed to various pressures. These came from friends and relatives, political parties, *ad hoc* pressure groups, foreign firms (which threatened to invoke the aid of their ambassadors), individuals from abroad who claimed to have helped Israel, heroes of the War of Liberation and so on—all of whom asked for special *rates* and conditions for their licences.

In the course of time the foreign currency controls of Israel progressively became more complex. Two causes may account for this; first, as the officials of the Ministry of Finance became more proficient in their tasks, they learned of the many ways in which their regulations were being evaded and consequently introduced new restrictions as a safeguard;[2] secondly, the more refined the multiple rate practices were, the easier it was, by the grant of favourable *rates* to reward "deserving cases" and to tax "excessive" traders' profits by less favourable *rates*.[3]

[1]"Large manufacturing concerns were forced to maintain full-time representatives in Jerusalem and Tel-Aviv to arrange for the granting of import licences. Criteria governing the acceptance or rejection of applications were usually not formalized in written instructions, and oral instructions were subject to considerable flexibility of interpretation" (231).

[2] In 1956 applications for an *IfE* licence underwent thirty-four distinct administrative treatments.

[3] An important exception was in the case of diamond exports. The Ministry of Finance adopted the realistic system called "Aforo" in post-Peron Argentine.

142

In time the foreign currency controllers prohibited Israeli traders from engaging in customary practices of international trade, and only those transactions were permitted which could be checked easily for their compatibility with the regulations. Most exporters were not allowed to send their goods "on consignment"; importers were not authorized to accept credit terms from their suppliers; applicants for *IfE* licences had to submit definite orders from foreign customers. (Only after a written foreign order had been received could the Israeli manufacturer apply for an *IfE* licence to import the raw materials required for the manufacture of the ordered article.) These and other hindrances to international trade were meant as additional guarantees in the endeavours to implement the foreign currency controls.

The Enforcement of the Foreign Currency Controls

Controls only have a *raison d'être* if they are enforced in practice as well as on paper. The experience of many countries with foreign currency controls shows how difficult it is to administer a system with a unitary rate. The foreign currency controls of Israel would have presented an impossible task even to the large efficient civil service of an economically advanced nation.[1] The staff operating the controls and the offices of the Competent Authorities was small in number and consisted of persons who, on the whole, had had no commercial experience and were served by a small police apparatus. Other Government departments resented their power and have been known to co-operate with the public against them. A considerable number of officials were incompetent or corrupt. An important aspect of the foreign currency controls is the ability of the customs authorities to check whether the goods which are cleared do, in fact, correspond

In theory the whole value-added of this trade was to be delivered to the authorized agents of the Ministry at the legal *rates*, but in practice, the foreign currency controls, as applied to the diamond exporters, aimed at about 90% of the net foreign currency income. It was an efficient system which worked, relative to the controls over other trades, to the satisfaction of the controllers and the controlled.

To instance this with the regulations in force in 1954: the department dealing with diamonds demanded of every dealer to deliver for *IfE* licences of £100 (with which to make purchases from the London Syndicate) $340 export proceeds (or $375 in the case of "chips"). If the diamond exporter delivered a sum of dollars which exceeded this ratio, no questions were asked and the controllers only intervened if the *IfE* allocation of Sterling was not coupled, after a reasonable time, with the receipt of dollars in the determined ratio (111).

[1] "The absence of adequate public information about import licences created an impression of disorder and confusion which lowered the prestige and morale of Government offices" (231).

to the quantity, description and value as set out in the import licence. The State Comptroller (56) commented upon the many discrepancies between the import licences and the goods actually imported. Israeli newspapers reported a number of convictions of customs officials who colluded with importers to evade the specifications of the import licences.

The Standard III black market was well organized and operated with relatively little risk of detection. The majority of business firms knowingly transgressed the controls. In one way or another, many of the banks, which were the authorized foreign currency agents of the Ministry, had recourse to the black market. However, I know of only one case (i.e. the Japhets Bank) where the licence to act as an authorized foreign currency dealer was temporarily withdrawn. In New York and Switzerland, banks openly advertised the sale of "IL transfers" (and, of course, IL banknotes) at Standard III prices.

The chief attraction of smuggling goods into Israel was not evasion of the low customs duty but the high prices obtainable from Standard IV goods. Goods which were smuggled over the land frontiers between 1949 and 1951 included crêpe-soled shoes, lighters, bicycle tyres, antibiotics and textiles; foodstuffs regularly confiscated were coffee, sugar, apples, eggs (!), poultry, and particularly live cattle and rice.

The falsification of invoices in connection with import licences (with or without allocation of foreign currency) followed rules of its own. Up to 1952 the following illustration was significant for the import of articles which were not Standard IV goods, and for which foreign currency had been allocated at the 0.357 *rate*. It became a gainful transaction to use a $100 import licence for imports of only $95, though excess customs duty on $5 had to be paid on the consignment invoiced at $100. The $5 (allocated by the Ministry of Finance for imports but illegally retained abroad) had a price on the Standard III market which considerably exceeded the 0.357 *rate* at which the dollars had been bought. After 1952 little incentive remained to engage in such reprehensible transactions.

When an import licence was given for a Standard IV article, it was at all times remunerative to undervalue the goods. Thus, with an import licence of $100, goods for, say, $105 were brought into the country. The profit of the importer, who had undervalued the Standard IV articles, was derived from the disparity between the Standard III *rate* at which he had to buy the marginal $5 and the Standard IV price which he received from the sale of his imports.

"Switches"

The economic theory behind the Israeli multiple rate system drove the foreign currency controllers to aim at the maximum number of *rates*, but the "switching" from one of these to another (by unscrupulous buyers and sellers of foreign currency) discouraged their zeal. The following are representative instances:

(I) Exports to country X were rewarded at a higher *rate* than exports to country Y—it was not uncommon for consignments destined for country Y to be shipped via country X.

(II) Immigrants from Brazil were given a higher *rate* for their capital than immigrants from Venezuela. It was not surprising that some immigrants concealed the country of their real origin from the bank officials who exchanged their foreign currency.

(III) The "sugar-pool", operated by the Food Division, laid down different *rates* for various purposes: 10.869 for the "grey" market; 5 for industrial users; 1.756 for distribution of price-controlled rations. In the summer of 1957, the police found a number of factories (privately-owned and from the Histadruth-kibbutz sector) engaged in the lucrative practice of selling their industrial sugar on the black market. About a year later "Tenuvah", the chief marketing firm of the Histadruth's farmers, was fined IL10,000 and kibbutz Givath Brenner IL40,000 for these offences. The prosecution did not demand prison sentences for the persons engaged in this "switching" as they did not act "for personal gain but for the good of their organization".

(IV) The Government, in selling foreign currency at Standard IV prices to the Amizan company, assured all the prospective buyers from this company, that it was preventing the commercial import of the articles—offered for sale by the Amizan company—through other channels.[1] Nevertheless, when the Government offered to sell import licences, via this company,

---

[1] The Brazilian authorities were faced with a similar moot point. Theoretically, Brazilian importers could buy foreign currency only on the Government auctions. The Brazilian Government thought that, as the monopsonist of foreign currency, it could practise price discrimination and charge high prices for the allocation of currency to finance the imports of luxuries. The Government price for "luxury dollars" was appreciably above the price of dollars on the money black market (in terms of cruzeiros). Brazilians who imported luxury goods attempted, therefore, to make large purchases of foreign currency on the cruzeiro-dollar black market rather than buy dollars at high—though legal—prices on the Government auctions.

for dried fruits with allocated foreign currency at the *rate* of 7, there were no takers. Although a Ministry of Finance investigation said (53) that dried fruits came into the country as the "capital transfer of immigrants", this was only a half-truth. Cunning merchants were buying foreign currency on the Standard III market—for IL2.450—and paying immigrants for the service of importing these goods. In this manner the immigrants and the merchants made a handsome profit and yet were able to offer dried fruits at an effective *rate* below the Government's offer of IL7.

(V) Exporters practised "switches" of a different nature.[1] The earnings of an exporter from the import of *pamaz* goods were up to IL12 per $1 of value-added. The law-abiding manufacturer could increase his proportion of value-added only by employing further local resources for the performance of additional processes. The unscrupulous exporter could create value-added artificially by increasing his export proceeds through the purchase of foreign currency on the Standard III market. It was usually cheaper for the exporter to acquire an additional *pamaz*-dollar by buying this on the Standard III market rather than by employing high-cost Israeli factors to create genuine value-added (*vide* p. 200). During 1958 the Histadruth's journal openly attacked the Ministry of Finance on this score and claimed to know that several textile exporters were buying foreign currency on the black market in order to inflate the amount of foreign currency which they had obtained from the sale of their goods in foreign markets.

(VI) Products which can be marketed abroad in different forms tend to be exported so as to yield the highest *rate* for the producers. Not unnaturally, there is a trend to "switch" from

---

[1] In 1953, the directors of the tailoring firm of Heilig were arrested when a case marked "export suits for Switzerland" was found to be filled with rags and stones (175). The directors pleaded in their defence that they had intended—there is no reason to doubt this—to remit foreign currency to Israel for the value of the suits allegedly exported.

In 1955, some cases marked "exports of religious items" were opened at the Lydda airport and found to contain sawdust. On further inquiry it was found that this company received *IfE* licences for expensive textiles to the value of 85% of the intended exports (190).

The local "manufacturers" of watches exerted pressure on the customs authorities not to sell the large stocks of confiscated watches in Israel. Consequently, a tender was published (180) inviting offers in foreign currency for the export of these watches. Police investigations show that the firm which won the tender did, in fact, transmit the contracted amount in foreign currency to the Ministry of Finance but sold the watches locally.

the avenue providing the economy with the highest export earnings to that which maximizes the IL profit of the exporter. Thus (280) the grapefruit growers transferred part of the crop suitable for sale as fresh fruit abroad—the most economical form of citrus exports—to the exporters of tinned grapefruit segments, this necessitating the import of syrup, metal sheets, etc. The reason was that the Government accorded the former a *rate* of 2.050 and the latter a *rate* of 2.650 (or even higher through *pamaz*).

Similar considerations applied to the payment of (cash money) premiums on the value-added of export earnings. In July 1957 the foreign currency controller's offices published a surprising communiqué in which they intimated that exporters were selling "too many dollars" to the Government, i.e. exporting too much and that, in future, checks would be made to prevent "switches" between the Standard III and the official export *rates*.

CHAPTER XVIII

THE AIMS OF THE FOREIGN CURRENCY CONTROLS

The foreign currency controls in the United Kingdom are concerned with the balance of payments difficulties of the economy; this defines their chief and—many would say—only purpose. Most British economists (though admittedly not all) have always favoured the repeal of the Exchange Control Act 1947, once these difficulties do not any longer justify the controls. But in many economies with foreign currency controls some subsidiary aims of the administration are connected to the declared chief purpose of the exchange regulations.[1] These subsidiary aims may at times assume such importance that, when conditions change and make the controls unnecessary, the latter are nevertheless retained.[2]

There is another relevant analogy to the exchange regulations of the United Kingdom. The influence of the Exchange Control Act is considerable and has left its stamp on Britain's external trade; yet the suggestion that British economic life was ever dominated by it would be an exaggeration. The situation in Israel is radically different. The high proportion of import content in Israel's products is a contributory cause to the preponderance of the foreign currency controls in its economy. The administration of the foreign currency controls is the most powerful unit in the civil service, and the methods by which the controls are applied dominate all economic activities, not only those pertaining to external trade. This book tells of the many tasks (imposed upon the foreign currency controls administration and Competent Authorities) which—by British standards—are quite remote from the duties of a staff administering exchange regulations. Perhaps it is not surprising that the names of the leading foreign currency controllers are well known throughout Israel and their utterances at press conferences and on other public occasions are sometimes given wider publicity than that accorded to the speeches of their ministers.

[1] Chalmers mentions South America in particular (90).
[2] Ellis, describing Central Europe of before 1939:
"The Treasury is always able in an exchange-control country to procure foreign devisen at the low official rate for its purpose . . . (this) might explain the continuance of exchange control and a wholly fictitious official rate in situations where they have otherwise lost their *raison d'être* (133).

148

The following is a list of some subsidiary aims:[1]

(a) Political philosophy dictated that middlemen, and especially importers, should be regarded as members of a parasitic caste. The controls were operated unofficially (and, during the Dov Josef period, by the Ministry of Trade and Industry officially[2]) to deprive private importers of their livelihood. Import licences were issued to Government corporations, to manufacturers (for self-use) and to trading organizations of producers' associations, but only in extreme cases were they given to import firms.[3]

(b) It was not expedient to tax philanthropic contributions (made abroad) to *institutions* openly. Discriminatory exchange rates for these were a more refined method of indirect taxation and less likely to offend.

(c) The Government was more concerned with the value of the IL as reflected in the movements of the cost-of-living index than with the general stability of its currency. The multiple rate system helped to manipulate this index by the import, at low *rates*, of goods which had a heavy weight in it.

(d) The policy of the Foreign Office was sometimes furthered by the workings of the controls. Although only soft currency articles were received in exchange, Israel supplied goods with a high import content to some countries whose friendship was worth cultivating. In some cases the Foreign Office persuaded the Ministry of Finance to issue import licences for goods from "friendly" countries though their prices were higher than those of other countries, while at the same time it blocked the imports from the cheaper supply centres.

(e) The policy of Tozereth Haaretz was aided to a considerable extent by the controls. Import licences were not issued for goods which competed with domestic products. (Export licences were refused in

[1] The Ministry of Finance thought that many of the subsidiary aims of the controls were served best if the external trade was concentrated in the hands of Government corporations. This was likely to realize the aims—to quote Viner (94)—"without need of special legislation, without publicity, and with all the flexibilities that there may be occasion to use."

[2] I have come across the case of a leading importer-merchant who was frightened by Dov Josef's open threat to his livelihood. He, therefore, invested some of his capital, together with a loan from the Development Budget, in a "phantom factory", i.e. a plant which treated raw materials without enhancing their value by any value-added. This gave the importer the status of a manufacturer and he now received import allocations (no longer in his old capacity of a parasitical merchant but) as a productive manufacturer.

[3] Manufacturers and others privileged to receive import licences worked in collaboration with import firms by engaging their services as "advisers" or "agents"; the authorities agreed to this practice provided the import licences were not in the names of these merchants.

149

some cases to enable local manufacturers to buy certain domestic materials below world market prices.)[1]

(*f*) The foreign currency controls acted as an important revenue agent of the Government. Some of the proceeds from its sale of foreign currency receipts at a price exceeding the 1.800 *rate* appeared as an income item in the ordinary budget. The profits from some sales of foreign currency, at prices exceeding official *rates*, were manipulated to cover unauthorized Government outlays.

It was accepted that the citrus exporters would be making excess profits if they were remunerated for their export proceeds at the ordinary *rates* applicable to exports. To obviate these anticipated excess profits, no special act authorizing the imposition of an export tax was passed nor were the income-tax authorities allowed to collect the larger part of these excess profits. Instead, the foreign currency controls allowed the imposition of special punitive *rates* for the citrus branch (*vide* p. 158).—When, in the view of even junior officials, unreasonable profits were likely to be made by exporters, it was hinted to the latter that by making voluntary contributions, *pro rata*, to the Exchange Equalization Fund, their applications for export licences would be granted.—The latest report of the State Comptroller castigates the Ministry of Finance for similar improper practices (290).

(*g*) The Government budgets, couched in terms of IL, were voted upon in the Knesset, but the controls gave the Government a greater control over real resources than parliament intended. The officials of the controls could transform IL1, in the case of one ministry, into an imported article of $3 and by applying another *rate* in the case of another ministry, to $0.50 of imports.[2]

Government departments favoured by the Ministry of Finance also obtained real resources by other means without the knowledge of parliament. The proceedings before the Supreme Court (10th September 1957) tell of an arrangement between the controls

[1] The proceedings before the Supreme Court in August 1957 confirmed that the Ministry of Trade and Industry had consistently refused to issue export licences for scrap metal until Solel Boneh granted the exporter a "clearance certificate". Solel Boneh exploited this Tozereth Haaretz protection by offering to pay only half the price which the exporters would have obtained c.i.f. European port, had they exported the scrap metal against hard currency.

[2] The following is taken from a semi-official report: ". . . by buying the foreign currency it required for its own needs at the lowest exchange rate, the Government kept at a minimum its own expenditure in the budget as registered in IL, particularly since the Foreign Exchange Equalization Fund is not included in the published budgetary accounts. In this way the Government is 'subsidizing' its own consumption (in terms of IL) . . ." (282).

authorities and the representatives of three shipping firms. The firms were promised that Israel would issue no import licences for Finnish timber except when the importers undertook to carry it in the vessels of these firms. The shipping companies, in turn, gave a secret pledge to the Ministry—the subsequent publicity of which embarrassed them—that Finnish timber imported by Government departments would be transported cheaper than the timber of other Israeli importers.

I have been told by several importers that the foreign currency controls administration has at times granted import licences only on condition that they grant a discount to certain Government departments. Agents of foreign suppliers have been informed that import licences for the goods of their principals (e.g. building materials for the Ministry of Labour's housing schemes) would be granted provided they charged only half of the ordinary commission for goods delivered to a Government department.

(*h*) Two of the main prestige aims of the Government were the encouragement of exports and a high rate of investment. The controls were operated to increase the nominal export volume (without thereby necessarily improving the balance of payments) and so help the responsible ministers in their political ambitions (*vide* Appendix VIII).

(*i*) The import of investment goods was encouraged by low *rates*. Taub, of the Bank of Israel (54), deduces correctly that in this way the country arrived at a larger proportion of investment out of "total resources" than if there had been a unitary rate. Taub believes that a large investment volume is desirable but that the public are not too enthusiastic about this aim. He expects the multiple rates to further this aim without the public being fully aware of the procedure.

CHAPTER XIX

A CLASSIFICATION OF EXCHANGE RATES[1]

A "Pure *Rate*"

ALTHOUGH Israel officially only had a system of multiple rates from 1952 to 1955, in fact, the system was in use during every one of the eleven years of the State. Israel does not publish a complete list of its effective *rates* and the investigator who wishes to enumerate them, meets three types of obstacles:

(*a*) Many foreign currency transactions in Israel are disguised as goods transactions. Neither the authorities, nor the importer nor the exporter (bringing in *pamaz* goods) will openly acknowledge that the IL proceeds from the sale of imported goods constitute a set of multiple rates. To ascertain the "pure *rate*", the investigator must know how to separate the importer's normal profit from the IL price of the (exchanged) foreign currency.

(*b*) For administrative reasons, the Ministry of Finance often calls dollar-pools (e.g. "private" equalization funds) into being. It makes up a group of import (and export) goods for which foreign currency is allocated through such a recognized pool; the allocation by the manager of the pools is made at multiple rates. The classic example is provided by the fuel pool (*vide* Appendix IV) which allocated, for example, foreign exchange for the import of kerosene at a *rate* of 1.522 and for petrol at 6.290. These pools do not always publish detailed statements enabling one to impute different *rates* to the goods for which they provide foreign currency. The Ministry of Finance, if challenged, will deny that fuel is imported at multiple rates; it claims that it puts foreign currency at the disposal of the Fuel Controller at the unitary official *rate* and any juggling of "private" equalization funds by the manager is not to be regarded as a function of multiple exchange rates.

(*c*) Some multiple rates are arrived at by tedious bargaining between the Ministry of Finance and importers-exporters. After a *rate* has finally been agreed upon, it is necessary to "dress it up" to hide its divergence from the official one. The foreign currency controls administration employs several techniques:[2]

---

[1] The *rates* quoted in this chapter usually refer to the value-added of the articles in 1957.

[2] The five techniques described all deal with *rates* above the official one. When *rates* are lower than the official *rate* it is easier to detect them, for the

I. The Ministry of Finance allocates foreign currency to a Government corporation at the official *rate* for the import of certain goods. The Government corporation "sells" the import right for the price of the official *rate* plus a profit determined by the controls administration. Thus the importer pays for the foreign currency at the *rate* originally laid down by the controls officials.

II. The officials impose surcharges on the imports or ask for "voluntary" contributions to the Exchange Equalization Fund.

III. The purchase tax authorities are instructed to collect, in the form of a special tariff, the difference between the official *rate* and the effective one demanded by the controls administration.

IV. The customs authorities are instructed to collect, in the form of a special tariff, the difference between the official *rate* and the effective one demanded by the controls administration.

V. (The Finance Committee of the Israeli parliament has been known to protest because techniques III and IV were employed before consulting it in advance. The technique outlined here is a subtle method which obviates the need to submit it for parliamentary approval.) The Ministry of Finance gives administrative instructions to the purchase tax and customs authorities to revalue the foreign exchange price of the imports[1] according to an "instructed" *rate* (*vide* Appendix IX). If this is done, the nominal (fixed measures of the) tariffs and indirect taxes remain unchanged, but the money burden, per $1 of imports, is adjusted to the design of the controls administration.[2]

When an importer pays, say, IL216 to clear $100 imports at the Haifa port, and this payment consists of IL180 (for $100 at the official *rate*) plus IL36 (for 20% customs duty) it would be inconclu-

subsidies on imported goods are usually listed in the "Explanations to the Proposed Budget", e.g. (107). The importers pay for the goods at the official *rate* but are reimbursed, on a *pro rata* basis, from the Food Equalization Fund or the Import Subsidies Fund. Sometimes these subsidies appear as "trading loss on imports of goods . . ." in the balance sheets of Government trading companies. In the case of fodderstuffs, the subsidy per dollar was, according to a Ministry of Finance report (107), "incorporated in the subsidies given directly for milk and eggs". In the case of medicaments for the Sick Funds, the foreign currency was sold at the *rate* of 1.800 and, on execution of the import, the Ministry of Finance "returned" IL0.800 per $1 to the importers.

[1] These were not instructions regarding a general devaluation, but specific orders to value the foreign exchange at different *rates* for different imports.

[2] I have unearthed two such instructions; in 1951 to the customs (by the Director-General of the Ministry of Finance) and in 1957 to the purchase tax authorities (jointly by the Foreign Trade Division and the foreign currency controls department); no doubt there have been other occasions on which such (unpublished) instructions were given.

sive to presume that he had paid a price for the allocated foreign currency at variance with the official *rate*. When, however, an importer is charged IL1,260 to clear the same $100 imports—and his bill is detailed: IL180 for the allocated $100, 300% purchase tax, 200% customs duty and 100% surcharge to some fund—it is not unreasonable to conclude that the import was executed at the *rate* of *12.600 less Y* (Y being the estimated margin for a "fair" indirect tax).

In some cases a 100% customs duty may have been meant primarily as a revenue-gathering tax and not as a function of the multiple rate system. In other cases even a low 25% customs duty may have originated in the foreign currency controls offices as a mode of making an importer pay (for some allocated foreign currency) at more than the official *rate*. There can clearly be no definite rule, though in Appendix IV I have illustrated how fiscal charges on imports can *arbitrarily* be separated into "compartments" belonging to the revenue and the controls authorities respectively. (For an alternate view on the "pure *rate*", *vide* Appendix IX.)

DIFFERENTIAL MARGINS

The system of multiple rates can be discerned in three distinct spheres and gave rise to differential profits (or losses) which are shared by various economic groups.

  I. IMPORTS were effected at *rates* of 0.500–15.
 II. EXPORTS (which yielded a net foreign currency gain) were rewarded at *rates* of 2–12.
III. TOZERETH HAARETZ (i.e. the protection of domestic products through the operation of the controls) was granted at *rates* of 1.500–17.

One must not presume that the whole of the margin between the official *rate* (or the *average rate*) and the effective *rates* (cited above in II and III) provided profits or windfall gains for the exporter or the heavily protected domestic producer. Often the high *rates* enabled the exporters and domestic producers to pay Israeli factors, inefficiently employed, a high price per unit of output and left them with only a nominal profit. The margin (cited in I) provided: (*a*) an (indirect) protective umbrella for some local producers, (*b*) a source of excess profits shared by importers and *IwP* transferrers, (*c*) a means of raising revenue for the Government and (*d*) (indirect) income for exporters to pay for their high production costs.[1]

[1] In the summer of 1957 serious "differences of opinion" were said to have existed between the foreign currency controls administration of the Ministry of Finance and the Foreign Trade Division of the Ministry of Trade and Industry

A CLASSIFICATION OF EXCHANGE RATES

"Private *Rates*"

Gilboa (67) propounds that the foreign currency controls administration should minimize the price of the foreign currency it buys and maximize the price of that which it sells. The Ministry of Finance imagined itself to be an absolute monopolist and monopsonist in this field; hence it practised price discrimination by splitting the markets until—in the final stage—a "private" price was laid down for almost every single large transaction. The making of thousands of individual decisions was justified by the foreign currency controllers as a technique which cheapened the purchase of foreign currency (in terms of IL) and optimized the Government's (IL) profits from the sale of foreign currency. Not unnaturally, the public entered into the spirit of the game and—before buying or selling a large block of foreign exchange—interviewed the responsible official of the foreign currency controls to secure the most favourable *rate*. A foreign consultant to the Government summarized the situation in an unpublished memorandum (4/9/53):

"... the consequence of the prevailing system of administrative discretion is that entrepreneurs find there to be no more profitable way to spend their time than in negotiating with Government."

It may be added that the real profits of exporters were made by conferring with Government officials in Jerusalem and not by competitive selling in the world markets.

Import *Rates*[1]

Import *rates* can be classified according to: I—country of origin of the goods; II—nature of the goods; III—recipient of the goods; relating to the import of certain luxurious textiles that sold at a *rate* of 8. The Ministry of Trade and Industry wanted these imports to be "reserved" for the *pamaz* imports of textile exporters who needed this *rate* to cover high production costs. The Ministry of Finance thought this was an expensive way of inducing artificial exports and wanted to "auction" these import licences (with allocation of foreign currency) and thus recruit extraordinary revenue for the Government.

[1] The following are four examples of the (undisguised) allocation of foreign currency for the same types of goods at different *rates*:

Rice in 1956 via the Amizan company at 6—for rationed distribution to children at 0.450 (107);

Meat in 1957 for grey market at 8—for rations at 0.500 (107);

Textile fibres, tissues, etc., in the spring of 1957 at 3 to 9—imported by the army for the manufacturing of uniforms at 1.800;

Imports of films (35 mm. used in towns by commercial cinemas) in 1957 at 3.150—imported by the Histadruth (16 mm. used mainly by kibbutzim) at 1.800.

IV—form of payment demanded by the Ministry of Finance; V—marketing conditions of the imported goods.

I—Import licences are issued in terms of IL and nominal-dollars. Goods are not necessarily bought in the cheapest market, but in those countries from which the Israeli importer is ordered to buy by the authorities.[1] The clearing-dollar and the dollar, although they may have the same IL price, have different purchasing powers and a set of disorderly cross-rates is brought into existence by the linking of imports to purchases in a particular country. The Ministry of Finance gave an agio on the purchase of goods with clearing-dollars in certain countries but (*vide* p. 140) this agio only partly compensated the importer for (being deprived of the right to buy from the cheapest source and) being forced to buy at an effectively high *rate* in a soft-currency market.

II—Goods with a heavy weight in the cost-of-living index were accorded low *rates*.—A *rate* of 1.400 applied in 1958 to the imports of books and newspapers under the International Media Guaranty programme.—Investment goods, in general, and implements for agriculture, in particular, were favoured with low *rates*.

III—Foreign currency at low *rates* was often preferentially allocated when the imports were destined for Government departments (particularly the army) and agriculture. In some cases the Histadruth received priority treatment.[2]

IV—The foreign currency controllers borrowed a technique from South America—e.g. Bolivia (90)—that helped to form a further set of heterogeneous *rates* which could be adjusted to the individual application for an import licence[3]: (*a*) the Ministry of Finance could permit the importer to obtain credit from his suppliers and let him pay for the allocated foreign currency, say, 120 days after the receipt of the goods. (*b*) Import licences could be issued "cash against documents" and the importer's bank might then open a letter-of-credit with a deposit of, say, only 25%. (*c*) The foreign currency

---

[1] "Many industrial raw materials are more expensive in Israel than elsewhere because the purchaser cannot exercise a free choice in buying from the cheapest source. . . . In recent years more than 70% of our industrial raw materials were bought from those sources which were from 5% to 30% more expensive than international sources from which raw materials may be freely purchased" (233).

[2] Until this discrimination was abolished in January 1959 the Sick Funds of the Histadruth and of some other groups were allocated currency at the *rate* of 1 for the import of medicaments and other similar articles, while imports of the identical articles destined for private pharmacists were charged at *rates* of 1.800 and higher.

[3] Its real significance can be gauged by referring to the prevailing interest charges—*vide* p. 91.

controller's office could demand that the importer deposit on receipt of the letter allocating the foreign currency . . . 10%, 50%, 100% of the IL value of the allocated currency, although the goods might not arrive for, say, four months and the Israeli bank might be instructed to pay the supplier only "against documents". (*d*) The Ministry of Finance could mark an allocation of foreign currency as being available only within the framework of one of the "tied" foreign loans or the Reparations agreement.[1] Such import licences, depending in each case on the credit arrangements and the price level in the countries making the "tied" loan, could mean an effectively low or high *rate* for the applicant.

V—The form of marketing imported goods was often the decisive element which determined the magnitude of the *rate*. Some licences were marked with the proviso that the imported goods were to be sold only according to instructions of the Competent Authority, which controlled the profit margin. Still others could be marketed unconditionally. (Many licences had instructions appertaining to a part of the consignment.)

EXPORT *Rates*[2]

The remuneration of the exporter is effected by hybrid *rates*. These are composed of the variable aids (outlined in Appendix VIII) plus either (1) the variable benefits of the *pamaz* technique or (2) the payment for the net foreign exchange receipts according to the official uniform *rate* plus a variable money premium.[3]

The aids, enumerated in Appendix VIII, are variable and not

[1] Many goods of the Reparations Company were (between 1954 and 1956) dearer than similar goods available from other countries. The Ministry of Finance did not wish to proclaim a special *rate* (in terms of the Mark) and forced Israeli merchants to buy the dearer German goods by refusing to issue import licences for competing goods from other countries. The effectively higher *rate* (of the Mark) was "lowered" for non-investment goods by the following liberal credit terms: only $12\frac{1}{2}\%$ of the value of the order had to be deposited with the receipt of the licence; a further 25% was due on arrival of the goods and the Reparations Company demanded payment for the remainder only after 90 and 180 days respectively.—Some privileged importers induced the Reparations Company to bring the goods in the latter's name to Israel, store them and release them on credit terms ex store Israel. The State Comptroller (56), (290) makes some pertinent remarks on the differential credit terms granted to importers by this Government corporation.

[2] This section deals with visible exports but similar conditions applied to invisible and "internal" (*vide* p. 277) exports.

[3] Since 1954 "premium" was not the official term and the phrase "participation of the Government in the costs of export production" was used to parry the charge of having more than one official *rate*.

proportional to the quantity of foreign currency earned by an exporter. The benefits of the *pamaz* technique and the export money premium are also variable but they are gained *pro rata* with the declared foreign currency receipts. I have not taken into account the incalculable benefits (enumerated as indirect export aids in Appendix VIII) in the classification below of export *rates*.[1]

The foreign currency controls department had other powers over and above the right to change the numerical size of *rates*; it could, *inter alia*, refuse an export licence or limit the export to only one of several named countries; it could grant an export licence with the express proviso that the exporter was not entitled to the privileges of the premium or *pamaz* system or apply these benefits to part or the whole of the net export proceeds or (exceptionally) to the gross receipts.

The decisions of the foreign currency controls department as to which conditions and *rates* were to be marked on the export licence depended on various factors. These were (I) the subjective qualifications of the exporter; (II) the type of product; (III) the designated export country and/or kind of currency; (IV) depth of value-added of the export product; (V) quantity exported; (VI) "ex post" calculations.

(I) Government corporations were granted special export terms. Kaiser-Frazer at one time also enjoyed a favoured status. The behaviour of producers in voluntarily obeying the orders of the Ministry of Trade and Industry was often rewarded by favourable *rates* for their export products.

(II) The export *rates* for different goods were usually varied through the heterogeneity of the *pamaz* privilege and, of this, more below. But the cash *rates* were also sometimes varied and in 1958 we find deviations from the standard cash *rate* of 2.650; there are discriminatory lower *rates*—varying again—for citrus,[2] diamonds and scrap metals and generously higher

---

[1] One of several exceptions: the Ministry of Finance subsidized certain exports to some countries—in Africa and South America—by participating in the transport costs, by air, or in specially chartered ships. (A premium of ILO.800 per $1 was granted on 40% of the cost of air freight for some Israel exports carried by EL–AL Airlines.) For goods like cement, in the export price of which transport-cost is an important element, this subsidy was so significant that it provided a calculable set of additional *rates*.

[2] The *rates* for the value-added of fresh citrus were as follows:

1948–49 season	0.391		1951–52 season	0.714
1949–50 ,,	0.400		1952–53 ,,	1.650
1950–51 ,,	(0.411)		1953–54 ,,	1.800

rates for groundnuts—2.750 (285); cotton—3.000 (286) and some textile products at *ad hoc* cash *rates* above 2.650. The officials of the foreign currency controller were given wide discretionary powers in the interpretation of the *pamaz* privilege. Some agricultural exporters, for example, were allowed to dispense with the "line of production" condition (*vide* p. 139) and permitted to utilize their *pamaz*-dollars (which originated in the export of farm products) for the import of white cement and other Standard IV articles yielding a high *rate*. In other cases the Ministry of Finance punished exporters by limiting their right to import Standard IV products (the value-added portion of the *pamaz*-earnings) by directing them to make such purchases exclusively in the relatively dearer countries with which Israel had trade agreements. In May 1958 the *pamaz* privilege was modified for some products in the following fashion: henceforth, only a part of the export proceeds could be paid into the individual exporter's *pamaz* account. Thus, by exporting tinned food to some countries, the exporter obtains 70% for his *pamaz* account, whilst for exports to other countries, he retains, as before, 100%. Exporters of radios can retain 60% and 100% respectively; those who send bathing suits to foreign markets may, irrespective of the country of designation, retain only 55%; the producers of religious articles 35%; artificial teeth 22%; but exporters of furs to any part of the world can retain 80% of the export earnings for their *pamaz* account.

(III) In December 1957 the maximum non-*pamaz* remuneration was composed of the official *rate* of 1.800 plus (or minus) the money premium (or disagio) fixed for each designated country or currency. The *rates* per nominal-dollar were as follows: West Africa,[1] 3; Belgium, Canada, Western Germany, Sweden,

1954–55 season	1.800	1957–58 season	2.050
1955–56 „	1.800	1958–59 „	2.160
1956–57 „	1.800		

The punitive *rates* for citrus export earnings were supplemented by a refusal to grant the citrus farmers most of the (indirect) aids of Appendix VIII. The attitude of the foreign currency controls administration was unmistakably demonstrated during the negotiations with the Swiss Government. The latter agreed to impose a levy of 3% on all Swiss exports to Israel, the receipts of which were to finance a 5–10% subsidy on Israeli exports to Switzerland. The Israeli representative pressed the Swiss authorities to exclude a small group of products, particularly citrus, from the articles which the Swiss were to subsidize.

[1] Cement was excluded from this *rate*.

Switzerland, United Kingdom and United States, 2.650; trade agreement countries, 1.260–2.650.[1]

(IV) The export *rate* was varied in October 1957 according to the depth of value-added in exports to Brazil, Denmark, Finland, Greece, Norway, Poland and Roumania—and, since the summer of 1958, Hungary and Uruguay. One nominal-dollar of export proceeds was exchanged at IL2.600 if the value-added exceeded 40%; at IL2.400 when the value-added was 20%–40%; and at IL1.750[2] if the value-added was less than 20%. The tool of value-added played an important role in the formation of a multitude of export *rates* at the discretion (unofficially) given to the foreign currency controls administration to alter the magnitude of the value-added. The Government has always strenuously denied any juggling with the official estimates in the magnitude of the value-added. These denials are not to be fully trusted. This can be learned by referring to a report of the head of the department in the Ministry of Trade and Industry engaged upon the "scientific" measurement of value-added. In the Goren report (95) on the Phoenicia works, it is stated that if premiums (and other export subsidies) are granted to this firm only in proportion to the foreign exchange which is attributed to value-added, the enterprise cannot cover its IL costs on export production. The senior investigating officer realized the impropriety of favouring this firm by a large premium. As, in his view, the export of Phoenicia was nevertheless worth encouraging, he suggested that the foreign currency controls administration should—by grace—"attribute" a greater proportion of the firm's product to value-added, than he arrived at in his measurements, and thus enable the firm to export without involving it in any IL losses.

(V) The tendency in the economic ministries is to accord relatively higher *rates* to those manufacturers who export a considerable proportion of their output or send abroad goods in (what is

---

[1] The *rates*, in terms of nominal-dollars, set for clearing-dollars (cledos), were not directly related to the real value of these currencies in terms of the dollar; hence exporters were faced with a set of cross-rates. The softest cledo, that of Turkey, was exchanged at IL1.260, i.e. 1.800 less a 30% disagio. The hardest cledo, that of France and Italy, was exchanged at IL2.600, i.e. IL1.800 plus the maximum premium of IL0.850 less a disagio of 2%. Some products could be exported to cledo markets only after the exporter had renounced his *pamaz* privilege for these exports and offered to sell the whole amount of his cledo earnings to the Ministry of Finance.

[2] As a rule such exports were not permitted.

officially regarded as) "large" quantities. Thus in 1958 exporters of books were paid at a *rate* of 2.300 if their annual foreign currency earnings were above $5,000 and only at a *rate* of 1.800 if exports netted less than this amount. Similarly with invisible exports; a special tourist *rate* was operated for those travel agencies (which organized conducted tours) that netted foreign currency proceeds in excess of $15,000 annually. Whilst the agencies earning less than this amount were credited by the Ministry of Finance at the *rate* of 1.800, the larger agencies were paid at the "1.800 *rate* plus a bonus of 22% less certain deductions", i.e. a *rate* of just below 2.196. In February 1959 the Israeli Government announced a series of new measures that will *ipso facto* create a further set of favourable export *rates*; it was stated that these *rates* will only apply to exporters who had in the preceding year exported for more than 100,000 nominal-dollars (289).

(VI) The "ex post" *rate* is used by the foreign currency controls department when it wishes to ensure that exporters are paid no more than a "fair price for their labours". As sometimes the "fair price" cannot be calculated before the consignments leave Israel, the *rate* is left in abeyance till the results of the sales become known. Many citrus growers believe that their export *rate* has sometimes been determined by the first prices of Jaffa oranges on the London Fruit Exchange. (It has been said that the low *rates* given by the Ministry of Finance for citrus between 1955 and 1959 owe much to the frost which had affected the competing Spanish crop.) The Ministry of Finance has cheerfully admitted that it would determine only in April 1959 the *rate* for the foreign currency earnings from citrus exports made in the latter part of 1958.

The Ministry of Agriculture used this "ex post" approach and, together with the Ministry of Finance, laid down "sliding scale *rates*" for the export proceeds of grapes, fresh vegetables, etc. The higher the sales prices per ton of produce, the lower were the export *rates*.[1]

In 1958 the Ministry of Trade and Industry wanted to force

---

[1] This "ex post *rate*", not unlike the variable exchange *rate*, is operated with a "fixed premium" mechanism (by the Ministries of Agriculture and Finance) for products like canned tomato purée. The gross IL export premiums paid per ton of tomatoes, utilized in the manufacture of purée, do not depend upon the foreign currency proceeds from the export of one ton of purée. The higher the foreign currency export proceeds per ton, the lower the effective *rate*. This technique subsidized exports at a cost of IL7.600 for every $1 of value-added (143).

the cotton spinners to export about 200 tons monthly *irrespective of the foreign currency price* which they would receive. The following agreement was, therefore, drawn up: (*a*) if the spinners succeed in selling their yarn at $1.20 per kg. or above, they would receive a *rate* of 2.650 for the net export earnings; (*b*) if the price of $1.20 was not reached, the Government undertook either to finance the storing of the yarn at home; or (*c*) to increase the *rate* to that point which would give the cotton spinners the same IL income (per kg.) which they would have received at a price of $1.20 (234).

An even more complicated "ex post *rate*" was fixed in the 1957–58 season for the groundnuts exporters. They were promised a "normal" *rate* of 2.650 for their value-added with the proviso that, should the export price fall below £110 and the local price below IL460 per ton, the *rate* was to be increased to 2.900.

MISCELLANEOUS *Rates*

Institutions: Low discriminatory *rates* were fixed for the *institutions* during 1952–58. It has been noted that these low *rates* were not infrequently evaded, but, by 1955, the foreign currency officials succeeded in checking most of these illegitimate practices. Until 1958 the larger *institutions* (e.g. the Jewish Agency) received a special *rate* of 1.500, but the smaller ones were given the official *rate* of 1.800. This latter *rate* also applied to foreign currency transfers by the larger *institutions* for building projects.[1]

Seamen: When the seamen's union negotiated wage agreements, the most important item on the agenda was not the wage rate but the proportion of the wage to be paid in foreign currency. This foreign currency was used abroad by the seamen to buy Standard IV goods which were then imported and sold in Israel. Smuggling via this tolerated channel assumed such dimensions that the Government forced the seamen's union in the spring of 1958 to agree that the import of Standard IV goods by seamen be prohibited. A union representative declared: "We intend to change the nature of the seaman's job so that he can live only from his work. This new policy, however, means that the seamen have to be compensated for the

[1] The State Comptroller complains that the Ministry of Finance—notwithstanding the "official" *rates* of 1.500 and 1.800—bargained with individual *institutions* and laid down varying purchasing IL prices for the philanthropic dollars (290).

termination of their trading income, as the income from the latter forms an integral part of their effective wage . . . compensation can be given either by increasing the wage or by paying a premium for the foreign currency exchanged by the seamen when returning to Israel" (170). A Government commission found in favour of the creation of a new exchange rate known as the "sailor's *rate*". As from the 1st October 1958 the Ministry of Finance pays at the *rate* of 2.300 for all foreign currency exchanged by sailors provided that this amount does not exceed 50% of that portion of their wage which is paid in foreign currency.

Transfers by non-residents: If a non-resident who wished to transfer foreign currency to Israel (for the purpose of investment or aid to relatives) approached a Consulate of the Israeli Government in January 1952 and asked what *rate* applied, he was explicitly told, 0.357. In practice, however (apart from the many illicit channels available to the non-resident), the Ministry of Finance was prepared to acquiesce in effectively higher *rates* by allowing non-residents to transfer all, or part of their foreign currency, via the *IwP* of Standard IV goods. The only unequivocal legal *rate*, above the official one, was that offered by building societies (e.g. Rassco) for the acquisition of a flat or house in Israel.

Tourists: (Most of the foreign exchange of the tourists was exchanged at Standard III and IV *rates*.) During the major part of the 1949–59 period the Ministry of Finance had special tourist-*rates*, applicable to hotel bills, restaurants and certain shops. In January 1959 a special tourist-*rate* of 2.160 was instituted for the tourist who undertook to exchange only a limited sum at this *rate*; if the tourist wished to expend a larger sum, then the *rate* of 1.800 still applied to his marginal currency exchanges.

Special receipts of Israeli residents: Israeli residents, in receipt of inheritances, insurance awards, or income from invisible exports, bargained with the Ministry of Finance to obtain a special *rate*. They contracted to sell a part of their foreign currency receipts at the official *rate* in exchange for licences to transfer the remainder in the form of Standard IV goods for self-use (or sale).

Until 1956 the individual restitution payments received by many Jews from Western Germany were exchanged by the Ministry of Finance at the official *rate* and this induced, in part, the emigration of thousands from Israel. Alarmed at this development, the foreign currency controls department announced at the end of 1956 that 20% of the restitution money could be paid into a special foreign currency account (277). This account could be utilized for foreign travels, the purchase of foreign securities and the import of certain Standard IV

THE ECONOMY OF ISRAEL

articles.[1] On 1st June 1957, the Ministry of Finance instructed the banks that all restitution Marks not paid into such a special foreign currency account, were to be exchanged at a *rate* of 1.800 and Government bonds—with a face value of 20% of the exchanged Marks—were to be given to the sellers of such Marks "as a bonus from the Government". (It may be asked why the Government did not instruct the banks to pay at a *rate* of 2.160. Unofficially it was explained that such a course might be interpreted as a deviation from the principle of a unitary *rate*.) These Government bonds, given to those who offered restitution Marks, could be sold immediately on receipt as they were bearer bonds freely negotiable. The effective *rate* of these Marks, therefore, depended on the daily fluctuations of these bonds on the Tel-Aviv exchange. In May 1958 the Ministry of Finance decided that henceforth recipients of monthly restitution pensions of Marks 350 or less, would be paid a straight money *rate* of 2.160. The foreign currency controller issued a further decree which laid down that the privilege of using a part of the restitution money for journeys abroad had been extended from $1,200 to $2,000, but only those who had not been abroad for three years or more were entitled to avail themselves of it! At the beginning of 1959 the right to pay into a special foreign currency account part of the restitution (and other) payments was raised to 33% thus giving an effective *rate* of about 2.400. Small rentiers were indirectly granted an even higher *rate* for they were allowed to pay into this account up to $50 per month even if this exceeded 33% of their total receipts.

Immigrants: Most immigrants arrived penniless, and the few with means solidly resisted any suggestion to exchange their foreign currency except by illicit means. The effective *rate* for most immigrants was determined by the Standard IV goods they brought in as "personal belongings". At times the Ministry of Finance issued special orders concerning the volume of Standard IV goods (apart from "personal belongings") which immigrants were allowed to bring into the country. This ranged from $500–3,000 (*vide* Oleh Hamashkiah, p. 191). There were also liberal allowances for the import of Standard IV foodstuffs; in 1950 immigrants arrived from Turkey and Poland with several hundredweights of food, nominally for self-use, but, in reality, for sale.[2]

[1] A list issued by the Ministry of Finance permitted the free import of one camera with six (!) films, one vacuum cleaner, medicaments up to $50 yearly, one tape recorder with six tapes, one piano, one electric razor, etc.

[2] The irony of the situation was that immigrants who had smuggled gold and dollars out of Iron Curtain countries—thereby endangering their lives—did not bring them to Israel, but (in the transit camps or on the Jewish Agency boats) exchanged them for Standard IV articles that provided them with a higher *rate*.

On the 1st July 1957 the most complex of all Israeli *rates* was introduced; immigrants from all countries were to receive a *rate* of 1.800 for cash transfers of any sum above $10,000; immigrants from Venezuela,[1] Western Europe, the British Empire and North America were also to receive a *rate* of only 1.800 for the first $10,000. Immigrants from the rest of the world were to be given a *rate* of 2.500 by the Ministry of Finance for their first $10,000. However, lest this new *rate* become publicized as a digression from the principle of a unitary one, the banks, while paying out—for each $1 exchanged —IL2.500, gave a receipt relating only to IL1.800. With the receipt was a note that the Ministry of Finance had granted the immigrant a present in the form of a premium of IL0.350. In addition, the banks made the immigrant sign a promissory note concerning the further sum of IL0.350, which was formally a 3% interest loan by the Jewish Agency.

On the 10th August 1958 the Israeli press reported a strange speech made by the Minister of Finance at the executive meeting of the Jewish Agency. He is alleged to have said that because of the bad impression which multiple rates were making on the International Monetary Fund, he had decided to cut down on his Ministry's grant of IL0.350 per "immigrant-dollar". Consequently the Jewish Agency, in order to maintain the effective *rate* of 2.500, offered to give all immigrants (up to $10,000) a ten-year loan of IL0.700 per $1 exchanged.

Blocked Accounts: In an English-language publication, in 1958, sponsored by the Jewish Agency (269), immigrants, temporary residents, tourists and foreign residents are informed that "by acquiring a blocked account . . . it is possible to obtain a higher rate for the dollar than the official rate of exchange, depending on stock-exchange fluctuations. Such fluctuations depend on the demand and supply of blocked accounts on the open market. At the end of December 1957 the rate for a dollar was IL2.070". This source further informs the aspirants to a higher *rate* than 1.800 that the use "to which such blocked funds may be put depends on the objective". The Foreign Exchange Division of the Ministry of Finance which considers each case on its merits, generally authorizes unblocking of such funds for "purposes of investment in some enterprise,

---

[1] A spokesman of the Jewish Agency who was asked why (of all the South American Jewish immigrants) only the Jews of Venezuela were punished with a discriminatory *rate*, replied ". . . the Jews of Venezuela are very wealthy." This discrimination between immigrants from different countries was so ludicrous that it was abolished after a few weeks and all immigrants, including those from Venezuela, benefited from the higher *rate*.

establishment of a business . . . In addition . . . unblocking of funds for current living expenses up to a total of IL50 per person per day, provided the blocked account was acquired six months before". This Jewish Agency report omits to mention that these regulations refer to only one type of blocked account, but there have always been sets of blocked accounts, the selling rates for which varied with the willingness of the foreign currency controllers to permit their non-resident owners to sell them for foreign currency to other non-residents.

Imported cars: On the 9th December 1958 the import of cars was liberalized and the Ministry of Finance offered to sell foreign currency for the import of many types of new and second-hand cars at *rates* varying between 8 and 11. The foreign currency and the accompanying import licence would be allocated after the formal payment at the *rate* of 1.800 plus a lump sum (in practice of IL6.200–9.200 per $1) calculated according to the year of production of the car and its weight.

Ship repairs: Ship-repairing companies in the Haifa port were paid at the *rate* of 2.650 since 1957 for repairs made to foreign ships that paid in foreign currency. Israeli shipping lines were not allowed by the Ministry of Finance to pay in foreign currency and hence were charged a higher price by the local repair companies. In the spring of 1958 the Ministry proposed that the *rate* of 2.650 for the repair of foreign ships should, in future, only apply to *non-urgent* repairs, i.e. the kind of repairs that the foreign shipping line could have executed either at Haifa or at an alternative non-Israeli port. For repairs of an *urgent* nature (i.e. of the kind that had to be made in Haifa because the ship was in such a state that it could not safely be brought to another port) only a *rate* of 1.800 was to apply, and the ship-repairing companies were urged to raise the foreign currency price for this type of work. (I have not been able to establish whether this change was actually effected or whether those who thought it administratively too difficult carried the day.)

"Ticket-dollars": The *rates* which applied since 1954 to the foreign currency value of travel tickets to and from Israel have undergone frequent changes. They have also varied as between travel tickets by air and by sea, and, at one time, divers *rates* applied to different classes on ships. Incidentally, for most purposes of foreign currency control, tickets on Israeli shipping or air lines are treated as if they are foreign currency expenditure and their IL prices are graded according to the *rates* in force for "ticket-dollars".

During 1958 the *rate* for this category was 1.800 if the traveller

166

was entitled to this privilege as a recipient of restitution funds from Germany. If the traveller could prove that the funds for his journey originated in the exchange of foreign currency sent to him from abroad for this purpose, he could purchase the "ticket-dollars" at the *rates* of 2.007 (return ticket) and 2.160 (single ticket). All other travellers had to pay at the *rate* of 2.520 for air, sea and (foreign) train tickets. (Since then the *rate* for train tickets has been reduced to 2.250 and new *rates* are being planned.)

"Travel Allowance Dollars": Until December 1958 Israeli residents, who wished to journey abroad for a non-approved purpose, had to purchase the foreign currency for their subsistence abroad on the black market (Standard III). On 8th December 1958 the foreign currency controller described this situation, which had lasted for more than a decade, as "shameful" and stated at a press conference that henceforth every resident who wished to travel abroad could purchase, per annum, foreign currency to the value of up to $100 at a newly-created *rate* of 2.300. Two days later, however, the banks were instructed that this new *rate* was temporarily "frozen". This was because some owners of value-linked securities had publicly announced that the creation of this new cash *rate*, which had been officially declared, had set a precedent, and in their view, the official partial devaluation of the IL had been proclaimed. Consequently on 16th December 1958 a new circular was sent to the banks from the foreign currency controller. The legal advisers of the Ministry of Finance had produced a gimmick which frustrated the claims of the owners of value-linked securities and deprived the new *rate* of its official nature. It will be recalled (*vide* above) that the recipients of German restitution money were permitted to purchase foreign securities with 20% of their foreign currency income. It now became legally possible for these foreign securities to be sold, at market prices, to Israeli residents entitled to a travel allowance. When this new circular was published, indignation was expressed by both bankers and intending travellers, because it was obviously clumsy (and the commission charges were extremely high) for travellers to have foreign securities and not money in their possession. The banks therefore refused to implement this new *rate*. After further deliberations in the Ministry of Finance, the following instructions were issued after which the new *rate* became effective from 25th December 1958: The recipients of German restitution money instruct their bank to purchase foreign securities on their behalf and immediately offer these for sale through the bank to those entitled to a travel allowance. The traveller may purchase the securities but can resell them to the Israeli bank for foreign currency only after thirty days.

167

The *rate*,[1] which fluctuates, was on the average 2.250 in early January 1959. In February it was announced that the waiting period had been reduced to fifteen days—the effective *rate* becoming 2.450. —If, however, a traveller, who had purchased dollars at the *rate* of 2.450, returned to Israel with unspent foreign currency, he was obliged by law to sell it at the *rate* of 1.800.

"*Macy-dollars*": In the early part of 1959 buyers from the American department store Macy visited Israel. The Government was interested, for prestige reasons, that this store should buy Israeli products; hence the Ministry of Finance indicated to exporters that it would be prepared to institute a specially attractive, i.e. high, *rate* for exports to Macy.

[1] Barclays Bank described this unique exchange rate as follows: "Israeli residents going abroad will be allowed to purchase foreign securities up to the value of $100 per year which they will be allowed to take out of the country or sell for foreign currency which may be taken abroad" (281).

CHAPTER XX

TOZERETH HAARETZ

> The foreign currency controls provided most Israeli entrepreneurs with a protective umbrella by either entirely prohibiting the import of competing products or by granting allocations of foreign currency for competing imports only at a high *rate*.
>
> Such practically unlimited protection led to abuses and efforts were made to apply the Tozereth Haaretz defence merely to products below a defined *rate*, i.e. below a ceiling of IL costs (to manufacture a product the import substitute of which is priced $1).
>
> The degree of protection was usually based on the gross value of the Israeli article and not on its value-added.

PROTECTIVE tariffs enable the unambiguous gauging of the degree of intended protection for domestic producers. As in countries, like Israel, such protection is ordinarily provided in the form of restrictions on the import of competing products, the degree of protection cannot be accurately measured. With the tool of value-added (*vide* Chapter XVI) a guess can, however, be hazarded as to the degree of protection attributable to the foreign currency controls.

Horovitz estimates the highest *rate* for the protection of value-added in industry and agriculture in the spring of 1957 to have been 10 (61); this is commensurate with a protective tariff of 456%. The highest *rates* for which I can find evidence are 16[1] and 17[2] respectively.

Tozereth Haaretz protagonists succeeded in protecting producers without linking the degree of protection to the proportion of value-added in the product. Hence, many adaptable importers and agents of foreign firms induced their suppliers or principals to allow them to

---

[1] After the Sinai campaign the army complained that the local crêpe rubber shoes had been of deficient quality, and it was suggested that in future the crêpe be imported. The Ministry of Trade and Industry investigated the factory, which for years had enjoyed monopolistic rights under the Tozereth Haaretz umbrella, and found it to be a dignified packaging station for imported crêpe. To maintain the fiction of a factory, six workers were paid to "manufacture crêpe" but, in fact, besides packing the crêpe, found useful employment in the garden of the factory (62).

[2] The production of canned sardines has an imputed value-added of 25% at a *rate* of 17 (143).

"produce" the foreign goods locally. In practice this meant that the foreign supplier would send, instead of a finished product marked "Made in country X", assembly components or semi-manufactured goods which were assembled or finished in Israel and then marked with the magic stamp "Made in Israel". Thus importers received import licences with greater ease—as manufacturers—and could demand that the goods of foreign firms (not domestically assembled) be excluded from the Israeli market on the grounds of Tozereth Haaretz. Several small plants, each employing up to a dozen workers, were put up by astute importers for the purpose of disguising their machinations.

Less scrupulous, though more commercially minded, firms secured Tozereth Haaretz protection for their traditional imports by bringing in the finished goods, specified on invoices and import licences, as raw materials or semi-finished articles.[1]

The existence of "factories", owned by importers, gave them power to blackmail other importers. Owners of such "dummy plants"are known to have demanded a share in the profits[2] of the imports of finished, competing products with the threat to denounce their competitors' proposed imports to the Tozereth Haaretz commission as being damaging to the interests of a local "manufacturer".

[1] The Baracork company was generously supported with *IwP* licences from the Investment Centre, when this Swiss company claimed it would develop a large export trade. In the autumn of 1954 criminal proceedings were instituted against the company after its representatives had attempted to release ready-made "insulating boards", which had been invoiced as "raw cork", from the Haifa port (128).

In 1953 and 1954 two firms applied for *IwP* licences from the Investment Centre saying they intended to open new departments for the production of certain electrical appliances. They were granted licences for the components of these appliances which they were supposed to assemble. The customs authorities discovered that the licences were, in fact, used to bring in fully-assembled appliances (187).

[2] A special case was presented by the paper mill in Hadera which had been put up with an investment of IL10 million and $2½ million. When it started producing in 1954 the Government promised that all paper imports would be stopped. With this backing, the plant produced, uneconomically, small quantities of different types of paper from middle-fine for stationery to newsprint; the *rate* of its value-added was exceptionally high (79). As newspapers were among the victims of this Tozereth Haaretz protection—they had to pay dearly for bad-quality Hadera paper which replaced the cheap good quality Finnish imports—a successful press campaign was launched and forced the Government to appoint a commission of inquiry in 1956. The main recommendation of the commission was that the Hadera plant should, in future, limit itself to the production of a few types of paper and that the import of the other types should be renewed. In 1957 the firm informed the Government that it was prepared to act on these recommendations provided it was recognized as the sole importer of paper.

170

In 1953 a Tozereth Haaretz commission was constituted in Jerusalem, the members of which were officers of the Ministries of Finance, Trade and Industry, Agriculture and the representatives of producers' organizations. Any manufacturer likely to be aggrieved by a proposed import had the right to turn for a hearing to this commission, which then instructed the Competent Authority to hold the proposed import licence in abeyance until the hearing. Sometimes months passed before this instruction was revoked or confirmed.

Goldberger reports that, at a meeting of the Ministry of Trade and Industry in September 1953, it was decided to protect (by not issuing licences) those local producers whose *rate* was 2.500 or less—"except in those cases where the foreign goods are dumped or enjoy an export subsidy"; in such cases the *rate* could exceed 2.500 (80). These *rates*, and others quoted in this chapter, are meaningless guides to the real degree of protection as the reference is to the gross value of the product and not to the value-added.

Goldberger also claims to know that the secretary of the Tozereth Haaretz commission had laid down a rule,[1] according to which goods were not to be imported into Israel when the local goods were only up to 50% dearer than the import substitutes. The secretary admitted, however, that the Tozereth Haaretz commission had successfully prevented imports even though the locally produced goods were dearer by more than 50%.

In time the commission abandoned the search for objective criteria and absolutely rejected most competing imports if the affected local manufacturer was sponsored by a strong pressure group. Apart from the case of the *IfE* goods already mentioned, some other exceptions must be noted. The import, for example, of staple products with a heavy weight in the cost-of-living index was not seriously challenged; thus in September 1957 the import of 20 million eggs, for index manipulations, was permitted despite heavy opposition from poultry farmers. On at least two occasions the Government representatives on the commission forced through a decision permitting imports of cotton yarn and woollen blankets—these imports were meant to be punitive measures against two private cartels which had not complied with "suggestions" put to them by the Ministry of Trade and Industry concerning the local prices charged by them.

Tozereth Haaretz was an ideal which many groups planned to serve, each in its own way. The Reparations Company, for instance,

---

[1] This rule was amended, for *IfE* goods, to 25%. The Foreign Trade Division fought many a battle within this commission to allow the exporters the right to buy their raw materials from the cheapest source, i.e. to import goods for *IfE* purposes which were produced more cheaply abroad than they were in Israel.

171

followed a procedure of its own. The State Comptroller (55) complained that the company was not guided by an objective criterion, but examined each application individually, "and checked it, on the basis of its own experience and expert knowledge, to see whether such goods were produced in Israel or not . . .."

The army did not have to defend its import formula before the commission. At first it seemed as if its purchases were regulated by an objective criterion. The director of its supply department stated publicly, in the spring of 1955, that henceforth the army would purchase those goods abroad which were offered locally at prices exceeding a *rate* of 2.500. When I checked on the implementation of this policy (in 1956) I was told that it had never been put into operation and officers of the supply department instanced the purchase of (non-weapon) goods bought locally at *rates* exceeding 4 and 5.

The trade unions were often the most vehement defenders of Tozereth Haaretz both inside and outside the commission. Elsewhere I describe how the *rates* for the *institutions* drove the latter to turn their money donations into "presents of goods" (*vide* p. 184). When a concert hall was nearing completion in 1956, the *institution* (sponsoring the cultural body concerned) applied to the Ministry of Finance for an *IwP* licence for 3,000 (specially constructed) chairs, each costing $1.70 c.i.f. Haifa. The local price was IL8.300; if insurance, freight and packaging costs are ignored, the comparative *rate* is, therefore, 4.900. The official journal of the trade unions explains (81) that their representatives are actively engaged in frustrating imports of goods competing with domestic products, and a list of such imports is given in the issue from which I quote. In connection with the above chairs, the journal tells us that, at their request, the Tozereth Haaretz commission had held up the licence, but the unions ultimately agreed to the import, as the chairs were the "present of a well-known philanthropist in America". Whether this is true or not, the fact remains that the unions defended themselves against charges of having deprived local manufacturers of protection, not by mentioning the *rate* of 4.900 (which would be higher still if translated into terms of value-added), but by the argument that foreign donors must not be alienated.

By 1958 the Tozereth Haaretz policy began to be formulated in terms of the value-added of the protected article. The *rates*, however, were arbitrarily worked out and adapted to each case. (Thus we read on 5th August 1958 in the Israeli press, that a Tozereth Haaretz protection *rate* of 4 had been laid down for a certain article.) Only a few weeks before, the Economic Adviser to the Ministry of Trade and Industry had publicly (230) stated that in the "Government's view every investment is economically worthwhile provided the value-added of the products does not exceed the *rate* of 3". He, nonetheless, made the following qualifying declaration: "it is permitted to ignore this criterion—i.e. the *rate* of 3—when the new investment absorbs unemployed, who have hitherto been supported by the State or when important military considerations prevail".

It was revealed that during the summer of that year deliberations had taken place in the economic ministries because disquiet was felt when the Government had received proof that the effective Tozereth Haaretz protection *rate* had "reached the astronomical height . . . of 25". The Israeli public was startled when, in August 1958, a series of articles was published in *Haaretz* (229) charging the Government with having accorded the Kaiser-Frazer assembly plant a protection *rate* of 27. Even allowing for some mistakes in the calculation of this *rate*, and considering that the calculation was based on a marginal product, this series of articles left a strong impression on public opinion.—A commission of the Ministry of Trade and Industry, which was established to lay down exact rules for the protection of home industry, completed its work in November 1958, but its report has not yet been published.

CHAPTER XXI

IMPORTS

Imports into Israel require: (1) a licence from a Competent Authority and (2) an allocation of foreign currency by the Ministry of Finance which also lays down the specific *rate* for the allocation or, alternatively, an *IwP* licence.

Largely owing to the entanglements of the multiple rates, the Ministry of Finance failed—certainly up to 1954—to ensure that the actual imports corresponded to the Import Programme. It was unable to stop the consistent and wholesale breaches and circumventions of the foreign currency controls—most *institutions* were among the offenders.

The terms "low *rates*" and "high *rates*" are defined in relation to the *average rate*. The working assumption is made that foreign currency allocated below the *average rate* are "cheap dollars" and above it "dear dollars".

The import of essentials was regarded as an unavoidable evil to be hedged in by Ministry of Finance restrictions —the import of luxuries was viewed as a deadly sin to be rooted out by total prohibition.

The import limitations did not always achieve the aim of improving the balance of payments for they distorted the optimum allocation of factors and sometimes frustrated remunerative exports.

The low *rates* discouraged domestic production in some fields, encouraged the wasteful utilization of imports and, particularly, inflated the demand for foreign machinery.

When the restrictions on non-essential imports were not effectively evaded, they induced the local production of luxuries—not infrequently in an uneconomic way. The high "Domestic Protection" (Tozereth Haaretz) *rates* (*vide* p. 154) originated in the policy of excluding (efficaciously) luxuries.

GENERAL CONSIDERATIONS

UNTIL 1954, the foreign currency controls were directed on the lines of discouraging the import of luxuries and foreign exchange was allocated only for essentials.[1] Such a policy conformed with popular sentiment. Furthermore, the Ministry of Finance regarded imports exclusively in the light of the foreign currency resources of the country, and official thinking rejected all approaches based on "the total resources at the disposal of the economy". The interdependence of imports, domestic factors and exports was not considered relevant by the Ministry when framing its policy of selective imports.

This policy stimulated investments in high-cost luxury production (e.g. growing of apples, assembling air-conditioners) whilst it discouraged investments in the production of goods for which Israel was relatively well suited (e.g. potatoes, wheat). The misallocation of resources induced by the local manufacture of high-cost luxury goods would have proved even more detrimental if the walls of the foreign currency controls had not been regularly breached by illicit imports.

As goods considered by the authorities to be luxuries could, in fact, only come into the country as Standard IV goods, the *manner* of their (illicit) import represented a waste of foreign exchange. For example, rather than bring in sugar and cocoa ingredients for the manufacture of chocolate, ready-made chocolate was smuggled in and many of these luxuries arrived in Israel individually-packed. Picker (83) has estimated that if the foreign exchange, which financed the import of Standard IV goods during the years prior to 1954, had been placed at the disposal of Israeli importers for the legal import of the same articles, 40% more of such goods could have been purchased. The post-1954 situation (when the Government allocated foreign currency for the legal import of Standard IV articles) bore out the contention that bulk purchases by experienced merchants and the import of semi-finished goods and raw materials—for the production of the Standard IV articles in Israel—were more economical methods than the previous practices.

The policy of selective imports and Tozereth Haaretz considerations deprived Israeli merchants of those conditions required to manœuvre freely in the intricacies of international trade. It is not unusual for countries to export a commodity in one season and import it in another, and many countries, while exporting one grade of a commodity, import another grade of the same one. Such transactions were hardly ever possible in Israel because of the clumsiness of the foreign currency controls. (A notable exception

[1] Meade (75) reports that this policy is generally favoured in countries with a large deficit on their balance of payments. If Israel's economy had a structure which enabled it, relatively to the rest of the world, to produce luxury products at lower costs than essential ones, this policy would have been less damaging than it proved to be.

with wheat is noted on p. 256). The authorities also frowned upon such deals, for, in their view, exports served a gainful purpose, and hence deserved to be subsidized, while imports, an inevitable evil, were to be hampered.[1]

Import restrictions were imposed in order to husband the foreign exchange resources of the country but, in some cases, they thwarted the exports and thus led to a net loss of foreign currency. The following are two illustrations:

Israel has a comparative advantage in the cultivation of large groundnuts which are eaten uncrushed. An export of 1 ton of edible nuts, f.o.b. Haifa, sells for the import price, c.i.f. Haifa, of $1\frac{1}{2}$ tons of small nuts ordinarily used for the manufacture of oil (88). The export of large groundnuts rose from $70,000 in 1953, to $1\frac{1}{4}$ million in 1956. Despite this increase, the exported quantity in 1956 was no larger than a quarter of the total crop,[2] and half the amount suitable for export. In that year alone, therefore, export earnings of $1\frac{1}{2}$ million were forfeited. This loss of potential foreign currency receipts can be attributed to the refusal of the foreign currency controls department to allocate sufficient foreign exchange for the import of the cheaper types of oil seeds, with the result that the black market prices of fats and oils soared (*vide* p. 59). This black market was in part supplied with oil illicitly manufactured from large (export) groundnuts. Furthermore, the craving for fats (induced by the insufficient legal rations) augmented the local consumption of edible (export) nuts, Halva and oriental sweets (these last-named being made from local groundnuts). The (additional) import of edible oils

[1] Propositions to export eggs in one season and import them during another were rejected.

The same attitude prevailed with similar proposals for potatoes. Israel's favourable climate helps to produce a good crop of potatoes in the spring when Western Europe pays premium prices for them. The second (autumn) crop is poor and does not suffice for the ordinary demand of the local population. Hence, some merchants believed it would be a gainful proposition to export part of the spring crop at high prices to Europe and, with the proceeds, to import cheap European potatoes in the summer. The autarchic-minded officials of the foreign currency controls rejected this type of transaction. Instead the surplus spring crop is stored—for a period of up to seven months during the hot summer, in costly refrigeration—in order to supplement the potato crop of the autumn and thus obviate imports.

Proposals to export the maximum quantity of olive oil and edible groundnuts, and import, instead, increased quantities of the lower-grade oils were similarly rejected.

[2] In 1958 groundnuts were exported for $2 million; this was still only one third of the total crop and merely 60% of the export potential was exploited.

and oilcakes,[1] to the value of $$\frac{3}{4}$$ million, would have reduced the black market prices to that level at which the farmers would have found it more profitable to export all suitable groundnuts, rather than sell them locally for the production of oils.

Olive oil, f.o.b. Haifa, fetches an export price equal to the import price of twice the quantity of other vegetable oils. The average annual export of olive oil netted less than $100,000 in the 1950–55 period. In 1956 the Ministry of Trade and Industry announced that it had found means to coerce the farmers to export olive oil, and expected to receive $$1\frac{1}{2}$$ million that year. In fact, less than $300,000 of olive oil were sold. In 1957, $472,000 olive oil were exported, and in 1958 only $77,000. Conservative calculations show Israel's annual export capacity in this product to be about $2 million. What happened to this crop in the past? Some of it was smuggled over the borders to neighbouring Arab states (84). The major part was crushed, illicitly distilled and the oil sold on the black market.[2]—In 1952 Dov Josef's Ministry recruited several hundred policemen for raids on villages in the olive area in order to "rescue" some of the oil from the clutches of the black market. The "rescued" oil was, however, not exported but distributed in that year, as on subsequent occasions, as a fat ration replacing the usual issue of margarine. The foreign currency controller approved of this utilization of the olive oil as its replacement of the margarine ration "saved the necessity to allocate foreign exchange for the import of oil seeds".

IMPORTS BELOW THE *Average Rate*

What were the results of allocating the majority of the foreign exchange at low *rates*?

In certain categories of goods the low *rates* generated an overall demand for import licences with allocation of foreign exchange that greatly exceeded the amount of foreign exchange which the Ministry of Finance was prepared to supply for these imports.[3] The deflating

---

[1] By exporting groundnuts, the economy is not only deprived of a source of oil but also of oilcakes for feeding animals.

[2] Olive oil is more palatable than, say, soya oil. The black market prices for edible oils, however, are not determined by the shortage of palatable oils but by the scarcity of basic cooking fats and margarine. The economic absurdity consisted in satisfying a demand for cheap oils by the supply of dear olive oil.

[3] Import licences, *per se*, promised substantial profits, but licences with "cheap" foreign currency were the source of even larger capital gains. The heavy interest charges of Israel were never a serious impediment for the merchant who sought finance for such lucrative imports.

of the magnified demand for such import licences caused many administrative predicaments and enhanced the discretionary power of the officials of the foreign currency controls.

The "cheap dollars" deranged the optimum combination of local and foreign factors; the following are some striking examples:

(a) Those entitled to pay for their imports at low *rates* bought the maximum of foreign finished goods and spent the minimum on local labour. Kalecky (89) was struck by this distorted price structure when he studied the building industry in 1951. He concluded that Israel would save foreign currency—by importing less iron and cement—if it made more use of stones and domestically fabricated bricks. (The direct labour input in building with bricks is higher than with iron-and-cement construction; there is also a higher labour input in brick-making). The managers of the Government building department divested Kalecky of his theoretical precepts. They explained to him that for Government projects imported iron and cement were relatively cheaper than local products with a high labour input, because foreign exchange for imports of Government departments were allocated at the low *rates* which overvalued the IL.—For similar reasons, Israeli shipping and air companies were interested to buy the maximum of their supplies abroad.

(b) There was a tendency to use wastefully goods imported at low *rates*; the dissipation was not large in the case of products imported in small quantities and distributed by rations, but was weighty in the case of imports sold unrationed. Bread and kerosene are examples of the latter—their IL prices were so low that it paid to smuggle them to the neighbouring Arab states. The following are some excerpts from the press of 1952–54: ". . . because of kerosene smuggling, it has been decided to ration the supply of kerosene to Arabs living in the Wadi Arah . . ."; ". . . an Arab woman was arrested for smuggling kerosene to Jordan". ". . . white flour was smuggled to Jordan via the village of Teibeh"; ". . . Arab children were arrested smuggling sacks of bread to Jordan in a barter deal for meat and vegetables".

(c) The pernicious effect of "cheap dollars" is well demonstrated by the case of seed potatoes, which were imported at an annual cost of $500,000 and were sold—"to encourage agriculture"— at low *rates*. In 1950 and 1951 one-half of the imported seed potatoes (92) were resold by the farmers on the black market

178

as edible potatoes. Whilst the Ministry of Finance intended to favour agriculture by a low *rate* for seed potatoes, the Ministry of Agriculture knew that the artificially low IL price of these imports impeded agricultural development. Farmers queued to receive large allocations of seed potatoes; an immediate trading gain awaited them if they desisted from the laborious task of planting. The Ministry of Agriculture understood that only if the IL price of the seed potatoes was high enough to make their planting more profitable than their immediate sale, would the waste—which had already cost the Israeli economy hundreds of thousands of dollars—cease. The Ministry of Agriculture, therefore, increased the IL price of the seed potatoes by surcharges, etc.

(*d*) Many invisible imports were accorded the lower *rates*. Hence, at a time when the Standard III *rate* was 1.500, the Post Office charged at the 0.357 *rate* for international telephone calls, and Israel's foreign currency expenditure on this item went up considerably because the low *rate* encouraged the reversing of charges, etc.

(*e*) The absurdity of the low *rates* may be gauged by comparing the IL costs of maintaining an Israeli student at a British university (receiving a foreign currency allocation at low *rates*) with the IL expenses of studying at the Hebrew University. For parents in Tel-Aviv (who were allocated foreign currency at the lowest *rate*), it was 2½ times as dear to pay—in the 1949–52 period—for the maintenance of a student in Jerusalem as in London.

(*f*) Transport costs retained the 0.357 *rate* until 1952 and this led to many abuses. *IwP* licences were, according to the foreign currency regulations, issued on a c.i.f. Haifa basis, because transferrers of capital were meant to pay with the foreign currency at *their* disposal for the freight of the *IwP* goods. The State Comptroller reports (56) that "in many cases" this provision was evaded and *IwP* consignments arrived on an f.o.b. basis, the *IwP* transferrers being allocated foreign currency at the 0.357 *rate* to pay for the freight and insurance of their imports.

The import of investment goods[1] at low *rates* seriously interfered

---

[1] In the 1949–54 period, part of the productive capacity of Israel's transport, agriculture and industry was not fully employed because of the lack of spare parts. The Competent Authorities and the Ministry of Finance allocated foreign currency for machinery on a priority basis. Allocations for spare parts were

with the optimum combination of machinery and labour. Despite the abundance of unskilled hands, the Histadruth ensured that they were paid a wage not appreciably below that of a skilled worker. Whilst the price of the labour factor was thus kept at a relatively high level, the price of investment goods was artificially lowered by the Ministry of Finance's policy of lucrative credit terms and low *rates*. From the first Export-Import Bank loan to the days of the Reparations Company, there have been Israeli entrepreneurs who have made capital gains by selling their equipment for cash, and acquiring new equipment (on credit terms) at low *rates*. Clawson comments on this feature in so far as it affected agriculture, as follows:

> "Agriculture, including irrigation, has been lavish and wasteful in the use of capital goods. This is particularly marked on the older farms, especially kibbutzim, but even the newer settlements have not always used machinery efficiently. Israel . . . often uses more capital than would be used in the United States under the same circumstances. The kibbutzim I have seen, have far more machinery . . . than a farm of the same size with the same crops in the large-scale, heavy-machinery-using farms in California would have. Moreover, most kibbutzim follow a system of agriculture which requires, or at least customarily uses, much machinery" (147).

Public concern about exaggerated mechanization in agriculture has led to a relative decline in the import of machinery since 1951.[1]—Reports of foreign observers have described how machinery was only partially utilized because entrepreneurs had often ordered too large-

granted grudgingly, as these were considered consumption goods and the officers of the foreign currency controls thought that consumption should be cut to the minimum. The Ministry of Finance also placed spare parts into the category of goods which were imported at high *rates*.

There was a similar attitude towards the import of raw materials. The import of machines was encouraged, even though it was clear often in advance that the Ministry of Finance would be unable to allocate foreign currency for sufficient raw materials to utilize the new machines fully. Nonetheless, the import of machinery was furthered, as "it is a good thing to have modern machinery in the country".

[1] The Jewish Agency used to allocate expensive machinery to new settlements, and one of the delights of its public relations officers was to show donors how a semi-literate immigrant was driving a new tractor. The tremendous wastage and excessive breakdowns, which resulted from this policy of "distributing" machinery, induced the Jewish Agency to concentrate its heavy agricultural machinery in regional tractor stations; the property title of the machinery remained vested in the Jewish Agency. Under the new system, skilled, hired mechanics operate the machinery which is more fully utilized than before.

sized models.[1] There have also been some cases where machinery was ordered on credit because of the attractively low *rates* for investment goods but, when delivered, could not be installed because of the lack of working capital.[2]

The "cheap dollars" which were allocated for the import of goods with a heavy weight in the cost-of-living index, sometimes had a harmful effect on domestic production as can be seen from the following two examples:

The Ministry of Agriculture lavishly subsidized deep-sea fishing, and the Ministry of Finance allocated foreign currency at low *rates* for the import of boats and equipment. The public funds spent on this venture were largely misapplied because the Food Division persuaded the Ministry of Finance to import fish at low *rates*, and the efforts to develop an Israeli fishing fleet were frustrated on the altar of the cost-of-living index.

Dov Josef's ministry fixed a low price for edible potatoes in 1949 and 1950—a price which (according to the farmers) did not cover their production costs. The low price was, of course, determined by the aim to reduce the cost-of-living index, but Dov Josef was not unduly concerned when the local farmers responded to these maximum prices by not growing potatoes for his Ministry. With foreign currency—at the under-valued *rate* of 0.357—the Food Division imported potatoes, and agricultural factors were released to grow crops which were not as suited to Israel's soil (77).[3] This manipulation of the cost-of-living index was executed

---

[1] The partial use of expensive machinery is not only a waste of resources, but also increases production costs per unit of output. This is well illustrated in the report on the metal factories of the Solel Boneh industry (15).

[2] The influential owner of the Pallalum Aluminium company was given a loan from the Export-Import Bank in 1950 for $137,000. At a time, when four enamelling plants were producing and a fifth was under construction, this firm was prompted by the low *rates* to order another such plant. When the machinery arrived in 1951, the crates were left unopened as the owner had neither the working capital to operate it nor a building to house it. The machinery had been acquired on long-term credit at an effective *rate* of 0.452. In 1954, with the crates still unopened, the owner proposed to sell the equipment against Turkish clearing-dollars. The Turkish Government approved but the Ministry of Finance did not allow the deal to proceed because of a negative report by the Economic Advisory Staff (78). By 1959 the owner (with IL loans from the Development Budget) had put up a building and installed the machinery, yet was unable to operate it for bankruptcy proceedings were instituted against him. The $137,000 were paid for an unrequited import *par excellence*!

[3] The Ministry of Agriculture regretted the conditions which made farmers change over to the cultivation of less suitable crops. Yet—*vide* Amir (98)—the Government's policy was vindicated by the need for low prices for articles with a heavy weight in the cost-of-living index.

181

by importing limited quantities for the distribution of a small ration and this "allowed" a black market to flourish. Thanks to the black market and the unwillingness of some farmers to obey the maximum price orders, large quantities of potatoes were nonetheless grown in Israel.

The Food Division mitigated the damage of some of these food imports at artificially low *rates* by offering to purchase the whole crop of similar local products. There have been cases where farmers benefited by this subsidized bulk-buying, but for the most part, the Government did not offer sufficiently attractive prices, and the farmers ceased cultivating such crops. The Food Division did not regret this as it then "saved" IL subsidies.

Two anomalies are significant enough to be recorded in this context. Low *rates* have been known to apply to the imports of a finished article and high *rates* to the import of raw materials for its manufacture; this did not encourage domestic production. The other anomaly concerns the import of an article at a low *rate* and that of a near-substitute at a high one; e.g. at the beginning of 1956 (76) certain medicaments, imported for human consumption, were used for veterinary purposes because the *rate* of 1 applied to human medicaments, while veterinary products had a *rate* of 1.800.

The foreign currency controller raised revenue directly and indirectly for the Government. Owing to the low *rates* the Ministry of Finance could apply—unauthorized by parliament—public funds for purposes it considered deserving. Two cases are cited:

An Israeli manufacturer, Mr. K., entered upon a commercial venture for which he had been promised technical aid by a Government department. The support did not materialize and Mr. K. suffered heavy losses, whereupon he informed the department that he would claim damages. The responsible Minister was advised that Mr. K. would probably win his case and public criticism would be severe when the details of his claim were published. The Minister was also advised that a financial grant of compensation was likely to raise awkward questions from the State Comptroller. The Ministry of Finance helped the interested department by granting Mr. K. in 1954 an import licence for certain Standard IV goods at the *rate* of 1.800. Mr. K. made an immediate capital gain—for the sum of the agreed (unofficial) compensation—by selling the licence. He then withdrew his claim.

In 1957 a group of farmers suffered some financial loss through a disease which ravaged their cattle. The Ministry of Agriculture was eager to help these farmers, but parliament had not voted any funds from which the compensation could be paid. The Ministry of Finance again helped out by instructing the foreign currency controller to issue to this group an import licence for live cattle at the *rate* of 1.800. It was hoped by the two Ministries that the differential profit which the farmers were expected to make from the sales of the imported cattle on the grey market would compensate them for the loss described (149).

PUNITIVE *Rates* FOR *Institutions*

The low *rates* laid down for the *institutions* deprived them of the financial incentive to transfer their foreign currency receipts in cash. The Ministry of Finance occasionally confiscated irregular *IwP* consignments and prosecuted offenders of the foreign currency controls, but it did not act in this manner when the larger *institutions* wilfully transgressed the laws of the land. The Ministry had ample proof to prosecute the majority of them (and all the Israeli political parties) for serious offences against the controls.[1] It is established that, certainly up to 1954, all of these used the black market—in one form or another—to transfer some of the foreign donations.

Apart from resorting to the Standard III channel, the *institutions* also used their foreign currency to finance imports, both for self-use and for sale in the Standard IV market. Such imports arrived in Israel sometimes with and sometimes without regular licences. The Ministry of Finance knew how specious were many of the pleas of the *institutions* to justify the use of their foreign exchange for *IwP*, but no strong action was taken against them.[2]

The punitive *rates* also had a detrimental effect on domestic output, for they induced the import of articles which could have been economically produced in Israel. (An important exception to this rule concerns the limited right to buy Israeli products with foreign exchange—*vide* "internal exports", p. 277.)

[1] The governor of an important academic *institution* once confessed that although he knew it to have been an offence, he had illegally transferred some of the foreign currency proceeds of an American campaign to Israel. He explained that he regarded himself as the trustee of the donors, who wanted the true IL value of their foreign currency to be used by his *institution*. "When the Ministry of Finance issues immoral regulations which discriminate against charitable *institutions*, it is my moral right," he said, "to evade such regulations."

[2] The Jewish Agency, for example, once pleaded that the only way it could transmit funds collected in South Africa was to buy jam with the donations and sell it in Israel. On another occasion it was argued that funds collected in Argentina could only be transferred by buying woollen blankets. These blankets were brought to Israel; some were distributed to needy immigrants and the remainder sold on the Standard IV market to net the Jewish Agency IL funds.

The directors of several *institutions* were adept in asking subscribers *not* to donate money, but, instead, to contribute certain Standard IV articles. After the requested goods-contributions had been made, the *institutions* approached the foreign currency controller and asked for *IwP* licences. The applications were usually accompanied by a declaration that the *institution* making the application, preferred to receive cash donations but "it so happened" that one supporter had given, say, a printing press and another philanthropist had contributed, say, a vehicle. The officials of the foreign currency controls were entreated not to offend the donors, but issue *IwP* licences. Indeed, until 1954, the Ministry of Finance usually acceded to such requests.

The following are some excerpts from the press relating to imports by *institutions*:

12/7/50—Jewish Agency imports iron bedsteads and oil lamps; import licences for these goods are not usually granted by the Competent Authority to safeguard local producers.

20/6/52—Jewish Agency establishes the Ytarim company to import textile remnants from America. Some of the consignments are held up by the customs authorities as they include finished textiles.

3/12/52—Jewish Agency buys in Germany (with "Irso" funds) fittings and 6,000 wash-basins—all goods manufactured locally.

3/12/52—The "Malben-Joint" *institution* imports bedsteads.

25/3/53—The Jewish Agency admits that it has imported apples(!) honey, woollen blankets, jam, etc.

23/12/53—A public outcry as the "Hadassah" *institution* imports large quantities of textiles.

There were other forms of transferring collected funds to Israel apart from importing Standard IV goods. Many of the religious *institutions* used "Scrip Vouchers" (*vide* p. 192) to pay the teachers of the seminaries they maintained.—The "Friends of the Hebrew University" to some extent avoided the punitive *rates* by letting their New York agency send travel tickets to lecturers of the Hebrew University who wished to travel abroad. In 1954, for example, the lecturers paid only IL1.800 for a "ticket dollar" and none of the surcharges and travel taxes imposed by the Ministry of Finance on tickets bought locally with IL. The "Friends of the Hebrew University" gained by the arrangement as their foreign exchange donations were exchanged at the effective *rate* of 1.800 and not, as the law prescribed, at 1.300.

184

IMPORTS ABOVE THE *Average Rate*

This category of imports is more or less identical with Standard IV
goods. The Ministry of Finance legalized the import of these luxury
articles in 1955, and since then sells foreign exchange above *average
rates* directly to Israeli importers. This section will describe the
conditions that prevailed until 1954.

Most of the Standard IV goods came into the country on *IwP*
licences and most of the *IwP* goods[1] were Standard IV articles;
the majority of Standard IV goods came into the country illegally.
[I have drawn heavily on the Picker report (83)]. The four chief
organized channels for Standard IV imports were: *IfE* (for sale in
the home market), "Investment Centre", "Internal Exports" and the
"Scrip companies"; all of these will be dealt with separately at the
end of this section. At the outset I will note a miscellany of legal and
illegal methods by which imports, for which the economy paid at
prices above the *average rate*, were brought in:

I—The sale by Government (commercial) departments and
institutions of goods which they had originally imported for self-use.
In an official Jewish Agency report, the policy of the Government in
not permitting the import of goods competing with products of local
manufacturers, is described. The following euphemistic note was
added: "An exception were imports by the Government and national
institutions effected for budgetary reasons . . ." (233).

II—A semi-legitimate way of importing Standard IV goods was
that opened up by the various export-retention and *pamaz* schemes
concerning the value-added portion of the export earnings. (This
must not be confused with the illegal practice of selling *IfE* raw
materials on the domestic market.)

III—Standard IV goods, or raw materials from which they could
be locally made, were allocated for certain specified purposes, e.g.
exports and manufacture of arms. The Government, however,
allowed damaged goods or remnants (the "cabbage" of the textile
industry) to be marketed domestically. The incentive of the producers

---

[1] Official statistics tell us that, at the height of *IwP* in 1950 and 1951, these
imports constituted 19% of the total import volume. In those years about one-
half of the Israeli imports were Government imports of fuel, grains and investment goods for public corporations. Thus, Standard IV goods constituted more
than 40% of the total non-Government imports. (This estimate is arrived at by
making allowance for those *IwP* goods which were not of the Standard IV type—
e.g. personal belongings of immigrants and certain investment goods—and
taking into account some of the illicit imports.)

to have a high proportion of "waste" products was considerable.[1]

IV—Tourists (and some diplomats) financed the better part of their stay in Israel by selling imported luxury articles. According to one estimate 75% of tourist expenditure in 1951 and 1952 was financed by the sale of foreign currency on the Standard III and Standard IV markets.

V—The term "presents" covered a multitude of sins; most were sent without a licence through the post. Some were genuine presents, in the sense that the donors, rather than use the Standard III channel, found it profitable to provide persons, they wished to aid, with Standard IV goods.—It was a contravention of the law for the earners of foreign exchange from invisible exports to ask that the proceeds be sent to them in the form of "presents". Nevertheless, this was a widespread practice, e.g. foreign newspapers paid in this manner for the services of native correspondents.—Declarations by persons claiming to make "presents" to an Israeli resident were often false; this was so, particularly in the case of vehicles.[2]

VI—Immigrants were permitted to import some Standard IV goods provided they brought them into the country within a year of

---

[1] The Ministry of Finance allocated foreign currency for *IfE* to the Citrus Marketing Board. It was not economical to import uncut logs; cut lumber was, therefore, imported and local firms only assembled the citrus boxes. As timber for domestic purposes was a Standard IV article, the American Israel Lumber Mills, Nathanya, put the following proposition to the Board, and it was accepted: the same amount of foreign currency hitherto used for *IfE* of cut lumber would, in future, be expended on the import of uncut logs (101). The previous arrangement had cost the Board—for the manufacture of 100 "74" boxes—$69 *IfE* of cut lumber plus IL6 of local assembling costs. The Israeli Mill now arranged to import $69 of uncut logs, received IL6 from the Board and, in turn, delivered one hundred boxes.

This manipulation by the Nathanya Mill depended on the use of only $34 (out of each $69) as materials for the hundred boxes and the utilization of the remaining $35 "waste products" for legal purposes at Standard IV prices.

For the Mill this was a profitable venture but it was less beneficial to the economy. Whilst 100 boxes made from imported cut lumber cost $69, those manufactured from (imported) uncut logs had a direct *IfE* cost of $34 plus an indirect *IfE* cost of $20—hence their value-added was only $15. The local IL costs of the Mill were IL67 (in excess of the IL6 charged by firms making the boxes out of cut lumber). The $15 of value-added had a *rate* of 4.500 (101).

[2] The following is from a police report in January 1958 when *illegal* Standard IV imports had ceased to be an important economic issue: ". . . many of the taxi-cabs are smuggled into the country in the disguise of presents . . . this was revealed by a thorough police investigation . . . several taxi drivers admitted that they paid in local currency to intermediaries who arranged for 'affidavits of presents' . . . the police will not prosecute the taxi drivers . . . but will proceed against the intermediaries and those who arranged the illicit exchange of the IL into dollars" (99).

arrival. Local merchants[1] used indigent immigrants—whom they contacted in the transit camps at the ports of departure or in the Israeli immigrants' camps—to clear Standard IV goods through the customs for a small payment.

VII—Finally, one must mention the import of Standard IV articles by smugglers over the Arab frontiers and by way of the Haifa port.

IfE LICENCES

The Ministry of Finance was sensitive to the wishes of (real and phantom) exporters who wanted to import Standard IV articles for *IfE* purposes. As there were, at first, no proper records of *IfE* many sold their *IfE* materials on the home market and did not manufacture goods for export from them.[2]

After 1954 the records of the Ministry of Trade and Industry enabled it to check whether the promised exports had, in fact, been carried out. At a later stage the Government admitted that *IfE* allocations of $5–6 million had, over the years, been misused by exporters and sold on the domestic market. (I consider this to be an underestimate.) An investigation made in April 1956 (104) revealed that, a few years previously, seven prospective exporters of radios had applied for *IfE* licences of radio spare parts. When the applicants were asked to deposit promissory notes to back their export-undertakings, two of the firms cancelled their applications. Of the five who contracted to use these *IfE* for exports and were consequently granted their licences, four sold the radios assembled

[1] In 1951 the investigators of the State Comptroller (56) found that under the regulations, permitting *IwP* by immigrants, playing cards were being imported in large quantities. This was not the accidental import of an immigrant, who happened to have been the owner of a playing cards factory, but was a collusive arrangement entered into by Israeli importers of playing cards, who had previously been refused allocations of foreign currency for these imports on the grounds of "inessentiality". From proceedings before the Supreme Court, in January 1959, it can be learned how light were the sentences which were usually meted out to such offenders.

[2] The State Comptroller (55) found that the Ministry of Finance kept no satisfactory records from which it could be verified whether the exporters complied with the conditions of the *IfE* licences: "According to the records of the Foreign Currency Controller's department to which we have had access, some manufacturers, who were allocated dollars in considerable amounts up to the end of 1950, did not carry out their contracted exports by the check date of August 1952". Two instances are cited: "The Government granted an *IfE* licence to a shoe factory after an undertaking had been given that 50% of the plant's output would be exported. In fact, only 5% was exported. . . . A certain textile manufacturer received a $35,000 allocation to import *IfE* materials for a projected export of $84,000; he exported $12,000" (121).

from the *IfE* in the home market; and only one found it expedient to send a consignment of radios abroad.

Up to September 1953 applicants for *IfE* licences "undertook" to use these materials only for export. These implicit undertakings were consistently broken. Between September 1953 and March 1955 the Ministry of Trade and Industry demanded a promissory note to the value of IL1 per nominal-dollar of export obligation from every exporter. This was to be forfeited when the export was not executed. In March 1955, the value of the bond was raised to IL1.800 per nominal-dollar. Theoretically, therefore, an exporter who does not now carry out his obligations towards the Ministry of Trade and Industry is liable to pay IL1.800, plus a fine of IL1.800, per $1 of *IfE* goods. Many of these Standard IV goods are sold at a much higher *rate* than 3.600 and this stimulated "exporters" to give such promissory notes although they had no intention of using the *IfE* materials for export production. After 1956 the officials of the Ministry of Trade and Industry—as is learned from a revealing case before the Supreme Court in 1958 (4)—were apparently (unofficially) given discretion to demand promissory notes at *rates* of up to 7.200.

During May 1958 a report on *IfE* was completed for the internal use of the Ministry of Finance, but it was apparently thought proper to let the information from this report leak through to the press. The report (which, in my view, errs on the high side) stated that hundreds of exporters sold their *IfE* on the home market, and consequently unfulfilled export obligations of IL40 million were outstanding. This internal Ministry report gives details about the technical and legal tricks used by the "exporters" to evade their obligations. It relates how improper outside influence was exerted to prevent the Government officials taking proceedings against offenders, and charges the Foreign Trade Division of the Ministry of Trade and Industry with neglect in this matter.

Despite this sensational report, there is little doubt that the officials of the foreign currency controls have been successful in stopping many of these old *IfE* abuses during the last few years. (Nevertheless, the State Comptroller's Report of the spring of 1959 (290) is still very critical of the economic ministries for permitting extensive abuses of the *IfE* system). Lately, however, a new technique has been increasingly used by unscrupulous merchants who parade as exporters. Several cases have come to light in which *IfE* Standard IV articles were brought into the country, sold locally and inferior substitutes, bought in Israel for IL, were used to manufacture the contracted export articles. These (inferior) exports were sold at a loss abroad, and this loss was covered by the purchase of foreign exchange on the Standard III market (*vide* p. 200). A manufacturer of memorial lights, which are sold in glass containers, was given an *IfE* licence for glasses. When the customs authorities examined his *IfE* consignment, they found it to consist of beer glasses, clearly inappropriate for the declared purpose. It was then discovered that this exporter had planned to buy local plastic glasses and use them as containers. He had presumed that the authorities would not check the type of glasses which he imported and the type of containers he exported (115)—In August 1957 the effective import *rate* for matjes herrings was 15. In that month an *IfE* licence was given to an Israeli merchant for such herrings (126). When challenged to say what he intended doing with the herrings, he replied that he proposed treating them and exporting them in special containers. Fish merchants (who presumably were displeased at not being allowed to import such lucrative Standard IV goods) told the press that this particular exporter planned to sell the matjes herrings locally and buy cheap herrings—available for IL—to "fulfil" his export obligation. This was apparently a warranted suspicion, for the Food Division (at a press conference on 21st August 1957) declared that they had undertaken (1) to prevent the sale of matjes herrings locally, (2) to check the export consignments produced from this *IfE* and (3) to investigate what was a reasonable amount of "wastage".

Statistics which have just come to light show that the *IfE* for the textile industry—in the years of 1957 and 1958—exceeds the total gross export carried out by this trade. This has been interpreted to mean that, despite the increased watchfulness of the Ministry of Trade and Industry, illegal textile imports for millions of dollars are still coming into the country through the back door of the *IfE* system.

INVESTMENT CENTRE LICENCES

The Investment Centre was founded in accordance with the Law for the Encouragement of Capital Investments, but here we shall be concerned only with its status as a Competent Authority entitled to issue *IwP* licences. An official publication has described this Law as an "important factor in stimulating the flow of capital, both imported and domestic, into productive channels" (102). The activities of the Investment Centre, during the first five years of its existence, showed that nothing was further from reality. Its main function, unwittingly, was to provide a new channel for illicit imports.

Three types of *IwP* licences were granted by the Centre:

I—*Machinery:* The size of the foreign currency investment in the form of machinery (imported or planned to be imported) largely determined the *pro rata* loans from the Development Budget (in IL) and the quantity of the other two types of *IwP* licences. Hence, the invoices for these capital goods were often over-valued; not infrequently investors bought second-hand machinery.

II—*Raw materials and Semi-finished Goods:* "Confirmed" projects received, liberally, *IwP* licences for—Standard IV—raw materials, building materials, etc.

III—*"Working Capital":* Despite the official status of the Investment Centre, its directors were allowed to work on the assumption that no investor would transfer foreign currency at the official *rate.* Any investor who expressed a wish to provide the working capital for his project with his own foreign exchange was given, on application, *IwP* licences for Standard IV goods[1] *not for self-use but for the express purpose of selling them on the black and grey markets.*

The *IwP* licences, II and III, were so profitable that the underhand course followed by a few schemers—to establish plants and import second-hand machinery for the sole purpose of receiving such licences as "by-products"—was commercially not unreasonable. (Some evaded the spirit of the regulations and did not even bring into the country machinery to camouflage their machinations.) Many such cases are quoted in police accounts, State Comptroller reports and journalistic investigations. One case concerned a Mr. K. whose project—to build a hotel on Mount Carmel—was "confirmed". As he claimed to be constructing a hotel, the Investment Centre issued *IwP* licences for building materials and such Standard IV articles as coloured baths, fancy tiles, etc. The suspicion of the officials was aroused only when Mr. M. applied for a licence for a large quantity of fluorescent lamps. An investigator was sent to view the hotel, nearing completion. He found an empty plot of land, in the middle of which a deep hole had been dug (187).

It is perhaps not surprising that official statistics tell us that, at the end of 1956, only one-half of the "confirmed" investment projects

[1] The Minister of Trade and Industry announced in the Knesset on 1st December 1954 that ". . . during the last three years the Government has encouraged the construction of hotels. With this aim in view, investors in the hotel branch have been provided with import licences for building materials in excess of the quantity needed to construct the hotels. This was done (by the authorities) in the full knowledge that the excess quantities would be sold on the free market and the hotel builders would thus acquire their needed liquid resources."

of the 1950–56 period were actually working. If the Centre had studied the fortunes of the projects to which it had granted conditional "confirmation" certificates, it would have found that few only of the contractual undertakings were carried out when these proved unremunerative.

At the end of 1953, a new department of this Centre, the "Oleh Hamashkiah", was opened and given the right to issue import licences to immigrant-merchants, who had a minimum capital of $25,000 and had been for at least three years in the trade in which they wished to re-establish themselves in Israel. The Picker Report (83) lists a number of Standard IV articles which reached Israel through this new channel; the police are convinced that most of the declarations of the applicants were untrue. The State Comptroller (46) says that, despite the explicit opposition of the Ministries of Finance and Trade and Industry, the Investment Centre

". . . issued in many cases import licences although the law did not authorize it to do so. These transgressions were particularly prominent after the department of the 'Oleh Hamashkiah' was founded. . ."

At the end of 1955 the Government dissolved this department and the Ministry of Finance assumed effective control over the Investment Centre in order to close this gap through which *IwP*-Standard IV goods had, for years, come into the country. The immigrant-merchants were now limited to merchandise *IwP* licences of $3,500, but, despite control by the Ministry of Finance, these "rights" were being sold on the Standard IV market in 1956.

"INTERNAL EXPORTS"

The term "internal exports" has several meanings in the language used by the foreign currency controllers, but the only aspect which concerns us at the moment is that which enabled Israeli residents to purchase Standard IV goods illegally for IL. The import, by devious means, of Standard IV articles gave rise to the justified plea of Israeli manufacturers that some of these could be made locally: "if a person is not satisfied with the meagre chocolate ration, why must his black market purchase be a bar of American chocolate sent by an 'uncle' through the post; why should not the 'uncle' purchase a bar of Israeli chocolate for him?" The Ministry of Finance acceded to the request of local producers and allowed them to open sales offices in New York, which sold dollar vouchers, for mailing to Israel, where they could be exchanged for the specified (locally manufactured or assembled) Standard IV article. Barton-Elite for chocolates, Heilig for clothes, several radio firms, Amcor refrigerators and Kaiser-Frazer cars were among these "internal exporters". The Government soon sealed this import channel of Standard IV goods when it learned that many of the "internal exporters" sold their goods (surreptitiously via intermediaries) for IL to local buyers. The purchase of the vouchers was financed by Standard III foreign currency and the buyers invented a "dummy uncle in New York".

"SCRIP COMPANIES"

The economic section of the police estimated that in the years 1951, 1952 and 1953 about $12 million of Standard IV foodstuffs were imported, illegally, into Israel—the major portion through the Scrip and the Standard Food Parcels companies.[1] Picker surmises that 80% of the Standard Food Parcels were financed by black market currency; according to calculations by the police the proportion was even higher than 80%. The court case, in which the Japhets Bank was involved during 1956 and 1957, publicly revealed some of the methods by which Standard IV foodstuffs were imported in collusion with those banks, which supplied the finance in the form of Standard III dollars.

In 1951 Scrip food shops were opened in all the chief towns; their prices were marked in terms of Scrip-dollars and this currency, in theory, was obtainable only from the sales offices of the Scrip companies outside Israel. Donors were urged by a high-pressure advertising campaign in the Jewish press (outside Israel) not to send their relatives goods or vouchers (for specific luxury goods via the "internal exports" schemes) but to make gifts of Scrip-dollars with which the recipients could buy in the special shops. The Scrip companies undertook that $42\frac{1}{2}$% of the foreign exchange sales proceeds would either be sold to the Ministry of Finance for IL or utilized for

[1] This description of the operation of the Scrip companies applies in many relevant details also to the 40 Standard Food Parcels companies. These companies sold—allegedly against foreign currency outside Israel—vouchers for food parcels, which could be exchanged by Israeli residents at their warehouses in Israel. (This system was meant to save the individual donor the trouble of buying foodstuffs, making up the parcel and sending it.) The companies received *IwP* licences for Standard IV foodstuffs which were said to have been financed by the foreign currency of the alleged donors. In fact, these companies bought the foreign currency on the Standard III market and made up a list of fictitious donors.

Two political parties are known to have operated similar companies and, via the import of food parcels, transferred some of the funds, collected abroad by sympathizers, at high *rates*.

the purchase of Israeli goods. The Israeli Pounds, accruing to the companies from exchanging foreign exchange at the legal *rate*, were to cover the distribution costs and the payment of customs duty.[1]

After a few months of operation, the Scrip companies had cornered the black market in foodstuffs and some newspapers regularly published the IL price at which the Scrip-dollar could be illegally purchased. At first, the intermediaries, who bought up large blocks of vouchers with Standard III dollars for resale against IL, inserted the names of fictitious donors on the vouchers. In time, as the supervision of the foreign currency controls administration proved to be lax, the Scrip companies imported foodstuffs without even formally accounting to the Ministry for the names and addresses of individual donors of Scrip-dollars. The Scrip companies sold these Standard IV imports in bulk and consumers, as from 1952, could purchase Standard IV goods from most of their local grocers by paying IL and it became unnecessary to buy Scrip-dollars for IL in order to purchase foodstuffs in the Scrip shops. In the budget year of 1953 the Scrip and Standard Food Parcels companies are said to have sold vouchers for $8.3 million. The maximum amount of genuine foreign exchange (i.e. that currency not purchased by Israelis on the Standard III market) financing these imports is said not to have exceeded $2 million.

What were the net foreign currency receipts of the Ministry of Finance? (The reports of the State Comptroller speak of "faulty" supervision over these companies, and hence the minimum of $42\frac{1}{2}\%$ that they had contracted to sell to the Government was not adhered to.) In 1953 the companies bought goods for $1,750,000 locally but 84% of these were chocolates (*vide* p. 271); these had an import content of 85%. The amount of cash foreign currency exchanged at the legal *rate*, and the value-added—in terms of dollars—of the Israeli products bought by the companies, provided the Ministry with a net foreign currency income of $1\frac{1}{2}$ million as compared with $8.3 million of vouchers. In 1955 the Scrip shops were liquidated on the orders of the Government.

---

[1] Police investigations revealed that most of the Scrip companies were organized by Israeli food importers and run by men of straw in New York. It must, however, be said in defence of the economic ministries that the mirage of $42\frac{1}{2}\%$ of tens of millions of dollars appeared at a time when Israel's balance of payments crisis was at its worst. It is generally agreed today that the Government should not have agreed to this scheme, but those who made the decision in 1951 may justly plead that at the time public pressure was strongly in favour and the black market price of sugar, for example, was then 25 times the official price.

CHAPTER XXII

EXPORTS

An analysis of Israel's external trade statistics reveals an important divergence between the "net foreign currency export earnings" and the "export volume". Table XIV, p. 197, brings out in full relief that two-thirds of the earnings are due to the—chiefly unsubsidized—citrus and diamonds exports whilst the remainder is derived from the heavily subsidized trades.

In a few cases the official *rate*—appreciably below the *average rate*—is paid for export dollars and consequently the export potential in these lines is not fully utilized.

Most of the non-citrus and non-diamonds exports, however, received such substantial subsidies that the *rate* at which the economy pays for $1 of net export earnings is considerably above the *average rate*. They therefore become—by definition—unrequited exports. When only Israeli value-added is exported, the sales to the clearing-dollar markets are unrequited exports *par excellence*. When, however, the articles exported to clearing-dollar countries have a high import content, Israel's balance of payments is improved by the "switch gains" which result from the sale of the intrinsic import content.

THE SIZE OF THE EXPORT EARNINGS

OFFICIAL declarations proclaim that the earnings of visible exports constitute between one-quarter to one-fifth of the country's foreign exchange income. This misleading percentage is the result of the window-dressing of the external trade data and is devoid of any economic purport.

Table XIV has been constructed to present a true picture of the contribution made by visible exports to Israel's total foreign currency receipts. The official data is in terms of nominal-dollars[1] (which equate, for example, the Turkish clearing-dollar with the Canadian dollar); this distortion must clearly be set aside before significant comparisons can be made.

[1] The distortions which originate in not deducting disagios from the clearing-dollar export proceeds are "rectified"—in official statistics—by adjusting the values of the imports from clearing-dollar countries with the appropriate agios.

194

Also, in view of the high import content of the Israeli export products, it is more relevant for a study of the Israeli economy to calculate the value-added of exports—i.e. the net foreign currency earnings—rather than the gross export proceeds.

UNUSED EXPORT POTENTIAL

The foreign currency controls of Israel mostly induced unrequited exports. In a few fields, however, they had the opposite effect of diminishing the export volume by discouraging exports.

The dogmatic restrictions on imports, and/or the clumsiness of the regulations laid down by the Ministry of Finance for international trade, led to the domestic consumption of (latent export) articles at high foreign exchange prices as a substitute for (latent imported) articles with low foreign exchange prices. Elsewhere reference has been made to the unexploited export potential of eggs, hard wheat,[1] groundnuts, olive oil and potatoes.

The inimical effects of the discriminatory low *rates* for citrus exports were discernible between 1949 and 1953 in the marginal output of this branch. Citrus growers can modify (by 10–20%) the quantity of marketable fruit in their groves. They can decide not to pick the "dear-labour-cost-oranges" (i.e. those on the very tops of the trees) and they can vary the amount of certain inputs (e.g. fertilizers) in the months preceding the harvest. This, indeed, is how, until 1954, some of the citrus growers reacted to their low *rates*. Several million dollars of potential earnings from citrus exports are said to have been lost for this reason during the first five seasons after the establishment of the State.

On inexplicable grounds the export of waste products was always discouraged and accorded a low *rate*. This is surprising when one considers that it is an item which sells for hard currency, has a high proportion of value-added and no *IfE* licences are demanded by its exporters. Trade circles claim that, between 1949 and 1953, millions of dollars from this export potential were lost because it did not pay to salvage the waste materials, and trade statistics appear to substantiate this claim. Exports[2] rose steeply after this branch was granted the *rate* of 1.800 in 1954.

The multiple rate system of Israel encouraged exporters to apply in the Government offices of Jerusalem for special *rates* and to plead

---

[1] One example: In 1957 Israel exported hard wheat for $2,522,000. Before 1956 the same hard wheat grown on Israel's soil was fed to the chickens or—at best—used for the baking of bread.

[2] The f.o.b. Haifa value of exported scrap metal rose from 209,000 nominal-dollars in 1953 to 1,341,000 nominal-dollars in 1957.

their cases individually. Moreover, most exporters reacted to the foreign currency controls in a manner which deflected them from the legal course. There are manufacturers who, on the grounds of laziness or morality, were not prepared to adapt themselves to the prevailing practices—their consequent non-performance of exports must be enumerated amongst the damaging effects of these controls.

UNREQUITED (VISIBLE) EXPORTS

According to the criterion of this book, exports are unrequited when:

(a) their foreign currency proceeds are less than their import content (i.e. value-added is negative)—categories A–E below;

(b) the economy pays for the foreign currency proceeds (of the value-added) at a *rate* which is higher than the *average rate*—category F below.

By definition, therefore, the whole of Israel's export volume since 1948 consisted of unrequited exports—the important exceptions are: fresh citrus, diamonds, marble slabs, religious and sentimental articles (e.g. Jordan water, Holy Earth), scrap metal and waste products, stamps. Before classifying the unrequited exports, I shall deal with three possible objections to the usefulness of my definition.

There is a certain difficulty in connoting as "unrequited" those exports which deserve, in theory, to be subsidized. Coen (96) specifies the following articles: those the average costs of which exceed the marginal costs; those the social product of which exceeds the private product; those the private and social costs of which can be lowered by enlarging the scale of production. This implicit plea, that certain articles merit higher *rates* than the *average rate* is most impressive and I would subscribe to it in an academic evaluation. But can this be translated into practical politics? Is there a civil service capable of acting disinterestedly and intelligently according to these precepts? Limiting myself to the country of this case-study, I have no hesitation in rejecting these genuine claims for higher *rates*. A breach—theoretically justified—in the wall of a unitary *rate* is likely to be widened by powerful vested interests for the satisfaction of their—theoretically unjustified—claims to (subsidized) higher *rates*.

It has been said that "unrequited" is not an apposite term to describe those exports, an important attribute of which is to serve as tools of the Foreign Office and/or help to publicize the Israeli economy to potential investors and donors. Undoubtedly exports have played such a role, but my study examines exports only in the light of their calculable economic performance.

TABLE XIV

EXPORT PROCEEDS AS PART OF TOTAL FOREIGN CURRENCY RECEIPTS

	Row	1954/55	1955/56	1956/57	1957/58
Total foreign currency receipts	A	397.9	411.9	506.0	577.0
Total export proceeds	B	88.2	91.0	102.4	130.0
Exports as % of total foreign currency receipts	$C\left(\dfrac{B}{A} \times 100\right)$	22	22	20	23
(Direct) import content—IfE	D	(43.9)	(45.0)	(50.0)	(56.2)
(Indirect) import content—IfE	E	8.8	9.1	10.2	13.0
Deductions on account of over-valued clearing-dollars	F	(4.8)	(5.1)	(5.5)	(5.5)
Sum of factors (to be deducted from A and B)	$G(D + E + F)$	57.5	59.2	65.7	74.7
Total (Deflated) foreign currency receipts	$H(A - G)$	340.4	352.7	440.3	502.3
Value-added in all exports	$I(B - G)$	30.7	31.8	36.7	55.3
Value-added as % of deflated total foreign currency receipts	$J\left(\dfrac{I}{H} \times 100\right)$	9	9	9	11
Value-added in diamonds and citrus	K	21.2	27.4	27.1	34.7
Value-added in diamonds and citrus as % of value-added in all exports	$L\left(\dfrac{K}{I} \times 100\right)$	69	86	74	63
Value-added in all exports less value-added in diamonds and citrus	$M(I - K)$	9.5	4.4	9.6	20.6

Rows A, B, D, E, F and G—millions of nominal-dollars.
Rows H, I, K and M—millions of dollars.
The data for the years 1954/55, 1955/56 and 1956/57 are taken from (published) official statistics; the figures for 1957/58 are ex-ante estimates of the foreign currency controls division of the Ministry of Finance. Whilst all the data refer to the budgetary period of 1/4 to 31/3, those for citrus refer to the period of 1/7 to 30/6.
Sources: (20), (23), (37), (38), (39), (40), (41), (43), (45), (46), (47), (108), (113), (158), (169), (181), (186) and (239).

EXPLANATORY NOTES TO TABLE XIV [1]

[1] I circulated Table XIV (slightly amended) amongst those with an expert knowledge of the Israeli foreign currency controls. The table was published with a description of my working method in the Economic Supplement of *Haaretz* (25/7/56) and in the *Economic Quarterly* (October 1956).

Some of the foreign currency registered as export proceeds is in fact derived from illegal manipulations of Israeli merchants, who buy dollars on the Standard III market and thus artificially swell the amount of value-added in Row M. No account has been taken of this practice in these computations.

Row D: I have relied mainly on the data published by the Ministry of Finance in its current foreign currency budgets which give an estimate of the (direct) *IfE* allocated to potential exporters. (I have not included those materials imported by exporters via the export retention schemes for the production of Standard IV goods to be sold locally.)

Row E: Import content bought by the exporters for IL (e.g. fuel) is represented according to Government estimates by about 10% of the total export proceeds. This is an *average* figure. I have included in this item also the payments by Israeli exporters to their agents abroad for about $2 million per annum.

Row F: To arrive at the dollar value of the export proceeds, I have deducted from the clearing-dollars (in the case of the majority of currencies) the official disagio. I have taken slightly higher disagios for the clearing-dollars of Yugoslavia, Finland and Turkey.

Row G: When we deduct the import content and the disagio of the clearing-dollars from both the export proceeds and the total foreign currency receipts, we arrive in row I at the net foreign currency earnings of visible exports and in row H at the foreign currency receipts of the country available for the domestic economy.

Rows I and J: Value-added, in these rows, is not an imputed value of the exports actually executed. It is the residual item after the direct and indirect *IfE* bought in year X are deducted from the foreign currency proceeds of exports in year X.

Row K: Unlike rows I and J, value-added in this row is an imputed value of the exports actually executed.

Row L: This shows the important role played by diamonds and citrus in Israel's exports.

198

Finally, a few words concerning the approach of the Economic Advisory Staff (72) to the measurement of the *rate* of value-added in export goods. In my computation of *rates* I have empirically included *all* the pecuniary rewards, which the recipient of export earnings squeezes out of the economy. The Economic Advisory Staff calculated the *rate* of value-added only in accordance with the production costs of the article and, consequently, ignored the windfall gains, *pamaz* profits, etc., of the exporter. The *rate* of value-added calculated by the Economic Advisory Staff is, therefore, in most cases lower than my comparative *rate*. My method may be considered more relevant when one wishes to ascertain—ex post—which of Israel's exports were unrequited. The method of the Economic Advisory Staff is a more useful guide for surmising which of Israel's exports are likely to be viable if the present foreign currency controls are abrogated.

CATEGORIES OF UNREQUITED EXPORTS:

It will be assumed throughout this section that *IfE* goods can be re-exported, unchanged and untreated; furthermore, there are assumed to be no transport costs in conveying goods to and from Israel.

A—An exporter buys *IfE* goods at the *rate* of, say, 1 and exports them at the *rate* of, say, 1.800. In such a pattern of exchange rates he can afford to sell abroad $1 of *IfE* goods for $0.90. The result is that there is a net loss to the economy of foreign currency, but a net gain in IL for the exporter.

Similar consequences ensue when an exporter buys an undervalued imported commodity domestically. Many (indirect) *IfE* components can be bought at IL prices, which correspond to a low *rate*, and are sold (incorporated within the exported article) at a higher *rate*.[1]

B—An exporter buys *IfE* goods for $1 and re-exports them for, say, 1.10 clearing-dollars. If we assume that the real value of the clearing-dollar is only $0.90, the result is a net loss of foreign currency to the economy, but—if the official *rate* for this cledo is the same as for $1—a net gain of IL to the exporter.

Not infrequently this occurred with exports to Turkey, Yugoslavia and Finland, the clearing-dollars of which were deliberately over-

---

[1] The same pernicious effect, produced by multiple rates in Israel, can be studied in countries with a unitary rate when a product with a high import content is heavily subsidized. This is what happened to British eggs, which were sold for a smaller amount of foreign currency—during the spring of 1957—than their import content. *The Economist* commented that "it would be hard to find in the history of commerce a more blatantly irrational trade-flow than that of subsidized British eggs to the continent of Europe" (188). Apparently the commentator had never heard of Israel's system of multiple exchange rates!

valued by the Ministry of Finance to give exporters a disguised subsidy.

(The regulations issued in December 1957 by the foreign currency controls administration prohibiting the export to clearing-dollar countries of articles with a value-added of less than 20%—and to Turkey of less than 45%—are an official, retrospective confirmation that in the past some exports for clearing-dollar payments have not been meritorious).

C—An exporter buys *IfE* goods for $1 and sells them for $0.90 abroad. He sends his buyer an invoice for $1.20, however, and this sum is, indeed, remitted by the foreign firm and paid into the exporter's *pamaz* account. The Israeli merchant reimburses the foreign firm for the $0.30 by buying this amount on the Standard III market. This export deal is only profitable to the Israeli merchant, when the *pamaz* ("value-added") of $0.20 is sold in Israel at a higher IL price than the costs of buying $0.30 on the Standard III market. The economy clearly suffers a loss of foreign exchange. This is a widespread practice amongst those exporters, who are entitled to *pamaz* (and similar) privileges; in 1959 the State Comptroller (290) publicly criticized the economic ministries on this score.

D—There is a further type of export the foreign currency proceeds from which are smaller than the import content—the economy loses foreign currency but the firm also makes some IL losses. In the economic climate of Israel considerable prestige is derived by manufacturers from the performance of exports. Several firms, including public corporations, have exported (at a loss) in the hope of gaining the sympathy of government departments.[1]

E—There are exports—"forced exports"—which create a void on the domestic market that is filled by imports of the same or similar articles. In some cases the foreign exchange cost of these imports exceeds the foreign exchange earnings of the "forced exports".[2]

---

[1] The Histadruth economist, Ben-Nathan, complains that the export of phosphates, organized by a government corporation, constitutes a "free gift to the customers in the Far East". He relates that thousands of tons have been sold, c.i.f., for $12.10; the freight from Haifa costs $5 and the transport from the Negev (where the phosphates are mined) to Haifa comes to IL12.

[2] In 1953 (225) 82,000 tons of cement were exported—three-quarters of which went to Turkey. Yet it appears that the export of Israeli cement did not improve Israel's balance of payments, for it can be learned that "large quantities of cement were ordered from Germany . . . and will arrive in about four to six weeks. The decision to order the cement from Germany . . . was arrived at in view of the shortage of cement in the country and the unwillingness of the Government to cut down the amount of cement to be exported".

Those who will one day write the economic history of Israel will probably note with astonishment that, in the Dov Josef period, oranges were at times

F—The exporter uses local resources to turn $1 of *IfE* into export articles of, say, $1.20—the $0.20 of genuine value-added is paid for by the economy at a *rate* above the *average rate* (*vide* Appendix VII, p. 268).

The only thorough investigation of *pamaz* subsidies was carried out by Gottlieb-Golan and covers the years 1954 and 1955. The material rewards of the exporters are not all reflected in the *rates* of the following table, for this cited study does not take into account the financial aspects of the supplementary subsidies (2), (178).

PAMAZ-FINANCED-IMPORTS SOLD EFFECTIVELY AT THE RATE OF:

3.854	.	food
3.149	.	textiles
3.352	.	leather
2.605	.	chemicals
2.775	.	metals
2.500	.	plywood
2.000	.	tyres
2.995	.	miscellaneous
3.052	.	average

These figures are averages for classes of goods and hide the most

rationed, maximum price orders on fresh citrus fruit existed and offenders were brought before the courts for operating on a citrus black market. During the harvest a special constabulary of temporary inspectors was enrolled to help the police in the drive to export the maximum quantity of oranges. Press reports tell us: ". . . this week the black market price of grapefruits and tangerines fluctuated between 350–400 Prutoth per kg., whilst the official price is 260 Prutoth. No tangerines are released this week for the home market . . . as the fruit is reserved for export." The Marketing Board published, at its own expense, the following advertisement in the daily press to deter potential offenders in the farming community (216): "On a path off the main highway, near Ramath Gan, a cart with six sacks of oranges was discovered without the driver being in possession of a Movement Order. He was arrested and the fruit confiscated. Legal action is being taken against the farmer from whose grove the oranges are said to have come."

The artificial shortage of fresh fruit caused by this coercive policy of "forced citrus exports" was relieved, in part, by the devious *IwP* of fresh apples, pears, tinned fruit, dried fruit, etc., at *rates* of 4–7. It has been remarked, with some apparent justice, that if in 1953 $500,000 of citrus would have been diverted from the export markets to the Israeli domestic market, the diminished demand for alternative luxury fruit would have cut the import bill by more than $500,000 and there would have been no need to ration "Jaffas" in Israel.

In 1958 the following was reported: "Israel . . . was forced to introduce the rationing of oranges in the home market in order to meet the export requirements of the canning industry" (45).

extreme *rates*. Thus the *pamaz* value of a raincoat manufacturer (in the textiles group) was 3.908; the *pamaz* value of a beverages exporter (in the food group) was 6.311; the *pamaz* value of a radio exporter (in the metals group) was 5.917.—The *average rate* at the time of investigation was approximately 1.850.

The *pamaz* system led to the partial realization of Tsour's ideal (*vide* p. 127), i.e. the "deepening" of the productive processes in Israel's industry and an increase in the percentage of value-added in export goods.[1]

In 1956 the hitherto separate import and export departments of the Ministry of Trade and Industry were organized within the joint framework of a Foreign Trade Division. This administrative reshuffle was meant to help in the implementation of the policy of surreptitiously taxing imports (without the formal assent of parliament) in order to provide exporters with supplementary subsidies. The Foreign Trade Division informed the members of defined trading branches[2] (e.g. ball-points manufacturers) that in future the whole quota of raw materials (reserved in the Foreign Currency Budget for their branch) would be allocated exclusively to those firms which had exported part of their output. The Ministry quite deliberately intended manufacturers, who had not found it profitable even under the *pamaz* system to export, to incur losses and buy the privilege of receiving allocations for the home market by "forced exports".

This new technique, as well as the *pamaz* system, demanded administrative dealings with individual firms. The foreign currency controller's department preferred, however, the autonomous organization of branches into closely-knit cartels. The banana cartel is a case in point. The Government assured it of complete Tozereth Haaretz protection and the farmers, in turn, undertook to export a part of their crop. The farmers received the same price for their bananas whether they were exported or sold domestically. The cartel

[1] Assume that the *average rate* of 2.500 was in 1957 turned into a unitary *rate* and all export subsidies and import restrictions were simultaneously abolished. In such circumstances it would not pay any manufacturer to create value-added at a *rate* exceeding 2.499. Under the *pamaz* system, however, the ceiling on the production costs of $1 value-added is set by the price for which the *pamaz* imports can be sold domestically and the value of the other calculable subsidies. Limiting ourselves to the *pamaz* subsidy, the radio exporter in the Gottlieb-Golan study can clearly bid for domestic factors up to the point at which the marginal costs of $1 value-added correspond to the *rate* of 5.916.

[2] In June 1958 the Ministry of Trade and Industry gave similar instructions to the plate-glass and asbestos industries and in February 1959 the system was to be applied to many other industries (289).

202

imposed—what the State Comptroller has called (46)—"non-authorized" taxes on local sales and subsidized exports with the proceeds, thus releasing the Government from the necessity of making budgetary provision for subsidies to this branch.

The honey cartel enjoyed Government support "for it freed the Ministry of Finance from the obligation to allocate sugar to honey producers" (218). The cartel sold a ton of honey at home for IL1,200 and abroad for $380. With the proceeds from the export of 1 ton of honey, the cartel imported 3½ tons of sugar. In view of the dear price of sugar on the black and grey markets, this constituted a very high effective *rate*.

CLEARING-DOLLARS

Leaving out the special case of the Yugoslav–Finland–Turkey group, the signing of trade agreements has not helped to improve the balance of payments. Israel has not succeeded in exporting within the framework of the trade agreements appreciable quantities of goods with a high value-added. Those articles (e.g. citrus) which proved the exception would also, in the absence of a trade agreement, have been bought by most clearing-dollar countries and/or Israel could have sold them at competitive prices in other markets; the Citrus Marketing Board had to ration supplies to the United Kingdom (which paid in hard currency) in order to export to clearing-dollar countries. The goods which were sold for clearing-dollars often had a high import content (e.g. woollen yarn) and the net earnings from these exports were small. In return for the doubtful advantage of selling to the clearing-dollar markets, Israel bought in these countries at discriminatory prices. In practice, trade agreements countries (e.g. France, Holland, Italy) maintained two sets of prices; one against payment in clearing-dollars and one against payment in hard currency. Without trade agreements Israel could have bought more advantageously in these countries with its hard currency.[1]

[1] An important by-product and, at times, the *raison d'être* of trade agreements is the provision of a framework for triangular trade. Trued-Mikesell (219) state in their report: ". . . a substantial volume of multilateral trade has taken place within the system of bilateral agreements through transit transactions. The financing of purchases for export to third countries through the agreements may have taken place with or without the agreement of both countries to the transaction." The soundest description of "switch markets" (97) is given by de Vries-Keesing. The authors appear, however, in their enthusiasm to establish economic generalizations concerning these consistent breaches of bilateral agreements, to treat too lightly the illegality of the transactions they describe. Some Israeli merchants engaged in "switch" transactions and, in so doing, returned to the Israeli economy through a back door, some of the advantages of

These general remarks apply to 15 of Israel's 18 trade agreements. As is evident from Table XV, p. 211, Yugoslavia, Finland and Turkey were by far the most important clearing-dollar markets and the special problems of exporting to these countries will be illustrated by an examination of the trade with Turkey. (The Yugoslav–Finland–Turkey trade agreements will be viewed, at this stage, only from the point of whether the Israeli economy recorded a net foreign currency loss or gain in its dealings with these countries; I shall not now consider the *rate* of producing $1 of marginal value-added.)

The first to make a quantitative study (covering the clearing agreements with Finland, Turkey and Poland during 1950 and part of 1951) was Golan (220). He concluded that by trading with these countries, Israel suffered a net loss of foreign currency. Israel paid a sum of 1,302,000 clearing-dollars in excess of the free dollar price of similar imports; Israel sold its exports to these countries for prices which were 737,000 clearing-dollars in excess of what it would have received in the free markets of the world had it been paid in free dollars.

In 1956 Kessler (221) concluded that, in effect, Israel made no overall gains or losses in its trade with Turkey. This was based on a detailed investigation[1] of the Israel–Turkey trade agreement in 1953, according to which Israel's export clearing-dollar prices to Turkey were 19% above the (world market) free dollar prices and the Turkish clearing-dollar export prices to Israel were 17% above the (world market) free dollar prices.

I have had access to the data in the archives of the Ministry of Finance from which it can be inferred that Israel, in 1954 and 1955, made a definite net foreign currency profit from its trade with

international trade which had been blunted by the knife of bilateralism. There have been unconfirmed press reports that the Israeli foreign currency controls administration was aware of some of these operations. It seems doubtful whether the Ministry of Finance, being aware of such triangular trade, would have approved of it.

[1] Kessler's data is derived from official trade statistics and information supplied by merchants. An Economic Advisory Staff member, who was handed similar data on comparative international prices, spurned them as inconclusive for, *inter alia*, he had "serious doubts as to whether they are truly the minimum U.S. prices" (222). In my view Kessler did not take sufficient account of the qualitative differences between free dollar and clearing-dollar purchases.

Actually, official trade statistics tell but part of the story concerning Israeli purchases for clearing-dollars. I have been able to check on two large purchases of foodstuffs by Israeli importers in Turkey and found that part of the payment was in hard currency and part in clearing-dollars. At times the Turkish Government officially made the export of certain Turkish goods to Israel conditional on the delivery by Israel of "hard currency goods" (e.g. sugar and coffee).

Turkey. I shall elaborate (*vide* p. 209) the nature of this gain after an indispensable digression.

A country sells goods for clearing-dollars (which are—legally—inconvertible currencies) on the assumption that it can buy suitably priced goods with the clearing-dollars and can sell the goods legally at home, or resell them illegally in the world markets. The true value of Israeli exports to Turkey is, therefore, the imputed dollar value of the Turkish goods that are bought with the clearing-dollar export proceeds. The value of the Israeli exports to Turkey can be ascertained by studying either the free dollar prices, in other supply centres, of goods similar to those imported from Turkey or (*vide* category D below) the free dollar prices at which these Turkish goods could be acquired on the "switch markets".

Assume that commodity Z is freely available in Turkey, in January 1955, for 7.60 (Turkish) Liras:

A—The black market price ("Standard III") of the dollar in Turkey was then 7.60 Liras (49). Hence the "*first*" price at which Z could have been bought was $1. (This is a theoretical price for most potential foreign buyers, because the Turkish authorities do not grant export licences for goods acquired in this manner. However it is an effective price for foreign residents, tourists and smugglers, who are able to take the goods out of the country without a licence. A case has recently come to light in which a famous Swiss company bought Turkish goods with Liras acquired in this type of transaction and had the goods smuggled to Syria and re-exported from there.)

B—The official exchange rate for all foreign currencies, at parity with the dollar, was 2.80 Liras. Buyers with U.S. dollars, however, received at that time an export premium of 50%. Thus the "*second*" price for Z was $1.81.

C—Buyers from countries that have a trade agreement with Turkey (except E.P.U. countries) received an export premium of 25%. Thus a "*third*" price for Z was 2.17. (Alternatively it is $1.95 Israeli clearing-dollars.[1])

D—An effective exchange rate for the Turkish Lira is that quoted in Switzerland (and other financial centres) for "retour switches", i.e. a selling price for Turkish Liras plus the required export licences for the goods which the buyer of the currency specifies he wishes to acquire in Turkey. Certain countries (for example Czechoslovakia, Finland, Yugoslavia and Poland) offered Liras at a discount, against

[1] In January 1955, when the official *rate* was 1.800, the Ministry of Finance imposed a disagio of 10% on the Turkish clearing-dollar. Whilst the Israeli exporter had his clearing-dollars transformed by his bank into $0.90, the Israeli importer bought his clearing-dollars for IL1.620.

dollars. (The discount rate must be applied to the effective buying price of \$2.17, category C and not to the official rate.) Pick (49) cites a discount rate of 28% in January 1955 and I have been shown a Swiss offer of 25% on approximately the same date. Therefore, by purchasing Turkish Liras in this manner the buyer, who is willing to offend against the foreign currency controls of Turkey, could buy Z at a "*fourth*" price of \$1.56–1.63.[1]

One can now catalogue the different prices at which the Israeli importer could have bought Z,[2] if he had been allocated foreign exchange at the official *rate* by the Ministry of Finance:

"First price"	IL1.800 : \$1.00
"Second price"	IL3.258 : \$1.81
"Third price"	IL3.510 : \$2.17
"Fourth price"	IL2.871 : \$1.59½

The "first" price may be disregarded for most commercial transactions. The lowest prices at which the Israeli importer could have acquired Z were the "second" and "fourth" ones, but the Ministry of Finance neither placed U.S. dollars at his disposal nor permitted him to buy on the "switch market". He was, therefore, forced to purchase Z at the highest, i.e. the "third", price: IL.3.510. Although this price already included the 10% disagio of the Ministry of Finance, it still over-valued the Turkish clearing-dollar. The Ministry compelled Israeli merchants to buy at this price (by issuing for certain goods import licences "valid only in Turkey") and exerted pressure on government purchasing agencies to buy in Turkey.

The overvaluation of the Turkish clearing-dollar was a boon to the Israeli exporters, who had to be restrained by the authorities in their eagerness to export to this lucrative market at the *given exchange rates*. In the following model, it will be assumed that there are no

[1] "In Turkey, last week, U.S. buyers of the new tobacco crop found their hard-cash deals being squeezed by satellite countries. Americans buy at the official rate of 2.8 Liras to the dollar. The Communists pay in barter deals at a rate of 14–15 Liras to the dollar, covering the cost by boosting prices of their goods. Much of the Red-bought tobacco does not go to satellite citizens, but is eventually sold in the U.S. for dollars. Since U.S. companies have recently found a better, cheaper tobacco in Greece, they are not worried by Red competition in Turkey. But the Turks are losing badly-needed dollars which the Communists are getting instead" (235). The exchange rates quoted in this journalistic account are incorrect but the trading operations are accurately sketched.

[2] These figures are no longer current. When the *ipso facto* Turkish devaluation, during August 1958, was carried out, the black market price of the Lira ("Standard III") had soared to \$1:14 Liras; the Swiss-quoted discount rates were then as high as 40% (11); the disagio of the Israeli Ministry of Finance was 30%.

transport costs between Turkey and Israel and that the IL costs to transform *IfE* goods into export articles[1] are nil:

(A) An Israeli exporter who turns $100 of *IfE* into 111 clearing-dollars or less, will not make any personal profit and will involve the economy in a loss of foreign currency. An Israeli exporter who turns $100 of *IfE* into an article selling in Turkey for 111 clearing-dollars, will have just covered his costs. The Ministry of Finance will exchange his 111 clearing-dollars for the IL equivalent of $100, i.e. IL180. The economy which values the clearing-dollar at the "fourth" price will, however, lose foreign currency unless $100 of *IfE* are turned into at least 136.05 clearing-dollars.

(B) An Israeli exporter who turns $100 of *IfE* into 111.01–136.04 clearing-dollars will make an IL profit for his private account, but the economy will lose foreign currency.

(C) An Israeli exporter, who turns $100 of *IfE* into 136.05 clearing-dollars or more, will make a large IL profit and a net foreign currency gain will accrue to the economy.[2]

The last type of export (C) merits a more detailed analysis. It is meaningless to search for "the" internal price level in countries such as Turkey and Israel. The vagaries of the multiple exchange rates gave Turkey, in January 1955, a series of price levels for imported goods, which stretched from the price of 3 Liras to 12 Liras per $1 of imports. The astute manipulators of currencies planned, therefore, to secure Turkish import licences for those goods which corresponded to Standard IV articles in our Israeli model. *There was a correlation between the import content of Israeli exports and the place of Israeli exports on the ladder of the Turkish price levels.* The lower the value-added of Israeli exports, the higher the rung on the ladder to which the article could climb (i.e. the higher the Liras remuneration per $1 of imports). Israel, from the point of view of its balance of payments, benefited most when the import content of its export goods remained, recognizably, *unchanged*. The highest rung on the ladder was reached when Israeli exports consisted of

---

[1] 90% of the *IfE* licences for exports destined for clearing-dollar markets were issued for goods from hard-currency countries (223).

[2] It is possible to arrive at the same conclusion by the following course: an Israeli exporter turns $$x$ (of direct and indirect *IfE*) into y Turkish clearing-dollars. The clearing-dollars are then sold on the Swiss "switch market" (or Turkish goods bought with them and re-exported to the world markets) for $$z$. If z is larger than x, the economy will have gained from this transaction. The foreign currency controls of Israel did not, in practice, provide opportunities to measure in this way the meritorious success of exports to Turkey.

hard-currency raw materials or re-exports of finished articles with the imprint of "Made in England" or "U.S. product".[1]

The *pamaz* system (*vide* p. 138) gave an incentive to producers to use, in the manufacture of an export product, as few direct *IfE* as was technically possible. The opposite occurred with exports to clearing-dollar countries, such as Turkey; the exporters aimed to incorporate within their clearing-dollar export articles as many—recognizable—*IfE* inputs as the Israeli authorities permitted. The reason, already implied, was the willingness of the Turkish consumer to be progressively more generous in his Liras-per-$1 payment when the *IfE* components of the Israeli export article could still be recognized. The laurels must, therefore, be awarded to that part of Israel's export industry which only "packaged dollar goods", for these "switch factories" netted the economy a larger foreign exchange gain than the factories with a high proportion of value-added.

The offices of the foreign currency controls department were well aware of the many rungs on the Turkish price ladder and, in their view, a high disagio should have been fixed for the Turkish clearing-dollar and/or only those goods should have been given an export licence which sold at prices corresponding to the highest rungs of the ladder. The net foreign currency gain from Israel's exports to Turkey could have been very much larger, had the foreign currency controls administration been permitted to pursue a policy of granting export licences to Turkey only for (Turkish) "Standard IV" articles. This notion of the Government's experts was too sophisticated to become the basis for official policy. In addition, a united front of the Histadruth unions and the Manufacturers Association pressed the Government, successfully, not to intervene unduly with industrial exports to Turkey.

One of the two assumptions with which we have hitherto worked, can now be laid aside, namely that which said that *IfE* goods are turned into clearing-dollar exports without any IL expenditure.— Let it be assumed that the wages of Israeli labourers to assemble a certain vehicle are IL2 and that the price of the assembled vehicle is 1

[1] In extreme cases genuine Israeli value-added lowered the Liras-per-$1 price of the article and the Israeli product was sold in Turkey at a lower price than would have been paid for its "pure" import content. (An Israeli merchant re-exports, without treating it, a $100 machine from Switzerland for, say, 1,000 Liras. The Swiss firm, for a second transaction, sends the Israeli merchant the components of the same machine at a cost of $90. The Israeli merchant assembles the machine under the supervision of the Swiss firm, making it qualitatively equal to that assembled in Switzerland. Yet the consignment of the second machine is more likely to fetch only 850 Liras. In this case Israel's genuine value-added is a negative factor in the "switch" of foreign currencies.)

clearing-dollar higher than the price for which the unassembled *IfE* components of the vehicle could have been sold in Turkey. (It is assumed in this case that Israeli value-added has a positive valuation in Turkey.) If the Israeli exporter receives from the Ministry of Finance only IL1.620 per 1 clearing-dollar, he has clearly lost by the application of Israeli labour to the *IfE*. Nevertheless, the employment of Israeli labour to process *IfE* (assembling machines or "packaging dollar goods") was a prerequisite for the transformation of hard currency into clearing-dollars. Although that transaction was most profitable to the Israeli merchant, in which "pure" foreign goods were turned into clearing-dollars, traders needed the stamp of "Made in Israel" to obtain an export licence from Israel and an import licence into Turkey. Whilst the employment of Israeli factors could, thus, not be dispensed with entirely, the commercial consideration of every manufacturer-exporter, in this type of trade, was to minimize the input of domestic factors in the preparation of export articles.

The net effect of the Turkish export-import trade upon Israel's balance of payments can be expressed in the following equation:

Gains from exchanging *IfE* foreign exchange into clearing-dollars

$$\text{at a ratio above } \frac{100}{136}$$

PLUS

positive value of Israeli value-added

LESS

losses from exchanging *IfE* foreign exchange into clearing-dollars

$$\text{at a ratio below} \frac{100}{136}$$

LESS

negative value of Israeli value-added

$$= \text{net foreign exchange gain or loss.}$$

The (unpublished) data in the archives of the Ministry of Finance leave little doubt that the equation denotes a foreign currency gain.

A guess can be hazarded as to the position if no clearing agreements had existed between the Yugoslav-Finland-Turkey group and Israel. In that case, certain unrequited exports, which led to a net foreign exchange loss for the economy, could not have been performed. Furthermore, by buying at the "fourth" price, Israel—to quote from our Turkish model—could have paid for its imports at free dollar prices $26\frac{1}{2}\%$ below the clearing-dollar prices at which it actually paid.

Yet the Ministry of Finance gladly forewent these two sets of advantages. They were more than offset by the advantage which accrued to those countries that knew how to exploit the latent opportunities of a trade agreement. Foreign goods (as *IfE* in Israeli products) which turned $100 into more than 136.05 clearing-dollars, were allowed into Turkey only by virtue of the trade agreements. The pre-condition for open and disguised "switches" was a mutual trade agreement. If Turkey had operated a unitary exchange rate or if it had refused import licences for Israeli consignments which (indirectly) transformed $100 into more than 136.05 clearing-dollars—the clearing arrangement with Turkey would have aided Israel's balance of payments as little as did its treaties with, say, Holland and Italy.

The trading, and not the manufacturing, abilities of Israel's exporters accounted for the net foreign currency gain in the trade with Turkey. Finally, one may inquire as to the price in local resources at which this income item in the balance of payments was earned. The assembly units and the "packaging plants"[1] attracted investment funds by the promise of quick and substantial returns, and its owners could afford to hire local factors for employment on uneconomic, high-cost production processes.

Some, who admit that Israel's balance of payments benefited in the past from these clearing-dollar exports, consider the trading gains (which accrued from the exchange of hard currency for the clearing-dollars of the Yugoslav-Finland-Turkey group) to have only been windfall profits of a passing phase. The recent internal changes in Israel's three main clearing-dollars markets appear to indicate that the establishment of many of the "packaging of dollar goods factories" has been a misallocation of resources.

---

[1] "A representative of the well-known French perfume concern P. is now in Israel . . . in order to organize the export of goods which cannot be marketed directly by the concern P. (from Paris). The export opportunities of Israel have encouraged the French concern to enlarge its base in Israel, so that cosmetics can be packed there and then sent to Turkey, Greece, Cyprus, Norway, Finland, Ghana and other countries" (17).

TABLE XV

CLEARING-DOLLAR EXPORTS AS PART OF TOTAL EXPORTS
(millions of nominal-dollars)

	Row	1953	1954	1955	1956	1957
MERCHANDISE EXPORTS						
All countries	A	56.5	86.2	87.4	103.8	136.1
Non-clearing-dollar countries	B	35.4	50.0	51.4	68.3	80.6
Clearing-dollar countries	C	21.1	36.2	36.0	35.5	55.5
YFT[1]	D	14.0	20.6	19.9	14.3	20.6
EXPORT TO CLEARING-DOLLAR COUNTRIES AS % OF TOTAL EXPORTS	E	37	42	41	34	41
MERCHANDISE EXPORTS WITHOUT CITRUS AND DIAMONDS						
All countries	F	22.2	35.3	35.1	39.1	55.6
Non-clearing-dollar countries	G	8.4	11.6	12.9	18.7	16.2
Clearing-dollar countries	H	13.8	23.7	22.2	20.4	39.4
YFT[1]	I	12.6	19.1	16.9	10.2	15.8
CLEARING-DOLLAR EXPORTS AS % OF TOTAL EXPORTS	J	63	67	63	52	71
YFT[1] EXPORTS AS % OF TOTAL EXPORTS	K	57	54	48	26	29
YFT[1] EXPORTS AS % OF CLEARING-DOLLAR EXPORTS	L	91	81	76	50	40

Sources as per Table XIV, p. 197.

[1] YFT: Yugoslavia, Finland and Turkey. A remarkable change in the destination of Israel's export volume is the decline of the exports to YFT (without citrus and diamonds)—from 57% in 1953 to 29% in 1957 (row K) and from 91% in 1953 to 40% in 1957 (row L).

211

CHAPTER XXIII

DEVALUATION

"I prefer twelve different exchange rates to one devaluation." (P. Saphir, Minister of Trade and Industry, 1/10/1957).

> So far I have advanced the proposition that a better use could have been made of Israel's foreign currency receipts if a unitary rate had prevailed.
>
> In this chapter I shall argue that, if the *average rate* had been chosen as the unitary *rate*, the IL, though freed from the distortions caused by the multiple rates, would still have been overvalued in relation to the dollar.
>
> The past devaluations of the IL are traced in terms of the movements of the *average rate* and their beneficial consequences are shown to be reflected in the changed composition of Israel's imports and the reshuffled Israeli production pattern.
>
> It is suggested that this commendable process of carrying the IL *rate* towards its true value could advantageously be continued.

THE first devaluation, in 1949, left no significant repercussions and the step was generally approved. The second and third devaluations were opposed by those who had been privileged to receive allocations of dollars at low official *rates* and had made handsome profits from this favourable treatment. The fourth devaluation is meeting with less opposition from these vested interests because the value-pegged clauses in Government loans and other measures have considerably reduced the differential profits of those who are allocated dollars at the official *rate*.

The consummation of the second devaluation—the progressive abrogation of the lower official *rates* and the initiation of the new set of multiple rates, which marked the beginning of the third devaluation—met with the resistance of members of the Economic Advisory Staff (B. R. Bell, O. Gass, A. P. Lerner and others). They argued along the lines of Alexander (196) that an (under-developed) economy is better served by import restrictions than by an outright devaluation. In their view the axiom postulated by Mikesell (217)

212

applied to Israel: "Until countries have achieved a reasonable amount of internal stability, an improvement in the trade balance through devaluation would be quickly dissipated by price rises". The discussion[1], in Israel, on the conceivable consequences of a devaluation centred in the traditional question of the effect on the balance of trade. I shall suggest below that this criterion was not a sound one by which to judge the merits of a devaluation *in Israel*.

Two arguments, specific to the Israeli scene, were adduced in favour of the Alexander-Mikesell position: one related to the disparity between imports and exports, and the other to the "value-pegging epidemics". A responsible official of the Ministry of Finance stated the first argument in the following manner: "If it is proposed to devalue the IL *in order to aid exports*, the Government can do the job better, without devaluation, by subsidizing $100 of exports and leaving untouched (the IL prices of) $1,000 of imports."

The second argument was advanced by several economists, but most zealously by Lerner. He maintained that the escalator clause in the national wage agreements would automatically raise the domestic price level and wipe out any temporary benefits derived from a devaluation. [Patinkin has been less outspoken than Lerner, but from passages in his writings (32) it can be inferred that he shared Lerner's views on the actual repercussions of the first two devaluations on the domestic price level.] Lerner's theory, to be found in several confidential memoranda to the Government, has been summarized by his assistant in the Economic Advisory Staff:

"It is now possible to go one step further and define the automatic cost-of-living allowance as an institutional device which is expressly designed to perpetuate for ever this fundamental distortion in the Israeli economy, come what may. Every devalua-

[1] The implicit assumption in the models constructed by most of the economists who have discussed the effects of devaluation upon the balance of trade or upon the terms of trade, is that the *volume of the imports of a country is almost exactly equal to the volume of its exports*. Two examples: ". . . a 10% depreciation of B's currency is equivalent to a 10% duty on B's imports, the revenue from which is used to finance a 10% subsidy on B's exports" (75).—". . . where the elasticity of demand for imports is just as much above zero as the elasticity of demand for exports is below unity, the sum of the elasticity is unity" (197). To measure the efficacy of a devaluation, we are asked to examine whether the sum of the two elasticities is more or less than unity. This, according to Lerner, will also give an answer to the question as to what movement in the import or export balance will occur in consequence of the devaluation. It is implicitly assumed in both Meade's and Lerner's models that total imports and exports are equal. I suggest that, on the score of the large disparity between Israel's imports and exports, many of the traditional theories on devaluation are not applicable to the Israeli foreign currency controls.

213

tion of the IL by forcing up the domestic price level automatically drives up nominal wage rates by a corresponding amount via the C-o-L. allowance and therefore brings us back bye and large to the former distorted relationship just at a higher turn of the spiral" (198).

In 1957 Lerner published in America the following comment on the Israeli devaluations:

"A tax on imports, just like the devaluation of the monetary unit, increases the domestic prices of imported goods and this raises the Cost-of-Living Index and the automatic C-o-L. allowance. This means an increase in costs, so that domestic prices are forced up, and with them the C-o-L. allowance, and again costs and prices, and so on. This process results in domestic prices rising as much as import prices and the effects of the devaluation, or of the taxes and subsidies, are completely negated" (226).

These quotations say explicitly that the rise in the domestic price level not only dissipates *some* beneficial results of the devaluation—as I shall suggest below—but that it *completely* dissipates them.

The Polak-Chang formula[1] (202) measures the efficacy of a devaluation by comparing the subsequent rise in the domestic price level with the rate by which the currency has been depreciated. I have applied this formula to Israel and the results are classified in Table XVI.[2] They show the *average rate* to have risen by 400% and the cost-of-living index by 169%; the three devaluations were—in the language of the Polak-Chang formula—58% successful. (The Polak-Chang formula measures only the rise in the domestic price level of the devaluing country. If its implicit assumption is dropped,

[1] Let us assume that the dollar has a constant value and the currency of country X, in terms of the dollar, is devalued by 50%. In the Polak-Chang formula this devaluation is expressed (in index form) by a movement of the index of currency X from the base of 100 (before devaluation) to 200 (after the 50% devaluation). If the domestic price level in country X rises subsequent to the devaluation by 100%, the "success" of the devaluation is nil. If the price level does not rise at all, the "success" is 100%. If the price level rises, say, by 40% after the currency was devalued by 50%, the "success" is 60%.

[2] The effects of the three devaluations can be studied by following the movements of the *average rates*—0.450 (June 1949) to 2.250 (June 1956). The repercussions of the depreciation of the IL upon the Israeli price level have been examined in relation to the Israel cost-of-living index. The rise of this index between June 1949 and December 1957 tells us about the "success" of the devaluations between June 1949 and June 1956. I have allowed for a time lag of eighteen months so that the full secondary and tertiary effects of the devaluations could work themselves out on the internal price level.

214

that the price level of the rest of the world has not changed and the fact that it has risen during this period is taken into account, the "success" is greater than 58%.)

TABLE XVI

THE MEASUREMENTS OF THREE DEVALUATIONS

Date	Average Rate		ISRAEL	U.S.
	IL	Index	C-o-L. Index	C-o-L. Index
		(June 1949 =100)	(June 1949 =100)	(Average 1947–49=100)
June 1949	0.450	100	100	100
June 1956	2.250	500	(254)	(116)
December 1957	(2.500)	(556)	269	122

How did the first three devaluations affect the preference of the Israeli consumers for Israeli products relative to imports? *Ceteris paribus*, the replacement ratio[1] appears to have shifted from IL0.450 : \$1 to IL2.250 : \$1. However, the replacement ratio has, in fact, moved from IL0.450 : \$1 to IL1.134 : \$1. The devaluations from IL0.450 to IL2.250 (followed by an increase—eighteen months after the last devaluation—in the price level by 169% in Israel and 22% in America) had the same results as if the *rate* of the IL had been moved from 0.450 to 1.134 without any subsequent change in the price level: $\dfrac{2.500 \times 122}{269}$. If it is assumed that the total effective money demand is suitably adjusted, and if the attendant changes in the Israeli and American prices are ignored, then the Israeli consumers who had in 1949 only found it profitable to buy domestic articles—similar to those that could be imported for \$1—when they were produced in Israel at a price of below IL0.450, found it, in 1957, advantageous to buy such articles at a price of up to IL1.134.

I must digress at this stage to interpose some remarks on the

[1] I use this term in preference to the more familiar, but possibly ambiguous, expression "substitution ratio".

peculiarity of Israel's external trade. In "normal" economies a devaluation affects the volume of exports because the foreign consumer can, subsequent to a devaluation, buy the local currency at a cheaper price, and because those exporters who are faced with an elastic foreign demand for their products can sometimes afford to reduce their export prices. However, apart from the buyers of goods which are smuggled out of the country, Israeli goods cannot be bought for IL as the foreign currency controls lay down that all exports must be priced, and paid for, in foreign currency.

The modifications of the official *rates* (Standard II) or the fluctuations of the *average rates* do not affect the exporter's decision on the pricing of his export goods—what matters to him are the varying pecuniary values of the indirect government subsidies and the changes in the *pamaz* values of Standard IV goods imported with the value-added portion of the export earnings. In this sense the official devaluations have left no impact on the major part of merchandise exports. Regarding the citrus branch, it did not receive the favourable treatment accorded to other exporters (e.g. no *pamaz*). The *rate* for its foreign currency earnings was determined by the Ministry of Finance, in each season since 1954, at a level which would just induce the marginal farmers to harvest their crop, and this *rate* fluctuated without any link with the devaluations of the Standard II *rates* or the *average rates*. The supply of fresh citrus is highly inelastic and seven years elapse before newly planted groves provide suitable export fruit; a higher *rate* would not have called forth a larger supply of fruit for export.—Consequently, it may be said of about 95% of Israeli products[1] that the four devaluations neither detracted from nor added to their export earnings.

How was the import volume affected? The Israeli demand for the available foreign currency was highly inelastic; although between 1948 and 1958 the *average rates* moved from 0.350 to 2.750 and the annual foreign exchange receipts increased considerably, the effective demand for foreign exchange was in no year below the available supply. Admittedly, the devaluations caused changes in the composition of the import volume; but had larger quantities of foreign exchange (at even higher *rates*) been offered, they would still have been taken up by the Israeli public. The total volume of imports into Israel has always been determined by the gross amount of foreign currency available to Israel for the financing of imports and not by

[1] Some exceptions are discussed on p. 195. Whilst the effects of the changes of the official and *average rates* on merchandise exports were practically nil, they caused the foreign currency income from invisible exports, exchanged legally, to rise.

the IL price for the foreign exchange which was paid by the Israeli importers.

Of the 577 million nominal-dollars anticipated (legal) foreign currency receipts for 1957/58, $380 million are political and charitable receipts from foreign donors who would not have materially altered the amount of their contributions had the external value of the IL been changed more often or to a smaller or greater degree; (i.e. the supply of "political and charitable foreign exchange" is inelastic in respect of Israeli exchange rates)[1]. If to these $380 million are added the foreign currency receipts from 95% of the merchandise exports (the latter also being uninfluenced by the movements of the official *rates* and *average rates*), a proportion is derived of 90% of the gross foreign currency receipts that are not directly affected by the devaluations. Thus, a general assertion may be made that Israeli's foreign exchange receipts would have been neither substantially larger nor smaller had the four devaluations assumed larger or smaller dimensions.

So far three features of the Israeli devaluations have been described: the dimensions of the import and export volumes were unaffected by changes in the official and *average rates*; the replacement ratio (between Israeli and foreign goods) was shifted to a more favourable position for Israeli products; the Polak-Chang formula shows the first three devaluations to have been 58% successful. The salutary results of the devaluations are reflected in an increased real value of Israel's domestic product and in a qualitatively modified composition of its imports. How were these results achieved and why did the dark prophecies of the opponents of devaluation not come true? The answer is to be found in two phenomena: the "resource allocation effect"[2] and Israel's idle resources.[3]

[1] The supply of "charitable and political foreign currency" is elastic and depends on such diverse features as the political fortunes of Adenauer, income tax exemptions for charitable bodies in the Western world, Jewish sentiments, American policy to build up Israel "as a bastion against Communism in the Near East", etc. In so far, however, as this foreign exchange flow is related to the exchange rates of the IL, it is highly inelastic; changes in the *rates* will make Jewish donors neither more generous nor more close-fisted.

[2] I first formulated the advantages Israel derived from its devaluations in two papers which I read in Jerusalem in December 1956 (204). Since then I have come across Machlup's analysis (203) in which he suggests that a devaluation may increase the real National Income by rearranging factors of production which, in turn, induce increased exports. I have borrowed his term "resource allocation effect" for use, in a more limited sense, in demonstrating that economies with foreign currency controls, such as Israel's, might increase their real National Product by devaluation.

[3] In the summer of 1954 I interviewed Bell (of the Economic Advisory Staff)

217

In 1948 as in 1958 the latent demand for foreign exchange to finance imports (at the prevailing prices) always exceeded the amount of foreign exchange at the disposal of the Ministry of Finance, and the foreign currency controllers licensed imports on a selective basis. Yet there is a significant difference between the first and the last year of this ten-year period. The "replacement ratio" was such in 1949–51 that there was then hardly an article which did not have a cheaper IL price when imported at the official or *average rate* than when it was produced in Israel. The rationing technique of the foreign currency controllers selected those articles that were considered essential, or necessary for the manipulation of the cost-of-living index.

In the early years of the State the licences for practically all the goods selected by the Ministry of Finance as being suitable for import were taken up by eager importers, for, at the low *rates*—which were asked by the Government for the allocated foreign currency—the profit on importing an article was always bound to be larger than on producing it domestically. Whereas, therefore, at first the foreign currency controller was able to determine absolutely the composition of Israeli imports, this power was progressively whittled away as the years advanced. As production costs in Israel for identical or similar articles were lowered, the "replacement ratio" rose, causing more categories of goods to be placed outside the range of profitable imports. The Ministry of Finance had increasingly to face the position that, although the total demand for its foreign currency still exceeded the supply, there were no takers of foreign currency that was tied to the import of certain goods.

Israel's economy underwent a dual development: with each devaluation the composition of (official) imports changed; step by step, a higher proportion of imports consisted of those goods which Israel was only capable of manufacturing at a relatively high *rate* domestically, and ever fewer goods were imported which could be produced at a relatively low *rate* domestically. In consequence, the resources of Israel which had in the past been employed indiscriminately on production of goods with low or high *rates*, were now (in some cases) released from high-cost production and transferred to employment on low-cost production. If Israel's domestic product is measured not in terms of IL, but according to its imputed dollar

to ask why, in his view, the forecast of the Economic Advisory Staff that the domestic price level would rise commensurate with the devaluation of the IL, had proved false. He attributed it to their underestimation of the idle resources of the economy, some of which were gainfully employed after the second devaluation.

value, these changes in the employment of some of its resources will be seen to have augmented its real value.

The second element which restrained the rapid rise of the domestic price level, was the reserve of idle and partly-utilized resources, particularly machinery. With each step of the devaluation a further stimulus was given to a more intensive and rational employment of the given resources.

The meritorious results of the past devaluations lead one to speculate whether this healthy development could not be continued. The devaluation of the IL can profitably proceed until the "equilibrium-*rate*" is reached, i.e. that *rate* at which the Israeli demand for foreign goods is just matched by the (inelastic) supply of foreign currencies. In theory, such a *rate* is consistent with a system of multiple rates, in which case the "equilibrium-*rate*" would become the *average rate*. If, however, the "equilibrium-*rate*" is a unitary exchange rate,[1] it would optimise Israel's domestic National Product—measured in terms of its imputed dollar value—and cause the import volume to be composed only of those goods that are complementary to Israel's productive capacity.

The argument of this chapter implies that a further devaluation of the IL would be advantageous. This is argued on two explicit assumptions that the internal and external resources at the disposal of the economy are constant and that the standard of living would not thereby be lowered. (Actually, of course, the standard of living is more likely to rise subsequent to any devaluation which brings the IL *rate* up to the "equilibrium-*rate*".) It is not within the sphere of this book to make detailed conjectures on a workable policy of foreign currency controls for Israel. Here I only want to indicate the view that once the above two postulates are dropped, the process of devaluing the IL need not, and should not, be halted at this "equilibrium-*rate*".

It might well be propitious for Israel if some of the foreign political and charitable aid was refused, and, by lowering the standard of living in the short run, a new *rate*, appropriate to this (voluntarily) reduced foreign exchange income, was established. Alternatively, Israel might wish to accumulate some foreign currency balances abroad, and this again would necessitate the institution of a *rate* above the "equilibrium-*rate*". These are clearly but two out of several

---

[1] At first sight it might appear as if a unitary "equilibrium-*rate*" would obviate the system of licensing imports and exports. If, however, the foreign currency controls are to be retained, e.g. to prevent unauthorized movements of capital, it is unlikely that the authorities could agree to the dismantling of licensing.

possible courses that would make it desirable to devalue the IL above the defined "equilibrium-*rate*".

Limiting myself to the economic aspect of the present foreign currency controls, I believe a case has been made out that Israel's material fortunes would be enhanced by the institution of a (unitary) *rate* that is not lower than the "equilibrium-*rate*". The considerations which make me suggest that Israel's moral fortunes could be raised by instituting a *rate* above the defined "equilibrium-*rate*" are of a non-economic nature. However, I am sceptical about the ability and willingness of a government in a political democracy to lower the standard of living of its citizens (even if meant only as a temporary measure) by refusing part of unrequited external aid or maintaining part of the "political and charitable" foreign currency as a reserve outside the country.

PART C

CHAPTER XXIV

A SUMMARY

D URING its first decade the State of Israel has proved that, notwith-standing its location in the Middle East, it belongs to the Western World and, as such, has equipped itself with many of the levers of a twentieth-century Welfare State. During this period it has absorbed one million immigrants and maintained a costly military machine. The National Income, in real terms on a per capita basis, of the young State has grown every year and the population has experienced a continual rise in its standard of living. These, undoubtedly, are the marks of Israel's material advancement.

It may be said in parenthesis that some of this progress can be attributed to the willingness of the Israeli Government to allow with-in the country free criticism of its economic policies. It has not hesitated to invite foreign experts to publish their detailed and, in some cases, unfriendly strictures on official policy. Much of the credit goes to the pioneers of the Economic Advisory Staff. Agri-cultural experts like Clawson and (the delegate of the Food and Agriculture Organization to Israel) Black often felt frustrated because their advice did not seem to be heeded. But their indirect impact on farming policy proved to be powerful. Similarly, many Israeli economists who felt that they were like voices in the wilderness found that in the course of time government policy was modified as a result of their criticisms. By 1959 the autarchist plans for agriculture and food supplies have been ignominiously dropped; many of the excesses of Tozereth Haaretz protection have been checked; a host of physical controls have been abolished; the subservient attitude of the Government to the economic institutions of the Histadruth has been moderated; some unrequited exports have been stopped—and these are but a few of the decisive changes that have taken place.

Despite these encouraging signs, however, Israel has gained little ground, if any, on the march to what its politicians call "economic independence". During this first decade the gap in the balance of merchandise trade widened from year to year. Furthermore, far from decreasing, the volume of political and charitable aid has, in fact,

221

increased, whether this is calculated in absolute, or in per capita, terms. In 1949 the 1,061,000 inhabitants of the Jewish State received $130 million of such support, i.e. $123 for every man, woman and child; in 1957 the 1,950,000 inhabitants received something like $380 million, i.e. $195 per capita. However, if we make the realistic assumption that only the Jews of Israel were the beneficiaries of this support, then the per capita aid has increased in this period from $143 to $218.

How true is it to describe Israel as a socialist society? I estimate that about 30% of the National Income is generated in enterprises and activities of which the managerial controls, and the majority of the capital, are in the hands of the State and the municipalities. (The State has a legal title—through debentures, unsecured loans, mortgages and equity holdings—to more than 30% of the entire capital of the country. However, I have not counted enterprises as belonging to this sector if the Government, though it owned the majority of the capital, did not exercise managerial control over them.) Income generated in enterprises and activities organized within the framework of the Histadruth amounted to 29% of the National Income in 1956 (166) and is said to have risen to about 33% in 1957. A rough computation of the portion of the National Income generated in enterprises and activities controlled and financed by the *institutions* suggests about 10% of the total. (The major part of this is accounted for by employment directly with the Jewish Agency or with its agricultural, building, banking, shipping and other subsidiaries.) The remaining, private sector, therefore, generates about 27%.

Israel's economy has a severely distorted price-and-cost structure. This has been illustrated by numerous instances in Part B; here I only wish to recall the extremities by which the value of $1 of foreign currency was represented in terms of the local currency: at the *rate* of 0.450 for imported rice and at the *rate* of 17 for locally-canned sardines. The economic ministries have had to draw policy conclusions and make detailed decisions amidst the Babel-like confusion of different "price" and "cost" languages, a confusion stemming from the operations of the multiple exchange system; this confusion has parallels in few other countries. To minimize the effects of this confusion various expedients have had to be followed. Thus, for example, most of the official data concerning international trade are not registered in the IL denomination, but a currency is used which the Ministry of Finance calls "the dollar" and which I have in this book connoted the "nominal-dollar". Again, the earnings of exporters are registered by the banks—*inter alia* for purposes of operating the *pamaz* technique—in separate foreign currency accounts. The proper appreciation of the Israeli concept of value-added is feasible only when those using it write out their calculations in the language of non-Israeli currencies. In Israel today judges do not fail to mete out prison sentences to persons convicted for transgressions of regulations made by the foreign currency controller. Yet, when the statisticians of the official Central Bureau of Statistics wished in their recent Statistical Abstract (239) to provide a complete survey of economic data on Israel, they published a series of black market prices of the Israeli banknotes in Zürich and of the Standard III *rates* of the Tel-Aviv money black market. It is doubtful whether the Ministry of Trade and Industry realized the strangeness of the order it made in September 1958 concerning the sale of long-staple Israeli-grown cotton. This commodity (which, incidentally, has a relatively low import content) was to be sold *within Israel* only against foreign currency. Thus the only way in which Israeli manufacturers of cotton yarn could purchase Israeli cotton was by using foreign currency which had accumulated in their *pamaz* accounts.

The first ten years of an independent Israeli economy robbed the IL of more than two-thirds of its 1948 purchasing power. Parallel to the abandonment of the IL as the currency in which Israel's external trade was carried out, the IL is no longer used as a standard of measurement within the country for medium or long-term contracts; the epidemic of value-linking (*vide* p. 93) has spread to all spheres of economic life.

One may ask which single feature most impeded the healthy development of the Israeli economy. In the views of A. M. Bernstein of the International Monetary Fund (138) and of D. Horovitz, the Governor of the Bank of Israel, the inflationary policy consistently pursued by the Government for ten years deserves this crown. The economists associated with the Economic Advisory Staff, and also Mosak (167), regarded the system of linking wages to the cost-of-living index as the most important factor which retarded the country's economic growth. I have attempted in this book to substantiate the thesis that the main obstacle to the optimum employment of Israel's external and internal resources has been the manner in which the foreign currency controls were exercised. In particular, I have highlighted:

(*A*) the over-valuation of the IL both by the official *rates* and the *average rates*;
(*B*) the inefficient system of import licensing;
(*C*) the multiple exchange rate technique with the concomitant

administrative discretion given to officials to fix individual *rates* ad hoc;

(*D*) the almost unlimited protection given through the Tozereth Haaretz policy;

(*E*) the cynical disregard for the sanctity of government regulations which the operation of the foreign currency controls engendered.

Although occasional references will be found in this book to punishments meted out by Israeli courts to those who contravened the foreign currency regulations, it is a fact that the enforcement of the regulations was extremely lax and few of the multitude of offenders were apprehended. The historian who, in the future, attempts to evaluate the foreign currency regulations in force during Israel's first decade, may well conclude that the moral harm bred by these regulations has been more detrimental to the country than even the economic damage which they caused.

Today already some observers dare to assert that those Israelis, who frustrated the aims of the foreign currency controls by evading the regulations and "switched" for personal gain from one *rate* to another, have performed the praiseworthy task of lessening the distortions injected into the structure of the economy by the rules and regulations of the controllers of Israel's external trade. Ignoring the moral consideration of how a citizen should behave towards his government in a democratic society, the offenders against the Israeli foreign currency regulations may pride themselves on having forced the controllers to abandon some of their more absurd techniques.

"It is curious how little notice has been taken of one of the most obvious gaps . . . in economics . . . the unwritten section on graft . . ." (213). Though I have not elaborated on this theme, it will have been obvious to the reader that a not inconsiderable amount of graft was and is a feature of Israel's administration. I would not, however, venture to compare its quantitative aspects with the volume of corruption in other countries. Yet it is highly relevant to say that corrupt practices in the Israeli civil service do not always provide material benefits for the offending officials. The desire of officials to serve their political ideals and religious convictions probably accounts for more malpractices in the administration of the foreign currency regulations than the craving for personal material rewards.

CHAPTER XXV

MULTIPLE RATES AND POLITICAL DEMOCRACY

IN the Israel of 1959 the multiple rate technique has become respectable. In the past this system was associated with windfall gains and differential profits to favoured importers and exporters. Today it is different.[1] Now, the absolute profits (per one allocated dollar) from imports which are marketed at, say, a *rate* of 12 are meant to be no larger than those derived from imports financed with dollars allocated at a *rate* of 1. Similarly in the case of exports: a staff of Government statisticians, investigators and accountants studies the actual costs of producing one (value-added) dollar; the Ministry of Finance may still confirm that certain exporters be paid at, say, a *rate* of 8, but it is intended that their gain shall not exceed that of the exporters who are given a *rate* of, say, 2.500.

From the criterion of the optimum distribution of factors, it matters little whether the anomalies created by multiple rates incidentally provide large profits for individual merchants or are a source of revenue to the Ministry of Finance. The chief characteristic of the Israeli foreign currency controls, as illustrated in Part B, is the manœuvring of resources into uneconomic patterns of production and, in other cases, the frustration of production in economic patterns for which the country is suitably equipped. The number of multiple rates is in 1959 much larger than in 1949, and the dissipation of resources—on account of unrequited exports and Tozereth Haaretz protection—is still very considerable. Yet, now that personal profits from the system are smaller, public opinion has reconciled itself to the multiple rate system.

The Israeli foreign currency controls often effectively serve the stratagems of politicians. Israel is sufficiently a democracy to make most politicians want to camouflage their machinations for fear of public opinion, but it is not enough of a democracy to have adequate parliamentary controls to preclude such contrivances. An American economist, E. Rolph, says that

" . . . in a democratic society, people should be aware of what their government is costing them. Such information is indispens-

[1] Important exceptions and breaches of the foreign currency controls are still current, but their weight in economic life has greatly diminished.

THE ECONOMY OF ISRAEL

able for intelligent judgements about the desirability of expanding
or contracting particular government functions. . . . Public
accounting should ideally provide the cost information in an
unambiguous manner" (118).

What chance is there to exercise "intelligent judgements" when the
relationship between the figures in a budget presented to parliament
and the command over real resources is deliberately vague? In one
case IL100 stands for the command over $x of resources, and in
another case the same amount represents a different real value of
foreign resources. Admittedly, there are other factors besides the
foreign currency controls which envelop the economic activities of
the Government sector (and other sectors) in a fog and thus deprive
the public and the administration itself of the "cost information . . .
which is indispensable for intelligent judgements"; but there is little
doubt that the multiple rate system is the chief offender.

The concept of the "average" is sometimes astutely used to pull
the wool over many people's eyes. Often the legislature and the State
Comptroller may only be able to check whether the executive com-
plies with the laws "in the long run" or "on the average". The
executive is thus given much unbridled power to distort effectively
the price-and-cost structure. The Israeli foreign currency controller
has at times appeared before the Finance Committee of the Knesset
and informed its members that the exchange rate for a certain
category of dollar receipts was currently at the *rate* of ILx. Formally
this has been true, because the average price in the equalization
fund established for this category of foreign currency was indeed x;
what the outside investigators did not always know was that this
average *rate* of x was arrived at by selling, say, one-half of these
foreign currency receipts for $2x$ to one group of Israelis and the other
half at $\frac{1}{2}x$ to another group of Israelis.

The following throws light upon the methods used by Israeli
Government departments—in this case the Transport Division of the
Ministry of Defence—to increase effectively its control over real
resources without a categorical financial vote of parliament: In
1950 the Standard IV *rate* for foreign exchange transferred to
Israel via the import of vehicles was about 2; the army was allocated
foreign exchange at the *rate* of 0.357. This may help to make more
comprehensible the suggestion made in that year by a general that
the army be given the complete monopoly for the import of all
vehicles. This general proposed that the Ministry of Finance place at
the disposal of the army the total amount of foreign currency ear-
marked in the foreign currency budget for the import of vehicles;

226

the army would execute this import and use the vehicles for one year only and then resell them on the civilian market. Thus, it was said, the army would have the benefit of a large fleet of vehicles which would need little servicing, and it would make a large IL profit on the resale after one year. This suggestion was not accepted though the fact that a responsible general could make it, in all seriousness, indicates the prevailing attitude in Government departments concerning budgetary appropriations by parliament.

In 1955 an influential merchant approached the Ministry of Defence with a proposal that was based on the same reasoning, and in this case an agreement was actually signed. He was to supply the army with 400 *new* Ford lorries in exchange for 400 *old* Ford lorries which the army intended to discard after years of intensive use. This commercial agreement was in the end not carried out, for public criticism centred on the fact that this merchant would be making an excessive profit even after paying customs duty on the old vehicles he intended to sell to civilians. It is not pertinent to this study to inquire whether the Ministry of Defence itself, or through an intermediary, should have carried out this transaction. However, it is relevant to report that when in 1955 the army paid for its currency at the *rate* of only 1.800, it was able to command a higher IL price for discarded vehicles than it cost the Ministry of Defence to purchase new ones abroad.

The Ministry of Defence, however, was not content to employ only the multiple rates system to gain command over transport resources without a specific parliamentary vote; it also resorted to a wasteful form of "recruiting". To illustrate this argument by figures the arbitrary assumption will be made that the Israeli army has an annual requirement of 2,000 lorries. Parliament votes funds to enable the army to buy only 1,000 lorries, but other regulations permit the Ministry of Defence "to recruit for one month every year all lorries of the country"—a yearly call-up of, say, 12,000 lorries. (The data are imaginary but not the regulations cited.) Large firms solve the resulting difficulties by maintaining a fleet of 12 lorries when their commercial requirements are only for 11 lorries. During the yearly call-up of their vehicles smaller firms hire lorries from outside contractors to perform the work of the "recruited" lorries. Thus the civilian sector carries a reserve of 1,000 lorries for the constant use of the army. There are apparently well-founded complaints that the army which has a good reputation for looking after its own pool of vehicles, is not too particular in its treatment of these 12,000 "recruits" (206). This call-up represents a (disguised) specific tax on lorry owners, and an appropriation of sufficient funds to let the army acquire 1,000 additional vehicles would leave everyone better off even if the additional taxation was openly imposed on only the lorry owners. In practice, however, the voting of a money appropriation necessitates specific parliamentary consent; the call-up of 12,000 lorries does not.

It is not difficult to demonstrate that the distortions deliberately introduced into the Israeli economy are not only undemocratic—in Rolph's sense of the word—but also adversely affect the economic allocation of resources. It does not follow, however, that the leaders of Israel, once they are made aware of the opportunities to augment the national product by eradicating these distortions, would necessarily wish to act accordingly.

Many implicitly assume that after a social scientist has analysed a situation he has set out to study, it is incumbent on him also to suggest means of improvement when he has noted (what seem to him to be) deficiencies. How often have I been told that it is not proper for me to limit myself to a depiction of the distorted price-and-cost structure of the Israeli economy, if I do not simultaneously prepare a positive solution and express a view on what ought to be done to repair the imperfections. To me, however, description and prescription are two tasks which need not necessarily be jointly performed. A doctor may feel quite certain of a diagnosis that he has made and yet not tell the patient how he is to be cured. Several reasons may induce this attitude: he may not know of a cure; the only cure of which he can think may be beyond the means of the patient; the patient may be happier not to be told how ill he is; the doctor may think it a waste of time to elaborate upon a remedy because the patient does not wish to become well; the curing of the malady that has been diagnosed may bring on an even worse ailment—clearly, therefore, there can be numerous (reasonable) explanations for the refusal of a diagnostician to prescribe. He may thereby incur the displeasure of those who regard such behaviour as unethical or cowardly, but does the refusal to prescribe impugn his professional standing and invalidate his diagnosis?

To turn from these general observations to the specific case of Israel, it is true that one might engage in the dangerous game of outlining an economic programme, the implementation of which depended upon the Jerusalem Government having dictatorial powers and being able to execute it without fear of being overthrown by a political opposition. In such circumstances a list of "oughts" may be meaningful but I, for one, am not prepared to play such games. If one, however, proceeds from the assumption that the present framework of political democracy is to be maintained in Israel (or even

228

extended), then the preparation of a programme of "oughts" is a futile task. I do not believe that the Israeli Government is pursuing an economic policy which is "wrong" or "misguided" because its leaders are not aware of the structural deficiencies and are merely waiting for some critics to formulate a "correct" programme.

The men who head the Israeli Government are inspired as if by a vision and are filled with the fervour of missionaries. With (almost) no selfish thought to their own welfare, they believe that the community must expend the major part of its resources on investment, defence and agricultural colonization, to mention the three chief aims. No one in the country, apart from the small Communist Party, is prepared to organize active political opposition to the implementation of these aims. Yet the leaders of the State rightly ask themselves what the attitude of the population would be if, by proper accounting, the real burdens of investment, defence and colonization were exposed to view in plain figures. Would they vote, voluntarily, for a lowered standard of living in order to provide more steel plants, more tanks and more settlements on hilly land?

There have been few candid expressions on this subject. It will be recalled that Taub (54) proved an exception; he quite explicitly favoured the multiple rate system because it enabled the Ministry of Finance to hoodwink the public. He thought that the Government policy of subsidizing investment served a noble purpose, but he feared that most voters, once they knew the real costs in terms of their own standards of living, might be less favourably inclined to pursue this noble end.[1] How helpful the multiple rates are in such a dilemma! Large-scale investments, a strong army, colonization, a socialist economy—when it has proved to be uncertain whether ample public support would be forthcoming for all these aims, the political missionaries of Israel have sought to further them, *inter alia*, by burdening the country with the load of the multiple rate system.

---

[1] "There is no other road to economic development than a compulsory rise in the share of the National Income which is withheld from consumption and devoted to investment. . . . Under-developed countries thus need real democracy even at this early stage to break down the existing impediments to economic development; but undoubtedly democracy, at the same time, makes it more difficult for governments to hold down the level of consumption in the degree necessary for rapid development" (278). Myrdal's advice to under-developed countries may be well-meant but is accompanied by undemocratic sentiments; the word "compulsory" in the first line of our quotation should be particularly noted.

CHAPTER XXVI

ISRAEL AND OTHER UNDER-DEVELOPED COUNTRIES

ISRAEL is one of the group of countries on the African and Asian continents that have attained political sovereignty since the end of the last war. Most if not all of these countries have under-developed economies (to use a current all-embracing term). Elsewhere in this book it has been argued that Israel, though geographically situated at the crossroads between Africa and Asia, belongs truly to the Western World when judged by its cultural and political performance. But economically—how far are its problems similar to those of its under-developed neighbours? An Israeli economist who defends the official policies has asserted that "the economic activities of the Jewish population of Israel cannot be measured by the yardstick applied to the accomplishments of other nations. . . . It is therefore difficult to compare our social and economic conditions with those of any other country; it is equally hard to find amongst any other nation a parallel to our situation . . ." (240). This view on the uniqueness of the Jewish economy seems to me to be open to serious challenge because the similarity of some important economic issues, facing Israel and its African and Asiatic neighbours alike, is too obvious to be dismissed as a fortuitous phenomenon. Before considering the spheres (there are nine of them) in which Israel's economy exhibits characteristics similar to those of other under-developed countries, it may be helpful to mention some distinct features of the Jewish State.

During the first years of its existence as a sovereign state, Israel has borne the extraordinary burden of mass immigration. (At present this is no longer a noteworthy characteristic of Israel; some of the African and Asian under-developed countries today record an increase in their population through a large birth-rate which exceeds the immigration rate of the Jewish State.) Throughout the years, the Jewish National Home has also taken upon itself the maintenance of an expensive military machine; the expenditure on military preparedness (when measured in real terms) is probably larger than the military load carried today by any other nation. Whilst Israel, in common with all the other under-developed countries, receives international economic assistance, it alone enjoys in addition the generous contributions of Jewish sympathizers in the diaspora.

Many under-developed countries aim at expanding industry at the expense of agriculture and considerable resources are spent in order to transplant farmers to an urban environment. In Israel an opposite process is taking place; agriculture is favoured by the executive organs and farmers receive more lavish subsidies than any other group.

Reference must also be made to the uniqueness of the Histadruth. No other under-developed country—outside the Soviet sphere—can boast of an analogous trade union movement that serves the political régime so faithfully. During the pre-State days the Histadruth had built a comprehensive system of social and cultural services; when the State was proclaimed in 1948 the nucleus of an Israeli Welfare State already existed, and the Government either took over some of these services from the Histadruth or commissioned the Histadruth to administer them on its behalf and on behalf of the Jewish Agency. The entrepreneurial section of the Histadruth empire proved a convenient prop on which the socialist Government of Israel could lean, when the private sector organized anti-Government strikes; these were usually frustrated by the joint resources of the Government and Histadruth sectors.

The new sovereign states of Africa and Asia stand in awe before learning and place a high premium on the service of university-trained persons, especially when they are also nationals. This high regard for professionally trained persons is not a mark of Jewish life in Palestine-Israel and there are several economic and historico-sociological reasons explaining this. Until recently there was a relative over-supply of managerial skill and academic knowledge in this Jewish community; the persecution of Jews in Europe had brought to the National Home many persons who had fled there, despite the fact that they would not be able to find employment befitting their experience and learning. One must also not underestimate the anti-intellectual philosophy that was implied in the ideas which inspired the early Socialist-Zionists and from which the political *élite* of the country has not yet emancipated itself. (This anti-intellectualism has spread deep roots in Israel and while, like in other countries, it is also a prejudice prevalent among the masses, primarily it is a heritage from the early days of Zionist colonization that is proudly cherished by the leaders of the State of Israel. Ben-Gurion has publicly demonstrated on frequent occasions that he regards it as a healthy sign to foster a mild type of anti-intellectualism; he differentiates, however, between law, economics and similar worthless occupations on the one hand and praiseworthy professional activities like veterinary surgery and hydraulic engineer-

231

ing on the other.) Whilst the task of training managers is one of the most burning issues in under-developed countries (241), Israel has only lately begun to pay attention to this need, and even now does not regard it as a pressing problem. The shabby treatment extended in the past to many experienced managers and the anti-intellectual trends have contributed to the fact that of the 100,000 Jews who have emigrated from Israel during the last ten years an unduly large proportion consisted of those who could perform professional, managerial and entrepreneurial functions.

I now turn to an assortment of unconnected elements that are present in the majority of under-developed countries; foreign currency controls and investment policies are discussed towards the end.

(1) The nationalist movements in Africa and Asia were, as a rule, led by men who subscribed to some form or other of socialist philosophy. The heads of many new sovereign states, after reaching independence, have approached the Soviet Union and Soviet China (or have been approached by them) with proposals for close cultural and political relations; this is no doubt of considerable significance in some fields but has not been the decisive factor, explaining the trend towards public ownership in these states. It is certainly not an inevitable course of events which dictates that the dynamic growth of under-developed economies must be accompanied by rapid and large-scale socialization; but it is a matter of observation that in all the sovereign African and Asian countries the wings of the private sector have been clipped.

(2) The influence of nationalism on economic conduct has exceeded in importance all other influences and considerations. Failure to reconcile themselves to this has caused much frustration to some Western economists who have served as advisers to the governments of the new states. Myrdal has put this succinctly (278):

> "Economic nationalism does not need to be preached to the newly liberated under-developed countries. . . . In many cases the people in an under-developed country feel that they have been so maltreated by the world as a whole, or by a particular country among the richer ones, that they consider themselves right and just in using all political means at their disposal. Emotional nationalism will usually provide what would be lacking in rational motivation for feeling self-righteous."

An optimization of the National Product, or planning for the maximum material welfare, are not the primary aims of policy-makers in Africa and Asia today.[1] "Independence from outside

[1] This is well elucidated by the authors of (161).

suppliers", the psychology behind the "international demonstration effect" in the public sector, considerations of national pride, the prestige of the government in power—all these are of far greater force. The recitation of textbook arguments about the evils of autarchy and the benefits to be derived from free international trade may be listened to in silence and will often be treated with suspicion. It is not always easy to persuade the masters of these new countries that the professional services of experts—though white in colour—may be given disinterestedly. (Experts are treated in Africa and Asia today in a manner in which the Soviet authorities treated American engineers during their service in Russia in the 1921–29 period.) The memories of colonialism are hard to eradicate in one generation! It is even more difficult for the governments of the new sovereign states to believe that the international economic assistance which they are offered by the Western powers is disinterested aid— disinterested in the sense that it does not purport to exploit the resources of the former colonial countries for the material benefit of the donors who, in fact, have to impose fiscal burdens on their citizens in order to finance the gifts. Sometimes the governments of under-developed countries, upon which richer nations wish to bestow aid, use a radically different approach; in this instance the leaders of poorer nations aver that it is their *right* to receive such endowments from the older and richer countries. Thus in some cases offers of assistance are spurned because the motives of the donors (or the conditions accompanying the grants) are suspect, whilst in other cases the international assistance is accepted but with resentment. The political philanthropists in Washington and Whitehall rarely reap appreciation and, even more rarely, gratitude.

(3) The accepted philosophy in most of the new states (most prominently illustrated by the case of Israel[1]) is to see an achievement

---

[1] Israel's chief exhibition piece is the Histadruth steel town, which is being constructed with public funds, near Acre. The project will finally demand IL121 million of which one-quarter has already been invested. The first operating unit, a steel-rolling mill, in 1954 replaced imports at the *rate* of 18; other units soon expected in production are anticipated to replace imports at the *rate* of 11. The prospects of saving foreign currency on completion of the IL121 million enterprise have been estimated at $1.1 million per annum; about IL100,000— of this one-half in foreign currency—will be invested per worker. Some assert that the *rates* of replacing imports will in the end prove to be even less favourable than those cited in this passage, but I have relied on the figures of the original Erdreich report (136) and on press accounts of his second report. The Histadruth has challenged these calculations of the Government adviser, Erdreich, but has not done so very convincingly. A Scottish economist who was shown the Acre steel town remarked on returning to the United Kingdom that he would advise the British Government to subsidize the planting of citrus groves on the Clydeside.

I

per se in the "creation of things and creating them within the shortest span of time". Foreign experts often complain that it is easier to obtain public funds for actual new construction that may cost, say, 1 million money units, than it is to be voted 25,000 money units for a pilot plant or an exploratory survey—the latter are said to "waste time and delay building". When Israelis want to pay a compliment to a member of their Government, they say of him that he is "engaged on actually *making* things", and this is supposed to elevate him to a platform from which he can look down condescendingly on his inferior colleagues who are merely administrators, intellectuals and despicable eggheads. This craze for the "making of things" is not unconnected with the ambition to construct undertakings that are larger than those of one's neighbours, or the biggest of the region, or the most colossal of the continent and perhaps even the most spacious or modern in the world. As Milton Friedman (244) has pertinently pointed out, this building of economic monuments is aided and abetted by the relative over-supply of financial resources in the hands of governments which do not have to explain before any meeting of shareholders or any banking forum what use they have made of them.

(4) The use of what Rolph (118) has aptly described as the practice of "tax forgiveness" is spreading rapidly throughout the under-developed countries.[1] Public corporations are given specific tax benefits or total exemption; they are permitted to recruit on the free money market loanable funds on which the interest payments are partially or wholly exempt from direct taxes; government departments and public corporations are allowed to purchase in the open market without having to pay the indirect taxes that are collected from other purchasers. At times these practices induce a distorted cost structure and a serious dissipation of resources, yet many of the governments resort to these tactics in order to hide from the public gaze, or the legislature, that command over additional real resources is obtained by the public sector without a detailed financial appropriation.

(5) Physical controls, or specific controls demanding individual decisions by government officials, are even more arduous to administer in the new sovereign states than in the older countries with a long tradition of applying justly and efficiently complicated laws.[2] Economic plans which depend on individual controls for their

---

[1] Some exceptional instances of these reprehensible practices can also be found in Western economies, but there the consequences are slight.

[2] The Israeli politician, Dov Josef, played a prominent role in the legal and illegal fight against the British administration of Palestine. Josef's ministerial

234

execution are not infrequently unworkable in under-developed countries, because capable staff (to man the second echelons of the administration) are either not available, or unwilling to serve, or likely to succumb easily to corruptive suggestions.

(6) Table XIV shows that more than two-thirds of Israel's net foreign currency earnings from merchandise exports were derived from two articles, viz. citrus and diamonds. This reliance on a few exports is not unusual for non-industrial economies (242) and often the export earnings of such countries are composed virtually of the sales proceeds of three or four commodities. These major export goods are in many cases marketed by government corporations, a single (private) concessionaire or a marketing board to which all producers must sell their exportable output. In such circumstances the government attains with administrative ease an *ipso facto* control over the country's most weighty sources of foreign currency. Not infrequently directions of a non-commercial nature are given to these monopolistic export organs.

(7) The negative balances of payments, on current account, of most of today's sovereign African and Asian nations, used to be redressed (when they were still colonies) by the inflow of private capital. The G.A.T.T. report, which has already been quoted above (242), states that "it seems that over the long run official aid has taken over part of the role previously played by private long-term capital". Indeed, it is not infrequent for the foreign currency controllers of some of the new nations to find 15–25% of foreign currency receipts being drawn from international economic assistance. Despite seemingly attractive "laws for the promotion of foreign investments", tax concessions and promises of favourable treatment, private risk capital has not flowed to these new sovereign states in considerable amounts and the prospects for the future are equally dim. In so far as there have been substantial private investments, they seem to have been made by the Burnhamite managers of large corporations; one cannot help feeling that the main motives for many (though not all) of these investments are ones of prestige and response to the entreaties of Western governments (for "private" foreign aid programmes); they do not aim at the optimizing of profits for the shareholders.

How much of the foreign aid and the foreign investment capital

career is indissolubly linked to the failure of physical controls and rationing in the State of Israel. His regard for the British civil service was as high as his mistaken belief that it could be successfully emulated on another soil; he used to say that if Britain "succeeded to ration its population during the war, so can we here in Israel."

235

is channelled into the private sector of the under-developed countries? The statistical data, which are often quoted on this subject, are unsatisfactory on many counts and do not faithfully portray the full government control over practically all these foreign receipts. The World Bank and (for internal political reasons) the United States Government have made it their declared intention to strengthen through such assistance the private sector of these new sovereign countries; they aim at placing few financial resources directly at the disposal of the public sector. What an illusion this has proved in most instances! Governments of many of the new states have not hesitated to employ devious subterfuges to frustrate this intention of the political philanthropists of the West. If some of this foreign aid is "tied", i.e. granted only if it is given to the non-public sector, the governments will gladly comply with the formal condition attached to the gifts by proposing as beneficiaries for the aid, government-owned (or controlled)—but legally independent—corporations, and this enables the administrators of the Western aid to denote the destination of the gifts as being the "private sector". It is a delusion to believe that a private company in any one of these semi-socialist economies could apply directly to the Western institutions for economic aid *against the wish of its Government*. There are, of course, a large number of genuine private firms which have acquired substantial funds from foreign investment resources, but these firms are permitted to make their applications only after they have convinced their governments of the economic justice of their claims and the control of the public planners over the aid (given by outsiders) to the private sector is almost as severe as if the government had directly allocated this aid. The endeavour of the Western World, in the granting of abundant economic aid, is to strengthen the economies of the under-developed countries against the socialist world of Russia and China; in the process of so doing they have succeeded in strengthening the socialist tendencies of the new sovereign states and enhanced the economic power of their public sector at the expense of the declining private sector.

(8) The majority of the investment funds, intended for larger projects, are spent in the under-developed countries subject to the direction of the governmental bureaucracy; many of the foreign grants and loans can only be taken up in the form of heavy machinery; the price for most investment loans is low, nil or (in the case of severe inflation and frequent devaluations[1]) at negative

---

[1] In some cases the long-term loans, which are offered as outside aid, become a foreign currency obligation of the Government whilst the latter may in turn lend the funds in terms of its local currency.

(real) rates of interest. All these have led to misinvestments or, in extreme cases, to the completion of enterprises which, by functioning, actually add a new burden to the economy. When loanable resources are used to construct an enterprise which gives a smaller economic return on the invested capital than an alternative project would have yielded, we may properly speak of a "misinvestment". Many public investments in under-developed economies have, however, more adverse implications. Leaving a return on the original investment entirely out of account, the country may find that a new project utilizes domestic resources that are drawn from production for foreign markets where they earn considerably more foreign currency than is saved by replacing the original imports through domestic production and foregoing the original exports.

The following are the chief criteria which appear to guide the public officials in their investment decisions:

   I. Funds are allocated on a priority basis for fixed equipment and only grudgingly for spare parts, technical training, liquid capital and merchandise stock.

  II. Large-scale schemes demanding long-term investments are preferred to small-scale, short-term projects.

 III. Projects are often selected in relation to the political aims promoted by the government and not in accordance with the anticipated return on the invested capital.

 IV. As much of the foreign assistance is "tied" to the purchase of equipment in the country of the donors, those projects must be preferred the completion of which can be hastened by the purchase of such "tied" machinery.

  V. When the state appears as the distributor of investment funds at advantageous terms it must contrive to appear impartial as between rivalling ethnic, religious and regional interests.[1] This

[1] Israel's Government and the Jewish Agency had to face the peculiar rivalry of the private and Histadruth sectors and, for political reasons, surplus productive capacity was created in the country in order to "deal justly" with both these non-government sectors.—In 1947 there was one privately-owned factory in Palestine, equipped with automatic machines for preparing tins for the food-processing industry, but, despite large-scale exports, the whole economy of Palestine could not fully employ even one shift of this undertaking. As soon as the State had come into existence, kibbutz Yagur applied to the Ministry of Finance for an allocation from the Export-Import Bank loan for the import of identical machinery *"in order to make tins for the Histadruth sector"* (15). After the machinery had arrived, the old and new plant—both working in 1950 to 30% of their capacity—acted like textbook duopolists and reached a tacit understanding on marketing, prices, etc.—Israel provides several other such instances; the best known concerns the allocation of public funds for the creation

sometimes leads to the establishment of several (uneconomically-sized) undertakings where one (economically-sized) unit is called for, or to the waste of resources by duplicating the number of enterprises to make two groups of citizens politically happy.

(9) Almost without exception the new sovereign states of Africa and Asia exercise some form of foreign currency control, and while the day of complete convertibility seems to come nearer for most countries in Western Europe, the under-developed countries are moving in the opposite direction. As explained above the greater part of the foreign currency receipts—i.e. the proceeds from the export of the three or four chief items and the international economic assistance—accrue either directly to the government or are placed at its disposal under conditions that permit it to resell foreign currencies at varying prices. No state has yet reached the "perfection" of the Israeli foreign currency controls, but most strive to operate a multiple exchange rate mechanism; this policy follows along the lines of the Israeli experiment of individual import and export licences, national and private barter agreements, currency manipulations (disguised as commercial transactions) of export marketing boards and government corporations, open discriminatory exchange rates for different currencies, the imposition of export and import taxes (not primarily for revenue purposes but as a function of foreign currency controls), etc. One can only hazard a guess as to why these practices have become so widespread in Africa and Asia, and my hesitant conjecture is to ascribe them—as feature (4) above—to the wish of the executive to procure a larger command over real resources than it intends the public to realize. If this is a correct interpretation of the inclinations of the rulers in the new states, Rolph's plea that "in a democratic society people should be aware of what their government is costing them" (118) will not fall on very fertile ground. Nonetheless, it is my contention that even under conditions, which are far removed from those associated with political democracy as understood in the Western World, a realistic unitary exchange rate[1] can be shown to be economically superior to the jungle of a multiple rate system.

of an Histadruth tyre factory in the same year that public resources had been allocated to an entrepreneur of the private sector for a tyre factory; they competed with each other for four years in the local market until they learned of the commercial benefits that accrue to collaborating duopolists.

[1] This is written on the assumption that the governments of these states would be unwilling to abolish foreign currency controls altogether. I confess to holding heretical views on the subject, for I am convinced that no correlation exists

Some, who consider the multiple exchange rate system as largely wasteful, nevertheless treat demands to abrogate the technique as impractical and/or futile when the government of such a country has a decisive control over its economy. They question whether the replacement of this system by a unitary rate does in fact alter anything, when the government has the power to satisfy the demand of the public sector for a given amount of foreign currency by modifying the budgetary allocation of local currency to the public sector, enabling it thus to purchase the foreign currency at the prevailing rate. If a state plans to build a dam for which $100 million of imports are required (and the foreign currency receipts of the country are larger than this amount), what difference will it make, it is asked, whether the internal budget of that country provides for an expenditure item of y or z local money units to enable the Ministry of Construction to purchase the said amount of dollars? As long as economic planners plan in physical terms and the Ministry of Finance adjusts the local currency budgetary appropriations in accordance with these physical plans, neither a realistic unitary exchange rate (say, modelled on the Israeli "equilibrium-*rate*", as defined in Chapter XXIII) nor a Brazilian system for auctioning foreign exchange will make the bidders for foreign exchange from the public sectors free economic agents in the sense, that an increase in price will induce them to lower their demand for foreign exchange and vice versa; their demand for foreign exchange—it is argued—will always be inelastic because the Ministry of Finance can adjust *ex post facto* the amount of local currency needed to pay for any given sum of dollars.

But while a "free" currency market under such conditions is a contradiction in terms, even it may prove serviceable in the furtherance of three ends. Firstly, to enable the governments in these countries to write their economic plans in the language of one currency, namely their local one, and thus to obviate the drawing up of two unconnected plans for capital requirements, in local currency and foreign currency respectively.[1] Thus a unitary rate with a single set of calculations may enlighten government officials (called upon to make the

between the economic development of a country and the need to institute foreign currency controls. Some under-developed countries—Israel among them—would be well advised to abrogate their foreign currency controls; this applies in particular to those economies in which the overwhelming majority of the foreign currency receipts accrue directly to the government or to bodies under its effective managerial control.

[1] The practices of commending an investment project "because we have the foreign exchange" and/or the rejection of a scheme, that demands the import of foreign machinery "because we want to save dollars", would then cease.

investment decisions) on the true costs of a project, knowledge which through the multiple rate system is often as unascertainable to the planners as to the public. Secondly, although the socialist theorists in the new African and Asian States have the ambition to plan their economy centrally, at present it is not true to assert even of their public sectors that these are monolithic. Public corporations and different government departments often compete for scarce resources in a manner that is reminiscent of the commercial rivalries associated with a free market economy. (In Israel many revelations about the wasteful use of resources on the part of one public authority have come from confidential knowledge possessed by a rival public body which "leaked" it to the press. Such behaviour will probably shock British readers more than American ones.) There is something artificial about this type of "socialistic competition"; but, in the circumstances, a realistic unitary exchange rate for foreign currency can act as an arbiter—though not a very learned one—between the competing claims of two public authorities. Thirdly, and this is perhaps its main virtue, a unitary price for foreign currency—and the allocation of financial resources for a project planned by a public or private body *exclusively in terms of local currency* (without tying it to the purchase of any specific foreign resources)—will enable a rational choice to be made by the spender between a foreign and a local purchase. Part B of this book has included many instances to show how the Israeli Government has deprived prospective investors, the army, the irrigation boards and others of the opportunity to make this choice between the employment of local or foreign resources. In many cases the Jerusalem authorities · have offered to allocate not foreign exchange, but machinery, for specified physical projects; what incentive was there to buy local resources in preference to foreign ones when the former had to be paid for in cash while the latter were offered on liberal credit terms and in prices that under-valued the dollar?[1] The new sovereign states of Africa and Asia might profitably

---

[1] Until 1955 the Ministry of Trade and Industry did not make loans from the Development Budget for working capital of industrial enterprises. There are several documented cases where Israeli concerns had been liberally supplied with foreign exchange on credit by the Ministry of Finance in order to purchase expensive machinery but the crated equipment remained unopened on arrival in the country, for the IL funds necessary to install it were missing. The Jewish Agency pursued a similar policy in the farming sector. It showered investment goods "in kind" on the new settlers but regarded the provision of IL funds for working capital as taboo. Thus it not infrequently happened that the furnished factors of production remained idle while the settler worked as a wage-labourer outside his village in order to accumulate liquid resources to operate the idle investment goods. The kibbutzim were more daring and did not hesitate to sell

study the havoc played with Israel's commercial strength by the distortions introduced in its economy through the multiple exchange rate system.

(illegally from the standpoint of the Jewish Agency) some investment goods so that they could operate the remaining equipment with the working capital obtained from these sales.

CHAPTER XXVII

A GLIMPSE INTO ISRAEL'S FUTURE

In so far as can now be foreseen Israel's Jewish population may well exceed three million by 1970. The Soviet Union does not at present permit any of its citizens to emigrate; it is difficult to make a reasonable forecast about the number of Jews who would leave Russia for Israel if they were allowed so to do, though, in that eventuality, Israel's population would probably increase more rapidly. Writing in 1959, one can only point to Eastern Europe and North Africa as the main reservoirs from which Jewish immigrants are likely to be drawn into Israel in the next decade; half a million to three-quarters of a million Jews may be anticipated to come to Israel from all parts of the world. In the future the high birth-rate of the Oriental Jews in Israel should be a more significant factor than immigration. The prospects are practically nil of Jews from the West coming to Israel in large numbers. How far emigration from Israel will assume sizable dimensions depends largely on a number of internal features, some of which are a function of the country's material fortunes.

Whilst one can estimate the future population with some degree of certainty, no such predictions can be made about three issues the outcome of which might radically change Israel's economy: oil, sweet water and relations with its neighbours. Geologists are in general agreement that Israel is part of an oil-bearing region, and indeed oil has been struck at a number of places since 1955. Specially-constructed pipelines bring the oil to the Haifa refineries, but this oil, as yet, represents less than 10% of the $60 million import bill. Many of Israel's leaders dream about oil discoveries that would enable Israel to export oil, crude or refined, and earn hard currency. This is obviously an imponderable factor, though one that crops up frequently in discussion on the future prospects of Israel's economy. Should the miracle of large oil discoveries occur, the benefits to Israel would be relatively larger than those today derived from oil by many of the states of the Middle East. Most of the royalties would stay in Israel, as little foreign risk capital is used in the financing of the prospecting and drilling. Whilst pipelines with a length of up to 1,000 miles are being constructed in other countries, oil produced in the Holy Land need not be transferred from any point more than 100 miles to a port at the Mediterranean or the Red Sea. There would consequently be none of the handicaps experienced by oil companies when their pipes have to cross the territory of several sovereign states.

A revolution in Israel's agricultural output would follow if it became commercially feasible to convert some of the waters of the Mediterranean into sweet waters to irrigate the semi-arid areas of the south. This would render unnecessary the costly movement of water from the far north to the south, and hence also the execution of projects involving the expenditure of several hundreds of millions of dollars of foreign currency. Furthermore, it would cause an immediate saving in imports (particularly of fuel) and cheapen the home production of food. The Jerusalem authorities rightly allocate large sums of money for research in this field, and if the scientists engaged in this work should succeed, this would also be a blessing to other countries.

Peace with its Arab neighbours? At the moment this seems as far distant as the coming of the Messiah, though some optimists believe recent developments in the Arab world to be conducive to some kind of political settlement. If real political peace could be made to prevail, the repercussions on the Israeli economy would be tremendous. As indicated on p. 69, I do not accept the exaggerated estimates of the damage caused by the Arab boycott, nor do I find the Israeli and Arab economies as complementary as is suggested by some publicists. Admittedly peaceful relations would make possible the execution of inter-regional development plans (tourism, irrigation, etc.), and make it worthwhile to erect assembly plants in Israel that would serve the whole of the Middle East. But these advantages are relatively small fry, when we consider that the chief material benefit accruing to Israel from peace with its neighbours would be derived from a substantial reduction in the military burden now borne by the economy of the Holy Land. If the drain on the country's internal and external resources could be eased in this manner, it would lead to important structural changes in the economic life of Israel.

Yet, abundant oil wells, desalinized sea water and friendly commercial intercourse with the Arabs are not round the corner. Without them, how will Israel fare in its second decade? My own reading of the situation is that the great powers, including Russia, are interested in the continued existence of the Jewish State as a counterbalancing element in the Middle East. It is useful to remember that whilst Israel is now receiving arms from the West—mostly in return for hard cash—the War of Liberation of 1948–49 was won, *inter alia*, because the Communist states had sold the Jews weapons. Whoever the future suppliers of armaments to the Jewish State are, it can be presumed that sufficient supplies will be forthcoming to make it a formidable task for the Arab armies to attempt to destroy Israel in open warfare. During the first official visit of Israel's Foreign Minister to London, I wrote the following: "Dr. Adenauer's willingness to withstand Arab pressure on Germany to cut down the reparations payments; the mood of members of Congress in America; the prejudices of Jewish philanthropists—these are factors determining the future of Israel no less than the acquisition of more arms and the guarantee of her frontiers by the big powers." Despite the severe criticism to which I was subjected at the time for publishing these sentiments, I still unrepentantly maintain today that the continuation of a large volume of charitable and political aid is the most decisive single factor acting upon Israel's physical existence.[1] The United Nations statisticians adopt a rather narrow definition of what constitutes "international economic assistance" and, in the case of Israel, for example, they do not take into account the restitution payments, donations collected by Jewish charities, the selling of government bonds on a non-commercial basis, etc. Yet, even according to the limited United Nations data for the 1953–57 period, Israel is said to have received more assistance than any other country in the world; it heads the list with $27.7 per capita, is followed by Libya with $18.3 and Laos with $16.6, whilst India occupies the place of honour at the bottom of the list with only $0.01 (243). For most of the countries, the included categories of economic aid represented their total unearned foreign currency receipts, whilst (*vide* p. 33) for Israel they constituted but a small portion of the total outside assistance which in 1957, for example, amounted to $195 per capita.

Throughout this book reference has been made to the socialist character of the Israeli economy, though a good case could be made out for labelling the system as merely "non-capitalist". A terminological discussion on the most appropriate label would be barren. However, it is essential to an understanding of Israel to appreciate that all sectors gear their actions to the distributed foreign aid and there is hardly any form of social activity which exists without staking a claim to the gratuitous receipts from abroad. A former leader of the Labour Party (Mapai), Eliezer Livneh, was the first to popularize the concept of a "supported society" and to point out the dangers of moral and social degeneration which threatened a society increasingly dependent on foreign alms. Livneh has described the activities of those who "cultivate" the suppliers of these unearned foreign currency donations, as workers in Israel's most notable export enterprise. The various parties differ on the form in which the aid

[1] Israeli cynics have said that a drought in their country need not be a tragedy for the farmers provided sufficient rain falls in the United States.

should be expended, but none challenge the sacrosanct practice of organizing Israeli society according to such standards as are likely to attract the optimum amount of outside support. This, in my submission, is the most serious of all the maladies which have afflicted the organism of the Jewish State. It is one of the paradoxes of history that the Jews, who in the diaspora have played such a prominent role as entrepreneurs and merchants, suffered such abysmal failures in these traditional activities in their sovereign state, whilst in those spheres in which (in most parts of the world) they had not been allowed to be active, they excelled themselves in the Holy Land. Israel's cotton yields and the proficiency of its parachutists are high—the economic performance of its trade and industry is low.

Official circles are not unduly concerned with the growing foreign aid and deny that it saps the strength to build an independent economy; they express the view that a large volume of unrequited imports is needed at this stage for the planned investment programmes, the completion of which will lessen the degree of dependence in the years to come. Diametrically opposed to this view is the argument of those extremists who maintain that only the cessation of the flow of philanthropic assistance will shock Israeli society sufficiently to force it to reorganize itself, drop plans for further socialization, abandon grandiose—but commercially unremunerative—investment projects and furnish those conditions under which private enterprise can function freely. A middle course has been suggested by those who reject these extreme formulations; they argue that foreign aid should continue to be encouraged, but that its flow should be regulated and that the donors should use their veto in order to exercise competent control over a more efficient utilization of the aid. Attractive though this proposal seems at first sight, it becomes less alluring when one examines who these potential controllers are to be.

For obvious reasons the German Government cannot fulfil this role, and would certainly be unwilling to make its restitution payments dependent on exercising control over the way they are to be used in Israel. The American Government has somewhat half-heartedly taken upon itself the task of acting as a benevolent imperialist. It staffed several of its Tel-Aviv agencies with economists and other technical experts who proffered advice on how to spend the gifts, and there have been occasions when appropriations have been held up until the Israeli Government has made certain slight changes in its commercial practices. But these attempts of the American Government (and similar ones by the World Bank) to link economic aid with pressure on the under-developed countries to spend the funds in a manner that is likely—in the donor's view—to bring the optimum benefit to the recipients of the aid, must end in failure. As soon as serious pressure is applied the cry "Beware, imperialists at work!" is taken up. In our age the giver of alms must often be thankful to the poor that they condescend to accept the alms; under-developed countries (and, to some extent, this includes Israel) usually do not feel like expressing gratitude for foreign gifts and are certainly not prepared to be told how to spend the alms.

All that is left then is the possibility of an appeal to the Jewish donors and well-wishers of Israel that they might perform the function of altruistic controllers. Many Hebrew-speaking critics of the Jerusalem authorities have begged the Zionists of the English-speaking countries to exert the power they are thought to possess, because of their philanthropic activities,[1] in order to influence, cajole, or even (in the last resort) threaten the Israeli Government, so as to induce it to conduct a changed economic policy. Before considering whether such appeals are likely to be heeded by Zionists in the diaspora, one must digress and look at the Israeli attitude towards Zionism. The Jews of Israel are today only interested in the Zionists in the diaspora in so far as they make material contributions to the National Home. However, it is not true that this has always been the attitude of the Jewish community of Israel (Palestine). Up to a few years ago the belief was genuinely held that there is a unity of purpose and thought between the Zionists who "already" live in the Holy Land and those "still" in the diaspora. Today, for instance, supporters of a certain Religious-Zionist group in Canada, who protest to the Israeli authorities against the opening of a mixed swim-

---

[1] Almost all the philanthropists who head the list of contributors to the funds of the *institutions* have refused to make even the smallest personal investment in Israel since 1948. There is the case of the generous British Jew whose family has over the years contributed millions of Pounds (Sterling) to the cause of Zionism, who explained his unwillingness to invest even a single Pound in the following way: "I do not want anyone to say of me that I am making money out of my love for Zion; hence I am limiting my support for Israel to the making of charitable donations." Another famous millionaire, who in the past confined his pro-Israeli activities to charitable contributions, seemed to be breaking the "rule" when in 1958 it was announced that he had invested in several enterprises in Haifa. However, it soon became known that this investment was, in fact, made to provide a charitable trust with income and did not offer any encouragement to those who publicized the opportunities offered by Israel to potential investors to earn reasonable profits there. This Big Business leader made the following impressive statement at a press conference in the Holy Land: ". . . I shall see to it that these enterprises are conducted on commercial lines but please don't imagine that I am doing this *because I need your profits*."

ming pool in Jerusalem, are told not to intervene in the internal affairs of a sovereign state. Such a disposition of mind was inconceivable fifteen years ago, and perhaps as short a time as five years ago; most Jews in Israel would not then have condemned as improper interference the wish of some Zionists in the diaspora to have a say in the internal affairs of "our" National Home. The world-wide Zionist Organization was built on the implicit assumption of equality of all who subscribed to its ideals. This was not a mere formality; hundreds of thousands of Zionists in the diaspora once felt what nowadays only a few elderly people feel, that they were part and parcel of the Jewish community in Israel (Palestine). Elections to the Zionist Congresses between the two wars used to be preceded by crowded meetings organized by the competing political factions. Zionists, who zealously urged upon others the justice of their own particular party, have been known to hit one another until the police of New York and Warsaw had to be called in to separate them. A labour dispute in Kfar Sabah, a political murder in Tel-Aviv, the threat to Jewish industrialists in Haifa by Japanese imports—all these aroused in Zionist circles throughout the world sincere interest and passionate feelings which were no less intensive than those experienced by the people on the spot. Compare the lively Zionist Press of before the Second World War with the nature of today's propaganda journals. Then the Zionist Press reported intimate details of happenings in Palestine which are neither comprehensible nor of interest to the present readers of Zionist papers; nowadays articles in such journals have often been processed by experienced publicity experts who judge news from the National Home in relation to its usefulness for raising charitable contributions. Until Ben-Gurion finally exposed it as a myth, most Jews in Israel thought that their brethren living in the Western hemisphere were prevented by the restrictions imposed on immigration by the Mandatory Government from settling in the Jewish homeland; schoolchildren were taught by their Hebrew teachers that, as soon as the sovereign Jewish State would provide the physical opportunity of doing so, millions of American, British and French Jews would come into the country. During the years 1951 to 1954 Israel suddenly recognized that the period was drawing to a close when immigrants sought a refuge in the National Home in larger numbers than could be accommodated and that in the future, the Jewish Agency would be seeking out Jews with an offer to facilitate their immigration if they so desired. The almost complete lack of immigration from the West deeply shocked Israeli society.

In the past Ben-Gurion and the Jews of the National Home had accepted it as the natural right of the Jews in the diaspora to co-

247

determine how the charitable funds should be spent. Kaplan, who was for many years the Treasurer of the Jewish Agency and Israel's first Minister of Finance, found nothing offensive in having frequently to travel to meetings in Switzerland, there to be told by the representatives of the Zionist Organizations how to expend the collected funds. In those days, Ben-Gurion never challenged the right of his Zionist partners in the diaspora to participate in the making of financial decisions—*it was a right acquired, not by virtue of the Zionists in the diaspora collecting most of the funds, but through their status as fellow-Zionists and potential citizens of the embryonic Jewish State*. There is another notable feature of fund-raising in the past; the old guard of Zionists had never regarded the collection of money for the National Home as an end in itself, but rather as a means of proselytizing for their cause. In many Zionist campaigns the emphasis was placed on the *personal* financial stake which a Zionist could acquire by purchasing a plot of land, a house, an orange grove, shares in a private industrial or commercial enterprise, etc. But even when funds were specifically collected for the Jewish Agency, the organizers regarded the raising of money as subordinate to the higher aim of general Zionist education and the recruitment of new members. There were even activities of the Jewish National Fund, the net money proceeds of which formed but a small part of the gross proceeds; yet such apparent failures in money-raising were justified on the grounds of preparing the minds of the small donors for a closer personal association with the National Home, a purpose which was then regarded as more vital than the amount of money collected. This old conception of how charitable campaigns should be conducted did not conform with the commercial criterion of high salaries for efficient professional fund organizers; Zionist functionaries in bygone days were paid in relation to the idealistic content of their organizations.

Ben-Gurion and his Government drew far-reaching conclusions from the changed status of the Zionist organizations in the diaspora; henceforth the old attitude towards fund-raising was treated as sentimental nonsense, and the one criterion by which Jerusalem began to judge all Zionist activities was in relation to the maximum amount of foreign currencies transferred to Israel. To the chagrin of the old generation, the administrators of the successful fund-raising drives were no longer chosen in accordance with their Zionist record and their inner convictions, but only in accordance with their professional claims to maximize the amount of money raised. If an individual, who privately might admit not to adhere to Zionist doctrine, could nevertheless show an excellent record in the promotion of toothpaste, he stood a good chance of being appointed as the organizer of an Israeli charity appeal. The film stars, beauty queens and stunt performers who were invited to address fund-raising meetings outraged those old Zionists who had not yet fully grasped the nature of Jerusalem's changed attitude towards Zionist philanthropy. However, both Israel's Ministers of Finance, the late Eliezer Kaplan and Eshkol, the present holder of this office, have made their position perfectly clear; they accept the logic of the new situation and judge the sympathy for Israel, of registered members of the Zionist organizations and non-Zionists alike, by the standard of how much aid is offered, and they care little about the means employed to gather this financial support for the National Home.

Gass (246) is delighted that American-Jewish donors do not behave like rapacious imperialists and are not in the habit of making their contributions to Israeli charities conditional on the State pursuing certain policies.[1] There is room to doubt whether this attitude is as laudable as it seems at first glance. In my view it is based upon apathy to happenings in the National Home; *diaspora Zionists do not wish to control the expenditure of their donations in Israel, and if they have an inner urge to make their charitable contributions and buying of Israeli Government bonds conditional upon something, it is that they want to be left alone and to be divested of responsibility for the conduct of Israeli affairs.* They do not wish to be partners but detached well-wishers. To them there is an identity of purpose between the State and the leaders of its Government, whoever they might be. Though some Israelis even now refuse to recognize the fact,[2] the Jews of the diaspora will not withhold support from Ben-

---

[1] Federated charity campaigns which were conducted in the United States in 1957 covered areas in which two-thirds of the population lived. The "United Funds" which include the Red Cross, raised $4.18 per capita; $2.91 per capita were collected by the Community Chests. As against these figures for America's largest charity organizations, the combined Jewish contributions to Israel in 1957 totalled about $30 per capita; in addition the Jewish community does not lag behind the non-Jewish citizens in contributing to general charities and, of course, collects additional amounts for American-Jewish charities. Regarded in this light, the charitable contributions of American Jewry are remarkable indeed when measured both in relation to their importance for the Israeli economy and in comparison with the charitable disposition of non-Jewish Americans. What, however, is the weekly, net (i.e. after deduction of some of the tax benefits) burden per capita? I estimate it at $0.45; it does not seem an excessively large *subjective* burden for a relatively wealthy community.

[2] In the summer of 1958 the Israeli Government convened a meeting in Jerusalem of the leading philanthropists for Israeli causes. The Hebrew Press reported that neither at the public nor at the closed sessions was one word of criticism uttered at the conduct of Israel's economic policy; the representatives of (mainly) American Jewry travelled thousands of miles only to declaim how

Gurion and his party because of disappointing economic and social policies.

To sum up: in the 1948–58 period the State of Israel has become a solid political unit and a recognized military power in the Middle East. Socially, the "ingathered exiles" have been integrated within the existing framework of the Jewish community which had been constructed during the British mandate over Palestine. Though the majority of Israel's citizens were born outside the National Home, Hebrew has become, in fact as well as in law, the unifying bond of the Israeli melting-pot. These have been great historical tasks and ten years seems a short time within which to have resolved them. Some of the present sources of foreign aid (e.g. from Germany) will dry up in the near future, but Jewish philanthropy and non-Jewish (particularly by the American Government) support are likely to continue to prop the Israeli economy. It will be interesting to watch how far subjective and objective elements will influence the Government of Israel to change the course of its economic strategy—for on such a change the fate of the whole country may depend during its second decade of life.

unreservedly and wholeheartedly they underwrote the manner in which their donations and the bonds proceeds had been invested. This docile behaviour of the delegates called forth this comment in Israel's most serious organ:

"The nations of the world are astonished at the readiness shown by diaspora Jews to extend a helping hand to the builders of the State of Israel. . . If only the Gentiles knew . . . how superficial is the interest of diaspora Jews in the manner in which their funds are expended, their astonishment might well grow. If we (in Israel) have always been amazed how it came about that the contributors to the Funds, collected by the Jewish Agency, were satisfied with the sort of report which emanated from its executive, we find it even more amazing that the dignitaries of the 'bonds drives' have not so far demanded to play even a humble role in the determination of that policy according to which the large sums—that have accrued due to their efforts—will be invested" (248).

APPENDIX I

THE JERUSALEM SHOE CORPORATION

The success of the Boston Zionist lawyer, S.,[1] in the "investment-conscious atmosphere" of Israel, has been the main topic of a Government commission, is referred to in numerous memoranda of the Competent Authorities (dealing with leather), has been the subject of several statements by economic ministers in parliament and has been widely commented upon in the Israeli press. A detailed factual (though not entirely reliable) account will be found in (139).

S.'s contribution to the establishment of the company (which was popularly believed to have been financed by him) was to act as its promoter—not in the old-fashioned sense of asking banks and private individuals to subscribe capital, but by using his influence to tap the loan funds owned and/or controlled by the Israeli Government. S., himself, by the allocation of a large block of shares which he managed to sell before the factory faced bankruptcy, profited from this recruiting of public funds. As S. and the other two partners provided only a small part of the capital they were not unduly concerned with the economics of the enterprise, which was later shown to have been built on shifting sand.

S. (in conjunction with a well-known hides importer and a noted American shoe corporation), with the official support of Dov Josef, in the early months of 1949 had a large-scale shoe factory constructed in Jerusalem. (Official support was given despite the surplus production capacity in the country; most shoe factories worked only one shift for about 8½ months a year.) S. promised:

(a) to give employment to several hundreds of workers in Jerusalem, a town the Government wanted to develop industrially;
(b) to reduce the price of shoes by 40% and thus help to lower the cost-of-living index;
(c) to export about 60% of his output.

The enterprise was in operation by the end of 1949 and the following non-Government investments were registered:

[1] S. was *persona grata* with many Israeli ministers, was appointed to representative positions (including the board of the Investment Centre) and became the Israeli representative of the Independence and Development Bond Corporations. In 1956 he reluctantly conceded to the Government's request to give up his public appointments.

	IL
The General Shoe Corporation of America (second-hand machinery valued at) . .	71,413
Various members of the Habas family .	152,501
S.	26,086
	250,000

What about public funds?

(*a*) The land on which the factory was built was placed by the Government at the corporation's disposal with a 99 years' lease.

(*b*) A Government-owned company built the factory. This was done with the allocation of building materials at low, subsidized prices. The corporation was given the option to buy the building in eighteen annual instalments totalling IL100,000.

(*c*) A loan from the Export-Import Bank for $300,000 became a liability of the company at the 0.357 *rate*.

(*d*) The Development Budget provided "working capital" estimated at IL350,000–650,000.

(*e*) The (Jewish Agency controlled) Bank Leumi (and some other banks) lent more than IL1 million.

(*f*) The chief benefit from the status of a favoured company in Jerusalem was the receipt of import licences—for sums said to exceed $3 million—between 1949 and 1953; these licences were accompanied by foreign currency allocations at low *rates*. In addition, the company was liberally furnished with *IfE* licences, although it did not carry out the corresponding exports.

(*g*) The Ministry of Labour paid the expenses (for a period of 6–9 months) of training the factory workers.

By 1956, the opportunities to exploit the status of a favoured factory and the making of differential profits on licences with allocations of foreign currency at low *rates* had come to an end. The corporation faced bankruptcy proceedings. The Government and the Jerusalem municipality were begged to assist lest the remaining 200 employees lose their livelihood. The Histadruth was asked by the Habas family to purchase the factory at a nominal price but refused because, *inter alia*, it did not think the plant had a commercial future. In September 1956 the Government prevented the closing of the factory by lending it IL50,000 from the Development

Budget and IL125,000 from the "Employment Fund" of the Ministry of Labour. Further "contributions" were made during 1957.

An investigation in 1956 showed that S. had kept none of his promises. The prices of his factory were not lower than those of its competitors as S. had come to an understanding with the shoe cartel. The Jerusalem Shoe Corporation did not export 60% but less than 1% of its 1949–1956 output.

APPENDIX II

THE ZILBERG JUDGEMENT

In 1950 a 9% two-year loan of party X to party Y was registered as a charge on some property of party Y. The contract was made with the express proviso that, if the value of the property should rise during the period in which the loan was outstanding, the loan and the interest were to be regarded—in terms of IL—as having increased correspondingly. On expiry of the two-year period, party Y refused to recognize that the value of the loan had risen, although it was admitted that the value of the mortgaged property had appreciated. When party Y was sued, he cited in his defence the provisions of the Ottoman law concerning interest; he also argued that the agreement had been contrary to public policy.

Party X maintained before the district court that the Lomax[1] decision applied in this case and that the increment on the value of the loan—for the payment of which he was suing—was only compensation for the depreciation of the IL and not interest. Judge Lamm decided against party X, saying that he found the Bates[2] case useful in arriving at his decision. Judge Lamm stated further that an IL remains an IL, according to law, irrespective of any depreciation in its purchasing power. He interpreted the Ottoman law to mean that the 9% maximum interest included compensation for a possible depreciation in the value of the loan (116).

On appeal against the decision, the judgement was reversed in 1955 by the High Court of Appeal. Judge Zilberg, who gave the judgement, provided a legal basis for the many value-pegged contracts of Israel. He said that in his understanding of American, British and Jewish Law, it is not usurious for the lender of money to receive compensation from the borrower for the depreciation of

[1] Lomax (Inspector of Taxes) v. Peter Dixon & Co., Ltd.; (1943) 2 All E.R. 255.
[2] Bates v. United States (108 F. 2d. 407. CC.A. 7th. 1939).

the original money loan. (Judge Zilberg added that, as the intentions of the Ottoman legislators were not known, he felt himself entitled to conclude that they would not have wanted to be more severe than those who formulated the American, British and Jewish laws.)

Reviewing the second argument of party Y, which was accepted as valid by Judge Lamm, Judge Zilberg ridiculed the claim that value-linked loans were contrary to public policy and, as an inflationary element, would damage the economy:

> "No wise man has as yet proved the proposition that the safeguarding of loans by value-linking agreements is harmful to the country. But, even if all the experts in the world would say so, even then I would not be persuaded that this universal axiom can be applied to the specific economic structure of the State of Israel. If, for example, it could be shown that the legalizing of value-linked contracts would aid in the attraction of foreign capital to Israel, I would not hesitate to say that such value-linked loans are beneficial to the economy" (117).

Appendix III

WHEAT GROWING IN ISRAEL

There are four types of land on which both wheat and barley can be grown as winter crops without artificial irrigation:[1]

A. Heavy land, where the yield of wheat per dunam is higher than that of barley, and, therefore, only wheat is sown.

B. Land, on which the yield of barley and wheat per dunam is equal and on which (under normal conditions) farmers would sow wheat, as the latter usually fetches a better price than barley.

C. Land on which the yield of barley is between 10–40% higher than that of wheat; the ratio between the effective prices of wheat and barley will determine what proportion of this land is sown with wheat.

D. Land, the soil of which is suitable for both wheat and barley, but which is situated in regions where there is no certainty of rainfall and on which the farmer, who wishes to take no undue risk, will (irrespective of the price of wheat) sow only barley.

---

[1] The argument is presented on the assumption that the production costs of wheat and barley *per dunam* are equal; in fact, the costs (per dunam) of growing wheat are 3–5% higher than those of barley.

During the Dov Josef period the Government[1] offered the following prices (per ton) for wheat delivered at the mills:

Year	IL
1949	45
1950	45
1951	65
1952	110
1953	165

To appreciate the absurdity of these prices one must compare them with the effective (black market) barley prices which moved from IL160 in December 1951 (official price IL35) to IL300 in May 1953 (official price IL125) and dropped to IL285 in 1954. These barley prices were derived from the black market demand for animal products.

Those agricultural factors—in categories B and C—which were best suited to produce *bread* grains were employed on barley production. The minimum area only was sown with wheat—category A—but even that crop was illicitly used as fodder. In 1953 the Histadruth's Agricultural Union pleaded in a circular letter with the managers of the communal villages not to dissipate the nation's resources by growing barley on land categories B and C—but such appeals were not heeded.

In 1953 the Government proposed a barter arrangement to induce the farmers to utilize the suitable local resources for the supply of bread grains. The Food Division of the Ministry of Trade and Industry was authorized to pay for wheat delivered to the mills, not in IL, but in barley at an agreed barter ratio. At the start, the farmers treated this offer with suspicion and their distrust was strengthened when the first consignments of bartered barley were low-quality Turkish and North African crops. In time the system worked so successfully that the area sown with wheat increased from 300,000 dunams in 1953 to 600,000 dunams in 1956—an expansion partly achieved by reducing the area (in category C) under barley.

At first the barter ratio was 1 ton of wheat against 1.2 tons of imported barley; in 1954 the ratio was raised to 1.3 and in 1955 to 1.4. (After 1955 the technique was changed; 1 ton of wheat was exchanged for 1 ton of imported fodder-grains plus IL60.) The following equations (on an index basis) illustrate the economics of these barter deals in 1955:

---

[1] Probably no one was more surprised than the authorities when 16% of the wheat crop was actually delivered by the farmers at these official prices to the Government-controlled mills (194).

$$\frac{\text{Dollar price of 1 ton of imported wheat}}{\text{Dollar price of 1 ton of imported barley}} : \frac{150}{100}$$

$$\frac{\text{Average (physical) yield of barley per dunam (land } C)}{\text{Average (physical) yield of wheat per dunam (land } C)} : \frac{125}{100}$$

$$\frac{\text{Tons of barley (or milocorn) bartered[1] by Food Division}}{\text{Tons of wheat bartered by farmers}} : \frac{140}{100}$$

These barter arrangements proved helpful to all concerned. They reduced the foreign currency costs of part of the wheat imports by 7%. (By expending foreign currency on the import of milocorn, Israeli wheat was acquired at $\dfrac{140 \times 100}{150}$ of the c.i.f. dollar price of wheat imports.) The farmers on land categories A and B were not in need of such high barter ratios in order to induce them to sell their wheat crops to the mills—they made differential profits. The farmers on land category C, on which the yield of barley—in physical terms— exceeded the yield of wheat by 25%, gained 12% by sowing wheat and bartering it for barley rather than sow barley. They sowed wheat which yielded them 100 units (rather than barley that would have yielded a crop of 125 units), but exchanged the 100 units of wheat for 140 units of barley—a net gain of 15 units of barley.

The distortions induced by the foreign currency controls in the price relation between wheat and barley were largely corrected by this barter arrangement. A similar barter technique had to be engineered by the Foreign Trade Division in order to execute a genuine Israeli export that would automatically have taken place on a monetary basis had a unitary exchange rate prevailed. Israel's high-quality wheat is suitable for the making of macaroni, noodles and similar products and achieves better prices in the world market than those grades of hard wheat used only for bread-making. Yet, for years, because of the inflexibility of the foreign currency controls, Israeli wheat was not exported but used as fodder and for bread-making. In 1956 the first export consignment of 3,000 tons was bought by a Swiss firm and in 1957 27,000 tons were exported. To

[1] This equation represents the ratio at which the Food Division bartered wheat (supplied by the farmers to the mills) for imported grains in 1955. It does not refer to the volume of the transactions.

avoid the intricacies of the multiple rates, the export contract provided for the bartering of 1 ton of Israeli hard wheat, c.i.f. Italy, against 1.62 tons of soft wheat, f.o.b. Italy; the local farmers were paid with barley in the appropriate barter ratio.

APPENDIX IV

THE *RATE* OF THE "FUEL DOLLAR"[1]

According to official records a unitary *rate* of 1.800 is charged for the allocated "fuel dollars" and Ministry of Finance returns show an income (in 1955) of IL30 million from excise and customs duties on fuel. Because of juggling by the able fuel controller, all categories of fuel (except petrol) were sold at prices which corresponded to *rates* of below 1.800. The deficit in the fuel controller's equalization fund and the total IL30 million taxation burden were borne by the sales prices of petrol. When the local distribution costs are deducted from the retail prices, the *rate* paid by the consumer for petrol in 1955 was 6.290 as against 1.522 for kerosene. Yet, this is not a "pure" *rate* (in the sense that it is the IL price for $1 allocated for fuel imports); the sales price must be presumed to include some margin for the fiscal taxes that are reasonably expected to be imposed on fuel. Three suggestions for computing the "pure" *rate* are given in the explanatory notes to the coming table.

There is a highly inelastic overall demand for fuel in Israel, because the larger part of the imported fuel feeds the electricity grid and the machinery of the mechanized economy. Higher *rates* for fuel (or heavier taxation) would not have appreciably reduced the amount of foreign currency expended on this group of imports—except in the case of kerosene.

Kerosene has always been favoured with a low *rate*, though it was the only major fuel category for which there was an elastic demand; a higher price would have stopped wasteful consumption and encouraged a more economical use.[2] Kerosene is used by the lower

---

[1] Sources include (23), (52), (66), (107), (140), (168) and (169).

[2] In an unpublished report (in 1955) a fuel engineer speculates on a 25% reduction in the consumption of kerosene if the price was raised by 75%. (The report speaks of "only a slight shift to electricity and gas".) The annual imports of kerosene demand an expenditure of $5½–6 million and there are additional foreign currency costs in its local distribution. Accordingly the waste involved is about $1¼ million annually.

income groups for cooking and heating and has a heavy weight in the cost-of-living index.

Between 1949 and 1951 smugglers were caught with drums of kerosene. These were bought in Israel at the effective *rate* of 0.150–0.300 and sold at a profit in Jordan.

In the summer of 1957 the Government received reports that the consumption of kerosene was rising and that of petrol falling. Furthermore, kerosene pumps made their appearance at petrol stations. It seemed that car owners had learned the art of "switching" between multiple rates and this applied in particular to taxi drivers. Some bought kerosene instead of petrol to run their vehicles according to one of two schemes: they either filled the tank half with petrol and half with kerosene, or attached a contrivance (produced in Israel) to the car so that the engine could be started with petrol, after which it ran entirely on kerosene. An engine becomes obsolete within nine months if kerosene is used continuously. Though it represented a dissipation of the country's foreign currency resources, the difference in the IL prices of kerosene and petrol made these schemes profitable to the vehicle owners.

In 1957 the cabinet dealt with this issue, for in the view of the Ministry of Finance, a revenue loss of millions of IL was involved. The Ministry of Health was anxious about the effects of the noxious gases emanating from engines powered by kerosene. On the 18th December an Emergency Regulation was published prohibiting the use of kerosene in vehicles without a permit from the Ministry of Transport. Offenders were liable to a maximum punishment of one year's imprisonment and a fine of IL5,000. The Director-General of the Ministry of Transport announced at a press conference that the inspectors who would supervise the implementation of this regulation were equipped with a specially manufactured apparatus which—when inserted in the tank—would immediately indicate the fuel category. On the 1st February 1958 the owner of a petrol station was fined IL2,000 for selling petrol diluted with kerosene. The prosecuting counsel said that the Israeli parliament had lately passed a law prohibiting such practices; the law had been passed, not because the legislators wished to safeguard the interests of the private car owners (whose engines would be damaged through the use of kerosene), but because these practices were harmful to the economy of the country, for increased amounts of foreign currency had to be allocated for the import of new engines.

TABLE XVII

THE MULTIPLE EXCHANGE RATES FOR FUEL

	Row	Kerosene, Paraffin	Petrol	Gas Oil, Solar	Bunker Oil, Mazut
Imported tonnage, thousands	I	136	196	184	691
Dollar c.i.f. price per ton	II	39.30	42.60	36.59	22.16
IL equivalent of row II	III	70.740	76.680	65.862	39.888
Local costs in IL per ton	IV	28.692	32.737	18.068	10.403
"Tax" (+) or "Sub-sidy" (—), in IL, per ton	V	—10.925	+191.234	—4.406	—5.391
Retail IL price per ton	VI	88.500	300.671	79.524	44.900
Rates of "fuel dollars":					
Assumption A	VII	1.522	6.290	1.680	1.556
Assumption B	VIII	1.522	2.770	1.680	1.556
Assumption C	IX	0.802	5.570	0.960	0.837

Row I: the data refer to 97% of the tonnage and to 91.5% of the dollar value of the fuel imports in 1955.

Row II: price data refer to 16th April 1956.

Row III: computed according to the *rate* of 1.800.

Row IV: local costs include all distribution, handling and profit charges. They have a high import content, but this is ignored in my computations and local costs are reckoned entirely in IL.

Row V: all deviations from the 1.800 *rate* are regarded as "taxes" or "subsidies"; they appear in the official nomenclature as surcharges, fuel customs duties, excise duties, contributions to equalization funds, etc.

Rows VII–IX:

Assumption A—*The imposition of taxes on fuel is entirely ignored*; the *rate* for the "fuel dollar" is arrived at by deducting local costs (row IV) from the retail price (row VI) and dividing the remainder by the dollar price (row II).

Assumption B—The actual fiscal income of the Ministry of Finance from the total fuel imports was approximately IL30 million and is assumed to be *imposed only on petrol*; this works out at about IL150 per ton. The *rate* for the "fuel dollar" is obtained by deducting from the retail price (row VI) the local costs (row IV) plus IL150 and dividing the remainder by the dollar price (row II).

Assumption C—The fiscal income of the Ministry of Finance from fuel imports, IL30 million, is assumed to be imposed in the form of an (equal) *ad valorem tax of 40% on all fuel categories*. The *rate* for the "fuel dollar" is computed by deducting from the retail price (row VI) the local costs (row IV) plus 40% of the import price (row III) and dividing the remainder by the dollar price (row II).

Judging by the fiscal practices of the Western World, the "pure" *rate* of the "fuel dollar" can be presumed to be between the *rates* of assumptions B and C.

APPENDIX V

THE *RATE* OF THE "MEAT DOLLAR"

Ordinarily, as the authorities regarded edible animal products as "luxuries", foreign currency was not allocated for their import. Only small quantities of frozen meat (or cattle), for the formal distribution of a small ration to satisfy the cost-of-living index statisticians, were legally brought into the country. This Tozereth Harretz protection gave farmers an opportunity to produce (uneconomically) animal proteins.[1]

The following are the ex farm prices of three animal products in 1953 as compared with the import price of frozen meat, ex port Haifa.

---

[1] The director of the Food Division reported that ". . . we know of cows, giving 4,500 litres of milk a year, being slaughtered for the meat black market" (22).

Product	Price per kg. of gross weight	Percentage of edible portion	Price per kg. of edible portion
Cattle meat (carcass) .	IL3.000	75	IL4.000
Chicken (live) . .	IL2.500	60	IL4.167
Carp (live) . .	IL1.700	45	IL3.778
Imported meat (carcass)	$0.51	75	$0.68

Despite this price relation between imported and locally produced meat, the Government did not import low-priced meat to satisfy the latent demand for animal proteins. Instead, as was explained officially in 1954, Government policy aimed at "the expansion of the poultry meat branch in order to combat the slaughtering of milk cows . . ." (22).

Notwithstanding this encouragement to raise chickens domestically as the chief source of meat, the prices for edible animal products would have risen even further if they had not been kept down by illegal imports: cattle were smuggled in from the neighbouring Arab states; Scrip and Standard Food Parcels companies imported tinned meat; the law courts were busy with litigation concerning black market consignments of cattle and frozen meat. In 1956, despite protests by the Ministry of Agriculture that this was a contravention of Tozereth Haaretz policy, the Ministry of Finance willingly accepted frozen meat from American surplus stores on a non-commercial basis. The ending of the latter type of import and the Sinai campaign drove up the (Tozereth Haaretz) *rate* of meat in the autumn of 1957 to the high level of 8.

Press reports in November 1958 attribute to the Minister of Trade and Industry a public announcement that no more meat would be imported during 1959.

TABLE XVIII

THE (TOZERETH HAARETZ) *RATE* OF THE "MEAT DOLLAR"
[(16), (23), (24).]

	1950	1951	1952	1953	1954	1955
Price ex farm per 1 kg. in IL:						
Chicken (live)[1]	2.5	2.9	3.4	3.1	2.8	2.5
Cattle (carcass)	1.5	1.9	2.4	3.0	3.4	4.0
Local meat replaces imports at *rate* of:[2]						
Chicken	4.9	5.7	6.7	6.1	5.5	4.9
Cattle	2.9	3.7	4.7	5.9	6.7	7.8

APPENDIX VI

THE WASTAGE OF BREAD

Bread is baked in Israel almost entirely from imported flour or flour made from imported grains; the annual import bill is $20–28 million. Bread supplies the Israelis with 45% of their calories and 47% of their proteins, but in 1953 they spent less than 12% of their food budget on bread.

Two kinds of bread—both price-controlled but not rationed—are

[1] The price of "live weight" chicken is lower than that quoted; in order to bring chicken meat on to a common denominator with local and imported cattle meat, the price given in this row has been computed by dividing the actual price by 60 and multiplying it by 75. (Cf. different percentages of edible portion, p. 261.)

[2] The distribution costs ex farm—for domestic meat—and ex port Haifa—for imported meat—have been assumed to be equal. The palatable differences between the various kinds of meat have been ignored; in a country where the legal meat ration is sometimes only 100 grammes per month, they are not very significant.

The *rate* of the "meat dollar" is calculated by comparing the local IL prices with $0.51, the latter being the unweighted average price for imported frozen meat during our six-year period.

baked under Government supervision: bread from standard flour[1] with an extraction rate of 87% and bread from white flour with an extraction rate of 74%. (Some dishonest bakers adulterate the white flour with the standard flour and sell the bread baked from this mixed flour, at the controlled prices for white bread.) If the different extraction rates and other factors are taken into account, the undistorted price ratio between 1 kg. of standard bread and 1 kg. of white bread would be 100 : 120. The keenest distortion was in 1950 when the actual price ratio was 100 : 233. In 1959 it was 100 : 142.

Because of the higher extraction rate of standard flour, the Government encouraged the consumption of standard bread hoping thus to reduce wheat imports. The nominal *rate* at which wheat was imported was 0.357 in 1952; 1 in 1954 and 1.800 in 1959. However, the Ministry of Finance paid an IL subsidy per "wheat dollar" to the Food Division. In addition, the Food Division introduced "internal" multiple rates for the different categories of wheat imports and, in fact, subsidized the price of standard bread through the higher price of white bread. I estimate that during 1949 and 1950 the effective *rate* for the "wheat dollar", that financed the flour for standard bread, was between 0.250 and 0.274; Beham-Rosenberg (214) arrived at an effective *rate* of 0.749 for 1954.

During the spring of 1954, one-half of the laying hens were fed with fodder not allocated by the authorities, and the breeding of ducks, geese, pigs and rabbits, for which no feedingstuffs were allocated, spread throughout the country. Between 1951 and 1954 the retail price of standard bread, per ton, was IL45–139. Smallholders and urban families with some chickens in the backyard fed their animals with bread, for they were officially allocated only small quantities of fodder. The larger farms and kibbutzim supplemented their official fodder allocations by buying black market barley at IL160–300 per ton. The demand for bread, as a substitute for fodder, and the black market barley prices were a function of the prices prevailing on the black market for edible animal products.[2] During

[1] Standard flour sometimes contained rye; the highest percentage was 25%.

[2] "But sometimes tensions arising from the unreality of Soviet prices become too great to be ignored. One such situation occurred after Stalin's death as a result of the excessively low price set for bread. Thousands of Soviet citizens, taking account of the high price of meat in the free market where peasants sell their surplus produce, calculated that good money could be made by buying bread, feeding it to livestock and then selling the meat in the local free market.

"The result was a run on bread. Whole businesses were apparently organized to take advantage of this opportunity. Every morning in many Soviet cities trucks would go from bakery to bakery buying up bread and rolls to feed to livestock. People, the Soviet press implies, quit their normal jobs to devote themselves to the more profitable work of raising a few pigs in the backyard.

this period the import price, c.i.f. Haifa, of wheat was $75–101 and that of milocorn $55–60.

The responsible minister, Dov Josef, could have stopped this dissipation of resources by any one of four measures: (1) to appreciably increase the price of bread; (2) to import meat; (3) to import large quantities of cheap feedingstuffs; (4) fight the barley black market and the wastage of bread by police measures. The policy of keeping down the cost-of-living index worked against measure (1). Measure (2) was not even considered as meat imports were "a wasteful expenditure for a poor country". Measure (3) was opposed by the farming lobby, because such imports—apart from stopping the wastage of bread—would also have lowered the price level of local grains.[1] Dov Josef, therefore, called upon the police to stop the wastage of bread. Policemen searched farms and the allotments of smallholders and confiscated sacks of bread whilst the courts imposed fines—all to no avail. (In places, like Migdal, bread was even unofficially rationed—$\frac{1}{2}$ loaf of standard bread and $\frac{3}{4}$ loaf of white bread per capita.) In March 1953 a newspaper account stated that:

". . . a sentence of six months imprisonment was meted out by

Bread itself became scarce as human consumers found themselves competing on unfavourable price terms with livestock. The situation became so intolerable that in August 1956 a special decree was issued making it a punishable offence 'to use bread, flour, groats, potatoes or other food products bought in state or co-operative stores to feed livestock and poultry'. Heavy taxes were laid on city workers who kept livestock, and if they proved inadequate, local authorities were authorized to prohibit city dwellers from raising livestock at all. And bread, in effect, was rationed; only limited amounts could be bought by a person at any time" (249). Israel's experience is clearly not unique.

[1] I can testify, from personal knowledge, that the director of the Food Division pressed Dov Josef to allocate part of the foreign currency—at his disposal for wheat imports—for the import of feedingstuffs. This was rejected by Dov Josef, who was not convinced that increased imports of feedingstuffs would automatically lead to decreased wheat imports.

There was also a more important reason why Dov Josef rejected this suggestion. The foreign currency controls administration had instructions to allocate, come what may, foreign currency for a sufficiently large import volume of wheat (and fuel) that would obviate physical rationing. The Ministry of Finance regarded the import of feedingstuffs as an import of semi-luxuries and did not hesitate, when faced with a shortage of foreign currency, to cut promised allocations. Dov Josef knew that, irrespective of the "chicken consumption of bread", the Ministry of Finance would continue to place foreign currency at his disposal for unlimited quantities of wheat. He feared that, if he voluntarily reduced his demand for foreign currency to purchase wheat, his sacrifice would be accepted, but the Ministry of Finance would not keep to the bargain of allocating, instead, more foreign currency for the import of fodder.

the Tel-Aviv district court to Ephraim Guttschalk, the owner of a cowshed in Shaich Munis, who had been found guilty of having in his possession bread for the feeding of livestock."

In the summer of 1954 the Government finally adopted a set of measures which put an end to the wastage of bread. The price of standard bread was increased (by 40%) to IL194 per ton, the price control on grains was abolished and feedingstuffs were imported in large quantities, becoming freely available at IL140–180.

The results were immediate: the consumption of bread in general (and that of standard bread in particular) dropped, and the de-controlled grains became cheaper. Bread was still used by marginal producers for fodder and considerable wastage remained in the households but the back of the problem was broken by these measures.

What had been the extent of the past wastage of bread?

(a) A report by a senior official of the Food Division, comparing the allocations of flour to the population before and after the decisive measures in the summer of 1954, shows the average consumption of flour to have declined by 10% and the consumption of standard flour by 27% (200).

MONTHLY ALLOCATION OF FLOUR BY FOOD DIVISION PER PERSON IN GRAMMES

	March 1954	March 1955	Changes
For Standard Bread .	7,970	5,830	−27%
For White Bread .	2,655	3,785	+43%
For Total Bread Con- sumption . .	10,625	9,615	−10%

(b) The trade association of the millers estimated that after the summer of 1954 the flour consumption had dropped by 15% (201).

(c) There are several authoritative Government estimates of the waste of bread, which all range between 15% and 20% of the total imports of wheat and flour. The director of the Food Division said at a press conference in 1952, that 15% of the wheat imports were diverted to the feeding of livestock.

(d) A survey was made in August 1950 among 1,000 households in

K

connection with the new cost-of-living index. The economic research department of the Ministry of Finance found that the data showed a 20% discrepancy between the per capita figures of flour allocated by the Food Division to the bakeries and the declared consumption of bread by the households (87).

(e) In March 1951 a second survey in connection with the new cost-of-living index was completed. The nutritionist, Bavli, analysed the data of this survey and compared them with the official flour allocations of the Food Division. She found that the households interviewed admitted to consuming 19% more white flour, and 27% less standard flour, than was said to have been allocated per capita. Bavli explains these discrepancies:

". . . the actual human consumption of standard bread is considerably lower than the quantity marketed. Some of the standard flour has gone into white bread and some to feeding animals" (193).

DAILY CONSUMPTION OF BREAD PER PERSON IN GRAMMES

	According to allocations of Food Division	According to Second Survey of C-o-L. Index
Standard Bread . .	286.6	207.6
White Bread . .	115.5	138.3
Total Bread Consumption.	402.1	345.9

This table shows the actual (human) consumption of bread and flour to have been 14% below that which formed the basis of allocations to bakeries.

It is not unreasonable to conclude from the above evidence that about 15% of the imported wheat and flour went to feed livestock: $3–4 million per annum. The dissipation of resources can be measured by the difference between this annual foreign currency expenditure upon wheat and the hypothetical expenditure upon an equivalent quantity of milocorn: one to one and a quarter million dollars. To this must be added the import content of turning the wheat into bread plus the IL resources expended in the process of feeding livestock with wheat turned first into flour and then baked into bread.

266

TABLE XIX

NEW PRICES OF BREAD IN TEL-AVIV

Type of Bread	Grammes	Date	Price in Prutoth
Standard .	1,000	May 1948	65
White .	750	May 1948	85
Standard .	1,000	November 1948	65
White .	750	November 1948	88
Standard .	1,000	May 1949	53
White .	750	May 1949	80
Standard .	1,000	July 1949	52
White .	750	July 1949	79
Standard .	1,000	February 1950	45
White .	750	February 1950	79
Standard .	1,000	September 1951	50
White .	750	September 1951	85
Standard .	1,000	December 1951	55
White .	750	December 1951	95
Standard .	1,000	February 1952	60
White .	750	February 1952	100
Standard .	1,000	March 1952	65
White .	750	March 1952	110
Standard .	1,000	April 1952	70
White .	750	April 1952	110
Standard .	950	June 1952	75
White .	750	June 1952	115
Standard .	950	November 1952	90
White .	750	November 1952	140
Standard .	950	January 1953	100
White .	750	January 1953	155
Standard .	900	June 1953	125
White .	750	June 1953	180
Standard .	900	July 1954	175
White .	750	July 1954	190
Standard .	900	April 1956	180
White .	750	April 1956	200
Standard .	900	November 1957	185
White .	750	November 1957	215
Standard .	900	December 1958	185
White .	750	December 1958	220

Appendix VII

SIX ILLUSTRATIONS OF UNREQUITED EXPORTS

A—GLASS

In 1952 the new Phoenicia glass factory near Haifa commenced production. This monopolist was protected by the Government's policy of not issuing any import licences for plate-glass. Investments, valued at December 1957 IL prices, exceeded IL15 million (including a $600,000 loan from the Export-Import Bank). The Histadruth and the Government financed this firm which in 1949, when the foundation stone was laid, forecast that one-half of its annual output of 2 million square metres would be exported.

There are two studies on the commercial aspects of exporting Israeli plate-glass. The first, by Baharal (122), showed that in 1954 the import content in one square metre of plate-glass packed for export was $0.38. The second, by Goren in 1955 (95), computes the import content of that year's export at $0.37. The better part of the exported plate-glass in these two years was sent to Turkey. Belgian producers[1] found it unprofitable to sell the glass for less than $0.80 (c.i.f. Istanbul); hence Eastern Europe and Israel captured the Turkish market by offering their glass products at dumping prices. Israel sold its glass in 1953, f.o.b. Haifa, for 0.40 Turkish clearing-dollars (per square metre); for 0.46 clearing-dollars in 1954 and for 0.50 clearing-dollars in 1955. When these clearing-dollar prices are transformed by the effective disagios into dollar prices, it becomes self-evident that the export proceeds were lower than the import content of the exported articles.

B—WORSTED WOOLLEN GOODS

Two of the largest branches of the export industry were the spinning of worsted yarn from imported "tops" and the weaving of worsted woollen cloths from imported fine yarn. In both cases the *IfE* materials were imported entirely from hard currency areas.

---

[1] The Phoenicia glass works suffered the misfortune of the discovery of glass sand in the Negev; because of the principles of Tozereth Haaretz this raw material could then no longer be imported. The import content of transporting the glass sand from the Negev to the factory was larger than the foreign currency cost of buying the material abroad and shipping it to Haifa. Whilst Belgian producers paid $1.50 for a ton of glass sand, in 1954 the Phoenicia factory paid IL20.

The export of worsted yarn was directed exclusively to soft currency countries. According to official sources (23) the import content was almost 90%. The Ministry of Finance permitted three factories to export to the value of 9 million nominal-dollars in the 1953–58 period.

The same official source calculated that the import content of the latter branch was 80%.

EXPORT OF WORSTED WOOLLEN CLOTHS
(In thousands of nominal-dollars)

1951	.	(3,000)
1952	.	2,020
1953	.	611
1954	.	524
1955	.	297
1956	.	307
1957	.	448
1958	.	346

Until 1953 the export of woollen cloths was permitted even in barter deals leading to imports of soft-currency goods. After 1953 the Ministry of Finance no longer encouraged this type of export. Nonetheless, because of the special *pamaz* technique of this branch, sales abroad continued and in fact flourished, because the Ministry of Finance ceased to issue to ordinary importers licences for fine worsted yarn. The *pamaz* technique enabled exporters to import, with the value-added portion of their foreign currency earnings, materials for sale in the domestic market. Consequently, exporters of woollen cloths became the sole legal suppliers of worsted woollen yarn for the weaving of cloths designed for the Israeli market. In 1955 the *rate* of the woollen-yarn-*pamaz*-dollar was about 3.500. The exporters of this branch knew that the price of their *pamaz*-dollar depended on the demand of the domestic market for woollen yarn. They realized, however, that they must not increase their export volume beyond that point where the offer of too many woollen-yarn-*pamaz*-dollars would bring down the price of the yarn and thus endanger the worthwhileness of export production.

It seems that some exporters also used unworthy methods to augment their foreign currency earnings and sold their exports, unofficially, at dumping prices. The press reported (195) that in 1952 the Swiss authorities were perturbed about the dumping of Israeli woollen cloths in Switzerland and threatened to impose sanctions. The report attempts to explain this dumping:

". . . Israeli exporters can afford to lose on sales of woollen cloths to Switzerland as they gain, in barter deals, on the imported goods."

C—"CHEMICALS AND FERTILIZERS"

One of the showpieces of Israel's industry is the "Chemicals and Fertilizers Ltd." in which are invested—valued at December 1957 prices—IL100 million. The Government has subscribed between 80 and 90% of the capital, a large part of it in the form of foreign machinery.

In 1956 a junior civil servant, Pollack, was sent to make a routine check on the working of the factory; he returned with a written (114) analysis of the export calculations of this enterprise. Even now the report is still a closely guarded secret but, immediately after it was privately circulated, the foreign currency controller ordered that no further export licences be granted to this firm for certain of its products.

Inter alia, the Pollak report revealed that the production of super-phosphates had a value-added of 32.4% at a *rate* of 6.557. Potassium sulphate was said to have a value-added of 50% with a *rate* of 2.750. Ammonium sulphate had a value-added of 26% with a *rate* of 5.756 and di-calcium phosphate had a value-added of 35% with a *rate* of 6.455.

D—WATCHES

In 1953 and 1954 three watch factories were established in Israel and their export proceeds were (in nominal-dollars): 1953—213,000; 1954—909,000; 1955—445,000. The factories engaged in the dignified ritual of "switching" by changing the Swiss francs, allocated by the Ministry of Finance for their *imports-for-exports*, into Turkish clearing-dollars. The official disagio on the latter over-valued the Turkish Liras in terms of IL and the watch manufacturers were assured of a handsome profit. The nature of these exports was soon apprehended by the Ministry of Finance but the firms were not immediately deprived of their foreign currency allocations. Public opinion favoured exports *per se* and the foreign currency controls administration felt that it could not prohibit the export of watches outright. After the Economic Advisory Staff had prepared a memorandum on the subject, the Ministry of Finance let it leak through to the press. The report by the Economic Advisory Staff (179) suggested the immediate closing down of two of the three factories:

"The Solga factory is engaged in importing already assembled
270

Swiss movements and already manufactured cases; the movements are inspected, cleaned and re-oiled, and repaired when necessary, then timed and inserted in cases."

". . . the Orlogin factory . . . performs the same operations as does Solga with the one difference that it imports material and manufactures its own cases into which it inserts the imported assembled movements."

The Ministry of Finance stated in a communique that the Orlogin factory was "in fact, a metal works which has a watch department that employs four people. This department packs finished watch movements which are imported from abroad" (208).

By 1955 the authorities had, in practice, suspended the export of watches. One of the last consignments (to Turkey) was checked (209) by the Lydda customs authorities and found to consist of *non-assembled* watch movements. It seems that in some cases the watch firms did not even artificially create value-added by casing imported movements, but merely re-exported the unassembled movements.

E—CHOCOLATES

Sugar was the basic foodstuff which had the relatively highest black market price. In 1951 the ratio of the sugar black market price to the official price was 25 : 1; in 1952, 20 : 1; in 1953, 8 : 1. This craving for sugar was exploited by the manufacturers of products in which sugar is an important ingredient (e.g. chocolates, cakes, ice-cream).

In 1953 (130) a ton of sugar was sold on the grey market for IL900; if the IL75 customs duty is deducted, the *rate* is equivalent to 8. The prospects of selling sugar (imported with the value-added portion of the *pamaz* proceeds) at *rates* of 3–8 induced exports of chocolates and allied products for several million dollars.[1] As early as 1949, Marcus (127) had challenged the economic feasibility of exporting chocolates, the import content of which he had calculated at 68%. Six years later a more thorough official investigation estimated the import content of this branch at 85%.

The "internal exports"[2] to the Scrip companies were even more remunerative than the ordinary chocolate exports. It will be recalled

---

[1] Such exports were made possible only because of the anomalous price-and-cost structure of Israel. However, I exclude from this generalization sentimental exports to Jewish communities, consignments of chewing-gum and the delivery of cocoa butter in "switch" deals.

[2] "Internal exports" is used in the fourth sense of this nomenclature as set out on p. 277. For the Ministry of Finance agreement with the Scrip companies, *vide* p. 192.

that the Scrip companies had undertaken to sell 42½% of their foreign currency receipts at the official *rates* of 1 and 1.800 to the Ministry of Finance. Alternatively they could discharge their obligations by purchasing Israeli goods. Their Israeli suppliers were regarded as "internal exporters" and paid the dollar proceeds into their *pamaz* account. Of 1,374 tons of food bought by the Scrip companies in Israel in 1953, no less than 1,166 tons were chocolates and sweets.

   This preference of the Scrip companies for Israeli chocolates was the result of a surreptitious agreement. Until the agreement, the factories had delivered chocolates to the warehouses of the Scrip companies and the latter had sold them on the black market. This incongruous arrangement was terminated when the Scrip companies agreed to let the chocolate manufacturers sell the chocolates through their own black market contacts. Henceforth, the Scrip companies paid foreign currency into the *pamaz* accounts of the "internal exporters" against invoices of goods allegedly delivered to them but in reality sold illicitly by the manufacturers. The chocolate manufacturers, in turn, paid (unofficially) in IL for these *pamaz*-dollars which provided them with automatic import licences for sugar and other ingredients. The price the chocolate manufacturers paid to the Scrip companies for the *pamaz*-dollars was at the *rate* of 2.500 to 2.700. The Scrip companies benefited by this agreement for it discharged their obligations to the Ministry of Finance, yielding them about IL2.600 for every dollar they would alternatively have had to exchange at the *rates* of 1 or 1.800. The chocolate manufacturers gained by this arrangement for they thus bought *pamaz*-dollars, at a *rate* of 2.600, and this compared favourably with the value of *pamaz* imports of sugar.

   In 1954 the marginal profits of the chocolate manufacturers were depressed by a change in Government policy. While, for obvious cost-of-living index reasons, the official sugar ration was also to be distributed in future at low prices, an uncontrolled grey market was to be allowed to function. The Ministry of Trade and Industry offered food manufacturers unlimited quantities of sugar (c.i.f. Haifa costing less than $100) for IL750. In addition, an IL450 customs duty was imposed on all sugar imports (with the exception of the monthly sugar ration) including those financed with *pamaz*-dollars. This reduced the effective *rate* of the chocolate-*pamaz*-dollar to 3. (Actually the *pamaz*-dollar, when used for the import of other articles which could be said to be "in the line of production" of chocolate manufacturers, was worth about IL3½.) Some concept of the marginal profits that must have been made between 1950 and

1954 by the ordinary and "internal" exports of chocolates can be gauged from the fact that, even after the effective *rate* of the *pamaz*-dollar was reduced from 8 to $3\frac{1}{2}$, the chocolate manufacturers continued to implore the Government to allow them to export with *pamaz* benefits.

F—KAISER-FRAZER[1]

The Kaiser-Frazer assembly plant for vehicles (not restricted to Kaiser-Frazer cars) was opened in Haifa in 1951. Before the plant was actually working, this Israeli firm had already "exported"; goods were sent with its invoices directly from America to the customers of Israel who paid in clearing-dollars. It is not unjust to describe this plant as a "switch factory"; certainly its sponsors had primarily intended it for triangular trade transactions. For several years Kaiser-Frazer was the largest single exporter in Israel, and cars were the biggest export branch after citrus and diamonds.

EXPORTS OF KAISER-FRAZER
(In thousands of nominal-dollars)

1953	.	5,430
1954	.	7,148
1955	.	3,459
1956	.	1,711
1957	.	2,136
1958	.	1,838

Practically all the exports went to clearing-dollar markets and of those Finland, Yugoslavia and Turkey accounted (in 1954) for 90%. For every $100 of *imports-for-exports* materials allocated by the Ministry of Finance, Kaiser-Frazer sold receipts of 136 clearing-dollars to the Ministry of Finance. The official trade statistics regard these 36 clearing-dollars as a net foreign currency gain for the country, and on that basis Kaiser-Frazer asserted that its exports have 26% value-added. Actually the foreign currency controls administration discounted these 136 clearing-dollars with a 10% disagio and accordingly the value-added is only 18%. The Economic Advisory Staff (191) calculated the economic disagio rate in 1954 as 15% and, if this is accepted, the value-added is only 12% of the exported products. Data, not available at the time to the Economic

---

[1] The Kaiser-Frazer plant has been examined in several analytical studies, the most important of which—though in some details inaccurate—is that of Erdreich (191); *vide* also (229).

Advisory Staff, make it appear that a 20% disagio would then have been a realistic discount for the Turkish clearing-dollar. Consequently, I estimate that the value-added of Kaiser-Frazer exports was not higher than 8% and (using the computations of Erdreich) export earnings were then rewarded at the *rate* of 3. The effective *rate*, paid by the national economy, was much above 3, as the Kaiser-Frazer plant imposed further penalties on the country which were not reflected in the production costs of tne firm.

In the first stages of the company's operation, the foreign currency controller accepted its claim that it be allowed to import goods with some of the export earnings. The Cyprus company was formed for this purpose and successfully pressed the Government to allow it to act as a food importer. (In 1954, for example, American Kaiser-Frazer cars, assembled in Haifa, were sent to Argentina and bartered for frozen meat.)

As a large firm which enjoyed the confidence of the officials of the foreign currency controls, Kaiser-Frazer received preferential treatment. The disagio technique was sometimes "adjusted" by the Ministry of Finance for this firm's benefit, e.g. in the case of Finnish, Argentinian and Norwegian clearing-dollars (178).

The Israeli automobile market was regarded as the exclusive domain of this firm. When the Government at times relaxed the operation of the Tozereth Haaretz principle, the powerful Kaiser-Frazer lobby was activated. (The labour council of the factory declared a "spontaneous" strike when the Electricity Corporation (209) ordered some vehicles from an American supplier and not from the Haifa assembly plant.)

The vehicles of this assembly plant (though of inferior quality to the American product) were always dearer in IL than imported assembled vehicles and the import content of a Haifa-assembled car sometimes exceeded the dollar c.i.f. Haifa price of an assembled, imported car. Erdreich reports that the Haifa plant sold locally-assembled Pick-ups 4 Wd at 10.1% above the c.i.f. price of a finished model; the Haifa-assembled Aero Aco 685 B were sold domestically at 32.3% above the c.i.f. Haifa import price of the finished vehicle. In June 1957 the Government appointed a commission to inquire into charges that Kaiser-Frazer had paid for certain knocked-down units, c.i.f. Haifa, more foreign currency than the dollar price of the finished units, c.i.f. Haifa. There have been public charges (the results of the investigations by the Ministry of Transport have not been published) that this firm sold vehicles in Israel that had faulty engines which had been acquired from cut-price dealers in America (183).

Kaiser-Frazer, Haifa, made a profit of 54.3% on its capital in

1953 and 43.8% in 1954. As an industrial producer of value-added the Kaiser-Frazer plant has not proved an economic asset for Israel, though, because of its monopolistic status, it has yielded large profits to its enterprising sponsors. Israel's balance of payments records a slight foreign currency gain as the result of the "switch" activities of this plant; it may be noted, however, that other traders, who "switched" American cars and spare parts in Europe, made more lucrative deals.

The Ministry of Finance wielded an important bargaining weapon in its dealings with soft-currency suppliers for the Israeli market through the large hard currency cash income at its disposal. In my view, this bargaining power was capable of more advantageous application than allocating millions of dollars in the form of *imports-for-exports* materials to Kaiser-Frazer.

By 1956 the difficulties of exporting "switched" cars had mounted, and there was also a greater awareness of the nature of these unrequited exports in the Ministry of Finance. Further, the Kaiser-Frazer factories in America ceased to supply assembly parts as they had stopped production; the Israeli Kaiser-Frazer plant began to produce the French Renault cars. Several Government investigators, and Tevet in his articles, charged that the value-added in the assembly of Renault cars was at the *rate* of 27; one model was said to have a *rate* of 42.

When the Kaiser-Frazer company received the Government's blessing in 1951 to establish a factory in Israel, it promised publicly to export 90% of its output. During the last three years this firm managed to export about 25% and the remainder was sold for IL to the Israeli public which was forced to buy the high-priced cars of this firm because the Government did not ordinarily give import licences for other models.

There is something ludicrous in the foreign currency regulations of the French and Israeli Governments. The French Government does not issue import licences freely to its colonies for American cars and the Israeli Government does not give import licences freely for French cars. An agreement was, therefore, unofficially entered into whereby Israel would assemble American jeeps in the (Haifa) Kaiser-Frazer plant and be allowed to export these to the French colonies; in turn the Israeli Government would give the required import licences so that French cars could be assembled in Haifa for sale in the Israeli home market.

The Ministry of Finance has apparently blessed the Kaiser-Frazer plans to export in 1959 and 1960 (with *IfE* foreign currency allocated by the Government) assembled vehicles for $2 million to Colombia.

The astute Colombian importers will pay, not in money, but in coffee. 20% of this coffee will be sold on the Israeli market and 80% of it will be exported to a soft-currency market behind the Iron Curtain. The recipients of the Colombian coffee will also not pay in money to Kaiser-Frazer, but in the form of sugar and the Haifa assembly plant will import it for resale on Israel's domestic market.

APPENDIX VIII

A CATALOGUE OF EXPORT PROMOTION

This catalogue lists most of the direct and indirect aids which, at one time or another, subsidized the majority of exports. An "aid" is defined as a material[1] consideration for manufacturers who are exporters or claim to be exporters. The burden of these aids is borne by the State (through the remission of applicable taxes and obligations or by financial outlays which are a budgetary charge); they also raise the price level of imported and locally manufactured goods.

Most of these material considerations do not apply to the citrus and diamonds branches. Export subsidies have the declared purpose of increasing the *net* foreign currency income of the economy, and one need, therefore, only consider their effect on the volume of additional value-added of the non-citrus and non-diamonds exports. If the total cost (in terms of IL) of all the aids were calculable and compared with the value-added in row M, Table XIV, p. 197, the *rate* of the export dollar would be known.[2] Basing myself on official indicators, I arrive at a minimum *rate* of IL 4 per $1 of value-added for the beginning of 1959. This only takes into account the calculable costs and the total social cost of earning an export dollar is appreciably higher.

Although the majority of the "internal exports" are not registered

---

[1] I have excluded such considerations as the theatrical distribution of certificates to the "best exporters of the year".

[2] Assume the following: an export order for IL100,000 is subsidized by a 12 months' credit of IL100,000 on a 6% p.a. basis; the equilibrium interest rate is estimated to be 12% whilst the effective black market interest rate for this type of entrepreneur is 18%; the (net) value-added of this export order is IL18,000. On these assumptions the exporter is subsidized by the economy with IL6,000, this being the difference in the interest payments due on a 6%, rather than on a 12%, loan. (In fact, the subsidy is IL12,000, the difference between the interest at 6% and 18%.) What is nominally "a 6% subsidy on an export order of IL100,000" is an effective subsidy of 33% (or 66%) on the value of the net foreign currency earnings.

by the statisticians of external trade, most of them benefit from these catalogued subsidies. The term "internal exports" is used by the foreign currency controls administration in four different senses:

    (*a*) The sale of Israeli goods in Israel to non-residents and tourists against foreign currency or foreign currency vouchers.

    (*b*) The sale of Israeli goods in Israel to residents or bodies allowed by the foreign currency controller to expend their foreign currency income or allocations in this way, e.g. Israeli export firms, the army, local shipping and air companies, some *institutions*.[1]

    (*c*) The sale of local goods to Israeli residents against foreign currency vouchers paid for by non-residents (*vide* p. 191).

    (*d*) The sale of local goods to the Scrip and Standard Food Parcels companies.

(1) The export subsidies paid in the form of premiums and the *pamaz* technique are not strictly within the province of this catalogue. These calculable rewards of the exporter (*vide* p. 157) were modified by the following indirect subsidies:

The money premiums are paid on the basis of the nominal-dollar and are supposed to be converted into the equivalent of the U.S. dollar by the official disagios, if any. The clearing-dollars are deliberately over-valued by attaching relatively low disagios to them or none at all.

The *pamaz* technique was so rewarding that exporters had every inducement to pay into their *pamaz* accounts the maximum amount of foreign currency. The economic ministries helped exporters—I have been told as a "deliberate measure"—to increase artificially the proportion of their export earnings which could be imputed to value-added. The "real value-added" of an export is the f.o.b. Israel price received for the article less the c.i.f. Israel price for the *imports-for-exports*. In fact, however, the Ministry of Finance permitted the exporter to pay into his *pamaz* account the c.i.f. foreign market price for his goods less the f.o.b. foreign market price of his *imports-for-exports*; the Ministry of Finance allocated foreign currency at the 1.800 *rate* to pay for the transport and insurance costs and these costs were not a charge on the *pamaz* account. I estimate that this increased

---

[1] This was particularly attractive for *institutions* with their discriminatory *rates* for money transfers. As the foreign currency payments for local goods were usually paid into the *pamaz* accounts of the "internal exporters", the manufacturers gave the *institutions* a substantial discount on the ordinary IL purchase price. This *rate* of the foreign currency of the *institutions* oscillated between the Standard III and IV *rates*.

the *pamaz* account on the average by 15%.—By December 1958 both
these additional *pamaz* subsidies were abolished and today only the
"real value-added" can be paid into the *pamaz* account.

(2) Export firms were granted cheap credit facilities:[1]

A. To combat unemployment the Ministry of Labour extended
cheap loans to subsidize the cost of labour in plants willing to
employ additional labour. This "Industrial Employment Fund"
gave priority allocations to export industries—the Afikim
plywood factory, for example, received such subsidized loans
because it exported the "major part of its output".

B. Applications from export firms for loans from the Export-
Import Bank and the Reparations Company were given priority
and—by the latter also preferential—terms. The same policy
was pursued by the Ministry of Finance in regard to IL loans
from the Development Budget.

C. Banks were often permitted to accommodate export firms
"below the line of liquidity". The Bank of Israel used its
limited re-discount IL facilities chiefly for (agriculture and)
export.

D. The Government and the banks jointly established a fund to
provide loans at 7% for "Working Capital of Export Industries". This revolving fund had a capital of IL14 million
in 1957 (181).

E. On recommendation of the Foreign Trade Division, the Bank
of Israel discounted foreign currency bills of Israeli exporters.
This revolving fund had a capital of $5½ million in 1957 and
charged 5% interest (181).

F. Certain exporters were granted the privilege, denied to
ordinary importers, to bring in their *imports-for-exports* with
"private lines of credit" of suppliers and foreign banks.

G. Most Israeli trade treaties were coupled with payments agreements. These agreements provided for the central bank of the
country, that was exporting more than it was importing from
its partner, to pay the exporters of its country for their
delivered exports and carry the credit swing as an interest-free
loan from one government to the other. Whilst British exporters
to soft-currency markets are concerned with the time lapse
between delivering goods and receiving the foreign currency,

---

[1] The parliamentary debate in July 1956 revealed that many of the cheap
export credits were diverted to other, less noble purposes (182).—In 1958 several
cases came to light where Israeli "exporters" asked their friends abroad to open
dummy letters-of-credit in order that the former could obtain subsidized export
credits.

and must take into account the possibility of default by the country of their foreign buyers, no such anxiety besets the Israeli exporter. The Israeli Government carried a net debt due to Israeli exporters of 8,300,000 clearing-dollars in June/July 1955; of this Turkey[1] accounted for 4,300,000 and Finland for 3,000,000 (184).

H. In order to provide medium-term credit facilities for Israeli export to Burma, Ghana and Liberia—which is regarded as politically important—a special IL5 million credit fund at low interest rates was established by the Bank of Israel at the beginning of 1959.

(3) Whilst importers were not necessarily issued licences for purchases in the cheapest markets of the world and were sometimes forced to buy dear goods in countries with which Israel had trade agreements, most exporters were released from such restrictions. This applied not only to purchases of *imports-for-exports* materials but also to the utilization of that portion of the *pamaz* account which financed the import of Standard IV goods for the home market.

Some exporters were permitted to pay for purchases in Israel with their *pamaz*-dollars.

Where the *pamaz* system did not apply and *imports-for-exports* were financed by allocations of foreign currency from the Ministry of Finance, these were made at low *rates*. The exporter sometimes profited because the Ministry of Finance paid—at high *rates*—for the foreign currency proceeds of articles which incorporated inputs that had been imported at low *rates*, e.g. fodder was imported during a certain period with a *rate* of 1, but exported eggs had a 1.800 *rate*. Such examples concerning direct *IfE* are frequent only up to 1954. Examples concerning indirect *IfE*, however, can be met with throughout the eleven years of the State.

(4) The Israeli Government has proscribed restrictive cartel practices but encourages cartels formed for export promotion and has pressed recalcitrant merchants to join them, e.g. citrus, groundnuts, bananas, honey, shoes, fats, etc. The Ministry of Trade and Industry favours cartels which impose surcharges on domestic sales to finance additional export subsidies.

(5) An entrepreneur who aims to establish a factory will act wisely if he describes the new project, when dealing with Government bodies, as one that will export the major part of its output:

(a) The Investment Centre grants *IwP* licences more generously, and on more favourable terms, to a factory with professed

[1] In February 1958 the Turkish debt to Israel was 6 million clearing-dollars.

export potentialities. In fact, some projects, which would not ordinarily have been "confirmed", received their "confirmation" only after they had promised to export. The rights to repatriate the foreign currency investment and to transfer profits abroad, have sometimes been linked to the foreign currency earnings of the enterprise.

(b) Land leases are given at nominal rent and factory buildings erected at public expense.

(c) Housing facilities for workers are provided and the Ministry of Labour has ample funds to train workers for export industries.

(d) The foreign currency controls administration sometimes gives an implicit promise that the new export firm will be given a monopolistic status on the domestic market. (During the negotiations for the establishment of the Kaiser-Frazer export plant, the Ministry even gave such an undertaking in writing.)

(6) Some Government corporations charge lower fees to exporters, e.g. port dues, port handling charges, railway rates. [The suggestion is being canvassed (103) to introduce cheaper electricity tariffs for exporters, specially low port charges for *IfE* consignments and lower water charges for export branches.]

The Ministry of Trade and Industry used the bargaining power of the Food Division—the sole importer of wheat—to extract from the main Israeli shipping lines a 33% reduction in the freight tariffs for cement exports by offering the shipping companies a long-term contract to carry wheat from America. (This may have been a useful subsidy for Israeli cement exporters to the United States, but it was attained by giving up the lowest freight tariffs for Israeli wheat imports.)

The Controller of Fuel allocates fuel at lower prices to the cement factories[1] in proportion to their exports. [The Ministry of Trade and Industry plans to extend this subsidy to other export branches.]

(7) The Ministry of Trade and Industry has considerable funds at its disposal to provide for indirect services to exporters: market research; preparation and distribution of export catalogues; advertising expenditure in foreign journals; participation at foreign trade fairs; the erection and maintenance of exhibition halls; hiring of foreign experts; preparing special designs for export products, etc. The Economic Department of the Foreign Office receives budgetary appropriations to maintain a large staff in many capitals of the world

[1] This is a peculiar subsidy for it links the payment of a premium to the use of an expensive imported input. On inquiry, I found that it was actually a subterfuge of the Ministry of Finance to pay additional cash premiums to producers without incurring the displeasure of the State Comptroller.

on the grounds that they are chiefly engaged in "aiding export". The same consideration applies to the administrative expenditure on trade treaties which are said to "promote exports". The Ministry of Agriculture and the Ministry of Religious Affairs have separate departments, and special promotion funds, for export purposes. The Economic Department of the Jewish Agency also expends funds on propagating Israeli goods.

(8) There have been occasions (e.g. in Australia and New Zealand) when the importers of Israeli goods have been reimbursed by the Ministry of Finance for customs duty imposed on Israeli exports.

(9) Until July 1957, when a cabinet decision confirmed the establishment of a Government export insurance company (on the lines of the British E.C.G.D.) with a capital of IL1 million, no such insurance cover was available, but the Government has unofficially participated in the export risks of some favoured firms.

The Ministry of Finance returns to exporters the costs involved in having a special insurance cover for sending consignments through the Suez Canal. Enterprises which can prove that at least 40% of their output is exported are reimbursed one-half of the premiums paid in accordance with the (compulsory) "War Damage Insurance".

(10) The Government subsidized the transport of certain export items and/or the export to certain destinations. It has, for example, chartered ships for special journeys to South America and the interior of Canada (69). Air freight to South Africa has been subsidized for many years. In January 1958 a 30% subsidy on air freight for textiles and agricultural products was introduced. Some exporters using the services of EL-AL received a special subsidy from the Government.

Government import/export companies have been formed (e.g. General Export company,[1] Agricultural Export company, West African trade company, Far East trade company) and function as general shippers. The Ministry of Trade and Industry has been known to charter vessels for these companies; it has financed most of their operations.

(11) At a time when there were severe travel restrictions in Israel, liberal exceptions were made for those wishing to go abroad on export business.[2] They could purchase their tickets at the official

[1] This government-owned corporation was enabled to make monopolistic profits from the sale of gold medallions and imported Swiss watches and this provided it with funds enabling the payment of additional subsidies to the exporters that used its services.

[2] According to Tsour (58) the 32.6 million nominal-dollars industrial export in 1954 was carried out by 1,152 exporters. 19 of these exported more than 250,000, 260 more than 10,000 and 873 less than 10,000 nominal-dollars. On

rates, and in some cases were exempted from the "travel tax". Foreign currency for maintenance abroad was allocated at low *rates*. (12) A drawback system operated for customs duties and/or purchase tax. Exporters had to pay the taxes but received 100% reimbursement on production of the C.D.3 which indicated that the materials had been re-exported. The Ministry of Finance gave exporters an interest-free loan to the value of the statutory deposit.

Gottlieb (178) contends that the drawback system represents a disguised export subsidy, but I do not share his view. However, it is true that the drawback system provides a source of considerable illicit gain to dishonest exporters. Some of the *IfE* goods are sold on the domestic market and indirect taxation on these goods is not infrequently evaded.

(13) According to an amendment in 1950 to section X of the Income-Tax law, the Ministry of Finance is entitled to exempt from income-tax, in part or whole, profits arising from exports. There is no record of the application of this subsidy.

The *pamaz* system is regarded by many exporters as more profitable than cash export subsidies because of income-tax considerations. *Pamaz* imports (usually finished or semi-finished goods) can be sold to distributors with undervalued invoices. This evasion of income-tax is not feasible when the subsidies are paid by the Ministry of Finance in the form of a money premium.

(14) The Histadruth has been known to agree to lower wage-rates in those industries which are engaged predominantly on export production (e.g. raincoat manufacturers).

(15) The Swiss Government (*vide* p. 159) provides, at the request of the Israeli Government, a strange service for Israeli exporters to Switzerland. Swiss exports to Israel are taxed by the Swiss authorities and the tax-proceeds used to provide Israeli exporters to Switzerland with a further subsidy, that varies between 5–10% of the gross value of their consignments.

(16) The economic ministries announced in 1959 that the list of subsidies was to be extended and further categories of new aids were to be introduced in 1960.

---

the assumption that every exporter travels abroad at least once a year, and that his ticket and foreign currency maintenance costs (abroad) are $800, the following rule applied to the majority of exporters: one-quarter to one-fifth of the value-added of export proceeds was spent on travelling abroad on "export business".— In 1955 the Government stopped these allocations of foreign currency and most exporters must now finance their maintenance abroad with *pamaz*-dollars.

Appendix IX

TWO LEGAL VIEWS ON THE "PURE *RATE*"

In the first section of Chapter XIX I set out some of the methods used by the foreign currency controller to camouflage the multiple exchange *rates*, and to prevent these practices from conflicting with the declarations that there is only one legal exchange *rate*—or, at the most, four *rates*. No one who has dealt, even superficially, with the economy of Israel can deny that there are, in fact, hundreds of exchange *rates* simultaneously in operation. Israel's learned judges (and particularly Judge Vitkon, the expert on exchange controls) are, of course, aware of this situation. However, they have no choice but to adopt a formalistic attitude when cases appertaining to the "real" exchange *rate* of the IL are brought before them.

In May 1958 an order nisi (236), which had been granted against the Director of Customs by the High Court of Justice in February of that year, was set aside. In the decision it was said that the complaint of the applicant was based on the assumption that the respondent had valued imported goods according to a *rate* of 2.400 and had accordingly collected the customs duties and purchase tax: "The applicant says that the official exchange *rate* is 1.800 and that, according to section 41 of the 'Law of the Bank of Israel', the exchange *rate* cannot be altered except by the Government after previous consultations with the Governor of the Bank of Israel. Therefore, the action of the respondent was not proper and he must return the balance of the amount collected illegally.

"The evidence before us shows that the assumption of the applicant is wholly erroneous. The respondent, according to sections 130 and 131 of the Customs Ordinance, valued the goods in accordance with their price on the open market at the time of import. Admittedly, he added 30% to the purchase price abroad; but he valued the dollar at the *rate* of 1.800 and the supplementary 30% represented—in his view—the difference between the purchase price abroad and the value of the goods on the open market in Israel. The reasoning of the respondent was, therefore, not based on an arbitrary devaluation of the IL but on the real value of the goods on the open market (of Israel); hence the assumption of the applicant is baseless."

Only a few weeks before, Judge Vitkon gave an important judgement in this field when the Tillinger claim against the Jewish Agency was brought before the High Court of Appeal (237). In 1948 the

Jewish Agency had issued bonds, the capital and interest of which were linked to the official exchange *rate* in force for "essential" goods at the time of the redemption of the bonds and coupons. The appellant asked the Jewish Agency to pay the coupons of 15th June 1953 in accordance with the *rate* of 1.800. On that date there were three official *rates*, i.e. 0.357, 0.714 and 1, and the Jewish Agency agreed to pay the interest at the highest official *rate* of 1. The appellant produced evidence to the court that an effective exchange *rate* of 1.800 prevailed at the time for most imports, and his witnesses included merchants who told how their applications for import licences were granted, and foreign currency allocated at the *rate* of 1 *plus a surcharge of 80%*.

In rejecting the Tillinger Appeal, Judge Vitkon said, *inter alia*:

"Can we regard this surcharge of 80% as helping to establish a *rate* of 1.800? . . . True, sometimes there is no substantial difference between the imposition of a tax on imported goods—be it through customs duty, purchase tax, an obligatory payment to the equilization fund or in any other manner—and the gathering of these sums by the establishment of a new exchange *rate*. When one institutes so many exchange *rates*, premiums and subsidies, it is difficult to trace the exact demarcation line between the fiscal and the monetary aspects of the matter. . . . I am not convinced that the provisions of a private contract, that tie a debt to the official exchange *rate* in force for a certain imported article, permit the lender to argue that a customs duty or a purchase tax—or a portion of same—are imposed on a certain article to compensate the Ministry of Finance for an abnormally low *rate* that is then applied to this article. If we would take such a plea into consideration, we would, in fact, place the value-linking conditions on such a shaky basis as to divest them of any measure of certainty. It may well be that under the circumstances of this case, the value-linking provisions (of the contract) failed in their function to maintain the full stable value of the debt, but this is not a sufficient reason to have recourse to outside factors in interpreting the meaning of the term 'official exchange rate'."

A similar judgement was given by Judge Zussman (288).

APPENDIX X

THE PROCLAMATION OF INDEPENDENCE

"The Land of Israel was the birthplace of the Jewish people. Here their spiritual, religious and national identity was formed. Here they achieved independence and created a culture of national and universal significance. Here they wrote and gave the Bible to the world.

Exiled from Palestine, the Jewish people remained faithful to it in all the countries of their dispersion, never ceasing to pray and hope for their return and the restoration of their national freedom.

Impelled by this historic association, Jews strove throughout the centuries to go back to the land of their fathers and regain their statehood. In recent decades they returned in their masses. They reclaimed the wilderness, revived their language, built cities and villages, and established a vigorous and ever-growing community, with its own economic and cultural life. They sought peace yet were prepared to defend themselves. They brought the blessings of progress to all inhabitants of the country.

In the year 1897 the First Zionist Congress, inspired by Theodor Herzl's vision of the Jewish State, proclaimed the right of the Jewish people to national revival in their own country.

This right was acknowledged by the Balfour Declaration of November 2nd, 1917, and reaffirmed by the Mandate of the League of Nations, which gave explicit international recognition to the historic connection of the Jewish people with Palestine and their right to constitute their National Home.

The Nazi holocaust which engulfed millions of Jews in Europe proved anew the urgency of the re-establishment of the Jewish State, which would solve the problem of Jewish homelessness by opening the gates to all Jews and lifting the Jewish people to equality in the family of nations.

The survivors of the European catastrophe, as well as Jews from other lands, proclaiming their right to a life of dignity, freedom and labour, and undeterred by hazards, hardships and obstacles, have tried unceasingly to enter Palestine.

In the Second World War the Jewish people in Palestine made a full contribution in the struggle of the freedom-loving nations against the Nazi evil. The sacrifices of their soldiers and the efforts of their workers gained them title to rank with the peoples who founded the United Nations.

On November 29th, 1947, the General Assembly of the United Nations adopted a Resolution for the establishment of an independent Jewish State in Palestine, and called upon the inhabitants of the country to take such steps as may be necessary on their part to put the plan into effect.

This recognition by the United Nations of the right of the Jewish

285

people to establish their independent State may not be revoked. It is, moreover, the self-evident right of the Jewish people to be a nation, as all other nations, in its own sovereign State.

ACCORDINGLY, WE, the members of the National Council, representing the Jewish people in Palestine and the World Zionist Movement, are met together in solemn assembly today, the day of termination of the British Mandate for Palestine; and by virtue of the natural and historic right of the Jewish people and of the Resolution of the General Assembly of the United Nations,

WE HEREBY PROCLAIM the establishment of the Jewish State in Palestine, to be called Medinat Israel (The State of Israel).

WE HEREBY DECLARE that, as from the termination of the Mandate at midnight, May 14th–15th, 1948, and pending the setting up of the duly elected bodies of the State in accordance with a Constitution to be drawn up by the Constituent Assembly not later than October 1st, 1948, the National Council shall act as the Provisional State Council, and that the National Administration shall constitute the Provisional Government of the Jewish State, which shall be known as Israel.

THE STATE OF ISRAEL will be open to the immigration of Jews from all countries of their dispersion; will promote the development of the country for the benefit of all its inhabitants; will be based on the principles of liberty, justice and peace as conceived by the Prophets of Israel; will uphold the full social and political equality of all its citizens, without distinction of religion, race or sex; will guarantee freedom of religion, conscience, education and culture; will safeguard the Holy Places of all religions; and will loyally uphold the principles of the United Nations Charter.

THE STATE OF ISRAEL will be ready to cooperate with the organs and representatives of the United Nations in the implementation of the Resolution of the Assembly of November 29th, 1947, and will take steps to bring about the Economic Union over the whole of Palestine.

We appeal to the United Nations to assist the Jewish people in the building of its State and to admit Israel into the family of nations.

In the midst of wanton aggression, we yet call upon the Arab inhabitants of the State of Israel to preserve the ways of peace and play their part in the development of the State, on the basis of full and equal citizenship and due representation in all its bodies and institutions—provisional and permanent.

We extend our hand in peace and neighbourliness to all the neighbouring states and their peoples, and invite them to cooperate with the independent Jewish nation for the common good of all.

The State of Israel is prepared to make its contribution to the progress of the Middle East as a whole.

Our call goes out to the Jewish people all over the world to rally to our side in the task of immigration and development and to stand by us in the great struggle for the fulfilment of the dream of generations for the redemption of Israel.

With trust in Almighty God, we set our hand to this Declaration, at this Session of the Provisional State Council, on the soil of the Homeland, in the city of Tel-Aviv, on this Sabbath eve, the fifth of Iyar, 5708, the fourteenth day of May, 1948."

BIBLIOGRAPHY

The following is neither a comprehensive list of works relevant to the subject matter nor a catalogue of all the books and other sources which I have consulted in writing this book. Its purpose is merely to list those sources I have quoted but not fully identified in the text.

Source material in English is marked (E), Hebrew (H), bilingual publications (E)(H) and German sources (G).

Publications by departments of the Israeli Government (or those sponsored by them) are cited with the name of the responsible ministry of division; in some cases the publisher is marked as "Government Printer".

The *Economic Quarterly* is a journal published by the Am Oved Publishing company.

Davar, Haaretz, Haboker, Jerusalem Post, Lamerchav, Zemanim and *Yedioth Achronoth* are daily papers from which quotations are reproduced.

The place of publication by all Government departments, the Bank of Israel (B.o.I.), Jewish Agency, Economic Advisory Staff (E.A.S.), Falk Foundation and the Hebrew University is Jerusalem. All other Israeli sources are published in Tel-Aviv unless Haifa or Jerusalem is stated to be the town of publication.

(1). Gruenbaum, A. L., *A Four-Year Plan*, Prime Minister's Office, 1950 (H).

(2). Gottlieb, S., and Honigbaum, Y., *Government Subsidies in Israel*, Falk Foundation, 1957 (E)(H).

(3). Baer, B., "The Water Potential and the Development of Irrigated Land," Economic Supplement, *Haaretz*, 8/6/1955 (H).

(4). *Judgements of Supreme Court*, XII–63, Ministry of Justice, 1959 (H).

(5). Halperin, H. "Considerations affecting our Settlement Policy," *Economic Quarterly*, September 1953 (H).

(6). *Haaretz*, 3/5/1951 (H).

(7). *Conditions for leasing Land to Communal Settlements*, Jewish National Fund, Jerusalem, 20/7/1951 (H).

(8). Noam, M., *National Income originating in Israel's Agriculture*, C.B.S., 1956 (E)(H).

(9). Tanne, D., "A Five-Year Plan for Housing," *Economic Quarterly*, July 1957 (H).

(10). Kotler, Y., "Who Receives Land Free?" *Haaretz*, 12/4/1957 (H).

(11). (Woechentliche) *Kurs-Notierungen fuer Spezialvaluten*, Bank Hofmann AG, Zürich (G).

(12). Kleinfeld, R., *A Comparative Study in Meat Consumption* (unpublished), Food Division, 5/11/1956 (H).

(13). Samuel, L. E., *Outstanding Issues in Agricultural Policy*, Ministry of Agriculture, 1955 (H).

(14). *Israel's Foreign Trade in 1956*, C.B.S., February 1957 (E)(H).

(15). Bavli, I., *A Survey of the Metal and Electrical Industries*, M.o.T. & I., 1954 (H).

(16). (Clawson, M. M.), *Israel Agriculture*, E.A.S. and Joint Planning Centre, Government Printer, December 1955 (E).

(17). "French Perfumes to be exported from Israel," *Haaretz*, 14/2/1958 (H).

(18). Meron, G., "The Arab Boycott," *Economic Quarterly*, January 1954 (H).

(19). (Horn, S. I.), *Data and Plans*, M.o.FI., October 1953 (E).

(20). *Annual Report*, B.o.I., May 1956 (H).

(21). Mayer, E. J. M., *Agricultural Development in Israel*, Manchester School, Manchester, September 1955 (E).

(22). (Halevy, A.), *Haaretz*, 15/4/1954 (H).

(23). *Foreign Currency Budget 1956/57*, M.o.FI., May 1956 (H).

(24). *Foreign Currency Budget 1955/56*, M.o.FI. (unpublished), May 1955 (H).

(25). *Supplementary Notes to Budget Speech*, M.o.FI., August 1953 (H).

(26). Blass, S., "The Price of Water for Agriculture," *Economic Quarterly*, May 1954 (H).

(27). Amir, A., "Land and Water," *Economic Quarterly*, October 1955 (H).

(28). Duvdevani, I., "The High-priced Water," *Davar*, 17/4/1957 (H).

(29). Levie, E. L., "Water Costs as a Factor limiting Production," Economic Supplement, *Haaretz*, 8/6/1955 (H).

(30). Amir, A., "The Price of Water in Agriculture," *Economic Quarterly*, October 1954 (H).

(31). Kariv, S., "The Price of Water in Agriculture," Economic Supplement, *Davar*, 3/6/1955 (H).

(32). Patinkin, D., *Monetary Development in Israel*, Scripta Hierosolymitana, Hebrew University, 1955 (E)(H).

(33). Gevati, H., "Agricultural Production in the Coming Years," *Economic Quarterly*, January 1954 (H).

(34). Hoffien, A. S., Annual Address, Bank Leumi, 1953 (H).

(35). *Davar*, 6/3/1957 (H).

(36). *Monthly Statistical Bulletin, Part A*, C.B.S., September 1957 (H).

(37). *Foreign Currency Budget 1957/58*, M.o.FI., May 1957 (H).

(38). *Export Bulletin*, 36B, M.o.T. & I., April 1956 (H).

(39). *Export Annual 1956*, M.o.T. & I., 1957 (H).

(40). *Israel's Foreign Trade in 1955*, C.B.S., February 1956 (E)(H).

(41). *Foreign Currency Budget 1954/55* (unpublished), M.o.FI., May 1955 (H).

(42). Sacher, H., *Israel: The Establishment of a State*, Weidenfeld and Nicolson, London, 1952 (E).

(43). *Explanatory Notes to Foreign Currency Budget*, M.o.FI., July 1956 (H).

(44). Kochav, D., *Imports-without-Pay* (unpublished thesis), Hebrew University, 1952 (H).

(45). *Jewish Observer and Middle East Review*, 28/2/1958, London (E).

(46). *State Comptroller's Report, VI*, 1/1/1956 (H).

(47). *Export Bulletin*, 42, M.o.T. & I., August 1956 (H).

(48). *Report of "Foreign Currency Commission"*, Prime Minister's Office, July 1953 (E)(H).

(49). Pick's *Currency Yearbook*, New York, May 1955 (E).

(50). *Industry Yearbook 1957/58*, Israel Publications, October 1957 (H).

(51). Rubner-Raviv, A., "The Real End of *Imports-without-pay*," *Haaretz*, 13/4/1951 (H).

(52). "Fuel Prices in Israel," *Kalkelan Journal*, Jerusalem, 4/2/1954 (H).

(53). *Davar*, 15/5/1957 (H).

(54). Taub, Y., "A Sound Economic Measure," *Haaretz*, 4/9/1957 (H).

(55). *State Comptroller's Report, IV*, 31/12/1953 (H).

(56). *State Comptroller's Report, V*, 31/12/1954 (H).

(57). Schocken, G., "Overseas Aid and We," *Haaretz*, 30/9/1951 (H).

(58). Tsour, M., "Problems of Industrial Export," *Economic Quarterly*, February 1956 (H).

(59). Erhard, L., *Germany's Comeback in the World Market*, Allen and Unwin, London, 1954 (E).

(60). Verlinsky, N., "Problems of Agricultural Export," *Economic Quarterly*, February 1956 (H).

(61). Horovitz, D., "Structure and Cycle in the Israeli Economy," *Economic Quarterly*, July 1957 (H).

(62). Ben-Nathan, N., "Disguised Imports," *Davar*, 24/7/1957 (H).

(63). Dulberg, F., "The Trade Balance and Economic Progress," *Economic Quarterly*, June 1955 (H).

(64). *Haaretz*, 24/7/1957 (H).

(65). Nizan, A., *The Standard of Living in Palestine during the last 20 Years*, C.B.S., 1952 (H).

(66). Kozlov, I. R., Eiger, I., Barzel, I., "Supply and Consumption of Fuel," *Economic Quarterly*, October 1956 (H).

(67). Gilboa, M., "The Price of the 'Saved Dollar'," *Davar*, 27/4/1956 (H).

(68). *Inflationary and Deflationary Tendencies*, United Nations, 1949 (E).

(69). *Haaretz*, 29/7/1957 (H).

(70). *Confirmed Protocol on Commercial Relations between Israel and Switzerland*, Ministry of Foreign Affairs, October 1956 (H).

(71). Berger, L., "Value-added in Industry," Economic Supplement, *Haboker*, 27/4/1955 (H).

(72). Erdreich, E., *Memorandum on Export Promotion*, M.o.FI., 18/1/1956 (E).

(73). *Haaretz*, 8/9/1953 (H).

(74). Tsour, M., "Industrial Exports," Economic Supplement, *Davar*, 27/4/1956 (H).

(75). Meade, J. E., *The Balance of Payments*, Oxford University Press, London, 1951 (E).

(76). *Business Diary*, Haifa, 15/5/1956 (E).

(77). Gottlieb, S., *Price Control in Israel* (unpublished thesis), Hebrew University, 1951 (H).

(78). Erdreich, E., and Altschuler, E., *Proposed Resale of Enamelling Plant to Turkey*, E.A.S., 21/3/1955 (E).

(79). Altschuler, E., *American-Israel Paper Mills, Ltd.*, E.A.S., 27/7/1955 (E).

(80). Goldberger, Z., *Protective Tariffs in Israel* (unpublished), August 1956 (H).

(81). *Baigud Hamikzoi Journal*, 26/7/1956 (H).

(82). Cats, H., and Gabovitch, B., *A Study of Value-added in Terms of International Prices*, Falk Foundation, May 1957 (E)(H).

(83). (Picker, Y.), *Report on "Imports-without-payment,"* Prime Minister's Office, October 1954 (H).

(84). Barkai, C., *Consumption of Fats in Israel* (unpublished thesis) Hebrew University, 1954 (H).

291

(85). *Survey VI*, B.o.I., October 1957 (H).

(86). *Kalkelan Journal*, Jerusalem, 2/8/1956 (H).

(87). Baer, B., and Schweitzer, A., *Food Rations, Chikrei Kalkala*, M.O.FI., 1951 (H).

(88). Ettinger, J., "Peanuts and their Export," Economic Supplement, *Haaretz*, 8/7/1955 (H).

(89). Kalecky, M., *Report on Current Economic Problems*, M.o.FI., 1951 (E).

(90). Chalmers, H., *World Trade Policies*, University of California Press, Los Angeles, 1953 (E).

(91). Ezioni, A., "Agrarianism in Israel's Party System," *The Canadian Journal of Economic and Political Science*, Ottawa, August 1957 (E).

(92). *Knesset Proceedings*, X–A, 11/9/1951 (H).

(93). Dulberg, F., *The Development of the Real Wage* (unpublished), 1953 (H).

(94). Viner, J., *Trade Relations between Free Market and Controlled Economies*, League of Nations, Geneva, 1943 (E).

(95). Goren, M., *Export of Plate-glass*, M.o.FI., 1956 (H).

(96). Coen, E., "Decreasing Costs and the Gains from Trade," *Economica*, London, August 1951 (E).

(97). de Vries, B. A., and Keesing, F. A., *The Use of Bilateral Agreement Currencies for Trade with 3rd Countries*, Staff Papers, I.M.F., Washington, 1956 (E).

(98). Amir, A., "The Frontiers of Economic Planning," *Economic Quarterly*, May 1954 (H).

(99). *Haaretz*, 8/1/1958 (H).

(100). *Survey III*, B.o.I., July 1956 (H).

(101). Altschuler, E., *Citrus Packing Cases*, E.A.S., 6/6/1955 (E).

(102). *Israel Economic Bulletin*, M.o.T. & I., December 1955 (E).

(103). *Hataasiah Journal*, June 1956 (H).

(104). *Kalkelan Journal*, Jerusalem, 5/4/1956 (H).

(105). Michaely, M., "Domestic Effects of Devaluation under Repressed Inflation," *Journal of Political Economy*, Chicago, December 1955 (E).

(106). "How many IL for one Dollar?" *Davar*, 15/5/1957 (H).

(107). *Explanations to Proposed Budget 1956/57*, M.o.FI., February 1956 (H).

(108). *The Israel Economy in 1954*, E.A.S., July 1955 (E).

(109). *Report of the Public Commission on Government Value-linked Loans*, M.o.FI., January 1955 (H).

(110). *Haaretz*, 30/5/1951.

(111). Ben-Sussan, R., "The Diamond Industry," *Haaretz*, 20/1/1954 (H).

(112). Yang, S. C., *A Multiple Exchange Rate System*, University of Wisconsin Press, Madison, 1957 (E).

(113). Klebansky, M., "Balance of Payments for the Years 1955–1956," *Economic Quarterly*, July 1957 (H).

(114). Pollak, J., *The Worthwhileness of the Export of "Chemicals and Fertilisers, Ltd.,"* M.o.FI., 12/3/1956 (H).

(115). *Haaretz*, 11/9/1957 (H).

(116). *Judgements of District Courts, IX*, Advocates Association, 1954 (H).

(117). *Judgements of Supreme Court, XVIII*, Advocates Association, 1955 (H).

(118). Rolph, E. R., *The Theory of Fiscal Economics*, University of California Press, Los Angeles, 1954 (E).

(119). *Report of Public Commission on Bread-baking*, M.o.T. & I., 6/7/1955 (H).

(120). Goldberger, E., "Preis-Bewegungen in Israel," *Polygraphischer Verlag*, Zürich, 1956 (G).

(121). *State Comptroller's Report III*, 31/12/1952 (H).

(122). Baharal, U., *Phoenicia Glass Works*, Zemanim, Jerusalem, 26/4/1954 (H).

(123). *Haaretz*, 23/5/1956 (H).

(124). Horovitz, D., *The Economy of Israel*, Massada Publishing Co., 1954 (H).

(125). Baranyai, L., *A Monetary Mechanism of Israel* (B.o.I.), 1956 (E).

(126). *Haaretz*, 14/8/1957 (H).

(127). Marcus, A., *The Structure of Industry in Israel*, Am Oved Publishing co., 1953 (H).

(128). *Yedioth Achronoth*, 29/5/1955 (H).

(129). Gaaton, A. L., *A Survey of Israel's Economy in 1950*, C.B.S., 1952 (H).

(130). *Haaretz*, 13/1/1954 (H).

(131). (Swersky, A.), *Haaretz*, 20/3/1955 (H).

(132). *Haaretz*, 29/12/1954 (H).

(133). Ellis, H. E., *Exchange Control in Central Europe*, Harvard University Press, Massachusetts, 1941 (E).

(134). Lowe, Y., *Agricultural Credit in Kibbutzim*, Ministry of Agriculture, 1955 (H).

(135). (Barth, A.), *Haaretz*, 27/3/1955 (H).

(136). Erdreich, E., *Interim Report on Steel Rolling Mill*, E.A.S., 1954 (E).

293

(137). *Report on Reasons for Increase in Means of Payment*, B.o.I., 1957 (H).

(138). *Survey V*, B.o.I., August 1957 (H).

(139). Marsten, P., "Jerusalem Shoe Corporation," *Kalkelan Journal*, Jerusalem, 1/3/1956 (H).

(140). *Government Yearbook* (5714), 1953 (H).

(141). Halperin, H., *Changing Patterns in Israel's Agriculture*, Routledge, London, 1957 (E).

(142). Lubell, H., *National Expenditure and the National Accounts*, Falk Foundation, 1956 (E).

(143). "Ministry of Trade and Industry Investigations in Cost of Value-added," *Davar*, 15/1/1958 (H).

(144). Dulberg, F., "Investments in Israel," *Economic Quarterly*, January 1954 (H).

(145). Black, A. G., *National Agricultural Plans and Programs*, F.A.O., Report No. 161, Rome, 1953 (E).

(146). Kadar, G., *A Criticism of the Development of Agriculture*, Bank Leumi, 1952 (H).

(147). Clawson, M. M., *General Survey of Agriculture in Israel*, E.A.S., 12/11/1953 (E).

(148). Gaaton. A. L., "The Measurements of Economic Activity," *Economic Quarterly*, February 1956 (H).

(149). *Haaretz*, 6/11/1957 (H).

(150). Lubell, H., *Israel's National Expenditure (1952–53)*, C.B.S., 1956 (E)(H).

(151). Hansen, A. H., *Monetary Theory and Fiscal Policy*, McGraw-Hill, New York, 1949 (E).

(152). Gertz, A., "Statistics and Controls," *Haaretz*, 25/3/1952 (H).

(153). Hovne, A., *The Labour Force in Israel*, Falk Foundation, 1956 (E).

(154). Borochov, B., *Nationalism and the Class Struggle*, Poale Zion Press, New York, 1937 (E).

(155). Kaufman, Y., "Anti-Semitic Stereotypes in Zionism," *Commentary*, New York, March 1949 (E).

(156). Lipovetsky, P., *The Ideology of Work in Modern Hebrew Literature*, Hozaath Bamaaleh, 1933 (H).

(157). Greenberg, C., "The Myth of Jewish Parasitism," *Jewish Frontier*, New York, March 1942 (E).

(158). *Annual Report*, B.o.I., May 1957 (H).

(159). Creamer, D., *National Income of Israel (1952–54)*, Falk Foundation, March 1956 (E).

(160). *Industrialization in Egypt, Israel and Turkey*, United Nations Economic and Social Council, New York, July 1957 (E).

(161). Bauer, P. T., and Yamey, B. S., *The Economics of Under-developed Countries*, Cambridge University Press, London 1957 (E).

(162). Nizan, A., *Prices of Some Goods not included in Cost-of-Living Index* (unpublished), C.B.S., 19/8/1953 (H).

(163). Ramati, D., *Official and Free Prices*, E.A.S., 22/9/1953 (E).

(164). Dulberg, F., "Agriculture in the National Economy," *Economic Quarterly*, October 1956 (H).

(165). *Statistical Abstract of Israel (1955/56)*, C.B.S., October 1956 (E)(H).

(166). Cyderovitz, G., "The Labour Economy," *Economic Quarterly*, July 1957 (H).

(167). (Mosak, J. L.), *Inflationary Pressures and Price Control in Israel*, United Nations, New York, 1953 (E).

(168). *Government Yearbook (5715) 1954* (H).

(169). *Government Yearbook (5716) 1955* (H).

(170). *Haaretz*, 17/2/1958 (H).

(171). (Allen, Bredo, Robinson and Drexel), *The Industrial Economy of Israel*, Stanford Research Institute, California, 1955 (E).

(172). Horovitz, D., *The Palestine Economy*, Dvir Publishing Co., 1948 (H).

(173). Clawson, M. M., *Agricultural Planning in Israel*, E.A.S., November 1953 (E).

(174). Black, A. G., *Reflections upon Israel's Agricultural Develop-ment*, Hebrew University, June 1957 (E).

(175). *Haaretz*, 7/5/1953 (H).

(176). Clawson, M. M., *Estimated Future Cost of Irrigation Water*, E.A.S., November 1953 (E).

(177). Lowe, Y., "Agricultural Planning," *Economic Quarterly*, February 1955 (H).

(178). Gottlieb, S., and Golan, D., *Subsidies Classified*, Falk Founda-tion, 1956 (E).

(179). *Watch Industry*, E.A.S., 1954 (E).

(180). *Lamerchav*, 22/4/1956 (H).

(181). *Government Yearbook (5718) 1957* (H).

(182). *Knesset Proceedings*, 23–25 July 1956, XXXVII, October 1956 (H).

(183). Marsten, P., "The Motors of Kaiser-Frazer," *Kalkelan Journal*, Jerusalem, 23/3/1956 (H).

(184). *Foreign Currency Debts*, M.o.FI., February 1956 (H).

(185). Coltov, J. A., *Israel's Foreign Trade 1951*, C.B.S., 1952 (E)(H).

(186). Coltov, J. A., *Israel's Foreign Trade 1952–53*, C.B.S. 1954 (E)(H).

(187). *Kalkelan Journal*, Jerusalem, 5/1/1956 (H).

(188). *The Economist*, London, 4/5/1957 (E).

(189). Weitz, R., *The Development of Israel's Agriculture*, Jewish Agency, October 1953 (H).

(190). *Haaretz*, 29/5/1955 (H).

(191). Erdreich, E., *Profitability of Kaiser-Frazer Operations to the Israel Economy*, E.A.S., 30/3/1955 (E).

(192). Clawson, M. M., *Memorandum on Irrigation*, E.A.S., 25/4/1954 (E).

(193). Bavli, S., *Level of Nutrition in Israel 1951*, C.B.S., March 1952 (H).

(194). Levie, E. L., *Wheat in Israel* (unpublished), Ministry of Agriculture, 1956 (E).

(195). *Haaretz*, 26/12/1952 (H).

(196). Alexander, S. S., *Devaluation versus Import Restrictions*, Staff Papers, I.M.F., Washington, April 1951 (E).

(197). Lerner, A. P., *The Economics of Control*, Macmillan, New York, 1946 (E).

(198). Saaki-Erez-Ahuvah, "Israel's N.E.P. in Action," *Public Finance*, Holland, December 1954 (E).

(199). "Israel's New Immigration Problems," *The Economist*, London, 10/8/1957 (E).

(200). Jaffe, Y., "The Supply of Food," Economic Supplement, *Haaretz*, 8/6/1955 (H).

(201). *Kalkelan Journal*, Jerusalem, 17/11/1955 (H).

(202). Polak, J. J., and Chang, T. C., *Effects of Exchange Depreciation on a Country's Export Price Level*, Staff Papers, I.M.F., Washington, February 1950 (E).

(203). Machlup, F., "The Terms-of-Trade Effects of Devaluation upon Real Income and the Balance of Trade," *Kyklos*, Switzerland, IV, 1956 (E).

(204). Rubner-Raviv, A., "Four Equilibra Exchange Rates," Paper read to Economics Graduates Seminar (unpublished), Hebrew University, December 1956 (H).

(205). Eshkol, L., "Financing of the Four-Year Plan," *Economic Quarterly*, June 1956 (H).

(206). *Business Diary*, Haifa, 25/10/1956 (E).

(207). Riemer, S., *Index or Dollars*, Union Bank of Israel, 1955 (E).

(208). *Haaretz*, 2/9/1954 (H).

(209). *Haaretz*, 6/6/1955 (H).

(210). Darin, H., "Public Capital in Investments," *Economic Quarterly*, November 1957 (H).

(211). *Judgements of Supreme Court*, XI–29, Government Printer, 30/6/1957 (H).

(212). (Hobman, J. B.), *Palestine's Economic Future*, P. L. Humphries Publishing Co., London, 1946 (E).

(213). "Towards a Grammar of Graft," *The Economist*, London, 15/6/1957 (E).

(214). Beham, Y., and Rosenberg, L. G., *The Price of Bread*, E.A.S., 24/5/1954 (E).

(215). *Haaretz*, 23/11/1954 (H).

(216). *Haaretz*, 22/1/1953 (H).

(217). Mikesell, R. F., *Foreign Exchange in the Postwar World*, The Twentieth Century Fund, New York, 1954 (E).

(218). *Davar*, 3/8/1955 (H).

(219). Trued, M. N., and Mikesell, R. F., *Postwar Bilateral Payments Agreements*, Princeton University, 1955 (E).

(220). Golan, D., *The Trade Treaties of the State of Israel* (unpublished thesis), Hebrew University, 1952 (H).

(221). Kessler, A., *Terms of Trade of Israel's Clearing Agreements in 1953*, Falk Foundation, 1956 (E).

(222). Rosenberg, L. G. (*Prices in Clearing Agreements*), E.A.S., 24/1/1955 (E).

(223). Golan, D., "The Value-added of Industrial Exports," Economic Supplement, *Haaretz*, 8/6/1955 (H).

(224). Meade, J. E., *Trade and Welfare*, Oxford University Press, London, 1955 (E).

(225). *Haaretz*, 1/7/1953 (H).

(226). Lerner, A. P., "The Histadruth and the Israel Economy," *Midstream*, New York, Autumn 1957 (E).

(227). Cohen, D., "Abandoned Arab Property," *Haboker*, 7/1/1958 (H).

(228). Gilboa, M., "Employment and Surplus Value," *Economic Quarterly*, August 1958 (H).

(229). Tevet, S., "Kaiser-Frazer—the Reality versus Hopes," *Haaretz*, August 1958 (H).

(230). *Haaretz*, 29/5/1958 (H).

(231). Bernstein, M. H., *The Politics of Israel*, Princeton University Press, Princeton, 1957 (E).

(232). *Davar*, 8/10/1958 (H).

(233). Berger, L., *Industry in the State of Israel*, Economic Department of the Jewish Agency, 1958 (E).

(234). *Haaretz*, 10/8/1958 (H).

L

(235). *Time*, New York, 24/3/1958 (E).

(236). *Judgements of Supreme Court*, XII–28, Ministry of Justice, 1958 (H).

(237). *Judgements of Supreme Court*, XII–15, Ministry of Justice, 1958 (H).

(238). *Annual Report*, B.o.I., May 1958 (H).

(239). *Statistical Abstract of Israel 1957/58*, IX, C.B.S., October 1958 (E)(H).

(240). Marcus, A., "Some Problems confronting Israel's Industry," *Israel Economic Forum*, M.o.T. & I., July 1958 (E).

(241). *Management of Industrial Enterprises in Under-developed Countries*, 58/II/B5, United Nations, New York, 1958 (E).

(242). (R. de O. Campos. G. Haberler, J. Meade, J. Tinbergen), *Trends in International Trade*, G.A.T.T., Geneva, October 1958 (E).

(243). *International Economic Assistance and the Under-developed Countries*, E/31/31, United Nations Economic and Social Council, New York, June 1958 (E).

(244). Friedman, M., "Foreign Economic Aid," *Yale Review*, Yale University Press, New Haven, Summer 1958 (E).

(245). Baker, H. E., "Legal System," *The Israel Year Book 1958*, Israel Publications, 1958 (E).

(246). Gass, O., "Four Books on Israel," *Commentary*, New York, July 1958 (E).

(247). *Giving USA*, American Association of Fund-Raising Counsel, January 1958 (E).

(248). *Haaretz*, 26/8/1958 (H).

(249). Schwarz, H., "The 'Spekulyanti' Prosper in Russia," *The New York Times Magazine*, New York, 4/5/1958 (E).

(250). Ben-Nathan, N., "Government Corporations," *Davar*, 26/3/1958 (H).

(251). *Haaretz*, 21/10/1958 (H).

(252). Kariv, S., "The Price of Water," *Economic Quarterly*, August 1958 (H).

(253). Levie, E. L., "Water Costs as a Factor Limiting Production," *Haaretz*, 8/6/1955 (H).

(254). Eshkol, L., "The Israel Economy towards the Second Decade," *Economic Quarterly*, April 1958 (H).

(255). *Government Yearbook* (5719), October 1958 (H).

(256). Lahav, E., "At War with the Cow," *Jewish Observer and Middle East Review*, London, 19/12/1958 (E).

(257). Ellis, H. B., *Israel and the Middle East*, The Ronald Press, New York, 1957 (E).

(258). Hershlag, Z. Y., "The Economic Future of the Middle East," *The Listener*, London, 9/9/1958 (E).

(259). Eytan, W., *The First Ten Years*, Weidenfeld and Nicolson, London, 1958 (E).

(260). *The System of Taxation in Israel*, M.o.FI., 1957 (E).

(261). Schweitzer, A., "Investments," Economic Supplement, *Haaretz*, 8/6/1955 (H).

(262). Hyamson, A. M., *Palestine under the Mandate*, Methuen, London, 1950 (E).

(263). Koestler, A., *Promise and Fulfilment*, Macmillan, London, 1949 (E).

(264). *Monthly Statistical Bulletin*, Part B, C.B.S., August 1958 (H).

(265). Finch, D., *Purchasing Power Guarantees for Deferred Payments*, Staff Papers, I.M.F., Washington, February 1956 (E).

(266). Herzberg, C., Banking Supplement, *Jerusalem Post*, Jerusalem, 17/8/1955 (E).

(267). *Israel Economic Indicators*, C.B.S., October 1958 (H).

(268). Berger, L., "The Worthwhileness of not Honouring Obligations," *Haaretz*, 4/12/1957 (H).

(269). *The Israel Year Book 1958*, Israel Publications, 1958 (E).

(270). *A Study on the Problems of Working Capital Finance of Israel's Industry*, U.S. Operations Mission and B.o.I., August 1956 (E).

(271). Schocken (Bendam), G., "Israel in 5711," *Haaretz Annual* 1951/52, 1951 (H).

(272). Kidan, A., *The Story of the Israel Bank Notes*, Israel Economic Forum, Bank Leumi and M.o.T. & I., undated (E).

(273). Cyderovitz, G., "The Labour Economy 1949–1957," *Economic Quarterly*, April 1958 (H).

(274). *International Financial News Survey*, I.M.F., Washington, 5/12/1958 (E).

(275). Ginor, F., "The Aims of Development Policy," *Economic Quarterly*, December 1958 (H).

(276). Kreinin, M. E., "Israel's Export Problem and its Policy Implications," *The Southern Economic Journal*, North Carolina, October 1958 (E).

(277). *Review of Economic Conditions in Israel*, Bank Leumi, November 1958 (E).

(278). Myrdal, G., *Economic Theory and Under-developed Regions*, Duckworth, London, 1957 (E).

(279). (W. Z. Laqueur), *The Middle East in Transition*, Routledge and Kegan Paul, London, 1958 (E).

L*

(280). Horin, Y., "I Talk as I Please," *Jewish Observer and Middle East Review*, London, 30/1/1959 (E).

(281). *Overseas Review*, Barclays Bank D.C.O., London, January 1959 (E).

(282). Barkay, R. M., *The Public Sector Accounts of Israel*, Falk Foundation and C.B.S., December 1957 (E).

(283). Riemer, S., "The Supply and Utilization of Capital Funds in the Israel Economy," *Public Finance*, Holland, Winter 1958 (E).

(284). Kenaan, J., "The Right and the Left Hand," *Davar*, 14/1/1959 (H).

(285). *Haaretz*, 30/12/1958 (H).

(286). Luz, K., "I Talk as I Please," *Jewish Observer and Middle East Review*, London, 16/1/1959 (E).

(287). *Echo* (Israel's Economic Review), 28/12/1958 (E).

(288). *Judgements of Supreme Court*, XII–71, Ministry of Justice, 1959 (H).

(289). *Haaretz*, 24/2/1959 (H).

(290). *State Comptroller's Report*, IX, 1959 (H).

(291). *Export Bulletin*, 72 M.o.T. & I., February 1959 (H).

INDEX*

Abdullah, King of Jordan, 16
Acre, 80, 233
Adenauer, K., 217, 244
Akaba, Gulf of, 85
Alexander, S. S., 212–13, 296
Allenby, 10
Altschuler, E., 170, 181, 186, 291–2
America, 61, 68–9, 83, 93, 104, 112–13, 214, 233, 240, 253–4; aid by Jews of, 25, 32, 46, 133, 172, 183, 184, 191, 250, 298; aid by Government of, XVII, 24, 32–3, 89, 105, 130, 245; currency of, 120, 160, 165, 206, 215; Jews of, 2, 3, 5, 247, 249; political attitude by Government of, 15, 244; Israeli trade with, 18, 168, 208, 251, 274–5, 280
Amir, A., 113, 115–16, 118, 181, 289, 292
Anglo-Iranian Oil Co., 83
Arab Boycott, 16, 69–70, 83, 243
Argentina, 140, 142, 183, 274
Army (Israeli), XVII, 19, 22, 24–5, 28, 68, 73, 78, 155–6, 172, 226–9, 240, 277
Atzmon, Mt., 7
Australia, 281
Austria, 4

Baer, B., 114, 266, 288, 292
Baharal, U., 268, 293

Baigud Hamikzoi Journal, 172, 291
Baker, H. E., 8, 298
Balfour Declaration, 2, 10–11, 285
Banks:
    Agriculture, of, 88, 92, 110
    Barclays, 168, 300
    Japhets, 144, 192
    Leumi, 18–19, 22, 28, 91–2, 99, 163, 252, 299
    Post Office, 88
    U.S. Export-Import, 20, 24, 32, 37, 89, 180–1, 237, 252, 268, 278
    Workers', 44–5, 91–2
    World, 236, 245
Baranyai, L., 91, 293
Barkai, C., 177, 291
Barkay, R. M., 150, 300
Barth, A., 92, 293
Bar-Yehudah, I., 2
Barzel, I., 257, 291
Basle, 2
Bauer, P. T., 232, 295
Bavli, I., XXII, 237, 289
Bavli, S., 60, 266, 296
Beham, Y., 263, 297
Belgium, 21, 130, 159, 268
Bell, B. R., 212, 217
Ben-Gurion, D., XV, 5, 9–10, 14, 16, 20, 24, 31, 231, 247–9
Ben-Nathan, N., 36, 169, 200, 291, 298

* Individuals and companies, which are sometimes identified in the text only by a bracketed number, e.g. (100) that refers the reader to the Bibliography, are nevertheless listed here.—Only those publications will be found in the Index, from which *anonymous* quotations or material have been taken.—Israeli Government departments, and their publications, have not been registered in the Index.

Greenberg, C., 3, 294

Haaretz, IX, 31, 63, 123, 127,
141, 146, 161, 163, 183, 186,
200, 202, 210, 250, 269, 271,
274, 291–300
Habas Family, 252
Haberler, G., 235
Haboker, 31
Hadassah Medical Organization,
134, 184
Hadera, 170
Hagannah, 13
Haifa, XVI, 3, 8, 12, 18–19, 29,
37–8, 69, 70, 80, 83, 85, 105,
122, 125, 134, 153, 166, 170,
172, 176–9, 187, 200, 242,
246–7, 260, 262, 264, 268,
273–5
Halevy, A., 260–1, 289
Halperin, H., 92, 107, 110, 288,
294
Hansen, A. H., 98, 294
Hebrew University, 3, 96, 132,
179, 184
Heletz, 27
Hershlag, Z. Y., 69, 299
Herut (Party), 42
Herzberg, C., 95, 299
Herzl, T., 2, 10, 285
Hilfsverein, 1
Histadruth, XIV, 91–2, 103, 208,
255; *Davar*, journal of, 3, 32,
146; Economic Institutions of,
22, 25, 38, 41, 44, 48, 71, 81,
83–4, 85, 108, 145, 155, 233,
238, 252, 268; Mapai and, XV,
28, 45, 46–7, 56; Part of Public Sector, 36, 82, 94, 98, 221,
222, 337; Trade Union Activities of, 21, 25, 40, 42–3,
52, 58, 73, 180, 200, 282;
Welfare Services of, 74, 156, 231

Hitler, A., 12
Hobman, J. B., 108, 297
Hoffien, A. S., 99, 290
Holland, 203
Honigbaum, Y., 201, 288
Hope-Simpson (Memorandum),
11
Horovitz, Dan, 7
Horovitz, David, 21, 25–6, 28,
34, 67, 138, 169, 223, 291, 293,
295
Hovne, A., XV, 78, 294
Hule Basin, 118
Hungary, 5, 65, 66, 140, 160
Hyamson, A. M., 10, 41, 299

Income Tax, 28, 44, 75–9, 90,
94–5, 150, 282
India, 16, 244
Interest Law, 28, 89
International Labour Office, 65
International Monetary Fund,
26–7, 75, 91, 121, 165, 223, 299
Iraq, 92, 137
Italy, 66, 160, 203, 257

Jaffa, 12, 85, 161, 201
Jaffe, Y., 265, 296
Japan, 247
Jerusalem, 1, 7, 11–12, 14, 16,
20–1, 32, 58, 61, 64, 69, 84–5,
90, 125, 134, 142, 155, 171,
179, 195, 240, 246, 248, 249,
251–2
Jerusalem Post, IX
Jevons, W. S., 93
Jewish Agency, 62, 63, 92, 162,
164–5, 166, 184, 185, 231, 284;
Agricultural Activities of, 102,
107–11, 115–16, 180, 240–1;
during British Mandate,
11–14, 18, 25, 36, 40–1; Economic Institutions of, 81, 85,

For Product Safety Concerns and Information please contact our EU
representative GPSR@taylorandfrancis.com
Taylor & Francis Verlag GmbH, Kaufingerstraße 24, 80331 München, Germany

* 9 7 8 1 0 3 2 6 7 6 7 6 0 *